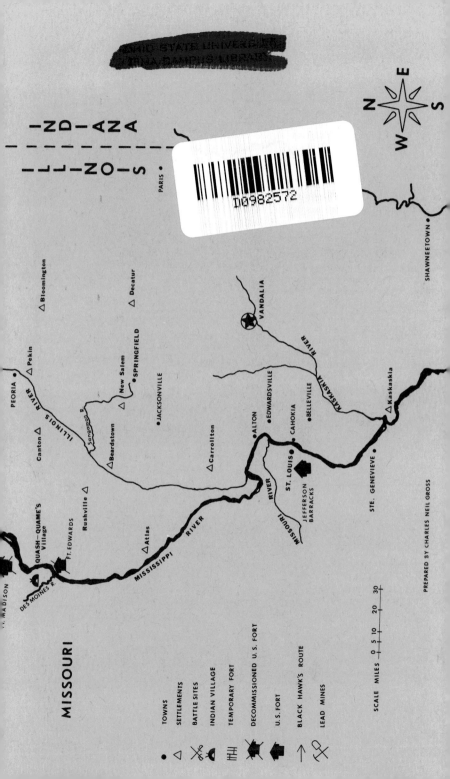

D0982572

INDIANA

ILLINOIS

N E S W

PARIS •

SHAWNEETOWN •

△ Bloomington

PEORIA •

△ Decatur

VANDALIA

• Pekin

ILLINOIS RIVER

• New Salem

Canton △

• SPRINGFIELD

Sangamon R.

• JACKSONVILLE

△ Beardstown

KASKASKIA RIVER

Rushville △

△ Carrollton

• EDWARDSVILLE

• ALTON

△ Kaskaskia

△ Atlas

MISSISSIPPI RIVER

• CAHOKIA

RIVER

• BELLEVILLE

QUASH-QUAME's Village

ST. LOUIS •

Ft. EDWARDS

DES MOINES R.

MISSOURI

JEFFERSON BARRACKS

STE. GENEVIEVE •

Ft. MADISON

MISSOURI

TOWNS •

SETTLEMENTS △

BATTLE SITES

INDIAN VILLAGE

TEMPORARY FORT

DECOMMISSIONED U.S. FORT

U.S. FORT

BLACK HAWK'S ROUTE →

LEAD MINES

SCALE MILES 0 5 10 20 30

PREPARED BY CHARLES NEIL GROSS

"That Disgraceful Affair," the Black Hawk War

"That Disgraceful Affair," the Black Hawk War

By CECIL EBY

W · W · NORTON & COMPANY · INC ·

NEW YORK

FIRST EDITION

Library of Congress Cataloging in Publication Data
Eby, Cecil D
    That disgraceful affair.
    Bibliography: p.
    1. Black Hawk War, 1832. I. Title.
E83.83.E29   973.5'6   73–6813
ISBN 0–393–05484–5

1 2 3 4 5 6 7 8 9 0

Contents

PHOTOGRAPHS APPEAR FOLLOWING PAGE 164

Acknowledgments

MY GREATEST DEBT is to Mrs. Ellen Whitney of the Illinois
State Historical Library, Springfield, who made available the
massive collection of Black Hawk War materials which she has
been assembling for nearly twenty years. As though this were
not enough, she gave me access to her own notes and memoranda
and pointed out the more hazardous sectors of the historical terrain. I wish to thank Mr. Paul Spence, curator of manuscripts,
for his astonishing display of archival surprises, and Mr. Howard
Rissler, formerly of the library staff, for assistance of a more
general kind. In any number of ways the Illinois State Historical
Library is a researcher's paradise.

The following were generous in answering questions or pro-
viding materials: Mrs. Marie T. Capps of West Point, New York;
Mrs. Lois Dugdale of Oregon, Illinois; Mr. Ellsworth Glick of
Galena, Illinois; Miss Josephine L. Harper of Madison, Wisconsin; Mr. Alvin M. Josephy, Jr., of New York; Mr. Donald Jackson
of Charlottesville, Virginia; Mr. Lawrence Oestreich of Galena,
Illinois; Miss Paula Richardson of Washington, D.C.; Mrs.
George Swart of Fort Atkinson, Wisconsin. At one point in my
research Dr. Frederick H. Wagman, director of the University
Library at the University of Michigan, cut through a mass of red
tape with admirable style.

For editorial and related assistance I thank Mr. Eric Swenson
and Ms. Mary Shuford of W. W. Norton and Mr. Perry Knowl-
ton of Curtis Brown. Finally I should like to offer extravagant
praise to members of my immediate family for having held up
so well during the course of my work on this book.

Chronology

1804	November	Treaty at St. Louis seizes lands of Sauk and Fox to the Wisconsin River
1806	Spring	Captain Zebulon Pike visits Saukenuk
1808	Fall	Construction of Fort Madison at Des Moines Rapids
1812	Summer	British Band joins British at Green Bay
1814	July	Sauk attack John Campbell's keelboats above Rock Island
	September	Sauk hurl back Zachary Taylor from Saukenuk
1816	May	Black Hawk signs peace treaty at Portage des Sioux
	Summer	Construction begins of forts Armstrong and Crawford
1822	Spring	White miners settle Galena area and launch lead boom
1827	Spring	White settlers arrive at Saukenuk
1829	Fall	Lands including Saukenuk sold by the government
1830	May	Sioux and Menominee ambush Fox party near Prairie du Chien
1831	June	First Black Hawk War ousts British Band over Mississippi River
	July	Sauk and Fox massacre Menominee above Prairie du Chien
1832	April 5	Black Hawk crosses Mississippi
	April 8	General Henry Atkinson's departure from Jefferson Barracks

"That Disgraceful Affair," the Black Hawk War

For the nation, there is an unrequited account of sin and injustice that sooner or later will call for *national retribution*.

—GEORGE CATLIN

Introduction

Ain't no game like Ingins—No, sir!
No game like Ingins.
                    —ADAM POE, pioneer

WHY SHOULD the contemporary American, already bending beneath the weight of the mass of recent revisionist history, be asked to accept the burden of yet another national calamity, the Black Hawk War? No one, not even with a scholar's devotion of a lifetime to its study would dare suggest that this four-month eruption in the Northwest produced more than a ripple throughout the rest of the nation. Other than slowing the flood of immigration into Wisconsin and Illinois briefly, the war had little effect upon American history as a whole. Measured in terms of human and monetary cost, the war shrinks to a pistareen. Only 70-odd whites were killed in the war and an estimated 450 to 600 Indians. It cost the United States less than $8 million (some calculations are as low as $3 million); today's Pentagon officials would call it a bargain-basement war, even after making allowances for the erosion of the dollar since 1832. And it might have cost even less had it not been, in the words of Colonel Zachary Taylor, "a tissue of blunders, miserably managed from start to finish." Junior officers unanimously agreed. Lieutenant Albert Sidney Johnston had cause to wonder whether it was a real war at all; what he chiefly remembered was "an affair of fatigue, filth, hunger, disease, petty jealousy, bickering, frustration, loneliness, boredom." Heroism must be stitched on finer cloth than this.

No pantheon commemorating the grand leaders of the Black Hawk War looms out of the cornfields of Illinois to remind native sons of the sacrifices of their forebears. Indeed, the names of these warriors are now almost unknown. Reynolds, Atkinson,

Whiteside, Posey—surely at least a generation of whittlers and loafers throughout the Northwest must have pronounced these names with veneration, or at least with derision; but they are not heard today. No post office contains a mural depicting the tumult of Stillman's Run or Bad Axe; no backwoods bard launched his literary career with tales of this war.

The most distinguished alumnus of the Black Hawk War, Captain Abraham Lincoln, is remembered not because of his campaigning, but in spite of it. A reasonably honest man, Lincoln in later years never denied that he had served in the war; but, when he alluded to his campaign at all, he mentioned the slaughter of mosquitoes, not Indians. Yet he had volunteered eagerly. Only hindsight permits us to see that his pursuit of Black Hawk proved to be but the first leg of a public career that eventually ended in the White House. If a man of Lincoln's humanity found it impossible to resist the lure of an Indian purge, then the bloodletting impulses of his fellow volunteers may be more easily understood. Many years later Governor Reynolds, the principal architect of the war, playfully characterized his militia, "They also entertained rather an excess of the *Indian ill-will*, so that it required much gentle persuasion to restrain them from killing indiscriminately all the Indians they met."

Historians, even Western ones, have generally joined in denouncing the heralded causes of the war as fraudulent and its prosecution as farcical. To Benjamin Drake of Ohio the war "had its origin in avarice and political ambition, . . . was prosecuted in bad faith and closed in dishonor" (1838). To Reuben G. Thwaites of Wisconsin, it was "a tale fraught with dishonor to the American name" (1892). To Perry Armstrong of Illinois, it was "simply a cold-blooded series of murders without cause or justification" (1887). These verdicts, while well intended, suggest that the Black Hawk War marked a kind of hideous aberration which was alien to normative American experience. According to this line of reasoning, the war was a strange anomaly rather than symptomatic of the national psyche.

The essential plot of the Black Hawk War is so familiar that any American must surely experience a sense of *déjà vu* as he watches the drama unfold. The script had been favorite since the seventeenth century. The villains, and victims, are non-whites, in this case, Indians. The massacre takes place in or near a swamp, stream, or ditch. The slaughter symbolizes the eradication of an entire race of enemies, whether the Pequot at Mystic, the Mohican at Gnadenhutten, the Sauk at Bad Axe, the Minneconjou at Wounded Knee, or the Vietnamese at My Lai. Had there been only one version of this drama, we could call it tragic and expect catharsis; but it has been played and replayed so many times through the centuries that fear and pity have been extruded from it. We learn nothing from the performance because its purpose is to justify the hunt, not to arouse sympathy for the hunted. To move either backward or forward in time from the Black Hawk War is to be locked within the same moral dimension, forced to view endless revisions of this American revenge tragedy.

Today, however, we can avoid personal responsibility for faraway deaths by heaping the blame upon the industrial-military complex. This comforting fantasy exonerates The People from complicity in the tragedy. Unfortunately, if we allow ourselves to see what truly happened in our Indian wars, it contradicts this simple thesis. The professional army was called in, often against its wishes, to perform what The People demanded. There would have been no Black Hawk War, for example, if The People had not trespassed on Sauk land and forced Black Hawk to the edge of a precipice where he had no choice but to fight. And it was the militia, not the regular army, which opened fire on the Sauk while they were advancing under a white flag to give themselves up.

Although, by the end of the nineteenth century, the regular army was responsible for Indian disturbances, during the Black Hawk War, civilians had the power to mobilize themselves. It should not be assumed that they fought to defend their homesteads and families against the onslaught of maniacal Indians. What menace was rumored lay far to the north; and it is difficult to believe that The People simply accepted their governor's report of an invasion, especially since the attackers were outnumbered by a ratio of two hundred to one. In most cases, they joined the militia army for personal and acquisitive motives: to scout new country for eventual homesteading; to pick up easy money from federal paymasters; to obtain that supreme badge of frontier manhood, an Indian scalp.

The volunteers of 1832, two-thirds of whom were of Southern extraction, came from frontier stock, but were not themselves frontiersmen. Their clothes had been cut from bolts of store-bought goods, not from animal skins; they subsisted on settlers' fare like pork, corn, buttermilk, and greens. Though they had been raised on tales of Indian wars, the great battles had been fought nearly half a century before. The frontier itself had jumped over Illinois, leaving them in the shadow line between wilderness and civilization. Having inherited the frontier ethic without a proper channel to express it, Illinois males of 1832 must have felt in the governor's call for volunteers an opportunity to emulate the derring-do of their sires and grandsires, to become part of that frontier legend which heretofore had been experienced only vicariously. For the warrior *manqué,* the prospect ahead must have also been vaguely disturbing: Civilization meant agencies of discipline and control—banks, churches, schools, laws—it meant building rather than destroying. The Black Hawk War seemed to offer a last chance for a man to acquire his heroism by the old rule, which required nothing more complicated than shooting an Indian.

Installed in the White House at this time was Andrew Jackson, the epitome of the Western man. His six predecessors had been more aristocratic, paying little mind to the clamor of urban mobs or frontier boors. With the ascension into power of Jackson, the Westerners believed, the people's millenium had arrived. There were whoops of delight in the back country as "Old Hickory" joined battle with Eastern banking powers and instituted policies that would eventually remove all Indian tribes west of the Mississippi. It was no accident that the Black Hawk War occurred during Jackson's tenure in the presidency.

In the Western states Jacksonism was less a political ideology than a religious belief in which Indulge Thyself appeared to be the supreme commandment. The rallying cry "Jackson forever— and damn everybody else!" captured, in a single phrase, the essential tenets of the new religion, which was based on immortality for one side and eternal perdition for the other. Jacksonian iconography was displayed everywhere. In Ohio a traveler counted thirty hamlets bearing the name of the new saint. In Wisconsin one zealous Democrat trained his parrot to shout, "Hurrah for Jackson!" In Illinois an English traveler, querying a local resident about the reasons for naming a budding settlement Palmyra, received the astonishing reply, "I expect it likely that Jackson gave the British a most complete whipping there." So the achievements of Jackson, and the Western man, were always celebrated in terms of violent encounters with his enemies, no matter whether the Indians, the British, the Adamses, or the banks. The Westerner was even prepared to revise Hammurabi's Law to read, "take the other fellow's eye before he takes yours."

Jackson did not create the climate of brutishness that prevailed in the West; it was rather that his rise to power was construed by these creatures of fang and belly as license to do whatever they pleased. It was every man jack for himself, "root, hog, or die." The milieu of Jackson encouraged the people's power in its most volatile form.

The pioneer of fiction has been so thoroughly imposed upon America that eradication of him is probably impossible. Today every hog kettle, puncheon table, and cedar bucket dating from the epoch of the doughty pioneer is a potential or actual museum piece; log cabins so clumsily made that they resemble gargantuan bird cages are embalmed in creosote or silicone and revered as temples; genealogists plunge into regional archives to trace affluent suburbanites back to pioneer forebears who, if now present in the flesh, would probably be fumigated and deported. According to the legends, in pioneer days rugged giants roamed the prairies and forests, helpful neighbors came for miles to lend a hand at barn-raisings, and contented folk amused themselves with pastimes such as quilting parties and spelling bees. This Currier and Ives idyl allows no room for the unsavory realities of pioneer existence: sallow, vermin-infested children, forced to drink their own urine as a cure for ague; unneighborly annual interest rates on loans calculated at 25 percent; entertainments like the gander pull in which the object was to yank off the head and windpipe of a live gander suspended by its feet from a tree limb, the screams of the bird providing, as a spectator explained, "a prominent part of the entertainment"; camp meetings where the chosen shook with holy seizure, while parsons shook with a different excitement as they pawed the young girls.

Accounts of the Western country written by outsiders are, almost without exception, derogatory. While Western propagandists alluded to back-country people as nature's noblemen, European visitors characterized them as "animals of an inferior type, dressed like men," "sons of Cain," and "Ostrogoths." Alexis de Tocqueville had been told repeatedly that honesty and hospitality were universal in regions west of the Alleghanies. Much to his disappointment he found that even the settlers regarded itinerant bands of Indians as more trustworthy than their nearest neighbors; he learned through experience that pioneer folk charged more for bed and board than innkeepers in the towns. His preconception that people who lived far from cities were less likely to be corrupted altered quickly as he moved about the West. "Everyone has come to make money," he wrote. "No one has been born there; no one wants to stay there." To obtain money the Westerner was prepared to trade "in everything, even morality and religion."

Many other travelers filled notebooks with similar observations of the blatant venality seen throughout the West. "A propensity to cheat and deceive pervades all classes of this people," William Faux wrote in 1823. "It is the boasted qualification of the *smart man*." Although thieves and liars existed elsewhere, what was unique about the West was that there villainy was transformed into a virtue. George W. Featherstonhaugh noted that a steamboat captain who had been caught in the act of cheating his passengers showed no remorse as he laughingly explained, "You can't get on no how on this river without lying a little." All was reduced to a desperate scramble for money. None of these travelers would have been surprised to learn that the first justice of the Illinois supreme court, in his zeal to get on, put his daughters out as prostitutes in the capital city of Vandalia.

Perhaps the most perspicacious observation of all came from

Charles J. Latrobe, an Englishman who, after watching several days of treaty negotiations between whites and Indians at Chicago, succinctly wrote, "The whites seemed to me to be more pagan than the red men." However reasonable this view may seem to us today, it would have sounded like madness to a citizen of Illinois in the 1830s, who accepted as God-given truth that he could put land to better use than any band of savages. To justify his extirpation of the Indian he borrowed the utilitarian principle of the greatest good for the greatest number. Under Jacksonism, that concept became the keystone of the American political system: It could justify anything, including robbery and murder. As one might expect, Governor Reynolds invoked it many years later to condone the white man's expropriation of Indian lands: "Providence will be best pleased in having a greater number of the human family in existence than a few."

One of the most regrettable aspects of the Black Hawk War was the failure of the white majority to see that its real enemies were not the Indians, but the land speculators who always grabbed the best land first and the merchants who realized the greatest profits on its produce. The white populace served as the cutting edge for a ruthlessly self-serving system which, in time, would mow them as close as it had mowed the Indians. Some few would escape the scythe by wielding one of their own; but, for the majority, the expectations of Jacksonian Democracy turned into a bitter joke at their expense. Competition may be the life of trade, but it is death to Indians and poor whites.

On the eve of the Black Hawk War, de Tocqueville called on John Carroll of Carrollton, the last living signer of the Declaration of Independence. The ancient patrician outlined the relationship between democracy and the frontier: "A democracy is but a mob," he said. "If we tolerate ours, that is because every year we can push our innovators out west." Here was an early version of what was later to be called the safety-valve theory (which held that the explosiveness inherent in the American political system could be relieved by permitting the combustible elements to dissipate in the empty spaces of the frontier). Although the Black Hawk War resulted from the movement of restless men to the West, John Carroll would probably have denied that his ideas and leadership were in any way responsible for the conflagration. So we have a curious phenomenon, a white man's war for which all white men disavow responsibility. Only the Indians had the perspective to put the blame squarely on white America as a civilization and nation.

There are no more safety valves. The West with its once boundless opportunities for escape and release has been bounded. To proclaim that the new frontier is either up in the sky or down in the earth is to avoid the crisis. The frontier now exists only in the American past in the form of a record of our mistakes. To dust off and to pore over these old account books might show us what investments to avoid in the future. That would certainly be one path evening the balance of the future, though the debits of former errors will remain forever old debts beyond reparations, atonement, or forgiveness.

ONE *Upriver with the General*

The people of St. Louis know as much about an
Indian as a cow does of a shilling.
—Thomas Forsyth

<<<<<<<<<<<<<<<<<<<<<<<<<<<<<<<<<<<<<<<<<<<<<<<<<<<<<<<<

ON APRIL FOOL'S DAY of 1832, Brevet Brigadier General
Henry Atkinson, who commanded the Right Wing of the Western Department of the United States Army with headquarters at
Jefferson Barracks below St. Louis, received from the Department of War a dispatch dated March 17 which ordered him to
chastise the Sauk and Fox tribes. The difficulty was largely an
Indian affair, having little to do with *Chemokemons* (as Americans were called in the West). Atkinson was charged with a
mission of pacification. He was to head off an Indian war which
appeared to be fomenting among the tribes of the upper Mississippi.

Seven years earlier the United States had compelled the
various tribes in the area to sign a treaty establishing their respective boundaries, assigning itself as guarantor of eternal
peace in the region. It was a well-meant, but foolishly bureaucratic, effort to put an end to the unceasing territorial wars
among the tribes concerned. In fact, no man of good sense in
the West—white or red—had ever really believed it could work.
(When asked why these boundaries had been set up, one of the
commissioners responsible for the treaty had shrugged and replied, "Washington will have it so.")

For years small war parties of Sioux and Sauk and Fox had
been ambushing one another on the hunting grounds claimed

by both tribes, but there had never been indications of a massive war impending. In May 1830, however, eighteen Fox invited to a government conference at Prairie du Chien were ambushed south of the settlement by a mixed war party of Menominee and Sioux; seventeen Fox were massacred. The attackers put the sole survivor, a youth, in a canoe, broke his arms, and set him afloat to carry news of the defeat to the Fox village at Dubuque.

The following morning the citizens of Prairie du Chien witnessed a shocking spectacle. The victors paraded through the streets of the village brandishing scalps, severed arms and viscera on poles. After "yelling and dancing like devils," they roasted the heart of the Fox chief, Kettle, chopped it into small pieces, and ate it. Instead of interfering with this barbarous celebration, the officers and men of the Sixth Infantry quartered at Fort Crawford, at the northern edge of the village, were eager spectators. In the whole community, a white woman reported later, "neither civil nor military authorities made any effort to prevent the exhibition." Nor was there any attempt by whites to bring the murderers to justice, as the 1825 treaty obliged them to do. One reason for this was the traditionally peaceful behavior of the Menominee, who almost alone among the Northwestern tribes could boast that they had never warred against the United States.

The Sauk and Fox were infuriated by the massacre; their rage was compounded by the do-nothing attitude of the federal authorities, especially when they learned that a former Indian agent at Prairie du Chien, John Marsh, had tipped off the Sioux about the conference—in effect, precipitating the massacre. The fact that Marsh, possessor of a Harvard degree and a Sioux common-law wife, had been removed from his $500 a year post as agent a few years before did not satisfy the Sauk and Fox, who were convinced that American authorities collaborated with the enemy. Adding to their outrage was the longstanding Indian custom that Prairie du Chien was respected as neutral ground.

Unlike the more malleable Menominee, the Sauk and Fox were a proud people whose culture had thus far resisted the erosion of contact with white men. Their decision was inevitable: If the Chemokemons refused them justice, they would avenge the massacre on their own. The opportunity for revenge came a year later, in July 1831, when a war party surprised and slaughtered twenty-five Menominee who were sleeping off a drunken frolic on an island half a mile north of Fort Crawford. Chanting and whooping, the victors moved down the river in the darkness—passing under the noses of the garrison—carrying with them many trophies which the Menominee had gathered from Kettle's band the summer before.

The score was even so far as the Sauk and Fox were concerned, but the U.S. government failed to see it that way. At a conference in the autumn, the United States, through its Indian agent Felix St. Vrain, demanded that the murderers of the Menominee be turned over to federal authorities for punishment. Such one-sided zeal for justice did not pass unremarked by the headmen of the Sauk and Fox, one of whom reminded St. Vrain that no comparable demand had been made to the Menominee and Sioux, even though Kettle's party had been carrying the American flag. "His flag, your flag," exclaimed the Sauk spokesman, "the flag of the United States was trod under foot and then burned!"

The substance of the Sauk and Fox argument, whatever its merit in reason and justice, mattered less to St. Vrain than his instructions, which were as explicit as they were arbitrary. Again he demanded the murderers. The headmen told him that the malefactors had to surrender on their own volition, which was tantamount to telling him that they would not surrender at all. The conference ended in anger on all sides: the Menominee because their tribesmen went unavenged, the Sauk and Fox because Chemokemon justice ignored their interests, and the whites because their authority had been rejected.

Thus, during the winter of 1831–32, reports of an imminent war among the tribes alarmed the settlements of the upper Mississippi. The Menominee strengthened their ties with the Sioux and reportedly patched up old quarrels with the Chippewa to the north, to protect their rear; the Sauk and Fox parleyed with the Potawatomie of northern Illinois. The Winnebago, who occupied the uncomfortable buffer zone between the two militant blocs, wisely gave lip service to whichever faction was nearer at the time, knowing well that they stood to lose no matter which side won.

In February "General" Joseph M. Street (the title was derived from militia service long before) who functioned as Winnebago agent at Prairie du Chien, warned his superintendent of the Menominee-Sioux entente, "if the Government is not early in stopping them, they will certainly go in considerable force, and a bloody contest may be expected." To head off this "bloody contest," which would surely ignite tinder long-smouldering in neighboring tribes and might spread to the white settlements, the Department of War called out General Atkinson, the first official act of the bloody contest, the bloody farce, known as the Black Hawk War.

General Atkinson was instructed to obtain eight or ten Sauk and Fox warriors who could be tried as Menominee murderers; further, he was to make a show of American strength so that the Menominee and Sioux would back down from their muted threats of war. Nothing in his orders indicated that white settlements were threatened or that the United States anticipated a war. The general was promised support, if he required it, from other military garrisons on the upper Mississippi, specifically Fort Crawford (Prairie du Chien), Fort Armstrong (Rock Island), and Fort Winnebago (Portage, Wisconsin). Counting his contingent at Jefferson Barracks, he had at his disposal about 420 regulars—infantry, for the most part—to bring the Indians into line and to "preserve the pledged faith of the Government unbroken," in the lofty phraseology of the original order from Washington.

The expedition was regarded as more nettlesome than hazardous—certainly not dangerous. The army had for twenty years been watchdogging the Indian frontier. Experience had revealed that in dealing with Indians a determined bluff was worth a thousand maneuvers. Further, among the regular officers, the Sauk and Fox were great favorites: They kept to themselves, they did not beg, and they were reputed to be the most civilized —and the most warlike—of all tribes along the upper river.

With their heads shaved close on each side and a great tuft of hair bisecting the skull—a defiant scalp lock brazenly exposed to an enemy—the Sauk and Fox resembled, at a distance, Roman legionaries helmeted for battle. A young American lieutenant summarized the army's attitude toward the tribe when he characterized them as the "fiercest Indians in our country, as their conduct during the last war exemplified. Some of them were killed at the very cannon mouth." Killed always, as he knew, by Americans, for the Sauk and Fox had been loyal to the British (*Saganash*) during both wars.

To this point the military career of General Henry Atkinson had been distinguished only by its plodding uneventfulness. Seldom in the annals of the United States Army had an officer gone so far and gotten so high by doing so little. The average American of that day had never heard of him, and with good reason, for Atkinson owed his rank not to heroic deeds on the battlefield, but rather to assiduous cultivation of the right people in the halls of Congress and the anterooms of the War Department. In a quarter-century of active service, Henry Atkinson had probably never even seen a thousand soldiers assembled together in one place, much less commanded them. No affectionate or contemptuous nickname like "Old Hickory" or "Old Fuss and Feathers" ever adhered to this man whose personality was so amorphous that his men seemed neither to like nor dislike him. (For a brief period he was called "Old Granny," but even this dropped from popular currency as thought mild abuse of the general was hardly worth the effort.) To the Indians he was "White Beaver," but whether this implied flattery or insult no white man could tell and no Indian would say. Physically he was imposing, in a broad-shouldered, potbellied way. With his thick wavy hair, his fine blue eyes, and his deeply cleft chin, Atkinson cut a fine figure at St. Louis cotillions; but to observers there was always a sense of not having engaged a real person behind the sleek façade.

Since General Atkinson never liked to talk about his family and early years in North Carolina, where he was born in 1782, his origins most likely were humble enough. The Atkinsons were probably piney-woods "white-trash" such as described by William Byrd in his *Dividing Line* history, folk who asked little more from life than an opportunity to "loiter away their lives, like Solomon's sluggard, with their arms across." However, Henry was bitten by the bug of ambition; when President Thomas Jefferson expanded the regular army in 1808, he cast aside his general store in Caswell County and applied for a commission. Though without any military training beyond an occasional backwoods militia muster, he nonetheless possessed sufficient political patronage to be posted as captain to the Third Infantry.

The War of 1812 came as godsend to young American officers eager to chaw up the British Lion, but Captain Atkinson was stalked by bad luck. During the opening year of the war, when most of the fighting took place along the Canadian front, he performed clerical duties in New Orleans. Later, just as the war swung into the South, Atkinson was transferred north! It seems that the only hostile shot that Captain Atkinson heard during the entire war came from the pistol of a fellow officer who called him out to duel in a chill Plattsburgh dawn. And, ironically, the ball which smashed Atkinson's right tibia provided him with the only wound which he was to receive during thirty-four years of active service. He ended the war convalescing in New London, a place bypassed, like himself, by military activity.

After the Treaty of Ghent, when more promising officers were being pared from army lists, Atkinson—by then a colonel —managed to hold on. Somehow he had acquired a sixth sense for survival in the peacetime army: He knew exactly how to butter the right people, to keep a tight set of books, and to avoid giving offense. Secretary of War John Calhoun, badgered constantly by kill-devil generals like Andrew Jackson and prima donnas like Winfield Scott, came in time to dote on Atkinson, who ruffled no feathers and did what he was told.

An opportunity for Colonel Atkinson to do something more than shuffle papers arrived in 1819 when Calhoun instructed him to establish a military post at the mouth of the Yellowstone River. Pushing off from St. Louis in late summer with three steamboats and a flotilla of keelboats, the Atkinson armada grounded out on sand bars almost within earshot of the point of embarkation. Refloated, they got as far as Council Bluffs where the colonel threw up a log compound for his men to winter over, while he retreated with his staff to St. Louis.

On returning to the compound in the spring, Atkinson found his men mangy, mutinous, and half-starved; part of his fort had been situated too close to the riverbank and had floated off in the spring floods. In addition, a tightfisted Congress, hit by the Panic of '19, cut his budget. To keep his men alive Atkinson went into the truck-gardening business; his official dispatches, filled with statistics about hay, corn, and potatoes, could have served as copy for a farmer's almanac. The colonel was proud of his four thousands bushels of turnips, and he was careful to send packets of fine seed corn to patrons like John Calhoun and DeWitt Clinton. Promotion to brigadier general came later in the year.

Though the Yellowstone expedition did not amount to anything tangible, at least it had exposed Atkinson's name in the newspapers. Andrew Jackson's faction in the War Department opposed Atkinson's promotion, arguing that it smacked of blatant favoritism; but President James Monroe upheld it, not because the officer in question much deserved it, but because "North Carolina had no one in military or civil status" and "this had weight." The real weight, of course, was the heavy thumb of John Calhoun on the scale. For the moment, the Jacksonists bowed to what was unpreventable, but ill will toward Atkinson —though he was but a dummy for the Calhoun machine— would rise to torment him again.

The year 1825 marked something of an *annus mirabilis* for General Henry Atkinson. Using newfangled paddle-wheel boats propelled by human feet, he established a post on the Yellowstone and supervised the construction—in stone—of Jefferson Barracks below St. Louis by soldiers of the Sixth Infantry. In the same year he took to his bosom the twenty-two-year-old daughter of a rich Louisville merchant. The Atkinsons established themselves as social bulwarks at "Shallow Water"—as the Indians called St. Louis—a place much in need of all the high tone it could get. An officer from Virginia, little impressed by such emblems of civilization as three brick warehouses hanging over a scraggly riverfront, noted that "*Rowdyism* was the order of the day." With the exception of minor annoyances such as chronic desertion and occasional Indian disturbances, his assignment was a pleasant sinecure.

As he prepared to move his command up the river in 1832, General Atkinson must have been struck by the similarity between this assignment and one which he had carried out five years earlier during the so-called Winnebago War. (In the West, if half a dozen Indians went on a rampage, the affair seems always to have been elevated into a war.) Then trouble had broken out when a band of Winnebago attacked a keelboat in the vicinity of the Bad Axe River forty miles above Prairie du Chien. At about the same time a Winnebago chief named Red Bird, an Indian respected by the whites, killed two settlers and scalped a baby girl. The two events, though apparently unrelated, unleashed a panic in the Lead Region. Miners, who had been in illegal occupation of Winnebago land, stampeded toward the settlements as though the Day of Judgment had prematurely arrived. At Galena, some three thousand refugees camped without food or shelter along the Fever River while the local citizenry desperately threw up a blockhouse on the hillside behind the town. Down on the waterfront crowds gawked at the battered keelboat—said to have taken 693 bullets in her hull and planking—and debated whether it made more sense to stand pat or to scamper. At Prairie du Chien the inhabitants barricaded themselves in the rotted-out fort and underwent an imaginary siege by a nonexistent enemy.[1] Each refugee made a pilgrimage to see the scalped baby, who was exhibited with much side-show éclat.[2] In Illinois, Governor Ninian Edwards exploited the uproar by

1. In 1826 Fort Crawford had fallen into such dilapidation that the garrison had been transferred to Fort Snelling (presently Minneapolis-St. Paul). Construction of a stone fort began after the Winnebago War and was in progress during the Black Hawk War.

2. The child lived to a ripe old age and was still remembered by many of the older citizens as late as 1930. She and her mother received a grant of land and a $50 payment for fifteen years at the conclusion of the war—all this deducted from Winnebago annuities.

calling for six hundred militia to drive the whole Winnebago nation across the Mississippi, without taking time to note that the belligerents resided in territory beyond his jurisdiction!

It was General Atkinson who had soothed the panic-stricken region. While Colonel Josiah Snelling hurried to the relief of Prairie du Chien,[3] Atkinson, with five hundred regulars from St. Louis, backed the Winnebago up the Wisconsin River to the portage and arranged for peace without firing a shot. Headmen handed over eight hostages to the Americans and three of them— including Red Bird—were sentenced to be executed. (As it turned out, Red Bird died in prison the following spring and the others were pardoned by President John Quincy Adams.) The Winnebago promised not to molest the miners encroaching on their land, even though it was this steady invasion which had been the major cause of their increasing frustration and militancy. Some nasty details came out at the negotiations, however. The keelboat had been attacked because the crew had abducted some Winnebago women, holding and abusing them during two days of carousal.[4] Nor was Red Bird's attack unmotivated. It came in retaliation for a report—false, as it proved—that two of his tribesmen had been summarily executed at Fort Snelling.

So far as the War Department was concerned, the Winnebago

---

3. On his arrival at the Prairie, the crusty Snelling immediately sent packing all the Illinois militia who had come to "defend" the town. Instead of preparing to attack the settlement, the Winnebago of the vicinity, terrified by the thought of reprisals to come, had fled in all directions.

When the Illinois commander, ruffled by Snelling's ill-concealed contempt for the militia, challenged the colonel to a duel, Snelling promptly placed the officer who delivered the challenge under arrest and forced him to deny knowledge of its contents. He then refused the militia transportation back to Illinois. Had it not been for the generosity of some private citizens who provided them with steamboat passage, the by then hangdog Illinois volunteers would have returned home on foot.

Snelling, like most professional military men, of course knew that the true aggressors were not the Winnebago, but rather the land-hungry whites with their gospel of squatter's rights.

4. Historians of the frontier have not been eager to accept this ugly detail. But St. Louis newspapers alluded to it, early settlers admitted it, and Governor John Reynolds of Illinois, no Indian apologist, freely confessed it in his memoirs.

War was the gaudiest feather in Atkinson's cap. He had put down an insurrection, yet had conducted a bloodless—and, perhaps more importantly, an inexpensive—campaign. This outweighed the grumblings among the settlers for whom a real victory was more luridly defined as skivvering Indians and taking another bite of their land; for such as these Atkinson was as insipid as milk and water.

In a sense the settlers were right about Atkinson. His tactic for settling Indian troubles was premised on making a show of force and waiting for the enemy to back down. And, further, he adhered to the classic rule that a white ought never to take the field against an Indian adversary without sufficient force to whip him; a setback invariably enlisted neutral tribes on the side of the enemy. These principles worked well in situations where the Indians' sense of outrage fell short of a determination to go to war, as was the case in the Winnebago War. But General Atkinson's policy had not been tested on a hard head; shortly he would learn how hawks differed from redbirds.

Before his departure from St. Louis, Atkinson received a disquieting note from Major John Bliss, commander of the sixty-odd troops garrisoned at Fort Armstrong on Rock Island. Rumors had reached him that a large faction among the Sauk and Fox led by Black Hawk was planning to cross the Mississippi into Illinois in flagrant violation of an agreement signed in 1831, the year before, in which members of the tribe had sworn never to occupy, or even to visit temporarily, land east of the river without prior approval by the government. Atkinson tended to discount Bliss's information. In a letter of April 7 addressed to his superior, General Edmund P. Gaines,[5] he wrote, "I can hardly think that Black Hawk and his Band have any serious intention of reoccupying their old village." He added, in a sentence he would come to regret, "If they have I shall be up in time to prevent it."

All the same, the ever-cautious Atkinson instructed his men to pack and store summer uniforms so that they could be readily

5. As commander of the Western Department, General Gaines would have led the American forces in the Black Hawk War had he not been on leave at the time. In his absence, responsibility for the department devolved upon Atkinson.

available if required. He did confess to Gaines that he might have more difficulty than he originally expected; there existed that off-chance that his expedition might entail not just defusing the Sioux and Menominee, but also ejecting the Sauk and Fox from Illinois.

On April 8 General Atkinson set out from St. Louis with six companies of the Sixth Infantry—the "Fighting Sixth," as they called themselves—aboard two chartered steamboats, the *Chieftain* and the *Enterprise.* The companies were understrength, counting no more than 280 men in all. In charge of the paper work was Atkinson's competent aide-de-camp, Lieutenant Albert Sidney Johnston, who had turned down a quick-promotion assignment in Washington because he preferred field duty on the frontier.

It took two days to reach the rapids of the Des Moines River (now Keokuk, Iowa) where a settlement of mixed-bloods and backwoods flotsam eked out their existence by preying on the river traffic. Here Atkinson learned that a band of Sauk estimated at four or five hundred warriors and an equal number of non-combatants had crossed into Illinois five days before. No whites had been provoked or molested. As was their custom, the Sauk had placed guards around Chemokemon houses near their camp-sites to safeguard the white inhabitants should any younger warriors get rambunctious. And, although the presence of women, children, and old people in Black Hawk's band suggested that the Sauk were migrating, not launching an invasion of Illinois, a sense of urgency swept through Atkinson's expedition. Against their wishes the boat captains were compelled to ascend the rapids at night in a race for Fort Armstrong to cut off the Sauk before they reached their old village near Rock Island. If not stopped there, the Indians might push up the Rock River and vanish into the interior of Illinois. Farther upstream, at a wood stop known as Yellow Banks (now Oquawka, Illinois), news came on board that about a hundred Kickapoo accompanied the Sauk.[6]

6. The Kickapoo were inveterate enemies of the Americans, and with good reason: They had been decimated by settlers pushing into central Illinois. This particular band had allied itself with the Sauk and established a village near Rock Island.

The movements of Black Hawk had little to do with the inter-tribal war that Atkinson had come north to prevent, however. The antecedents of the Sauk problem were more complex and the whites were more directly responsible.

TWO *The Sauk and Fox: The Rise*

THE HISTORY of any nation properly begins with the act of creation. Wesahkah, chief of the land, warred with the two chiefs of waters who, in retaliation, sent a flood to drown the world. Fleeing to a mountaintop with earth's creatures, Wesahkah built a raft and floated to safety. After ten days he dreamed that he saw dry land. Obeying Wesahkah, a muskrat dived into the deep and brought up clay in his paws. From yellow clay Wesahkah made the Asauwekie (Sauk) nation; from red, the Mesquakie (Fox). As brothers these tribes journeyed south, but each retained his own *meshaum,* or medicine bag. All their enemies and evil creatures died in the flood, though they quickly came back again.

This creation myth satisfactorily explained to the Sauk and Fox both the similarities and differences between them. Each was distinct and autonomous as a tribe. They might disagree or quarrel, but an outright war between them was unthinkable. They occupied separate villages and acknowledged different chiefs, but they fought common enemies and intermarried freely. The major difference lay in the superior political organization among the Sauk, who were ever more willing to adhere to decisions of their chiefs and council and who, because of this, offered greater resistance to the corrupting temptations—whiskey in particular—of the Chemokemons. Further, the Sauk always outnumbered the Fox by a ratio of about three to one, in a total population of approximately six thousand.

When the French arrived in North America, the Sauk and Fox tribes occupied the Montreal region. They were only loosely allied with one another and with other Algonquin language groups of the region. Both were driven west by ferocious Iroquois attacks in the seventeenth century, the Sauk to central Michigan where they left their name in Saginaw ("place of Sauk"), and the Fox to the Green Bay area of Wisconsin. For reasons still obscure, the Mesquakie became fierce enemies of the French—who gave them the name Reynards—and, by the middle of the eighteenth century, the tribe had become so nearly decimated that they accepted a Sauk offer of consolidation on terms of full equality.

Although the Sauk had followed the Fox to Wisconsin, their territorial aspirations lay to the south and west. They established a hunting domain that ranged as far as the Missouri River, waging a war of extermination against various Illinois tribes including the Kaskaskia who, by the early nineteenth century, had been reduced to a hundred-odd survivors begging and drinking themselves into oblivion near the Ohio River settlements.

The Sauk and Fox erected a fine town on the north bank of the Wisconsin River (near present Sauk City, Wisconsin), characterized by the British adventurer Jonathan Carver in the 1760s as "the largest and best built Indian town I ever saw." It consisted of ninety *wickeups*, each built of neatly fitted hewn planks and rainproofed with bark strips. The rich bottom land produced an abundance of corn, squash, and beans, shared equally by all members of the tribe. Jonathan Carver expressed surprised admiration of their sense of community, "They esteem it irrational that one man should be possessed of a greater quantity than another, and are amazed that any honour should be annexed to the possession of it." Scattered about the town lay large chunks of lead, which the Indians mined from lands south of the Wisconsin and sold to traders from Mackinac and Prairie du Chien.

Although Carver was shocked by their savage treatment of enemies taken in battle—he witnessed the execution of an Illinois Indian—he nevertheless found the Sauk hospitable and friendly toward strangers who came in peace. Other whites would endorse Carver's evaluation, "They are the worst enemies and the best friends of any people in the world."

By 1790 only rotting posts and leaching fireplaces marked this site. The new Sauk capital lay 150 miles south, 2 miles above the mouth of the Rivière de la Roche. This was Saukenuk, the most imposing town, Indian or white, in the Northwest. One hundred wickeups, some of them sixty feet in length and housing four families, lined regular streets from the bank of the river to the seventy-foot bluff behind the town. A child could ford the shallow Rock River, which abounded in fish. In season the valley teemed with birds: eagles, geese, pelicans, parakeets. Along the river spread eight hundred acres of rich cultivated loam protected from the horses by wattle fences lashed together with hickory bark. The bluegrass pasture around Saukenuk was reserved as a communal grazing land. From April until October some three thousand Sauk occupied Saukenuk.

Smaller villages belonging to the more fragmented Fox tribe lay scattered along both shores of the Mississippi as far north as the Wisconsin River. Along the Fever River bands of Fox dug galena with deer antlers and smelted the ore in crude log furnaces. On the Iowa bank of the river they also worked with Julian Dubuque at the "Spanish Mines," which the Frenchman had established with Indian cooperation in the 1790s.

When the geese flew south, the Sauk and Fox moved to their winter hunting grounds between the Des Moines and Iowa rivers. Before leaving, they buried dried vegetables in bark-lined caches dug in the ground and sold their surplus grain to the traders from Prairie du Chien. During the annual migrations, many tribal "constables" instructed each head of family where he should camp and kept the flock tightly together. Old people too feeble for the trek were supplied with food and a boy or two and left behind to winter over at Saukenuk.

With their industrious mining, trapping, and agriculture, the Sauk and Fox belied the perennial complaints of shiftless back-woodsmen about the "lazy, thieving Redskins." Indeed, the average Sauk enjoyed a standard of comfort—not to mention a code of ethics—beyond the reach of most frontier riffraff. White men's pastimes, like drinking, stealing, and evangelizing, had not yet debauched them—but this was soon to change. Though dependent on traders for guns, powder, and ball, the Sauk and Fox did not behave like a subservient or exploited people. Each spring a small mountain of peltries stacked before the trader's cabin was tangible measurement of the stature of the Sauk and

Fox. Their skill in hunting and trapping, one aspect of which was the warfare required to drive rival tribes out of hunting lands, was considerable. At a single trading post, for example, the tribe delivered in one year some 60,082 skins netting them $58,800; and this yield was only a portion of their profit for that season.

Long contact with Spanish officials west of the Mississippi and with British traders east of it had accustomed the Sauk and Fox to the presence of the white man, but without giving them a taste for changing their way of life. Spaniards aboard the gunboat that sporadically appeared at Saukenuk were greeted as friends. Neither they nor the British traders from Mackinac attempted to wrest tribal lands from the Indians. In 1800, the Sauk and Fox attitudes were doubtless more favorable to whites than adverse. But they had had almost no contact with the pioneering Americans. With the Louisiana Purchase and the crushing weight of settlements that accompanied it, the Sauk and Fox radically altered their assessment of white men.

Almost at first sight a natural antipathy marked relations between the Americans and the Sauk and Fox. When Captain Amos Stoddard, with eight soldiers from the Kaskaskia garrison, arrived in St. Louis to take possession of upper Louisiana in March 1804, he found a band of Sauk taking leave of the Spanish governor, Don Carlos de Lassus. Without sign or greeting, the Indians—among them an unimportant warrior named Black Hawk—passed through one door as the Chemokemons entered another. Stoddard soon discovered that the Sauk, unlike other tribes, which sent begging envoys to St. Louis, seemed in no hurry to shift their allegiance to the United States. Writing to the secretary of war, the captain complained, "The Saucks . . . certainly do not pay that respect to the United States which is entertained by the other Indians—and in some instances they have assumed a pretty elevated tone." He was angry because a party of Sauk had attacked some Osage who had been riding on a boat belonging to one of the fur companies, ostensibly under the protection of the American flag. The Sauk, however, construed Stoddard's wrath as a sign that the Chemokemons had

sided with the Osage in a war between the two tribes over conflicting claims to winter hunting grounds.

Far more unsettling to the Sauk were reports in the summer of
1804 that Americans were already occupying their lands without
permission, chopping down trees, driving off game, insulting their
women. This was their first exposure to a frontier phenomenon
known as squatter sovereignty, a concept that every white
American male had a God-given right to a tract of land even if
this entailed dispossession of its original owner. When moral
sanction was needed, the "greatest good to the greatest number"
was invoked. The Sauk and Fox were beginning to experience
the process of thievery—later called Manifest Destiny—that had
characterized American dealings with every tribe to the east of
the Mississippi for the past two hundred years. In time they
would have a proverb for the process: Americans, they would
explain, were like a spot of raccoon grease on a blanket—at first
imperceptible, then spreading until it covered the entire cloth.

When the United States acquired new territory from a foreign
power it had to extinguish tribal claims by treaties with the
Indians in possession. The purchase of Louisiana, for example,
actually bought nothing more than a promise that France would
not assert any further claim to it. It is ridiculous to suppose that
Napoleon had the right to sell—or Jefferson the right to buy—
lands held by tribes for countless generations in regions never
seen, much less charted, by white men. Recognizing this, the
government was always careful to obtain cessions of land from
those tribes about to be overrun by the frontier juggernaut. Always the government could point to a legal document which
authorized its occupation of Indian lands.

The methods used to obtain such documents were various.
Thomas Jefferson encouraged chiefs to go into debt because "they
become willing to lop them off by a cession of lands." Lacking
both the patience and the subtlety of Jefferson, William Henry
Harrison obtained signatures of whatever Indians were at hand,
even of those with no authority to act in behalf of the tribe or,
in some instances, even of members of a wholly different tribe.
Andrew Jackson, contemptuous of such trumpery, simply thun-

dered about American firepower and pointed to the space where the Indian was to sign. In defense of the national honor, it might be argued that the United States did not actually steal land from Indians, only cheated them of it. In most cases, Indians living in the ceded tract could remain until the land had been surveyed and put up for sale at land offices; but, as soon as private citizens bought the land, the Indians had to leave.

The hidden villain of this process—the invisible enemy the Indian never saw—was the land speculator. He bought up vast tracts and refused to sell until prices skyrocketed; settlers without ready capital, therefore, had to push to the extreme verge of the frontier to find the cheapest land. Because of the land-hog, the entire frontier surged westward faster than it had to, leaving great pockets of undeveloped land far behind.[1]

Manifest Destiny was a dog-eat-dog process by which the poor whites, to avoid being devoured by the speculator, frenetically pushed beyond the settlements, in turn, pushing back the Indian. Strictly interpreted, most treaties promised that squatters would be evicted whenever they strayed onto Indian land; but, in fact, the government found it impossible to enforce this prohibition. Responsibility for driving off squatters fell to the United States Army, which had no relish for waging war against whites in behalf of Indians. Occasionally, conscientious officers cooperated with equally conscientious Indian agents in ejecting intruders from federal land; but such zealous attention to the fine letter of the law usually resulted in public execration and even, from time to time, prosecution in the courts for assault and other trumped-up complaints.

Since the army represented authority—an abstraction abominated above all others by Western men—an act of hostility toward the military was regarded as an honorable deed among

1. In the 1829–30 session of Congress, Senator Samuel Foot of Connecticut pin-pointed the problem: "The disposal of the public lands has been . . . absolutely wrested from the Government, and monopolized by speculators and squatters. . . . Instead of legislating for them, we are to legislate after them, in full pursuit to the Rocky Mountains, or to the Pacific Ocean." To halt Squatter Destiny in its tracks, Foot proposed forcing speculators to unload their hoards. This failed, and the cross-country race continued.

many squatters. (The history of the Lead Region includes so many anecdotes about settlers hurling insults and taking pot shots at officers that it may have been safer in such areas to have a red skin than to wear a blue coat.)

Even though squatters were themselves victims of the speculator, their exploited status does not command much sympathy or compassion when one sees how they treated the Indian, the other victim of the frontier. For the most part, squatters were a proliferating and destructive nemesis, no more worthy of folk deification than a gang of border ruffians or a plague of grasshoppers. Had they surged onto an Indian tract openly and demanded, at the point of a gun, that they be given a piece of land, they might have at least earned the reputation of being honest men, albeit ruthless. But the tactic was quite different. Usually a single family arrived and begged for permission to build a cabin, pasture a cow, plant a crop. Since Indians had only a vague concept of individual property, they rarely objected; after all, the request was modest enough. Within a season or so, other settlers— friends of friends, cousins, in-laws—began to appear with that unerring instinct that fetches the whole colony of ants to a broken sack of sugar. Next came a rash of disputes and fights with the Indians, invariably climaxed when the squatters cast the Indians out and claimed the district as white man's country. If the Indians protested, a governor or military commander was certain to receive a petition charging that the tribe had become "hostile" or "threatening" and requesting that the government intervene.

In any dispute it was a given that the Indian lose, for the squatter, as an American citizen, held in readiness a full inventory of his rights for any and all politicians willing to listen.[2] If the matter went to court, the legal process favored the white because the trial proceeded by rules written by whites for whites and

2. The settlers' treatment of the Indian aroused no guilty conscience; it was rather a matter of amusement, as the following story which circulated in Illinois makes clear: In the woods a white and an Indian set up camp and prepared to eat the game which they had shot that day, a turkey and a buzzard. "You take the buzzard and I'll take the turkey," said the white. When the Indian objected, the white gave in. "All right, I'll take the turkey, and you can have the buzzard."

with settlers as jurors. *Realpolitik* on the frontier boiled down to a uniform essence: Whites in, Indians out, reasons afterward.

Once the Indians had been removed and the land put up for sale, the squatter had three possibilities open to him: Sell his "improvements," to a newcomer and follow the frontier, claim pre-emption rights based on occupation of his section for a period of seven years, or, much rarer, buy his own claim from the government.

The Indian had no such options. By a peculiarity of American law, foreigners could buy land but Indians could not. Perhaps the government considered it unfair to make them buy back their own land. Instead, dispossessed tribes were given land beyond the frontier where they could settle until inundated by the next wave of squatters—provided, of course, that they could oust those tribes already located there. Significantly, at this time, Indian affairs were administered through the Department of War, presumably because, if negotiations failed, artillery would be close at hand.

The Sauk and Fox were about to learn for themselves these strange habits and customs of the Chemokemons.

In late August of 1804 violence erupted at the Cuivre River settlement, fifty miles above St. Louis on the western bank of the Mississippi. Much confusion surrounds this relatively minor frontier ruckus, but the general pattern conforms to the traditional confrontation between Indian and white. Although the Cuivre River lay well within Sauk and Fox territory, squatters had been pushing into the region since early spring. Trouble broke out at a dance when an American took what a white historian called "undue familiarities" with an Indian girl. Her father interfered and the white kicked him out the door "like an offending dog." Accustomed to avenging insults blow for blow, the Indian— presumably a Fox—brained the ruffian on the spot; before the scuffle ended, some three or four whites were dead.

The squatters hastily threw up a blockhouse and petitioned St. Louis for aid. Rumors of imminent war sped up and down the river, panicking Indians as well as whites.

Those Sauk and Fox residing nearest Shallow Water (St. Louis) abandoned their village for the security of ground closer to Saukenuk. Genuinely alarmed by the prospect of a war that could bring in the Osage on the side of the Americans, the tribal council conceded to a white demand that a delegation be dispatched to Shallow Water. Expecting that the affair would be settled according to Indian custom, whereby the family of the victims accepted gifts as pledge of peace, the peacemakers were surprised by the whites' refusal to parley with them. Instead, they were turned back and ordered by the American negotiator Pierre Chouteau to fetch "the chiefs of your villages with some important men." (Chouteau was a fur trader who would shortly merge with the Astor interests and become the first St. Louis millionaire.) The Sauk did not suspect that the United States planned to barter a few dead squatters for several million acres of Indian land.

Overseeing American interests in upper Louisiana at this time was William Henry Harrison, governor of the Indiana Territory, who had just arrived with authorization from President Jefferson to open negotiations with tribes occupying land in the Louisiana Purchase.[3] The Cuivre River Massacre, as it was by now being called, provided Harrison, a notorious hawk in Indian affairs, with just the gambit he needed.

Representing the Sauk and Fox were Quashquame ("Jumping Fish"), chief of the band residing at the Des Moines Rapids, and three smaller fry. After handing over one of the "murderers" to white authorities, the four-man delegation roamed about the city pleading for his release. (One source claims that Quashquame was a relative of the prisoner who may have been a hostage picked at random to placate the Chemokemons.)

Pierre Chouteau, no doubt jittery about his own position as a Frenchman in territory now belonging to the United States, entertained Governor Harrison lavishly in his home, while at the same time giving the Indian delegates credit at his store (mainly

3. Apparently Jefferson never consistently adhered to a single solution of the Indian problem. Early he had advocated amalgamation; but, perceiving that this would not work, he toyed with the policy of removing all Indians west of the Mississippi and the creation of a separate Indian state. Later he seemed to have despaired of reaching any solution. Governor Harrison's instructions doubtless reflected Jefferson's removal phase.

for Monongahela whiskey, as it turned out). The citizenry of St. Louis knew that Quashquame and the others were about to be shaved close by Governor Harrison; as one of them recorded later, "The writer has no doubt, from his own personal knowledge of Quas-qua-me, that he would have sold to Gov. Harrison, at that time, all the country east of the Rocky Mountains, if it had been required." (In other words, Quashquame was a drunk.[4]) On November 4, 1804, the five delegates[5] scratched their marks on a treaty that must certainly rank (among some tough competition) as one of the most notable swindles in American history.

According to the terms of the treaty, the Sauk and Fox relinquished claim to all their land east of the Mississippi between the Illinois and Wisconsin rivers and to a great chunk on the western shore, including the Cuivre River country, as well. What the Indians got in return—other than the unmarketable froth of the "friendship" and "protection" of the United States—is quickly itemized: They were promised an annuity of $1,000 in trading stock (reckoned at retail prices F.O.B. St. Louis). If they wished

4. The following account of Quashquame passed into the oral history of the tribe and was recorded many decades later: "It was known to all that he had gone to spend the winter near Shallow Water. His object was to be near a trading-post where he could dispose of his pelts as fast as he got them. But it was rumored that he spent much time at the post, and that he hunted little; that he hobnobbed with the big official there, and that he had much money to spend; that he drank a great deal. . . . Kwashkawami and the men whose names were on paper denied ever having touched the pen. They must have lied, or else they were drunk at the time and did not know they had touched the pen."

This bears out Black Hawk's own laconic disavowal of the treaty because of the condition of the negotiators: "They had been drunk the greater part of the time they were in St. Louis."

Poor Quashquame, who suffered nearly thirty years of abuse and a gradual stripping away of his chieftain status for his part in this contemptible treaty, doggedly held to the story that he had been drunk at the negotiations. Better to be condemned as a drunkard, he must have thought, than as a crook or a fool.

5. These were Quashquame, Pashepaho, Ouchequaka, Hashequariqua, and Layowvoia. The last-named is a man of mystery. Apparently no members of the tribe had ever heard of him, then or later. It is not impossible that he was the hostage in jail or that Harrison dragged him in off the street to add his signature to the others.

to have a blacksmith or agricultural agent, the government would provide both, but with wages and expenses to be deducted from the annuity. Further, the five Indian delegates received a mysterious lump sum of $2,234.50, which presumably settled their account with Chouteau, who just happened to be one of Harrison's witnesses to the treaty. Thus the United States, obtained title to fifteen million acres of Sauk and Fox land for $1,000 per year.

According to Indian law and custom the treaty had no validity whatsoever. None of the principal chiefs of the Sauk and Fox, Black Thunder or White Skin, for instance, even attended the conference, much less signed the document. Nor was the treaty submitted to the tribal council for debate and approval by the tribe as a whole, a procedure mandatory in matters of land cession.[6] Not one word in it alluded to the release of the captive, which was the sole item of business that Quashquame's group had been authorized to bargain for. Evaluated in terms of United States law, the treaty was preposterous. Had Governor Harrison, for instance, given the Sauk and Fox a deed to the Indiana Territory, his action would have been, rightly, repudiated as the irresponsibility of a madman. Yet, when an Indian delegation gave up fifteen million acres, with no authority to do so, the treaty was accepted by whites as a binding legal document!

Though incidental to the land cession, there were also other provisions of the Treaty of 1804 that would cause difficulties in later years. In one article the Sauk and Fox agreed to end their long-standing war with the Osage tribe of Missouri. (Chouteau

6. Harrison, who plumed himself on his knowledge of Indian matters (in later years he authored a book on Indian culture), must have known that no individual chief possessed the authority to give up land. Jonathan Carver, a casual traveler among the Sauk and Fox had gleaned this much forty years earlier. He stressed that the chief was not head of state, in the Western sense: "Whole assent is necessary in all conveyances and treaties to which he affixes the mark of the tribe or nation."

The oral history of the Sauk and Fox has always stressed that Quashquame had no authority to participate in the treaty: "The man was not a chief; he had no power to make a treaty with another nation; his act was not known before or at the time he did it; he was not made a delegate to make a treaty on behalf of his people; what he did, he did as an individual."

and other traders must have very much wanted the Indians to cease their nonproductive intertribal killing and concentrate on that activity which had been left to the "ignorant savages," filling white warehouses with furs and white pockets with money.) Unfortunately this gave the United States the role of peacemaker and placed the Americans in the uncomfortable position of imposing law and order by coercive means.

Article Seven caused serious misunderstandings a generation later: It gave the Sauk and Fox permission to live and hunt on the ceded tract until the land was put up for public sale.

In another article the government promised that if any white intruded upon territories belonging to the Sauk and Fox, he would "forthwith be removed" and, further, that if a white murdered or robbed a member of the tribe he would be punished "as if the injury had been done to a white man." This last was mere claptrap included in almost all treaties. No judge or jury in the western country took such promises seriously, unless the malefactor was a free Negro or Frenchman.[7]

In obtaining this agreement from the Sauk and Fox nation, Governor Harrison must have been most pleased with himself.[8] Almost at once he returned to Vincennes, the seat of his adminstrative duties in the Indiana Territory, leaving the imple-

7. A famous case in early Wisconsin dealt with an Indian girl charging a white man with rape. Much to the amusement of the Green Bay settlement, the judge sentenced her assailant to buy her a new frock, replacing the one torn in the scuffle, and to work for one week in the judge's garden. The implication seemed to be that a preposterous accusation demanded a preposterous sentence. Since Indians were subhuman, the terms *rape* or *murder* were inappropriately used in describing crimes against them.

8. Though more famous for his exploits as an Indian fighter at Tippecanoe (1811), Harrison had consistently shown a talent for extortion. In his 1809 treaty with the Shawnee, for example, he arranged to have their lands ceded to the United States, even though no Shawnee attended the negotiations. In their place, Harrison got some Kickapoo to sign. In his later years Harrison ran for president. He won, in large measure because his campaign tacticians within the Whig party were able to prevent him from speaking to the people at large and thereby revealing, on the stump, the nonentity that William Henry Harrison really was.

mentation of his treaty to others. Behind him he left the seeds of the Black Hawk War, although it would take twenty-eight years for them to germinate. Commenting on the injustice of the Harrison treaty, Black Hawk said everything that need be said, "I will leave it to the people of the United States to say, whether our nation was properly represented in this treaty? or whether we received a fair compensation for the extent of country ceded by those *four* individuals?" The compensation for the four pathetic delegates, remarked an Illinois historian of the 1880s, consisted of "wet groceries and gewgaws."

President Jefferson accepted the transfer of land eagerly enough, although he did issue an order for the release of the Sauk hostage, on the ground that he had killed in self-defense. It arrived too late, however. The hostage had already been shot in the back while attempting to break jail. (Quashquame and others always insisted that he had been shot after his release.[9])

In a solemn ceremony, the new governor of the Missouri Territory, James Wilkinson, delivered the pardon to the brother of the deceased and advised him to keep it as a warning against "Bad Deeds." The governor's *double-entendre* seems to have been unintended.

For a short time the government seemed prepared to honor its part of the Treaty of Shallow Water. In 1805 an agricultural station was established opposite Quashquame's village at the Des Moines Rapids (the present Nauvoo, Illinois) to teach the Sauk and Fox farming. The agent, a youth from Pennsylvania named William Ewing, came highly recommended as "a sober, honest, faithful young man." If Ewing ever possessed these virtues, they withered quickly on the frontier. The ever-obliging Quashquame loaned him a squaw, and the agent promptly began to supplement his stipend of $400 a year by purchasing guns from Indians for whiskey and selling them back for twice their value in horses and fur. In time the Indians became so enraged that they swooped

9. Quashquame's account is supported by the editor of the Harrison papers, who wrote in a footnote that the hostage was shot "supposedly by the guard but more probably by some personal enemy."

down on the agency and filled Ewing's livestock with arrows. The government meanwhile had become so disgusted with conduct "degrading to the institution" that it dismissed him. With this failure to bring the blessings of agriculture to the Sauk and Fox, the government allowed the tribe to return to its old diet of catfish, blue geese, mallard, and buffalo. This first close contact between Chemokemon and Sauk had desposited grit in the mouth of each.

Meanwhile the United States began exploring and mapping the upper Mississippi River. Captain Zebulon M. Pike, who took twenty men to its headwaters in 1805, found the Indians of the lower river friendly enough. They shouted "How-do-you-do" in English at the keelboat and invited the explorers ashore. In the vicinity of Saukenuk, however, Indian canoes avoided the American boat. "It is astonishing to me," Pike recorded in his journal, "what a dread the Indians have of the Americans in this quarter." Yet there were no signs of overt hostility. When two whites strayed into the wilderness, a party of Fox came upon them, fed them, and escorted them back to the keelboat.

After wintering above the Falls of St. Anthony, the Pike expedition started downriver in the spring of 1806. Visiting Saukenuk again, this time they encountered undisguised belligerence. In the village at the time was an army detachment looking for some Osage prisoners; the Sauk probably regarded Pike's men as reinforcements. They hovered about with pistols under their blankets, called the captain a "Bloody American," and expressed anger at the plume in his hat—for them a provocative emblem of war.

Furious to discover the British flag flying over the village, the Americans gave the Indians the Stars and Stripes. They were aghast when the Sauk hoisted it without pulling down the other. This defiant behavior so offended Captain Pike that he later recorded in his journal his regret that he had no authorization to attack the village. In his autobiography Black Hawk gives a different perspective to the incident, which he remembered clearly: "He presented us an American flag, which was hoisted. He then requested us to pull down our *British* flags—and give him our *British medals*—promising to send us others on his return to St. Louis. This we declined, as we wished to have *two Fathers!*" [10]

From the Sauk point of view, a gang of white bullies had appeared in their village without invitation and begun giving unreasonable orders. On the other hand, the Americans, subsequently reported in St. Louis that the Sauk were hostile and disobedient.

After Pike had mapped the upper Mississippi, the government began its "conquest" of the region by projecting a series of forts. During the fall of 1808 a company under Lieutenant Alpha Kingsley landed on the western bank a few miles above Quashquame's village and fell upon the tall timber with axes and mauls.

Kingsley had absolutely no right to build on this site, which had not been included in the 1804 cession. To allay mounting dissatisfaction among the local bands, he paid out $300 in baubles and explained that he was building a trading post which would sell them goods very cheaply. Asked about the soldiers, Kingsley concocted a story that they would remain there only to keep the trader company. Spurred by the approach of winter and by the extras which they got for construction work —$.10 a day and a gill of whiskey—the soldiers threw up three blockhouses surrounded by a lopsided pentagonal palisade which was christened Fort Madison.

Meanwhile Indian pranksters amused themselves by surrounding the work parties, emitting bloodcurdling war whoops, and watching with delight as the Chemokemons scattered like poultry. No blood was shed, but the nerves of the garrison were rubbed raw. Lieutenant Kingsley, a dour Vermonter newly

10. Indians loved flags, as much for their color as their talismanic effects. They preferred the British flags because these, being made of silk, lasted almost indefinitely, while the American flags, of cheap worsted material, quickly ragged out. Further, the British upstaged the Americans by distributing brass medals of George III to all Indians who would wear them. As late as the 1840s George Catlin found such medals, burnished by decades of hard wear, hanging around the necks of Indians located hundreds of miles from Canadian spheres of influence. Pulling one of these medals from his bosom, a chief told a visiting Englishman, "Tell my Great Father that we keep his face bright."

arrived on the frontier, might easily have gained the Indians' affection by countering with a few forceful pranks of his own. Instead, he incurred their dislike and distrust by behaving as if his entire command hovered on the brink of imminent disaster.

For nearly a decade Fort Madison—called by one visitor a "wretched pen, improperly called a fort"—remained the ultima Thule of the American empire on the upper Mississippi. It was a festering sore, a sorry advertisement for both the dignity and the potency of the United States.

Their political naïveté, and hardheaded individualism contributed as much as anything else to the piecemeal destruction of the Indians, tribe by tribe. For instance, although the Sauk and Fox had scant respect for, and less love of, the Americans, the tribe resisted the overtures of the Shawnee Tecumseh with his dreams of a vast Indian confederation powerful enough to hold the Long Knives (whites) east of the Wabash. The council at Saukenuk listened in disbelief when Tecumseh's emissaries told them, "If you do not join your friends on the Wabash, the Americans will take this very village from you." They felt too remote from the "seventeen cities" of the Chemokemons ever to be directly threatened by them. As Black Hawk later commented, "I little thought then, that his words would come true!" Many Winnebago joined Tecumseh, however; and, when some of them were killed at Tippecanoe in November 1811, isolated Sauk war parties joined with the Winnebago in retaliatory harassment of Fort Madison. But the tribe as a whole remained uncommitted.[11]

After Tippecanoe, Indian-American relations in the western country eroded. Americans believed that the Indians planned wholesale attacks on the settlements, citing as evidence the fact that the Indians had struck Governor Harrison's army without warning. On the other hand, few Indians who heard about the battle were foolish enough to think that Harrison, having crossed

11. When Winnebago attacked a small group of American miners on the Fever River in January 1812, a Sauk hid George Hunt, a trader, and later escorted him through a blizzard to the safety of Fort Madison nearly two hundred miles downstream. Nothing better illustrates the hazard of generalizing about Indians on the basis of the tribe to which they belong.

seventy miles of territory belonging to Indians, had a mission of
peace on his mind. Before long Harrison was calling for a "war
of extirpation" against the Indians. In Congress the faction of
War Hawks—Western men like Henry Clay and Felix Grundy,
for the most part—began to drum harder for the conquest of
Canada and a general mop-up of "hostile" Indians. Realists in
the War Department, however, begged in vain for a policy that
would keep the Indians "quiet and friendly," knowing well how
bad were Western defenses. It was a bit late, in any case, for
retroactive peace pipes.

When Congress declared war on Great Britain in June 1812,
the Northwest Indians swarmed to the support of the Saganash.
Black Hawk reflected the sentiment of most of them when he
said, "*I had not discovered one good trait in the character of
the Americans. They made fair promises but never fulfilled them!
Whilst the British made but few—but we could always rely
upon their word!*" [12] American mistreatment of the Indians contributed, within two months, to the loss of Mackinac, Chicago,
and Detroit. The American frontier receded to the lower Wabash,
and companies of rangers had to be extemporized in Missouri
and southern Illinois to protect the Mississippi River settlements
because the regular army was busy elsewhere.

The War of 1812 split the Sauk and Fox into two factions.
The majority, known thereafter as the Peace Party to Americans,
took no part in the conflict. About fifteen hundred of these even
moved their villages far down into the Missouri Territory to
prove their peaceful inclination. (Among these émigrés was
Quashquame, ever willing to placate the whites, even though a
party of rangers had shot down his brother a short time before.)
A cadre of about two hundred warriors, largely from Saukenuk,
joined the war against the Americans and became known as the

12. Embalmed in history texts is a great deal of pious nonsense about
how the United States refused to employ Indian mercenaries against the
British in the War of 1812 out of humanistic motives. The truth is that
few tribes respected the Americans enough to want to support them and
that those tribes which offered assistance were usually turned away because American commanders believed—with good reason—that the Indians
would turn against them at the first opportunity.

British Band. By this time the tribes had become so dependent upon credits from traders for supplies that strict neutrality was almost out of the question.

Had it not been for bureaucratic bungling, the British Band probably would not have existed. According to Black Hawk, an American official promised the Sauk extensive credits payable at Fort Madison.[13] Arriving there in late summer they found nothing. Without supplies for the winter hunt, they faced starvation; without weaponry, they faced extermination by the Osage. Deliverance arrived in the form of a British trader who reached Saukenuk with two boats crammed with supplies. Little wonder that an American Band never materialized among the Sauk and Fox.

Coerced into the British orbit by necessity, the Saukenuk Indians went up to Green Bay, the assembly point for those Indians of the Northwest being collected by Robert Dickson, a British trader. The Sauk were still not eager to fight the Americans, however. When their war chief Black Hawk attempted to back out, Dickson took him aside and issued the warning, "If you do not immediately strike upon the Americans, I will turn all the other Indians against you and strike you to the ground." [14] Yet Dickson, who understood the Indian psyche, did not overplay his threatening role. Placing a medal around Black Hawk's neck, he gave him command of all Indians recruited at Green Bay. Moreover, he flattered the Sauk leader by addressing him as General Black Hawk. Somewhat reluctantly Black Hawk committed his band to war with the Chemokemons.

No white American would have been much intimidated by the appearance or the credentials of Makataimeshekiakiak, "Black Sparrow Hawk." At forty-five he was an old man by In-

13. During the spring of 1812 a Sauk and Fox delegation visited Washington, where they were deluged with promises by the government, eager to neutralize the Northwestern tribes in the war then being hatched.

14. In his autobiography Black Hawk did not allude to this incident, probably because it showed him in a poor light. But the minutes of a conference with the British after the war at Prairie du Chien record Dickson's threat, which Black Hawk quoted in order to show how his band had been coerced into the war and to obtain additional rewards from the British.

dian standards, and he was not a chief. Excluded by birth from those clans from which the tribal chieftains were elected, Black Hawk owed his influence to an outstanding military career that went back to his fifteenth year when he first wounded an enemy. In thirty years of warfare, most of it directed against the Osage, he had personally killed thirty of his enemy, exclusive of boys and squaws. Even before the Americans arrived at Shallow Water, Black Hawk had led five hundred Sauk and Fox braves deep into the Missouri country "determined," as he later said, "on the final etermination of the Osages." War was his natural element. It was as though his entire intellectual endowment had been channeled into this highly specialized function of tribal existence. A poor orator, he usually remained silent at councils, appearing to accept his subservient role in the tribal hierachy.

For Black Hawk the customs of Saukenuk, where he was born in 1767, were sacrosanct and inviolable. Even by Sauk standards he remained from beginning to end parochial and reactionary. When his father was killed by Cherokees, his period of mourning extended to five years—ten times the minimum length of time. At a time when many Mississippi Indians were drifting toward the moral shoals of Shallow Waters Black Hawk sensed, with a kind of outraged instinct, the contamination being spread by white Americans, and adopted from them only their superior weaponry. He abominated firewater with all the zeal of a later temperance fanatic.

While some tribal leaders, like Quashquame, collected wives like horses, Black Hawk remained faithful to his wife, Singing Bird. ("She is a good woman and teaches my boys to be brave.") Though his sons Nasheaskuk ("Whirling Thunder") and Wausaumesaw ("Roaring Thunder") impressed even white men by their superb physiques and carriage (a governor of Iowa in the 1840s called the former "probably the handsomest man in the world") Black Hawk himself would have been overlooked in a crowd. He was slender and of medium height, his wide mouth bent downward over a receding chin, his pierced nose and ears seemed ungainly protuberances on his small, shaved head. Unlike Tecumseh, who collected followers fanatically loyal to him, Black Hawk was always more respected than loved. He was a tactician rather than a strategist; his vision rarely extended beyond the next day or the next scalp.

Five hundred Northwestern Indians, with Black Hawk as puppet commander, marched by way of Fort Dearborn to join the British Army south of Detroit. At the River Raisin (now Monroe, Michigan) they virtually annihilated the Kentucky volunteers commanded by General James Winchester, an incompetent politico who had taken it upon himself, without orders, to probe the defenses of Detroit. Sauk took part in the siege of Fort Meigs on the Maumee River in May 1813, but it is not likely that they realized that the author of the infamous treaty of 1804, William Henry Harrison, was inside the fort.

Although many Indian allies, including the great Tecumseh, remained with the British to the end, Black Hawk left for home after the unsuccessful attack on Fort Stephenson in August. "I was tired of being with them—our success being bad and having got no plunder," he reported twenty years later. Moreover, he had become disillusioned with the manner in which white men waged war. Instead of approaching the enemy by stealth and killing with minimum exposure of one's own warriors, the Saganash and Chemokemons "march out, in open daylight, and *fight*, regardless of the number of warriors they may lose." Then each side made meaningless statements in writing and claimed the victory. Black Hawk failed to fathom the purpose of the war as he had seen it fought in the Ohio country: "Our maxim is, *to kill the enemy*, and *save our own men*. Those chiefs would do to *paddle* a canoe, but not to *steer* it."

When Black Hawk returned to Saukenuk in the early fall of 1813, the Americans had been sorely thrashed on every front and had lost control of the entire region of the upper Mississippi. Blackened chimneys marked the site of Fort Madison, the garrison having fired the place and fled to St. Louis. Prairie du Chien was occupied by an assortment of British traders, their Indian allies, and indifferent half-breeds of putative French extraction. The Americans had mounted a campaign in Illinois by pushing a disorderly gang of rangers—described by a federal agent as "a banditti of ruffians"—into the Peoria region, where they had burned Potawatomie villages and thrown up a vast pen called

Fort Clark. A mild scare had occurred at Saukenuk in July when news arrived that a hundred rangers, under Major Nathan Boone (son of Daniel), were reconnoitering toward the Rock River; but these cavaliers apparently had little stomach for engaging a solid mass of Indians and turned back forty miles from the Sauk village.

The prospects for the Sauk and Fox looked bright. In view of the American setbacks, Black Hawk's participation in the war with the British gave him a strong position in tribal councils. It was all too easy for simple woodland minds to conclude that because the Chemokemons had vanished from the river they were completely gone.

Not content to lick their wounds from behind the ramparts of Shallow Water, the Americans sought to recover in 1814 what they had lost during the two preceding years. The result was a series of blunders that punctured the gasconading self-importance of the would-be soldier frontiersmen.

The governor of the Missouri Territory at this time was William Clark (of the Lewis and Clark expedition), who had given up exploring for more lucrative activities. Clark viewed the occupation of Prairie du Chien by British traders with a not wholly disinterested aversion, for he was a partner in Auguste Chouteau's Missouri Fur Company. Though the governor was nearly a functional illiterate, he nevertheless knew how to add and subtract.[15] Whoever controlled Prairie du Chien, visited by ten thousand Indians yearly, controlled trade in the upper Mississippi. While patriotism may have provided the public explanation for the expedition which poled upriver in May, the real reason was protectionism. Probably fearing that General Benjamin Howard, military commander of the region, would disapprove (as he did when he heard about it), Clark organized his expeditionary force while the general was conveniently out of town.

The Dog Prairie Campaign of Governor Clark, while richly

15. A specimen of Clark's literary style, with all its misspellings and malapropisms is the following extracted from his journal of the Oregon expedition, dated June 17, 1804: "The party is much aflicted with *Boils*, and Several have the Deassentary, which I contribute to the water."

comical in its own right, demands only a brief summary here. A flotilla of five barges passed Saukenuk without incident and occupied Prairie du Chien without resistance early in June. The British traders had skedaddled and the local population readily swore allegiance to the American flag and bayonet. Governor Clark, who accompanied the expedition in person, immediately confiscated the buildings of the Mackinac Company, his British rival in the fur trade, and set off for Shallow Water leaving sixty regulars of the Seventh Infantry under Lieutenant Joseph Perkins to fend for themselves. Left behind, presumably as naval support, was one barge, fittingly named the *Governor Clark*.

By the middle of June, as the governor was reporting on his improvised expedition to General Howard, Lieutenant Perkins was moving his men into a double-blockhouse stockade which he christened Fort Shelby. Although General Howard must have been lavish in expletives when he learned how Clark had reopened the war in the Northwest, he had no alternative but to dispatch reinforcements to Perkins, isolated and beleaguered in a hostile wilderness full of British and Indians. Collecting forty regulars and sixty-odd rangers, he put them under the command of Lieutenant John Campbell, who set off from Shallow Water on July 4. While Campbell's force were poling upstream, a rag-bag force of Canadians and Indians arrived on the bluffs overlooking Prairie du Chien and opened fire with a three-pounder. After but a few salvos, the *Governor Clark* hauled anchor and ignominiously fled downriver. "I had no idea that she had gone off and left us," wrote Perkins in his official report.

For three days Fort Shelby sustained a siege of British fire and Indian war whoops; the ferocity of the bombardment was reflected in the American casualty lists—five men slighty wounded, none mortally.[16] Finally, on July 20, Perkins capitu-

16. Local tradition contradicts the official report by claiming that no Americans were wounded. Joseph Rolette, a trader of the place, carried news of the battle to the British outpost at Michilmacinac, where a throng gathered round to hear of the fight. "A great battle, a sanguinary contest," began Rolette, with histrionic solemnity. "How many were killed?" shouted the crowd. "None." "How many wounded?" "None." "What a bloody contest!" hooted the crowd.

lated and the Union Jack was again hoisted at Prairie du Chien.
The British commander, whose force numbered fewer than the
Americans, had greater difficulty in preventing his Indian allies
from massacring the garrison than he had had in taking the fort.
But he succeeded in getting the prisoners away safely and in
paroling them home.

Apparently no Sauk took part in the Prairie du Chien battle;
but their contribution to the American debacle was about to
begin. On the evening before the surrender of Fort Shelby,
Lieutenant Campbell's force, in three keelboats, reached the
mouth of the Rock River, nearly two hundred miles south of
Prairie du Chien. Invited ashore by the Sauk, who had not yet
heard of the British presence far upriver, the Americans "used,
and gave us, plenty of whiskey," Black Hawk later reported.
After the Chemokemons had returned to their boats for the night,
a messenger reached Saukenuk bringing news of the fight at
Prairie du Chien—and a gift of six kegs of powder so that the
Sauk could join battle. After a year of peace, Black Hawk entered the war again.

Throughout the following day parties of Sauk and Fox
stalked the keelboats from the dense willow undergrowth along
the Illinois shore, waiting for an opportunity to strike. After a
day of hard poling, and two nights of hard likkering, the Campbell flotilla had gotten above the rapids north of Rock Island.
On the following morning, July 21, most of the Americans were
under the weather, in more than one sense. Gale winds blew up
from the west and dispersed the keelboats; Campbell's dropped
far astern. The boat went hard aground on a boggy island
bristling with Indians who opened fire at point-blank range
from behind a screen of underbrush. Black Hawk himself set the
sail on fire with a flaming arrow. Because of the wind, the other
keelboats heard no shots; but when Lieutenant Stephen Rector
saw smoke billowing over the island behind him, he returned,
dropped anchor, and swung in close to the burning boat. In attempting the same maneuver, Lieutenant Jonathan Riggs, in the
third keelboat, dragged anchor and went ashore a hundred yards
below Campbell.

To provide cover, Rector raked the thicket with his swivel

gun and took off the still able-bodied of Campbell's men, leaving the dead and the seriously wounded on the burning craft. Campbell himself, who subsequently confessed that he was ill —that is to say, drunk—during the fight, was badly wounded as he was being hoisted aboard Rector's boat.[17] Cutting his cable, Rector then promptly headed for St. Louis under oar, leaving Riggs to fend for himself. Riggs waited, playing possum, before opening fire when the Indians rushed his boat en masse. The attackers fell back with two dead (one of them a squaw)— the only American kills of the encounter. Later Riggs's men pushed the boat off and returned to St. Louis, much to the surprise of Rector, who had reported the keelboat destroyed. Twenty years later Black Hawk, who recalled the fight vividly, had high praise for Riggs's ambuscade: "I had a good opinion of this war chief—he managed so much better than the others. It would give me pleasure to shake him by the hand."

The fate of the wounded men left behind on Campbell's boat was vividly described by a British officer at Prairie du Chien: "to give an idea how disparate [sic] the indians were, the women even jumped on board with their Hoes &ca, some breaking heads, others breaking casks, some trying to cut Holes in her bottom to sink her." Black Hawk himself knocked in the heads of whiskey barrels to pour out what he called "the bad medicine." Among the plunder the Sauks found enough blue coats to outfit many of their band. Hoisting the British flag, they danced over their scalps, decked out in American uniforms. This curious spectacle was briefly witnessed by the men aboard the Governor Clark, which happened to pass by, providing those on board with yet another lurid tale of Indian ferocity along the upper Mississippi. The Indians fired at the barge from their canoes and hooted with delight as it vanished down the river. All told, the

17. While a fearless giant of a man, Lieutenant Campbell was nonetheless a notorious drunkard. For many years afterward the "Hero of Campbell's Island" was a featured exhibit in many a Missouri grogshop. Today the site of the battle, surrounded by trailers and shanties on Campbell's Island in East Moline, is marked by a commemorative stone and plaque, making no mention of the besotted condition of the lieutenant or his crew.

Americans lost sixteen dead and twenty wounded at Campbell's Island.

Reports of the fiasco at Prairie du Chien and the humiliation at Campbell's Island sent shock waves through the administrative chambers of Shallow Water. The Americans were especially angered by the behavior of the Saukenuk Indians. Stung into activity—and doubtless damning Clark for having poked the hornet's nest in the first place—General Howard resolved to burn the Sauk village to the ground. He assembled 430 men for the job, picking as their commander a crusty Virginian named Zachary Taylor. Major Taylor, a twenty-nine-year-old regular officer, was widely admired in the West. While commanding the garrison at Fort Harrison (now Terre Haute) in 1812, he had beaten back repeated Indian attacks at a time when most American forts were capitulating. For his gritty defense Taylor had received congratulations from Congress, grateful for any victory, however small. Prominent among his militia officers was Captain Samuel Whiteside, a no-quarter Indian fighter from southern Illinois.[18] The expedition embarked in eight keelboats from St. Louis in late August. Their plan was to feign a movement on Prairie du Chien by proceeding past the mouth of the Rock River and then to drop back on Saukenuk, taking the village by surprise.

Unfortunately for the Americans, the British commander at Prairie du Chien decided to engage the flotilla at the rapids above Rock Island. He sent Lieutenant Duncan Graham, a militia officer, to Saukenuk with thirty whites, a hundred Indians, two swivel guns, and a three-pounder. Graham reported that his arrival among the Sauk was greeted with more pleasure "than if all the goods in the King's store in Mackinaw had been sent

18. Fighting Indians seemed to be a trait bred into the Whiteside clan. As early as the French and Indian War they were in the thick of it, and a Whiteside commanded the Seventh Cavalry at Wounded Knee, the last Indian battle in American history. They so crowd the annals of border warfare that it is sometimes difficult to tell one from another. This particular man was a friend of John Moredock's (the celebrated Indian killer treated in Herman Melville's novel *The Confidence-Man*) and he later commanded the first levy of Illinois volunteers during the Black Hawk War.

them." Black Hawk's people planned a warm reception for the Americans, who expected to meet nothing more formidable than musket shot and arrow.

On September 5 the Chemokemon fleet was sighted along the Iowa shore opposite the mouth of the Rock River. Gale-strength winds had compelled Major Taylor to alter his plan of attack so that he now planned to hoist white flags as though to arrange for a parley and then to attack the Sauk during the conference. Dropping anchor at the head of Credit Island (off present-day Davenport, Iowa), he sent aloft his flag of truce, which the Indians ignored. They darted about in canoes like skimming insects but fired no shots. Early the next morning some Sauk fired at some American sentinels from the island. Captain Whiteside, tired of Major Taylor's pussyfooting delay, at once hoisted a red flag—the signal for a no-quarter fight—and unleashed a load of canister into the shrubbery. The battle was joined. Taylor's whole fleet opened fire against the handful of Sauk concealed in the undergrowth of the island, while the main body of Indians jumped up and down with excitement on the beach of Rock River, over half a mile away. As Taylor's boats milled about the island destroying Indian canoes, solid shot rained down from Lieutenant Graham's battery on the Illinois shore. The Americans were so flabbergasted by this unexpected attack that they never succeeded in locating the British guns. Whiteside's boat was hit repeatedly—fifteen shots went through her in forty-five minutes. The survivors finally chucked their dead overboard and rowed downstream out of range. The other boats quickly tailed after Whiteside's.

The Sauk were beside themselves with delight at routing the hated Chemokemons. "The satisfaction afforded the Indians," wrote Lieutenant Graham in his report, "can only be imagined. Their shouts and acclamations of joy at every shot from our guns, drowned the report of the guns." Black Hawk expected the enemy to land and put up a fight: "I was prepared to meet them—but was soon *sadly disappointed.* . . . They did not stop until they got below the Des Moines rapid." As a matter of fact, Major Taylor overtook the other keelboats and ordered the officers ashore for a brief conference three miles below Rock

River. He tried to induce them to go back and finish the job, but his arguments carried no weight with a militia convinced that they were outnumbered three to one. Reluctantly Taylor led his force back to Shallow Water. Eighteen years would pass before he would settle his account with Black Hawk.

With three American expeditions on the upper Mississippi repulsed during the summer of 1814, the authorities wisely abandoned further attempts to re-establish outposts in the region. The War of 1812 ended with the British and Indians in firm control of all territory north of the Des Moines Rapids.

For a time it appeared that the Sauk had nullified, by force, the contemptible treaty of 1804. No one at Saukenuk could have predicted that American diplomats at Ghent would obtain what American soldiers at Shallow Water had been unable to secure for themselves. The successful defense of Saukenuk proved to be the high-water mark of Sauk and Fox history.

THREE *The Sauk and Fox: The Fall*

AT GHENT it became clear that the British, having lost interest in contending for the Northwest, were prepared to throw their Indian allies to the Americans. Talk of an independent Indian state came to nothing. All that the United States would concede was a restoration to the Indians of all rights and possessions enjoyed in 1811, which meant that they had fought for nothing.

When the British commandant at Prairie du Chien explained the treaty to an assemblage of loyal tribes in April 1815, their wrath was so great that for a time the British garrison feared an attack. Black Hawk rose to demand a "large gun" for his village as protection against "treacherous Big Knives." When even this was denied him, he told the council, "I shall fight the Big Knives till they are off of our lands." Failure to comprehend that the British had really withdrawn from the Northwest led Black Hawk to underestimate the American capacity for doing his people harm. That supreme moment when a big gun along the beach of Rock River had sent the Chemokemons in full flight from Saukenuk had been etched into his mind for many years to come.

The ink on the treaty was barely dry when the United States began to consolidate its control of the upper Mississippi. To implant respect for the American might among the Indians, as well as to break the near-monopoly of the British fur-trading interests,[1] the government projected, during the summer of 1815, a

1. At the instigation of John Jacob Astor, Congress banned all British traders from United States territory in 1816. But the prohibition nearly backfired, for the American Fur Company could not find a sufficient num-

series of forts which would stretch from the Great Lakes to the Mississippi. During the next five years log forts mushroomed in the virgin timber and peat bogs of the region: Fort Edwards at the Des Moines Rapids, Fort Armstrong at Rock Island, Fort Crawford at Prairie du Chien, Fort Howard at Green Bay, Fort Snelling at the Falls of St. Anthony. Further, Fort Dearborn and Fort Mackinac, both of which had capitulated during the war, were reactivated. At the same time, to advance the frontier, the prairie region lying between the Mississippi and Illinois rivers was decreed a military tract, out of which land grants were available for veterans of the late war.

Surveyors tramped the vast domain with rod and chain, hammering stakes into ground hundreds of miles from the nearest white. But there were suggestions of settlement throughout the West. Speculators gobbled up the military tract from veterans unable to pay taxes on land which less than a handful had ever seen. And behind the speculator came a new and more formidable enemy of the Indian—not the soldier in his blue coat, but the squatter in linsey-woolsey. Multiplying like bacteria in warm milk, they began to crowd into the Territory of Illinois at a time when hunting preserves necessary to sustain Indian life were already vanishing.

To assert its hegemony over the tribes of the Mississippi Valley, the government held a conference in June of 1815 at Portage des Sioux, a few miles north of St. Louis. Noting that few Sauk attended, Governor William Clark dispatched a warning to Saukenuk that, unless a delegation of headmen appeared within thirty days, he would construe their absence as an act of war. When the Rock River chiefs still failed to appear, Clark negotiated with the remnant at hand, most of them, like Quashquame, prepared to agree to anything for a gallon of whiskey. Clark made them assent to the land cessions of the treaty of 1804 and promise to hold themselves apart from the Saukenuk hos-

---

ber of experienced traders with American citizenship. Astor's factors solved the problem of granting licences to dummy applications who then "hired" British traders to perform the real work.

tiles. This was a clever maneuver, for it drove more deeply the wedge splitting the Sauk and Fox into the two factions called by federal authorities the Peace Party and the British Band.

Although Clark, still smarting from Sauk counterattacks in 1814, sought to foment a war against the Rock River bands, the Department of War insisted that he pursue a peaceful policy toward them—that he wrest concessions from them by chicanery rather than by violence. Accordingly, "Red-Head"—as the Indians called Governor Clark—called the dissidents to a parley in May of 1816. Black Hawk attended but remained silent.[2] When Clark accused them of "heinous crimes" in joining the British during the recent war, a Sauk chief replied with jolting defiance: Alluding to the broken promise of supplying them with traders' goods during the first summer of the war, he said that the Americans spoke with two tongues. His tribesmen stamped their feet in joyous approval of this oratorical stroke, but Clark testily broke off negotiations.

Timothy Flint, a New England writer and pedagogue observing the treaty making, explained how his countrymen overawed the Sauk: In the afternoon of the same day, a detachment of artillery deployed in full view of the Indian camp, gave an exhibition of their parade-ground maneuvers, and fired a few pieces in the air as a grand finale. The following morning the Sauk requested a continuation of the conference. The offending chief apologized, explaining that he meant only that the Americans spoke in two languages—French and English. With the encouragement of American artillery, the Rock River Sauk signed a treaty which confirmed the land cession of 1804.

Even Black Hawk inscribed his mark to the document, although he always insisted in later years that he had not understood that he was handing Saukenuk to the Americans. "What do we know of the laws and customs of the white people? They

2. Later Black Hawk claimed that the Saukenuk band had started for the 1815 conference, but had turned back after one of their chiefs had died en route—a very bad omen. Yet, since Black Hawk had been attacking Missouri settlements during the spring of that year, long after the Treaty of Ghent, it is unlikely that he wished to put himself within the clutches of avenging Chemokemons at a parley.

might buy our bodies for dissection, and we would touch the goose quill to confirm it, without knowing what we are doing. This was the case with myself and people in touching the goose quill the first time." [3] Black Hawk was evolving rapidly into a hostile (any Indian with an unwillingness to forget or to forgive the brutal injustices inflicted by the Great American Father).

Even as the Saukenuk band returned home, they trod the heels of military engineers staking off future forts and work parties of blue coats felling and hewing timbers. On a bluff below the Des Moines River (present Warsaw, Illinois) Fort Edwards was nearing completion. And on Rock Island, less than two miles from the council fire at Saukenuk, Chemokemons were stripping the western tip of the island of its timber and constructing Fort Armstrong, a stockade 270 feet square with three blockhouses. The Sauk and Fox were not only distressed by the proximity of the fort but were sorrowed by its particular location as well. The Chemokemons had placed it on a limestone abutment directly over a cave inhabited by a good spirit honored by Indians of the river. The spirit was white with large wings like those of a swan, but ten times larger. "But the noise of the fort has since driven him away," Black Hawk complained, "and no doubt a *bad spirit* has taken his place!"

At Prairie du Chien, Fort Crawford was being built the same summer, while American officers purged the settlement of treasonous elements. Houses near the fort were burned down or converted into warehouses, former British sympathizers were carried to Shallow Water under guard, and threats of flogging reached even into the home of a ninety-year-old Frenchman accused of lewdness. Thereafter Prairie du Chien remained solidly loyal to the United States and to the American Fur Company.

The economic conditions of the Sauk and Fox deteriorated rapidly under the empery of the Americans. To settle their ac-

3. His complaint seems to have been genuine. According to Thomas Forsyth, the Sauk agent, Black Hawk refused to accept his share of the American annuity after 1818 when he learned that the goods were payment for ceding Saukenuk in 1804. For a time Forsyth had difficulty in obtaining signatures for receipt of goods, because the Indians had come to associate touching the goose quill with cession of their land.

counts with traders they had to range farther afield each fall in search of pelts, at a time when other tribes were competing for the same grounds. Horses became a necessity, and the horse market was controlled by whites, ready to charge a fantastic price for even the most broken-down nag. Bills at the trading posts swallowed up their annuities. In one year, for example, $1,900 out of a government disbursement of $2,000 went to a single firm, Farnham and Davenport of Rock Island (factors of the American Fur Company), while the remainder went to squatters claiming Indian depredations. As a later sheriff of Prairie du Chien remembered, pay-outs at annuity time were "a great jubilee, in most cases got up at the expense of the Indians," who returned to their villages "*sans* land, *sans* money, *sans* everything but a deep conviction of having been cheated."

Traders had nothing to lose when their clients ran deeply into debt, for outstanding accounts invariably were paid off whenever the tribe ceded its next tract of land to the United States. It was a hawk-eyed Redskin who ever caught a glimpse of even a copper or pistareen at annuity time. Yet the Indian had to trade or starve, for the self-sufficiency of the old hunting economy had collapsed under the pressure of encroaching white settlements.

As the Sauk and Fox independence waned, the tribe adhered more uniformly to those headmen who believed that their sole hope for survival lay in propitiating the Americans. The man who came to dominate the Peace Party was Keokuk ("He who has been everywhere"), the best friend among the Sauk that the white man ever had. Initially the warrior elite regarded him as an unimportant upstart, but tolerated him because he took on certain jobs no self-respecting Indian wished to do—such as negotiating with the Chemokemons. He had no stature whatsoever as a brave. When Black Hawk led the British Band to Green Bay in 1812, Keokuk stayed at home to tend the council fire. Much to everyone's surprise, when news arrived that Major Nathan Boone's scouting party was moving toward Saukenuk, Keokuk volunteered to take charge of the defense. His subsequent boast of having saved the village was more rhetorical than real, for Boone had turned back on his own volition. If Keokuk took part in the Sauk attacks upon John Campbell's keelboats and Zachary Taylor's armada, he wisely refrained from telling his white friends about it. Keokuk did not belong to the clan from which chiefs were chosen, but he became a kind of ombudsman on whom the tribe became dependent. And the Americans, more at ease with an Indian whose blue eyes were a visible sign of white blood (his mother's line went back to French-Canadian forebears), fostered the Sauk inclination to employ Keokuk in negotiations.

As Keokuk rose in influence among the Sauk and Fox, Black Hawk fell, until by the mid-1820s the Americans passed over him completely when negotiating with the tribe. When William Clark, who became superintendent of Indian affairs in 1823, picked out ten Sauk to take to Washington, Black Hawk was not included. Keokuk not only went, but was allowed to take his wife. Tama, another friendly Indian, was accompanied by both wife and daughter. It seems likely, however, that had Black Hawk been chosen and thereby made aware of the boundless resources and population of the Chemokemons, there probably would never have been a Black Hawk War.

Although the period when Keokuk would rule the Sauk like a Persian despot—with $300 horses, epauletted uniforms, and a harem—still lay in the future,[4] the foundations of his political edifice were laid in the 1820s with the connivance of William Clark.

Especially irritating to the Americans was the unflagging loyalty of a small faction of Sauk to the British. Since the Revolutionary War many tribes of the Northwest had made annual treks to Fort Malden, the British post at Amherstburg, across from Detroit. There they received gifts in recognition of assistance to the crown during the war. By the 1820s the custom had languished for various reasons, among them that the British au-

4. The artist George Catlin accurately took the measure of the man during a visit to the Sauk camp in the 1840s. Asked whether he had ever seen the Pipestone Quarry in Minnesota (a sacred place among the Indians), Keokuk said he had not, that it was located in enemy territory. "I wish it was in ours," he added. "I would sell it to the whites for a great many boxes of money."

thorities, having no further political interest in retaining the Indians' loyalty, discouraged the pilgrimage, while American agents warned their charges against showing such patent preference for the Saganash. Fort Malden posed no threat to the United States, but in the popular mind it was denounced as the "British scalp-market" where American hair-pieces were featured in a ghastly museum of mayhem and immolation.

Each spring Black Hawk led several hundred Sauk from Saukenuk to Fort Malden, a beeline march across Illinois and Michigan along what came to be known as the Great Sauk Trail. They passed through white settlements, glancing neither to right nor left, supremely oblivious to the gawking spectators along their route.[5] Although the quality and quantity of their presents declined every year (what had once been a musket and twenty pounds of powder for every warrior had become a bolt of cloth and frying pan for each family) nevertheless Black Hawk stubbornly persisted in making the annual journey. Never forgetting how the great gun of the Saganash had scattered the hated Chemokemons, he apparently believed always that the British Father, whose medallion he wore around his neck, would intervene to drive off the Americans. All his visits accomplished, however, was a stockpiling of complaints against the British Band by frontiersmen whose hierarchy of rancor placed Englishmen a close second to Indians; yet Black Hawk's Sisyphean labors affected the British policy toward the Sauk and Fox nation not one jot.

The beginning of the end for the Sauk and Fox nation came in 1822 when the United States began to lease land in the Lead Region. In April Colonel James Johnson, the brother of Vice-president Richard M. Johnson, obained a government permit to establish a mine on the Fever River. Anticipating resistance from the Fox and Winnebago of the area, who had zealously

5. One Michigan settler described how Black Hawk's band spent an evening near Ypsilanti in 1827. After a war dance, "a wild weird scene," a citizen brought out a decanter of whiskey for them, certain that this spoke a language all Indians understood. "Black Hawk's face darkened, he spoke a few earnest, authoritative words to his band. . . . The proferred whisky was promptly rejected, not one of the Indians could be induced to drink."

guarded their rich lodes against encroaching whites, Johnson took the precaution of bringing along military support from Fort Crawford when he arrived to stake out his claim.

Thomas Forsyth, the Sauk and Fox agent at Rock Island, was furious when he learned about this latent subversion of Indian property rights.[6] Though a government employee, Forsyth was an honest and an honorable man who had attempted to build confidence in the United States among the Sauk and Fox. At this outrage, he wrote to his superior, William Clark, warning of trouble ahead and explaining, "I cannot see how the major part of the Foxes, and some of the Sauk, could exist without those mines."

Even had he cared about the plight of the Indians, it is unlikely that William Clark, who could turn deaf, dumb, and blind when confronted with a moral dilemma, would ever have questioned an edict from Washington. He shared the official view that, if mere savages could produce four hundred thousand pounds of lead per year with pick and shovel, there was no predicting what white Americans could extract with modern machinery. If the Indians could not adjust to the presence of whites, let them move across the river.

The matter was settled by an agreement whereby both Indians and Americans were to operate mines side by side. This meant, of course, that within a few years the latter would be in undisputed possession of the entire region. Forsyth was correct in predicting trouble, for the boom in the Lead Region brought on the Winnebago War of 1827.

With the opening of the Lead Region to whites, the flush times of northern Illinois and southern Wisconsin had arrived. Miners swept up in both bonanzas have argued that lead fever

6. Forsyth probably knew more about the Sauk and Fox than any other white man. Agent at Rock Island from 1817 to 1831, he wrote a brilliant report on the tribe for William Clark, who apparently learned nothing from it. The son of a British officer, Forsyth was born in 1771 at Detroit and grew up on the frontier. He had only contempt for Clark, of whom he once wrote, "In Indian affairs he is a perfect ignoramus. But he is superintendent and can do no wrong." His habit of informing his superior of the latter's mistakes led finally to his removal from office in 1830, just before the outbreak of the Black Hawk War.

produced expectations as high as the gold fever in California twenty years later. Lured by prospects of instant wealth, thousands of men gouged millions of holes around the mushrooming settlements of Shake-Rag, Hardscrabble, New Diggin's, and Buncombe. From a population of less than fifty whites in 1822, the region grew to ten thousand a decade later.

Every spring whites poled up the Mississippi, when the river was high, or beat paths through the high prairie grass between Fort Clark (Peoria) and Galena. Those wintering over in dugouts were called Badgers; those returning south in late fall were known as Suckers, after the migratory bottom fish that was a staple in the diet of both groups.

By 1829 the town of Galena boasted two hundred fifty houses strewn about the steep hillsides above the Fever River. It advertised itself as the seat of the newly created Jo Daviess County (named atfer a Kentucky martyr at Tippecanoe) and publicized its economic promise in Eastern newspapers.[7] Steamboats unloaded cargo and passengers at the Galena wharf (though they had some difficulty in turning around in the shallow, mucky river), where ragamuffin youngsters hawked the *Miner's Journal,* the only newspaper in the Northwest. With progress had come an academy offering Latin; fraternal lodges like The Friends of Ireland, and of Civil and Religious Liberty; and a Methodist preacher of short tenure (he was expelled after raping a schoolgirl).

By the late 1820s the frontier, always elusive, had slipped farther west, to the vast spaces of the plains. Though there were great gaps in the white penetration of the upper Mississippi, the population explosion in the Lead Region was the concussion that

7. In this year R. W. Chandler's map of the lead mines, a chamber of commerce affair emanating from Galena, was published and circulated in the East. It charted (none too accurately) the region between the Rock and Wisconsin rivers. The boom was shortly to attract Thomas Melvill, who took over the chamber of commerce post in Galena and who, in 1840, enticed to the Lead Region his grandnephew, Herman Melville. To his credit, the younger Melville remained only a month, but his Western adventures formed the basis for his bitter indictment of American values in *The Confidence-Man.*

opened the country. Racing far ahead of the settlin' folk, the miners had hacked out crude communities in the vicinity of Galena, leaving in their wake hundreds of miles of empty tracts. But word drifted back from them of rich bottom land and tall stands of timber in the Rock Valley, and the squatter host of would-be farmers, more interested in loam than ore, began to march on Saukenuk—that pageant of American history (with the Indians cast as villains) called "Westward the Course of Empire Takes Its Way" or, as Mark Twain subtitled it, "Westward the Jug of Empire . . ."

As early as 1823 a few squatters had occupied land in the Rock Valley and cleared farms near Saukenuk. But, since they were unobtrusive, the Indians made no objection. The trouble began in 1827 when Goveror Ninian Edwards, the dick-horse of Illinois politics, began to petition the Department of War for the removal of the Sauk and Fox from the state.[8] He possessed no authority to remove them on his own, for the tribal lands were still federal property and, by the treaty of 1804, the Indians retained rights to use them until surveyed and sold to private individuals.

The following year agent Forsyth conferred with the chiefs, who rejected all proposals that they cross over the Mississippi. "They would not move from the land where the bones of their ancestors lay," the agent wrote Clark, "and would defend themselves against any power that might be sent to drive them from the present villages." Such defiance, even though 90 percent bluff, infuriated Edwards, who warned Clark that if the national government "declines acting with effect, those Indians will be removed, and that very promptly." Caught in a crossfire between the chiefs and the governor, the secretary of war, Peter B. Porter, capitulated to Edwards by promising that all Illinois Indians

8. Born in Maryland and educated at Dickinson College, Edwards drifted about the frontier functioning as doctor and lawyer until he discovered politics. His various offices included territorial governor, United States senator, and governor (1826–30). His son, Ninian W., and Abraham Lincoln married sisters, both men having served together as Sangamon County representatives in the state legislature.

(with the exception of some Kickapoo, who somehow had acquired such airtight guarantees that even the secretary lacked the presumption to remove them) would be ousted in 1829.

When the Sauk left on their winter hunt in the fall of 1828, news spread downstate that they were gone for good and that the land was about to be put up for sale. In the Jacksonville area a part-time Methodist parson named Rennah Wells passed on the information to John W. Spencer, a young man who later wrote an account of the early settlement in the Rock River Valley. In December, Spencer went up to Saukenuk, joining a drifter named "Judge" Pence, who had installed himself in the most comfortable wickeup in the village, a sixteen-by-fifty-foot lodge belonging to Black Hawk. Brother Wells soon arrived with three families, all of them kinsfolk; and, by spring, about a score of whites were squatting at Saukenuk.

One morning two Indians appeared, saying "Saukie wickeup." They proved to be Black Hawk and a companion. While on his hunting grounds, he had heard that Chemokemons had taken possession of the village and had hastened back. Though not happy at what he found, he was nevertheless not discourteous or hostile. He showed the Judge where fire had burned the posts of his wickeup and explained how they should be protected. At this time, Spencer had never heard of Black Hawk; later he lived within a quarter of a mile of him and found him "a very quiet, peaceable neighbor."

When the main body of Sauk returned in April, they found that the squatters had fenced in much of the village and their cornfields. The Indians decided to frighten off the Chemokemons much as they dislodged evil spirits from an unhealthy body. Two hundred braves staged a shivaree around the Judge's wickeup, which sent the intruders racing to Fort Armstrong for assistance. When Forsyth arrived from St. Louis in May he advised the Sauk to leave—like the Fox, who had all departed for Iowa. Quashquame, the sole living signatory of the treaty of 1804, came forward to deny that any land north of the Rock River had been sold. When Forsyth read the treaty and showed Quashquame his signature, Black Hawk grumbled that the whites must have inserted it later. Working through Keokuk, Forsyth arranged for most of the Sauk to occupy a new village on the Iowa River in the spring and he told the dissenters that he would receive no more complaints from Indians choosing to remain at Saukenuk. Privately, however, the agent sympathized with the Black Hawk faction. "It appears hard to me," he wrote Clark, "that the Indian property should be stolen, their huts torn down and their persons insulted by strangers . . . who are now quarreling and fighting with each other about cornfields." [9] Even William Clark blamed the squatters for exacerbating the Indians needlessly, thereby hindering his plans for their peaceful removal.

The summer of 1829 passed in this volatile atmosphere of mutual fear and distrust, with Indians and whites farming side by side. When a squatter named Joshua Vandruff, a beefy Pennsylvanian with ten children, opened a grocery selling redeye liquor to the Sauk, Black Hawk demanded that he desist. Vandruff refused. Buying the liquor at $.25 and selling it at $20 per gallon was a profit margin too great to give up. Black Hawk and a band of Indians then took further measures, rolling his barrels outside and staving in the heads with their tomahawks, spilling the "sure-fire liquid pop" on the ground. Such violation of property rights put the settlement in an uproar.[10] Vandruff appealed to the commandant at Fort Armstrong. It is said that Major John Bliss did not interfere because he loathed the squatters and knew they deserved it. But Black Hawk was rebuked by Antoine LeClaire, the three-hundred-pound interpreter at Rock Island, who said that the government would subtract the spillage from Sauk annuities.

Knowing that, as citizens, they had the support of the government if a crisis developed, many squatters began to bully and insult the Sauk, who knew too well the cost of striking back. The

9. Black Hawk later recalled that when he arrived in Saukenuk that spring, the Chemokemons "were making fences and dividing our cornfields for their own use—and *were quarreling among themselves about their lines, in the division!*"

10. It is gratifying to report that not everyone in Illinois sided with the squatters. Writing of the whiskey rebellion in 1835, Isaac Galland, an editor at Carthage leveled his sarcasm at the white provocateurs: "the bare recollection of such extravagance, will doubtless draw water from the *mouths* of many, whose *eyes* refuse the sympathetic tear."

Wells clan clubbed an Indian for opening a fence which they had thrown across a tribal right of way. A squaw was beaten for pulling a few suckers of corn out of a white's field, her own having been expropriated. Frightened by Chemokemon violence, an old Sauk planted his corn on a vacant island in the Rock. A white, deciding the site must be a good one, ploughed up the man's field and replanted it himself, leaving the Indian in tears. Repeatedly Black Hawk reported these assaults to Thomas Forsyth, who could do nothing except fume inwardly.

Some settlers, like Spencer, agreed to stable their animals at night so that they would not push through the flimsy wattle fences of the Sauk and destroy their planting; but Rennah Wells met every Indian spokesman with a loaded shotgun and ordered him off his land. When some Sauk, gaining a small revenge, turned Wells's livestock into his own field one night, the incensed squatter-parson claimed damages from the annuity payment to the tribe. Although it must have occurred to Black Hawk that this white canaille richly deserved extermination, somehow he kept his young men under control, for Spencer recorded no cases of Sauk violence during that summer.[11]

One major result of the confrontation at Saukenuk was that Black Hawk, eclipsed for many years in tribal politics, became the leader of the dissidents, most of them very young braves unaccustomed to groveling. One of them, Neapope ("The Broth") came from a line of chiefs, and he played upon the pride of Black Hawk, perhaps making him the figurehead of his own movement. That Neapope and other war hawks were prodding the old Sauk into action is suggested by Black Hawk's statement in his autobiography, "I now promised this party to be their leader, and raised the standard of opposition to Ke-o-kuck, with a full determination not to leave my village." Unfortunately

11. Black Hawk was aware, of course, of the ruthless manner in which the Americans put down Indian insurrection. He told the ex-governor, Thomas Coles, and James Hall, who visited Rock Island during the summer, "We dare not resent any of these things. If we did, it would be said that the Indians were disturbing the white people, and troops would be sent out to destroy us."

Neapope hatched more schemes than he had the resolution to carry out, and he proved to be an inspired troublemaker rather than committed militant. Yet, because he held the rank of chief, Black Hawk was in awe of him. Whether, in the events to follow, the two acted in concert or one led the other cannot be deduced from the evidence available.

When the Sauk left their village in the fall of 1829, few whites expected them to return in the spring. In their absence, Saukenuk was sold at the General Land Office, most of it gobbled up by "Colonel" George Davenport, the American Fur Company factor at Rock Island, a so-called friend of the Sauk until that time.[12] Neapope's response was to plan a fantastic assassination plot which would do away with Davenport, Forsyth, Clark, LeClaire, Bliss, and Keokuk, the authors of their misfortune. But the ravings of Neopope amounted to nothing, beyond angering, and alarming, the Chemokemons when they heard of it.

After half a century of territorial expansion and prosperity, crises began to compound in the Sauk and Fox nation. That winter, for the first time in Black Hawk's memory, the tribe was in want. Those members who had tried to break ground at the new village in Iowa had found the task nearly impossible with hand tools. (Sodbusting on the prairie was a major enterprise even for whites, who used teams of oxen, a convenience not provided Indians moved to virgin land.) Moreover, on the national level, Andrew Jackson, the most Indian-hating president ever to sit in the White House, in his annual message asserted that the presence of Indians within state boundaries was a violation of states' rights. His policy of encouraging Power to the People

12. Davenport, an Englishman by birth, claimed to have been an officer under Andrew Jackson during the War of 1812, a claim not supported by the official records. Setting up as a trader on Rock Island in 1816, while Fort Armstrong was being erected, he professed great admiration for the Sauk, who trusted him completely. In all his years as an Indian trader he "never lost a cent's worth" by theft. By 1832, Davenport had grabbed 2,652.87 acres in the vicinity of Saukenuk—some 80 percent of all land sold. The Sauk were particularly angered by his purchase of their ossuary, for they believed that the souls of their ancestors resided in the bones of the dead.

dealt the squatters all the winning cards in their contest against the Indians.[13] (And one can imagine the wrath of "Old Hickory" when he heard that one group was called the *British* Band.)

Even more ominous, for the immediate future, were fresh confrontations with the Sioux on the winter hunting grounds. In their sporadic warfare dating back to 1818 the Sauk and Fox had usually come out a few scalps ahead, but the numerical superiority of the Sioux, all of them inhabiting lands west of the Mississippi, added to the desire among the Sauk to return to the safety of Saukenuk in the spring.

By the spring of 1830 the major Sauk problem, so far as Superintendent William Clark was concerned, was averting a war between the Sioux and the Sauk and Fox, for he doubted that the British Band would again return to Saukenuk. To this end, he notified his agents of a conference to be held at Prairie de Chien in May between the headmen of the conflicting tribes. As we have seen, the result was a disaster: Seventeen Fox under Kettle were ambushed and slain. Thomas Forsyth averted a retaliatory strike by convincing two hundred Sauk and Fox to talk with Clark at Shallow Water. Thousands of dollars had been expended in arranging for the peace conference, and Clark warned that if they refused to attend, "You will stand alone in the world." In other words, if the Sauk and Fox boycotted the conference, the government would stand by and watch the Sioux devour their enemy.

In Clark's grand council room, decorated with Indian curios and pelts that sometimes reminded visitors of gory scalps, Keokuk aired his people's grievances: "We always take notice of your words and our G. Father's words—twelve days after your letter was received, advising peace and a meeting at P. du Chien, our people were killed. . . . Our chief was sent for, and killed when thus obeying the instructions of the Agent." Clark listened with mounting impatience—when angered his florid face turned mot-

13. George Davenport later reported that during a trip to Washington in 1829 he asked Jackson for a delay in evicting the Sauk from the Rock, only to be told, "By the Eternal, every last one of them shall cross the Mississippi, or be killed." Though Davenport was always given to hyperbole, the quotation nevertheless has a truly Jackson ring to it.

tled white behind old acne scars—unable to comprehend this fuss over a handful of dead Indians.

During these proceedings, Thomas Forsyth, who had led the protesters to St. Louis, learned that at that moment squatters were swarming across the Mississippi and occupying the Dubuque mines, which the Fox had evacuated after Kettle's assassination. Worse, the leader of this illegal occupation was none other than Henry Gratiot, the subagent of the United States to the Winnebago. Forsyth aired his feelings about the whole despicable affair in a letter to Clark: "Permit me to observe to you that the Sauk and Fox Indians are sufficiently soured against the Whites by their own people having been killed going to Prairie du Chien last month, on an invitation of some of the Government agents. You must know what will be the consequence when they are informed that their mineral land is occupied by the whites, and permitted to remain. . . . This, in my opinion, is the moment for the Government of the United States to show their affection towards the Sauk and Fox Indians."

Clark had had enough of the effrontery of this man, who dared to imply that the United States was somehow responsible for all the intertribal bickering. He fired Forsyth, using as his excuse the fact that the agent had brought the Sauk and Fox to St. Louis without proper authorization. Thus, on the eve of the Black Hawk War, the government was deprived of the one man who possessed some sort of understanding of the Sauk predicament and who might have dissuaded Black Hawk from his hopelessly impractical scheme.

Almost totally absorbed in the Saukenuk problem, Black Hawk seems to have missed all the war dancing and treaty making which filled the summer of 1830 for most of the tribe.[14] He brought his followers to Saukenuk; then, desperate for help, he journeyed to Fort Malden to talk with his British Father. The

14. In July another foolish treaty was signed at Prairie du Chien after all. It expanded the demilitarized zone between the warring tribes—ignored by the Sauk and Fox the next summer when they massacred the Menominee above Fort Crawford. Further, Keokuk sold a twenty-mile strip in Iowa for $6,000 annually for ten years—most of it going into the pockets of George Davenport's fur company for debts owed by the tribe.

results were exasperating. The British commander advised him to apply to his American Father, who would do him justice. By the time Black Hawk had completed his peregrinations and returned to Saukenuk, most of his band had moved to Iowa.

According to J. W. Spencer, whose narrative seems fair-minded, there was less violence in Saukenuk that summer than in the one preceding. He noted that some Kickapoo had joined those Sauk remaining in the village—certainly not very formidable recruits to the Black Hawk cause. The squatters continued to flood the governor's office with letters itemizing each missing sprout of corn and displaced fence rail. Since the government no longer supplied the services of a smith at Rock Island, the Saukenuk group faced the prospect of the winter hunt with defective flintlocks and broken gun springs. It appeared that Keokuk had won. Although he still had his pride Black Hawk had few followers.

Meanwhile, the go-ahead men of Jacksonian temperament had taken hold of Illinois politics by the throat, and "Injun-varmints" would be the first to feel the pain. At Vandalia (the appropriately named capital of Illinois) John Reynolds, the newly elected governor, asked the General Assembly in January 1831 for powers to call out the state militia to drive Indian trespassers across the Mississippi. The governor's dander was up. Among petitions received was one from Rennah Wells of Rock Island, who asserted that during the previous summer his son, after chasing an Indian out of a cornfield, had been the victim of "an attempted stabbing." To authenticate this atrocity, Wells had journeyed to Galena to collect the signatures of witnesses who had seen the rent in the near-victim's vest.[15]

Although the legislature refused to grant the governor such executive power, they nevertheless did pass resolutions specify-

15. The petition was authored and signed by a Galena group which included James M. Strode, colonel of the Jo Daviess County militia (a fatuous opportunist described more fully below), and Thomas Ford, a young lawyer who became governor in 1840. Ford, who wrote a bold exposé of Illinois politics after leaving office, subsequently repudiated much of his jingoism during the Sauk crisis. As might be expected, neither Wells nor the other complainants owned any land in the Rock Valley—all were squatters with less right to be there than the Indians themselves.

ing that if any Indians henceforth violated the "rights of the citizens of the State," force would be justifiable in chastising them. This resolution was forwarded to the president, serving notice that Illinois would act alone if the national government delayed.

As the Western populace began to squeeze Washington, so Washington squeezed William Clark, who demanded that his agents among the Kickapoo and Sauk and Fox investigate squatter complaints. But before he received their reports, Black Hawk's band—now swelled to three hundred braves—had returned to Saukenuk.

The new Sauk and Fox agent was Felix St. Vrain, the thirty-two-year-old son of a French émigré, who was ill-equipped to handle the Rock Valley crisis. Squatters complained to him that the Indians had burned down a house, destroyed a fence, and pastured their horses in wheat fields. On investigation St. Vrain (called "Savary" by the locals who could pronounce about as well as they could spell) found no charred remains of a house—only a fence burned by an accidental fire. There were Indian ponies in a wheat field, because a white had pulled down a fence to haul lumber across a squatter's domain. After talking with Black Hawk, the agent wrote to Clark, "I had considerable talk with them on this subject and could discover nothing hostile in their disposition unless their decided conviction of their right to the place could be construed as such." He recommended negotiations to get them to move rather than calling in military force. St. Vrain, however, was little more than a frustrated, well-intentioned hireling without any influence with either Clark or Black Hawk. Since the departure of Forsyth, relations between the Chemokemons and Sauk had all but collapsed.

There can be little doubt that Black Hawk's band became increasingly militant during the summer of 1831. When the squatters ploughed up a few patches of Sauk corn, Black Hawk collected his braves and delivered an ultimatum: All Whites had to remove south of the Rock River. The principal troublemakers, Rennah Wells and Joshua Vandruff, had to leave at once; the others could stay one more season in order to harvest their crops. When Vandruff pointed to his ten children, Black Hawk relented and permitted him to remain, but Wells was given twenty-four hours to get out.

When St. Vrain and Major Bliss refused to intervene, the squatters ceased squabbling among themselves long enough to pen a petition to the governor, dated April 30, 1831. Thirty-seven signatures were affixed to this mendacious and preposterous document, which exaggerated the number of Indians, suggested that the Winnebago and Potawatomie were about to join Black Hawk, recounted how the hostiles "almost destroyed all our crops," and so on. Unless the governor came to their aid, the petitioners would be compelled to abandon "the lands which we have purchased of government," an assertion that might have contained a grain of truth had George Davenport signed the petition, but he did not.

When no reply was forthcoming, the same petition was redrafted and three squatters, led by Vandruff's barkeeper, bore it to the governor in person. This second missive was dated May 19.

Men of substance in Illinois knew, of course, that such petitions were compounded, for the most part, of caterwauling and flapdoodle, agonized cries not to be taken very seriously. August Kennerly, Clark's agent investigating putative Kickapoo depredations that same summer, made this point perfectly clear in a report to his superior: "In this place as well as other sections of the country through which I passed, it seemed to be the opinion generally of the better class of people, that the petition had been got up by some of that portion of the inhabitants who, being too indolent to work, depend chiefly upon hunting for their support, and who had resorted to that method to save the game, and get the Indians out of the way, as being too greatly their superiors in hunting the wild game of the forest."

However, "the better class of people" were not very numerous or influential in the state, relative to the population as a whole. They possessed neither the power nor the will to inculcate a sense of humanity into those frontier hordes beginning to clamor for Sauk scalps in the name of *lex talionis*. As someone observed at the time, Western society contained five kinds of people, quality, bob-quality, commonality, rubbish, and trash, with the last two categories predominating. Hence, Governor Reynolds had a vast reservoir of prospective recruits on which to draw, when he called out the militia on May 26, just hours after his conference with Ben Pike, Vandruff's trusty barkeeper.

On the same day Reynolds issued his call for seven hundred citizen-soldiers, he wrote William Clark, "Those Indians are now, and so I have considered them, in a state of actual invasion of the State. . . . There is no disposition on the part of the people of this State to injure those unfortunate and deluded savages if they will let us alone; but a government that does not protect its citizens deserves not the name of a government." The next four days saw a barrage of foolscap passing between Reynolds, Clark, and General Edmund P. Gaines—the white triumvirate of the spurious Black Hawk War of 1831 (not to be confused with the genuine war of the following year).

Less to assist the squatters than to avert a wholesale slaughter of the Sauk, General Gaines, commander of the Department of the West, collected six companies of U.S. infantry from Jefferson Barracks and set off on May 30 by steamboat for the troubled area.

Before his departure from St. Louis, Gaines penned Reynolds a letter, fairly bristling with patrician hauteur, in which he made clear his contempt for the governor's wildcat army: "Should the hostile band be sustained by the residue of the Sac, Fox and other Indians, to an extent requiring an augmentation of my force, I will, in that event, communicate with your Excellency by express, and avail myself of the cooperation which you pro-pose. But, under existing circumstance . . . I do not deem it necessary or proper to require militia, or any other description of force, other than that of the regular army." Gaines and his staff had no illusions about politicians of the Reynolds's ilk. Lieuten-ant George A. McCall (later distinguished in Mexico and as general of the Pennsylvania volunteers in the Civil War) spoke for most regular officers when he characterized the governor's military ardor as having "no other incitive than the promised advancement of his own political views." The issue, the young

West Pointer went on to say, was not whether land had been stolen from the Sauk, "for that was apparent to the most obtuse," but whether they would fight to regain it.

Whether Black Hawk intended to fight the Chemokemons is a complicated, and unproductively hypothetical, question. Had Black Hawk suddenly been joined by thousands of Indian allies ready to engage in an all-out war on the hated Chemokemons, doubtless he would have been delighted to lead them against the settlements. But this is pointless speculation, since no other tribes rallied to his banner aside from those few Kickapoo who had already been adopted by the die-hard Saukenuk faction.

More than likely any impetus for a pan-Indian entente came from Neapope rather than Black Hawk, whose political vision was myopically restricted to holding on to Saukenuk. There can be no doubt that Neapope and other Sauk envoys had spent part of the winter on what the old war chief called a secret mission to tribes of the Southwest, obviously a far-flung attempt to build a Tecumsean confederation.[16] Even as Gaines's force steamed toward Fort Armstrong, Neapope was en route to Fort Malden, where he had gone to solicit military support from the British. (Probably the battered old Hawk, who had not the vaguest sense of the colossal power and vast extent of white America, still hoped that a great gun borrowed from the Saganash would drive the Chemokemons helter-skelter down the Mississippi, just as it had in 1814.)

Black Hawk openly alluded to anticipated assistance from outside; and the whites were never sure whether the old man knew something they did not or whether he merely had an overly active imagination. Hints of secret allies proved to be a counterproductive tactic, however, for, instead of frightening the whites away, it produced a massing of force at Rock Island beyond any that was actually required to handle the "crisis."

Another bungling advisor who attached himself to Black

16. Black Hawk records this in his autobiography: "Runners were sent to the Arkansas, Red river and Texas—not on the subject of our lands, but a secret mission, which I am not, at present, permitted to explain." Since most of the envoys died on their journey or were killed in the 1832 war, little is known about the conspiracy except that it failed dismally.

Hawk at this time was Wabokieshiek ("White Cloud"), better known as the Prophet, a medicine man who had established a rat's-nest village thirty-five miles up the Rock River (now (Prophetstown). Half-Winnebago and half-Sauk, the Prophet carried a three-foot magical wand employed in healing, claimed direct contact with the spirits via his dreams, and gave political counsel whenever he got the chance. Promising his followers happiness in a future state, he damned the disobedient and ruled his village with his own concoction of voodoo gleaned from Indian and Christian lore. Physically the Prophet was an impressive figure, with broad shoulders, a narrow waist (in contrast to the Sauk, who ran to full bellies and slight shoulders), and a mane of hair neatly cut at the neck. At times he sported a moustache, going against the almost universal custom among Indians. His two or three hundred followers were a variegated rabble of little use in either peace or war consisting, for the most part, of outcasts and invalids from other tribes. (Caleb Atwater, an ethnologist who visited them in 1829, characterized most of them as deformed or dwarfs, a nightmarish aggregation adhering to the Prophet because they were unwelcome anywhere else.) For all this, the Prophet had strong medicine, and Black Hawk relied upon his interpretation of dreams.

General Gaines arrived at Rock Island with his relief force on June 4 and held a conference with the hostiles on the next day. The British Band arrived, as Lieutenant McCall phrased it, "bounding from the earth and whooping" in battle regalia and with bows bent, a defiant gesture. Sitting with the whites in the council house on Rock Island was Keokuk, who had established a camp close at hand under a white flag as large as a bed sheet; but, at the menacing approach of Black Hawk's band, he left in great haste. Davenport appeared extremely nervous as well. In actual fact, both groups were frightened; but the war dance, as Black Hawk confessed later, was a bluff. Before the conference Black Hawk had consulted the Prophet, who told him "all we had to do to retain our village, was to *refuse* any, and every offer that might be made this war chief [Gaines]."

General Gaines opened the conference by alluding to the 1804 treaty and to each succeeding one that confirmed the cession. The country was now filling up, the Great Father could tolerate no further delay, the Indians must move across the river. Guilt-ridden and ancient, Quashquame came forward to deny that his delegation had sold the site of Saukenuk. "I am a red-skin," he added, "and do not use paper at a talk, but what is said is impressed on my heart, and I do not forget it." [17] The whites received his disclaimer with respect (they had to, the bulk of their troops were one-quarter of a mile distant), but it failed to counter the original document with Quashquame's X-mark affixed.

Although he rarely spoke in council, Black Hawk said that since the Great Spirit had given the Sauk this land, they were unwilling to leave it. Gaines countered by replying that white men as well as red became attached to their birthplace, but that whites left without quibbling once it was sold. The Sauk received an ultimatum: Cross the Mississippi peacefully or be forced over.

Despite his unflinching demeanor, General Gaines was troubled. His regulars could speedily clear Saukenuk of all stubborn Indians; but, if the fugitives moved up the Rock River, he lacked means to pursue them. Infantry could not overtake mounted Indians, and he had no cavalry (because none existed in the United States at that time, Congress having refused to appropriate funds to maintain them).

Though reluctant to call upon Governor Reynolds, on June 5, the date of his first conference with the Sauk, he asked for a single battalion of mounted men. Gaines continued negotiations while engaging in a mild variety of psychological warfare: The regulars held musket and artillery practice. Reconnaissance parties charted the terrain in preparation for the impending Battle

17. This was Quashquame's last public demurrer; he died the following winter. In his last years Quashquame turned artist. Proudly he showed Caleb Atwater a bark carving strikingly prophetic. It featured a steamboat, cannon going off, United States officer with epaulettes, privates on the boat. It was as though he had envisioned the events that came to pass at Bad Axe in 1832. Quashquame, it appears, was a more accurate dreamer than the Prophet.

of Saukenuk. Steamboats dashed about on the river, decks spotted with fashionable ladies eager to watch the fun and officers eagerly watching the ladies. (Lieutenant McCall paid court to a beautiful Arkansas lady whose husband, an obese drunkard nearly double her age, never left the card table till carried by a waiter to bed.)

Discomfited by the deadlock, Black Hawk appealed again to the Prophet, whose scheme it was to use the Sauk women as negotiators. Because the task of clearing land fell to Indian women, Black Hawk's ranks had swelled with squaws set against taking up a new village enterprise in Iowa. "I had one consolation," the old leader remembered, "for all the women were on my side, on account of their corn-fields." Much to the surprise of the whites, a middle-aged squaw, the daughter of a deceased chief, appeared at the agency house to make her appeal to Gaines. Arguing that the men could not sell cornfields because "they belonged to the women," she went on, "Our women have worked the fields till they have become easy of culture, and they have come to tell you they will not leave them. Know then, that they have decided *not to move*." [18] Gaines replied that it was unnecessary to say anything more about the matter. The Indians had to leave. No further conferences took place. Black Hawk notified his villagers that if the Chemokemons came to eject them, no resistance should be offered. He had been impressed with Gaines's "manly conduct and soldierly deportment" and "felt conscious that this great war chief would not hurt our people."

On July 28 the first militia companies were spotted on the south bank of the Rock. Gaines sent Lieutenant McCall to pay his respects to the governor. Conducted to the vehicle bearing this honored freight, the lieutenant discovered the "linsey-

18. This testimony varies from Black Hawk's, which said the woman begged permission only to remain long enough to gather the harvest. There was talk, too, that Black Hawk expressed willingness to move across the river if provided with a face-saving payment of $6,000. If true, the government missed a real bargain, for the Black Hawk War of the following year cost hundreds of lives and uncounted millions of dollars.

woolsey Excellency coiled upon a truss of tarnished straw" in a battered caisson resembling "a Jersey fish-cart." The chalky-faced executive explained that he had been laid up for three days with chills and fever.

Although Gaines had requested only a single mounted battalion, he got nearly sixteen hundred men, all of them eager to "knock the Injuns into a cocked hat." Commanding this Sucker host, the largest military force ever assembled in Illinois, indeed, the largest congregation of human beings that most of the participants had ever seen, was Major General Joseph Duncan, M.C.,[19] who was soon closeted with Gaines in an extemporized war room aboard a rented steamboat.

On the following day the regulars, under Major John Bliss, swept across the peninsula and descended on Saukenuk from the bluffs to the north of the village. With him was a fifty-one-man outfit of local squatters, eleven of whom bore the surname Wells, calling itself the Rock River Rangers and under the captaincy of Ben Pike, the barkeeper. Concurrently, the Duncan force pushed up the slough on the south bank of the Rock, fording the river to Vandruff's Island and storming the Sauk fortress from the rear. Within this pincer movement, General Gaines brought up the center from his command post in the wheelhouse of the steamboat *Winnebago*. He opened battle by firing grape and canister into the dense undergrowth of Vandruff's Island where the enemy was supposed to be lurking. Initially the militia splashed forward with spirit, but they were soon milling about the river bank, unable to locate the ford. Duncan came up and reprimanded the local guide, who cursed the commanding general to his face, in front of all his troops, before showing him the way.

Despite the brief logjam at the ford, the operation succeeded wonderfully. The campaign was marred by only one detail—the village had been abandoned. The victors found not one brave,

19. Duncan (1794–1844), a native of Kentucky who had stumped his way to the House of Representatives by 1827, acquired great popularity when he succeeded in getting through Congress appropriations to pay the militia for their service. This, combined with his role in the 1831 war, elected him governor of Illinois in 1834.

squaw, papoose, or dog. During the previous night Black Hawk's entire band had crossed the Mississippi and set up camp on the Iowa shore below Rock Island. The old leader later explained, "I would have remained and been taken prisoner by the *regulars,* but was afraid of the multitude of *pale faces,* who were on horseback, as they were under no restraint of their chiefs." It was a wise move, for the Sucker army would undoubtedly have massacred the whole village, as evidenced by what did happen, as described by Thomas Ford (a future governor) who was an eyewitness: "The enemy having escaped, the volunteers were determined to be avenged upon something. The rain descended in torrents and the Indian wigwams would have furnished a comfortable shelter; but notwithstanding the rain the whole town was soon wrapped in flames, and thus perished an ancient village which had once been the delightful home of six or seven thousand Indians."

The squatters, overjoyed at first, soon found the presence of the Sucker militia cause for complaint and petition. The army from downstate shot their hogs, pastured horses in grain fields, and rooted about in their kitchen gardens. One of the same Rock River Rangers who had petitioned Governor Reynolds for aid against pillaging Sauk now begged the governor, face to face, to rescue him from marauding Suckers: "I had a field of twenty acres of corn and potatoes, and the volunteers went for the fence. We tried to stop them from taking the rails, but could not; going to the Governor and General Gaines, they went out to the field and told the men they must not take the fence. While they were present the men stopped operations, but as soon as they turned to return, the men, to the number of four or five hundred, took each a rail on his shoulder and marched behind them into camp. By this operation I lost all my crop for one year, for which I never received a cent, the soldiers doing me ten times as much damage as the Indians had ever done."

Twenty-eight chiefs and headmen, including Black Hawk, appeared without coercion at Fort Armstrong on June 30 to sign a document, pretentiously called Articles of Agreement and Capitulation, drawn up by Gaines and Reynolds. The terms compelled the British Band to submit to the authority of the friendly chiefs—

that is to say, Keokuk's party. They were forbidden communication and intercourse with any British post, garrison, or town. And, most astonishing of all, no members of the band were to cross to the eastern shore of the Mississippi without express permission from either the president of the United States or the governor of Illinois! The document had no legal authority,[20] but the Indians who signed it were never told that.

During the ceremony, Black Hawk evidenced grief and humiliation. Lieutenant McCall sympathetically described the moment when he came forward to sign: "The sound of his heel upon the floor as he strode majestically forward was measured and distinct." Taking the goose quill in hand he "made a large, bold cross with a force which rendered *that* pen forever unfit for future use." Then, returning it politely, he resumed his seat.

The Saukenuk question seemed disposed of by late summer 1831. Black Hawk appeared to be utterly crestfallen and defeated. His band took no part in the massacre of the Menominee at Prairie du Chien a few weeks later, although some of the malefactors took asylum with the British Band in the spring following. Most citizens of Illinois assumed that Black Hawk had been "chawed up pretty small" and that war had been grubbed out by the jacknife Caesarean of Gaines and Reynolds.

20. For two reasons: 1) neither Gaines nor Reynolds had been instructed to make a treaty, and 2) the document was never ratified by Congress. When Black Hawk recrossed the Mississippi the following year he was entirely within his rights, even as these were laid down by Chemokemon law.

FOUR

The People's Army

The country rings around with loud alarms,
And now in fields the rude militia swarms;
Mouths without hands, maintained at vast expense,
In peace a charge, in war a weak defense. . . .
Of seeming arms to make a short essay,
Then hasten to be drunk—the business of the day.
—DRYDEN

◄◄

AS EARLY AS April 5, 1832, Felix St. Vrain, the Sauk agent at Rock Island, had learned of the British Band's impending move across the river into Illinois. On that day the Prophet had come voluntarily to the agency house. He revealed that, during the winter, he had invited the band to join him and to live at his village thirty-five miles up the Rock. When St. Vrain, aghast at the implications of such an invitation, pointed out that it was in flagrant violation of the Articles signed the previous summer, the Prophet expressed ignorance of them, adding that, had he known of them, the invitation would not have been extended.

The agent immediately notified Major John Bliss, commander of the sixty-man garrison at Fort Armstrong, who arranged a conference with the Prophet the following morning. The shaman said he saw nothing wrong in fusing his group with Black Hawk's; after all, they would not be returning to Saukenuk and were dissatisfied with the new lands in Iowa. Again he denied knowledge of the treaty. When Bliss, a liverish man in the best of times, warned that there would be war if the Sauk crossed the river and advised the Prophet to prevent them, the quack Messiah stalked out of the agency, one of his followers explaining that he was very angry.

Whether the Prophet had sent his invitation to Black Hawk

out of the kindness to the Sauk or malice toward the whites no one could say, but his professions of ignorance about the prohibition were not convincing. Obviously he had received news of Black Hawk's arrival and spilled the story to St. Vrain in order to disavow his own responsibility for having broken the law. When the major got word that the British Band was indeed across the river, he patched together a defense for his fort, described by one pioneer as a "log pen [which] would have offered about as much resistance to a cannon ball as a sheep skin." He clamped a restriction on the discharge of firearms unless as signal of the Indian's approach. The settlers of Farnhamburg (now Rock Island), the scruffy hamlet on the mainland, remained calm until April 11, when the sound of gunfire down the river stampeded them across the slough to the haven of the fort. Only later was it discovered that the Vandruffs had been unable to restrain themselves from shooting at wild turkeys while on scout near Saukenuk. Thus to the infamous whiskey-seller belongs the distinction of having fired the first shot of the Black Hawk War.

Major Bliss must have been frustrated, indeed, as he took stock of the droves of human cattle, both soldiers and civilians, called out to defend Fort Armstrong. Drunkenness and venereal disease were so rampant that, at any given time, one-quarter of his garrison whiled away their time in the guardhouse. (Colonel George Croghan, inspector of frontier garrisons and himself a drug addict, estimated desertions at more than half the soldiers on muster rolls; he complained that the principal reading matter at frontier posts was Bell's *A Treatise on Gonorrhea Virulenta;* and he warned that proliferating dramshops about all the western forts had undermined the health of the army.) And further, the stockade and buildings, pocky with rot, would be a virtual tinderbox for flaming arrows.

The citizenry flocking into the fort, poor dubs for the most part, seemed to be roughly divided into two groups: those demanding that Bliss protect them and those hovering about a Presbyterian elder united in appeals to God. Divine intercession was not required, however, for signal guns on the river announced the arrival of General Henry Atkinson during the predawn hours of April 12.

All authorities agree that General Atkinson reached Fort Armstrong before the British Band arrived at the mouth of the Rock. Why he did not immediately deploy his troops, vastly superior in firepower and nearly equal in numbers, across the path of the approaching Sauk to prevent their march up the south bank of the Rock remains the great unsolved riddle of the Black Hawk War. He must have realized that once the Indians got past him, pursuit of them with mere infantry would be impracticable.

Black Hawk, in fact, saw the steamboats passing at night and became alarmed, "expecting to meet the soldiers at Rock river, to prevent us from going up." Probably only the assurances of the Prophet, who had come down to meet them, that the American war chief would not dare attack them so long as they behaved peaceably, kept Black Hawk from halting where he was.[1] Taking care not to cross over to Saukenuk on the north bank, the Sauk advanced "beating our drums and singing, to show the Americans that we were not afraid," a certain sign that they were. The Hawk, ever apprehensive that the Chemokemons were preparing an ambush from a ravine or bluff, could scarcely believe his good luck (or the Prophet's magic) in getting through so easily.

Had the likes of "Old Hickory," "Old Fuss and Feathers," "Old Tippecanoe," or "Old Boiler Balls" been in command of the federal forces at that time, the Black Hawk War would have been aborted. But Henry Atkinson was a paper general, unwilling to proceed until all risk had been eliminated from the territory ahead. Instead of moving out his troops, he called in the local authorities and Indian experts and, by the evening of April 12, had begun to believe that Black Hawk planned an all-out offensive. Incredible as it may seem, Atkinson did not even send one of his officers, under white flag, to call for a parley with the Hawk.

That nonaggressive whites were in no danger should have

1. Even while urging the British Band to remain peaceful, the Prophet added, according to Black Hawk, that "we were not *yet ready* to act otherwise. We must wait until we ascend Rock river and receive our reinforcements, and we will then be able to withstand any army!" Although this statement can be interpreted in many ways, presumably the Prophet alluded to support from other Winnebago tribes along the Rock should the whites attempt to oust the British Band from Prophetstown. It does not necessarily suggest that the Prophet envisioned an offensive against the settlements.

been plain enough from the experience of John Spencer, a local settler, who forded the Rock to talk with Nasheaskuk, Black Hawk's son. Asked where the Indians were going, Nasheaskuk replied, maybe Saukenuk, maybe Prophetstown. This appears to have been the sole contact between white and Indian, and the opportunity to stop Black Hawk's band slipped irretrievably away.

The stockade at Rock Island had become little more than a corral. Within it, each human creature was primarily concerned about deciphering the significance of the Sauk movements. Most finally concurred in the theory that they signified death and destruction for law-abiding white settlers. Rather than relying upon the limited good sense of agent St. Vrain, General Atkinson accepted the apocalyptic hypotheses of the settlers. In particular, he seemed hyponotized by the views of George Davenport and Nathan Smith, the latter a squatter who had married a Sauk woman and spoke the language fluently. He had each man put his predictions in writing for his official file. Both letters bear the date April 13.

Davenport claimed that men in his employ had wintered with the Sauk and learned that the British Band "is determined to make war upon the frontier settlements." They planned to establish a stronghold in the peat bogs of the upper Rock, pick up Winnebago and Potawatomie reinforcements, and then "make a descent and murder all the settlers on the frontier." In the same letter Davenport took care to assure Atkinson that Keokuk's party had nothing to do with the British Band. Davenport neglected to mention either his 80 percent holdings of land in the Rock valley or the $40,000 which he would subsequently claim as owed him by the Sauk, a debt that would be paid, as he well knew, only when the Sauk and Fox ceded more land to the United States.

Smith, one of Davenport's henchmen employed in the Wisconsin River trade, corroborated his boss, adding colorful details of his own. One warrior had told him, for instance, "that he would rather kill Genl Gaines than any other being on earth," and others said they were going to the British. It was this latter report that gave rise to the notion, which electrified the settlements as

far east as Detroit, that Black Hawk intended to break through
to Canada.

It was not that George Davenport hated Sauk; rather, his high
regard for them simply did not outweigh his greater affection for
$40,000 and 2,652.87 acres of land. Further, it is likely that mem-
bers of the British Band did discuss openly and graphically what
they would do to the Chemokemons if given half a chance. But the
gap between wish and deed is a vast one, and the angry vows
of Sauk warriors can be taken no more seriously than the pious
pledges of the Americans promising fairness to the Indians. Completely ignored was the fact that no Indians in history had ever
gone on the warpath taking their women, children, and old people, with them! This was not a recondite notion, as the April 26,
1832, issue of the *Sangamo Journal* (Springfield) made clear: "It
is well known that all ineffectives and helpless persons are sent
away after they have made up their minds to fight."

The overwhelming conclusion is that, having cheated, bru-
talized, and provoked the Sauk, the whites created a war in the
name of preserving peace. They then proceeded to blame their
victims for causing it.

On April 13 General Atkinson met with the Keokuk faction
to demand the murderers of the Menominee, only to be told that
the malefactors had joined the British Band. During this conference the drums and songs of the defiant Sauk could be heard
"so plainly that they seemed but a short distance from us," though
they were five miles distant. Keokuk seemed less cooperative than
usual, and the whites feared that large numbers of the Peace
Party might tail after Black Hawk if his movement appeared
successful. Some members of Keokuk's own family and of that of
Wapello, a principal Fox chief, had already defected to the
militants.

The situation seemed to worsen for Atkinson with each passing
hour. Major Bliss and others advised him that baggage wagons
could not be hauled up the Rock Valley during the wet season
and that the river was too shallow for steamboats. Pursuit by
infantry was therefore out of the question. The general outlined
an impossibly intricate campaign, involving the transfer of his
soldiers to Galena, whence they would march down Kellogg's

Trail with artillery to intercept the British Band before they reached Dixon's Ferry, a way station seventy miles up the Rock. To be sure of nailing the Sauk in his box, he needed a substantial number of mounted men moving out from Rock Island on Black Hawk's trail. That meant the Illinois militia.

Instead of buckling on his sword, Atkinson reached for his pen. ("Old Goose Quill" would have been an appropriate nickname for him.) He informed Major General Alexander Macomb, commander in chief of the army, of his precarious situation (without mentioning his missed opportunity to halt the Sauk) and warned that "if things assume a more threatening aspect, it will be necessary for the Governor to call out the militia to protect the frontier." Considering that no white had reported a single act of depredation or molestation, "more threatening" was an empty phrase.

His letter to Governor Reynolds was a minor masterpiece of equivocation. It suggested an urgent need for a militia call-up without ever saying so. While he confessed that Black Hawk had not yet committed any hostile act, he understood that the Sauk would "resist an attempt to remove them." He further implied that the situation was very grave by offering to go down to St. Louis to confer with Reynolds, who was summering at his home in Belleville, Illinois. One sentence in particular was calculated to arouse Reynold's indignation: "I think the frontier is in great danger, and I will use all the means at my disposal to cooperate with you in its protection and defence."

These letters dispatched, Atkinson and his staff steamed off to review the Fort Crawford garrison and to prepare for the thrust from Galena. In the two days since the general had arrived at Rock Island no message or envoy had been sent to Black Hawk.

Atkinson's missive to Governor Reynolds produced the desired effect, for one of his campaign promises had been to remove all redskins from Illinois. The legislature, loath to dip into the state treasury for wars it could ill-afford, had held "Old Ranger"— as he liked to be called—in check, but the Atkinson letter cut him free: When a state defended itself against invasion, the national government paid. With a celerity almost unprecedented in Western affairs, Reynolds wrote, printed, and posted a proclamation of war within hours of receiving Atkinson's equivocal authorization on April 16:

TO THE MILITIA OF THE NORTH-WESTERN SECTION OF THE STATE

Fellow citizens:

Your country requires your services. The Indians have assumed a hostile attitude, and have invaded the State in violation of the treaty of last summer.

The British band of Sacs, and other hostile Indians, banded by Black Hawk, are in possession of the Rock River country, to the great terror of the frontier inhabitants. I consider the settlers on the frontiers to be in imminent danger.

I am in possession of the above information from gentlemen of respectable standing, and also from General Atkinson, whose character stands high with all classes.

In possession of the above facts and information, I have hesitated not as to the course I should pursue. No citizen ought to remain inactive when his country is invaded, and the helpless part of the community are in danger. I have called out a strong detachment of militia to rendezvous at Beardstown on the 22d inst.

Provisions for the men, and food for the horses will be furnished in abundance.

I hope my countrymen will realize my expectations, and offer their services, as heretofore, with promptitude and cheerfulness in defence of their country.

In hamlets as far-flung as Canton, Paris, and Pekin this twelve-gauge prose evoked in the citizenry vivid images of besotted Redskins, smeared with human gore, burning and raping their way through the Rock Valley.

By happy concidence for the governor, the call-to-arms came the same week that newspapers throughout the state were reporting that Congress would honor claims for militia who served with General Joseph Duncan in 1831. (Duncan, now called in some quarters "The Hero of Vandruff's Island," had been pressing hard for these claims all winter before a less than enthusiastic Congress.) Thus an Indian war promised bacon, boodle, scalps, and likker for all patriots willing to follow Old Ranger "in defence of their country." With whoops and hollers the Black Hawk War was on.

To repel the invasion of his state, which counted 157,000 free citizens in 1830, by four or five hundred ragged and hungry warriors, Governor Reynolds made use of a militia apparatus designed to meet more serious crises. Since the state constitution of 1818 defined the militia as all free white males between the ages of eighteen and forty-five, the Old Ranger had at his disposal a numerous host indeed. Fortunately for the taxpayers of the United States and the State of Illinois, he called for volunteers only.

Because of a lack of crises in the public safety, the militia system had rotted through disuse. In theory each county supported a regiment. But, in practice, few citizens demonstrated much zeal for the militia, unless they were officers. In an epoch not yet blessed with fraternal lodges such as the Knights of Pythias or Odd Fellows, the militia satisfied a deep hunger for paraphernalia—whether titles, uniforms, badges, or epaulettes—which would distinguish them. An astute visitor in the West once remarked of these undemocratic yearnings that a Westerner fifty miles from his home alluded to himself as a major; at seventy-five miles, as a colonel; and at one hundred miles, as a general. The titles of captain and squire belonged to whoever wanted them, anywhere. Governor Thomas Coles reflected this when he reported to the Department of War in 1826, "The militia as now organized is a mere school of titles where honors are conferred more from a momentary impulse of personal kindness than from a sense of the qualifications of the individuals." In other words, service in the militia provided an avenue for a man to make a name for himself without having to do anything. And woe unto an aspirant to public office without military service! A generation of Illinois politics was dominated by "veterans" of the Black Hawk War.

Regulations called for four militia musters each year, but no one adhered to this requirement. The yearly muster which was announced by fife and drum, however, invariably fetched crowds of ragamuffins, idlers, and vendors of stale gingercake and molasses beer. Spectators from beyond the immediate locality were rarely impressed by the maneuvers or accouterments of units known as the Wolf Creek Cavalry, the Spoon River Sharp-shooters, or the Half-Moon Lick Rifles. Except among the officers, festooned in massive coils of gold braid, uniforms consisted of the calico shirts and tow-linen pantaloons worn everyday. Fortunate indeed was the officer who found a shotgun among his disheveled mob, described by one viewer, "some sitting, some lying, some standing on one foot, some on both—every variety of weapon, the corn-stalk, the umbrella and riding whip pre-dominating."

The citizen-soldiers selected their company officers as children chose sides for a tug of war: Candidates stood off to one side and collected behind them their supporters; the longest line won. More often than not the officer elected was the man who could thrash everyone else in the crowd or whose stump oratory was the best in the district. It was a foregone conclusion that two barrels of whiskey—known as the fixin's—guaranteed a man a captaincy. Although, according to the laws governing militia organization laid down in 1821 by General Winfield Scott, regimental officers were supposed to be selected by company officers and general officers by members of the legislature, such hierarchic preroga-tives were scorned in the West as the residue of feudalism: The men demanded, and usually got, the right to elect as general whomever they wanted. But, as reward for the faithful or carrot for the hopeful, Governor Reynolds doled out staff commissions without consulting the *vox populi*.

Although most of the volunteers mustered had been weaned on tales of doughty forebears beating off attacks of screeching savages, the most recent full-fledged Indian war lay a generation in the past. However, macabre stories of redskins thrusting in-fants into Dutch ovens (climaxed by such details as "all that was left was a heap of bones and a bit of gravy") or raping female captives till the poor souls went insane still circulated and were believed as gospel by Western folk. As an English traveler noted with dismay, Illinois youths demonstrated toward the Indian "an antipathy since childhood"; they were wont to boast that "they should not mind shooting an Indian more than a wild cat or raccoon." [2]

In addition to the satisfaction of fighting and killing Indians, whites found it extremely profitably as well. There was no money in it if a few hundred ruffians went out on their own initiative to chastise a hostile tribe. But, as Governor Reynolds had learned in 1831, if the militia were called out at the request of the United States government, they were paid liberally.[3] Such a war could be a profitable enterprise in at least two ways: In the short run, it brought federal money into the state, thereby helping to counterbalance the perennial flow of cash to New Orleans and the Eastern bankers. Over the longer run, it extinguished Indian claims to lands which were subject to taxation as soon as they had been sold by the federal government. Every politician worth more than a dozen votes knew the boodle to be made from an Indian war. Charles Fenno Hoffman, a New York writer who traveled extensively in Illinois two years later, found prominent citizens using the phrase "hooking from Uncle Sam" when they alluded to the Black Hawk War. Local wits said it had cost the United States over $2 million to thrash the Sauk, yet the war "would have been taken by contract for $50,000."

2. The Indian-hating syndrome, while visible enough, has eluded explanation. Herman Melville, who treated the phenomenon in *The Confidence-Man*, seemed unable to decide whether instinct or environment caused it, though he leaned to the latter: "The instinct of antipathy against an Indian grows in the backwoodsman with the sense of good and bad, right and wrong. In one breath he learns that a brother is to be loved, and an Indian to be hated."

It comes as no particular surprise to find that in 1814 the territorial government of Illinois offered a $50 bounty for the scalp of a hostile Indian (not to be confused with a friendly scalp lock) against a $2.00 bounty for the pelt of a wolf.

3. For many months after his martial junket against the Sauk in 1831, the Old Ranger was in agony, for the national government refused to honor his claim for the costs of the campaign. In a personal letter to Reynolds, President Jackson demanded that he submit convincing evidence that the militia had been needed. After a long correspondence, assisted by the Honorable Major General Duncan on the floor of Congress, Reynolds collected what he claimed, including payment for himself at the going rate for a major general.

Nor were the militiamen who volunteered to fight Indians entirely blind to the individual economic benefits of patriotism. Although the base pay for a high private amounted to only $6.66 per month, this sum tripled if he brought a horse with him, as most did. Added to this was a travel allowance and easy access to all the food a volunteer could eat and all the whiskey he could drink, both of which were usually considerable. Arms, bedding, and camp equipment came from government stores, and generally returned home with the volunteer at the conclusion of the campaign. Most lucrative of all were the land warrants issued to veterans (which included anyone not on record as a deserter) when new territories opened up for settlement.[4]

Because Governor John Reynolds's very existence and public career were so inextricably associated with the Black Hawk War, it is particularly relevant to examine this man of his time in greater detail. Generally speaking, history has been kind to the governor by not mentioning him at all. Even his contemporaries seemed more willing to bury than to praise him. Thomas Ford, who knew him well, credits him with a "kind heart," but observed that "no one would suppose from hearing his conversation and public addresses that he had ever learned more than to read and write and cypher to the rule of three." Henry Brown, one of the first Sucker historians, found more to say about the arrival of Columbus at the Spanish court than about the activities of the governor at Vandalia. For General Edmund Gaines,

4. It is instructive to compute the compensation received by Abraham Lincoln, the most famous volunteer of the Black Hawk War. For eighty days of service (a captain during the first month, thereafter he dropped to private) in what he called, according to his biographer and law partner, "a holiday affair and chicken-stealing expedition," Lincoln received a lump payment in 1833 of $125. In 1852 he got a land warrant for 40 acres in Iowa (which he sold during the Civil War) and in 1856 another warrant for 120 acres in Illinois. Land sold for $1.00 an acre when it came on the market and appreciated rapidly. Therefore it might be argued that Abraham Lincoln made more money per diem as a volunteer in the war than he did in any other job before or after, exclusive of the presidency.

In short, from a material point of view, the Black Hawk War was a generous employer not too choosy in selecting its employees. Indian fighting paid well and was considerably more diverting, and only slightly more dangerous, than chopping wood or slopping hogs back home.

the governor embodied the raw stuff from which humor is made. The general had such a repertoire of "Reynoldsisms," based upon their short acquaintance in 1831, that for a time there was talk of a possible duel between the two. Even the centennial history of Illinois, a work published under official auspices in 1922, dismisses the Old Ranger as a "pliant demagogue [who] endeavored to cover his meanness of spirit with dignified or distant phrases."

Fortunately Reynolds bequeathed to posterity an autobiography entitled *My Own Times, Embracing also the History of My Life* (privately printed in 1855), a work which would have stature in the history of American humor were not the author's comic banalities entirely unintentional.[5] It is remarkably honest, one suspects, largely because the governor lacked the sense to know what he ought to hide.

Born in 1788 somewhere on the Pennsylvania frontier, John Reynolds grew up in the Knob District of Tennessee, where hatred of the British was exceeded only by loathing of Indians. Reynolds's father often boasted that no drop of English blood tainted his Irish veins, and the earliest recollections of John Reynolds were filled with "the nightly alarm of hostile Indians."

In 1800 the senior Reynolds, a squatter by trade, set out with his brood for New Spain. En route they passed through Kaskaskia, the principal town of southern Illinois, and were enchanted by this metropolis of five hundred, mostly French. The town had a log cathedral with a real church bell, the first that young John had ever heard.

Learning that New Spain admitted only American immigrants willing to convert to Papism, the father settled east of Kaskaskia on Horse Prairie. This was the home country of celebrated Indian killers like the Whitesides, the Goings, and the Murdocks. (Later Reynolds described the notorious John Mur-

5. Consider what Mark Twain might have done with a character who, on a grand tour in his twilight years, painfully calculated the acreage of St. Paul's, located Paris for his readers by giving the latitude and longitude, visited Oxford to see a cattle fair and chanced upon a university (of which he had never heard), or expressed joyous enthusiasm for Antwerp because he had seen a vessel flying the Stars and Stripes.

dock, a man who literally hunted Indians as though they were varmints to be exterminated, as "one of the greatest men that was ever raised in Illinois; he was Nature's nobleman."

In later years John Reynolds looked back fondly upon the frolics of his boyhood: stoning darkies, kicking hats off boys' heads, putting woodchucks in his saddlebag and inviting a companion to reach inside. When he was seventeen he accepted on faith that the sun went around the earth and that the Declaration of Independence was "the greatest achievement of human intellect." With the passing of time, however, he repudiated the former belief.

On the invitation of an uncle, John Reynolds returned to Knoxville to enter college. At twenty-one he was a gangly lout in a wolf-pelt hat, moving clumsily among such opulent marvels as woven carpets, papered walls, and Windsor chairs. He studied enough Latin to become convinced, as he said, that as orator Henry Clay outshone Cicero. College addled his brain. He dropped out to read law, but had a nervous breakdown. In 1811 a Knoxville physician dispatched him home with instructions never to study again, lest it damage his mind. Back at Horse Prairie the population was preparing for war. A local soothsayer had spotted a red comet streaking across the sky—a cosmic sign that "caused" the Battle of Tippecanoe one month later.

Off and on, John Reynolds took up arms during the War of 1812. His most notable service occurred in March of 1813 when he joined William B. Whiteside's rangers in pursuit of some Kickapoo who had massacred a family with the singularly inappropriate surname of Lively. Half a century later, Reynolds remembered vividly how the youngest Lively boy had been disembowelled and decapitated. The rangers found no Kickapoo—as a matter of fact, they could not even find the boy's head. In the light of his gallant defense of the frontier, Reynolds adopted the nickname "Old Ranger" when he began to nose about courthouse politics a few years later. But the sobriquet never quite caught on.

After the war young Reynolds hung out his shingle at Cahokia, the old French town across from St. Louis. He was a miserable failure until a Creole widow took up with him. She ground off the rough spots, steered clients his way, and in gratitude Reynolds married her, despite her Catholic faith. The fruits of this alliance were a judgeship in 1819 and the opprobrious nickname "John of Cahokia," which caught on as "Old Ranger" had not. As a jurist he had, wrote a contemporary, "a pusillanimous fear of giving offense." On one famous occasion, after sentencing a murderer to be hanged, he told the offender, "Now I want you and all your friends down on Indian Creek to know that it is not I who condemns you, but it is the jury and the law."

By 1826 he was installed in the Illinois legislature, where he made his mark by calling for "internal improvements," which the state clearly needed, and by working for the overthrow of Governor Ninian Edwards, whose hauteur grated on the Jackson-forever men making their bid for political dominance in Illinois.

When no one of any consequence came forward as gubernatorial candidate in 1829, Reynolds entered the lists, kicking off his campaign with the aphorism, "I must stir or git beat. The people is with me." His opponent, Thomas Kinney, was an illiterate Baptist preacher who stumped the state with a Bible in one pocket and a bottle of blackstrap in the other—so that "he could preach to one set of men and drink with another, and thus make himself agreeable to all." In contrast to Kinney, John Reynolds might almost have passed for an intellectual giant.

There were no significant issues; the only political difference between them was that Kinney boldly announced himself as a "whole-hog Jackson man" while Reynolds contented himself with the more ambiguous "nominal Jackson man." Armed with what Thomas Ford was to call "all the bye-words, catch-words, old sayings and figures of speech invented by vulgar ingenuity," Reynolds concentrated on advocating improvements, especially the projected canal linking the Mississippi with Lake Michigan, and damning Indians. A frontier wag circulated the story that "John of Cahokia" had promised to make the Mississippi run upstream half the year and downstream the other half, for the benefit of the river trade.[6]

6. It is not wholly impossible that Reynolds said something to that effect, for his ignorance of rudimentary scientific principles was total. Years later, while a congressman in Washington, he attributed rising tide in the Potomac to a heavy rain upriver.

Faced with a choice between a fool and a damned fool, the Edwards machine chose Reynolds by default; and the populace did not so much vote for him as against Kinney. In any case, whatever his limitations, the new governor shrewdly guessed that the electorate was even less informed than he (and a frontier politician who understood this could go far). He did not have to worry about betraying his principles for the simple reason that he had none to betray: One solved problems; and, if problems did not exist, it was the job of a governor to create them. With a kind of backwoods instinct, the Old Ranger recognized that Black Hawk's return to Illinois provided him with the political opportunity of a lifetime. Having called out his legions, he planned to take his place at their head.

During the rainy weeks of late April the Illinois volunteers slogged through the mud of a hundred roadways toward Beardstown, their point of rendezvous. The diary of one of them, O. H. Browning (later U.S. senator and secretary of interior under Ulysses S. Grant) is sprinkled with crabby complaints: "heavy fall of rain. . . . Could not sleep. Stood in mud ankle deep till day. . . . Encampment much infested with rattlesnakes. . . . Took some refreshments. Got merry."

The importance of liquor in the Black Hawk War cannot be overestimated. The complaint of one lieutenant to his superior, "I found the company about 60 strong full of patriotism mixed with whiskey," became the trademark of the campaign, though in fact the latter proved to be the more powerful fuel. Captain William Ross of Pike County had collected his quota of volunteers by an ingenious device: His reading of the governor's proclamation in the hamlet of Atlas had inspired no enthusiasm. Nor had a band playing martial airs. As a last resort he formed the men into two lines facing each other and sent two buckets of whiskey down the column. By the third round he had picked up one hundred volunteers, more than the quota for the entire county.

Converging upon Beardstown, the volunteers set up their camps among the willows fringing the Illinois River and, voracious as wolves, descended upon the commissary stores stacked along the riverbank with cries of "Damn the fat-back! Where's the whiskey?" The responsibility for provisioning the rabble spreading out across the sandbars and sloughs of the river bottom fell to Reynolds's quartermaster general, Colonel Enoch C. March, who laid the foundation for a private fortune with his activities during the war, and deserved every penny of it. March's efficiency was praised even by officers of the regular army, who found almost nothing else to commend among the governor's entourage. The colonel picked over the country like a magpie, buying horses, grain, fodder, and even a cache of Prussian fowling pieces which a Beardstown merchant had acquired from a South American government which had rejected them. One local farmer swore March would get his horses only over his dead body, but changed his mind promptly when offered $350.

Conspicuously missing from the activity at Beardstown was even token instruction in the military arts. A volunteer from St. Clair County, William Orr, reported bitterly, "The whole time that I was out I never witnessed a company drill, a battalion drill, or regimental drill. . . . I never heard a roll-call in the whole Brigade from the time of its organization." The same young idealist had cause to wonder "whether we were not going on some frivolous holiday excursion, and not to encounter hostile Indians." [7] The painful fact was that few officers had the moral courage to demand that their men be subjected to drill or discipline, knowing that the same voices which had elected them officers could as well vote them out. Now and again an officer's voice could be heard crying out plaintively, "Fall in, men—fall in! Gentlemen, will you please come away from that damned whiskey barrel!"

Among the green officers unable to maintain discipline in his company was a pock-faced, stoop-shouldered, slab-sided assistant storekeeper from New Salem, a two-rut, hilltop settlement near Springfield. The first order Captain Abraham Lincoln ever

7. William Orr had been editor of the St. Louis *Register* and the Kaskaskia *Republican*. He wrote several astute reports contending that the war had been caused by the "electioneering mania" of Governor Reynolds. He sent them to the editor of the newspaper in Edwardsville, but they were not published until eighty years later.

gave to his men received the retort, "Go to the devil, Sir!" Some of his men later confessed that they elected Lincoln as their commander, rather than his rival, William Kirkpatrick, because they would be able to do as they liked under Abe.[8]

Lincoln, a tender-hearted fellow of twenty-three who was so averse to bloodshed that he had not pulled a trigger on a wild fowl in fifteen years, joined in the Black Hawk War more for political reasons than anything else. Six weeks before he had filed as candidate for the legislature (elections for which were coming up in August) and circularized his platform (in support of Sangamon River navigation and in opposition to usury laws, both sound Whig principles). But his captaincy provided him with the first taste of the satisfaction that could be derived from election to public office. (He was especially pleased to defeat Kirkpatrick, who had owed him $2.00 for a cant hook for far too long.) Although Lincoln always belittled, in a joking way, his service in the war ("I had a good many bloody struggles with the mosquitoes"), nevertheless he recorded this surprising reflection in an autobiographical sketch thirty years later: "Then came the Black Hawk War, and I was elected a captain of volunteers, a success which gave me more pleasure than any I have had since." Presumably winning the election was more pleasing to him than whipping the Sauk.

As a military commander Lincoln remained a hopeless amateur, but what he lacked in information he made up for in improvisation. One of the few bright anecdotes of this dreary war was told by Lincoln on himself: "I could not for the life of me remember the proper word of command for getting my company

8. In the 1870s J. F. Snyder, who later became president of the Illinois State Historical Society, interviewed men of Lincoln's company and discovered that they "never spoke in malice of Lincoln but always in a spirit of ridicule." He was a jolly companion, "indolent and vulgar," and utterly without discipline. "They regarded him as a joke, an absurdity, and had serious doubts about his courage. Any old woman, they said, would have made a more creditable commander than he did." Allowances have to be made for Snyder's alleged pro-Southern sympathies. But that Lincoln was something of a buffoon at this time is undeniable. Kirkpatrick, by the way, joined Lincoln's company as private, but within a few weeks was promoted to quartermaster sergeant on the regimental level.

endwise, so that it could get through the gate; so, as we came near I shouted: 'This company is dismissed for two minutes, when it will fall in again on the other side of the gate!'" [9] This story, in fact, typifies the conduct, if not the effects, of the entire war.

While waiting for the army to assemble its full strength (some early arrivals had to wait at Beardstown a week for laggard units), the volunteers turned the Illinois bottom into a political forum, shooting gallery, and sporting arena. Choice campsites were taken and held by brute strength. When Lincoln's company came into conflict with a contingent from St. Clair County over a campground claimed by both, the matter was settled by a wrestling match. New Salem put Lincoln forward, knowing that he had never been whipped. He knew all the regular tricks plus a few special ones of his own (for instance, temporarily blinding an opponent by rubbing dog-fennel in his eyes). Taking one look at his adversary, a smallish man named Lorenzo Dow Thompson, Lincoln told his men to bet everything they owned, assuring them that he could dust the stranger promptly. Thompson won the toss, took a "side-holt," and threw Lincoln. It was the best two out of three, and Lincoln said, "Now it's your turn to go down!" He used his formidable "crotch-holt," but Thompson easily broke it and both tumbled to the ground. The New Salemites clamored that this was a "dog-fall" (a draw) and stripped off accouterments for a free-for-all. But Lincoln said he had been fairly thrown, adding, "Why, gentlemen, that man could throw a grizzly bear!" [10]

9. Whether this occurred at Beardstown or earlier is not known. Lincoln was actually twice elected captain during the same month. On April 7, prior to the call for volunteers, he acquired this rank at the regular spring muster of the Thirty-first Regiment of Illinois militia. But when it appeared that the militia might have to do actual fighting, those who volunteered elected (in most cases re-elected) officers who were to lead them into battle. On April 21, at a farm near New Salem, Lincoln's earlier rank was confirmed.

10. After Lincoln's death there was no shortage of courthouse raconteurs who claimed to have outrassled Abe; but the Beardstown encounter alone is supported by some few scraps of evidence. In 1916 J. F. Snyder reported that three witnesses had pointed out to him the exact spot—di-

This grotesque-looking captain from Sangamon, blue-streaked about the shins from a lifetime of wearing trousers six inches too short, with his head encased in a frazzled straw hat several sizes too large, and sticking out above the host congregating at Beardstown, was later remembered by many there for his inexhaustible grab bag of quips and jokes and tall tales, many of them delightfully obscene.

It took many a barrel of whiskey to put this disorderly army of 1,694 men into marching order. There were mutinous murmurings even before they got under way. First, opposition arose when Governor Reynolds had the audacity to appoint Samuel Whiteside commander in chief without putting the matter to a vote. General Whiteside had killed his first Indian in 1795, but he had no notion of how to manage an army of men as irascibly independent as himself. It was "a heavy hog to hold" for the toothless old Baptist, who perched on his horse like a flustered bald eagle while younger men put the camp into motion. The volunteers were further outraged to discover that eighteen baggage trains had been pre-empted for officers' use, while they had to carry their own provisions. "The mighty Napoleon," fumed one rankled volunteer, "was often known to march on foot and to encounter all the fatigue and inconvenience of the common soldier. . . . Our officers availed themselves of every privilege their rank could give them; and were *hated* and *execrated.*"

Setting off for Yellow Banks on April 30, the army traversed a prairie so wide and empty that scouts had to steer either by compass or by landmarks such as Twenty-mile Timber. The euphoria of the Beardstown carnival was quickly snuffed out by weather "right cold and tempestuous." The men fell to cursing prairie mud and Whiteside's adjutant, Major Nathan Buckmaster, as well for billeting them in sites two miles distant from firewood. "Much dissatisfaction and murmuring among troops,"

---

rectly across the river from the village—where the match occurred. Since Snyder steadily fought the burgeoning Lincoln cult, which threatened to convert the man into Sucker saint at the turn of the century, his belief in the story carries weight.

O. H. Browning scribbled in his diary. "All cussing Buck for keeping them in the prairie."

As they approached the Mississippi, they found the whole face of the earth one level sheet of water, with creeks and sinkholes indistinguishable from the rest of the muddy surface. By midday of May 3, the advance reached the Henderson River, a stream so swollen that the governor himself described it as a "millrace." The army crossed "in great disorder" by felling trees to make "a show of bridges" and by swimming horses across to the wooded slough on the far side. Much to the merriment of the soldiers, two wagons disappeared in the yellow muck, carrying down their loads of officers' baggage. Several horses drowned, but the governor nevertheless waxed proud of this crossing: "I believe the same army in less than one day could raft and cross the Mississippi." (Probably it would have required considerably less time than that had a canoe full of Sauk made its appearance.)

The ruddy cheerfulness of the Old Ranger disappeared when his army wandered into Yellow Banks before nightfall and found no steamboat laden with rations and whiskey awaiting them. Since most of the volunteers had thrown away their provisions during the march from Beardstown, they foraged for wild onions and fell upon the local livestock. The local citizenry besieged the governor in his van, contrasting the butcherings of the militia with the good behavior of Black Hawk's band, which had passed through the community a month earlier without disturbing a grain of corn. Adding to his woes, hungry volunteers cursed him to his face and discussed how his appearance could be improved by a coating of tar and feathers. Although Fort Armstrong was now only a day's march distant, the governor dared not order his disgruntled army to march out on empty bellies. Instead, he dispatched a letter to Atkinson begging for supplies. Many years later he explained why he waited at Yellow Banks: "It was considered dangerous to swim creeks and the enemy lurking about." [11]

11. Adding to everyone's confusion was General Atkinson's switch in plans. Originally Reynolds planned to march to Fort Armstrong, as he had in 1831. But before leaving Beardstown he received an express from Atkinson ordering him to proceed to Dixon's Ferry. Reynolds could not take

For two days the people's army waited without food. General Whiteside used the delay to inject some sense of military order into the young, undisciplined troops he commanded. He demanded that any officer allowing his men to fire rifles in camp be demoted to the ranks; this order, had it been enforced, would have reduced practically his whole army to the level of private. He promulgated hopelessly complicated instructions, like the following system of conveying orders by bugle notes:

12 blasts — brigade will rise in the morning
 8 blasts — new guard will parade and relieve the old one
 6 blasts — men will catch horses and saddle up
10 blasts — men will parade, prepared to march
 4 blasts — brigade will march
 3 blasts — brigade will halt
14 blasts — officers will parade at the general's tent

The sound of a distant bugle sent scrupulous officers ransacking pockets for memos. The old Baptist's association of music with the devil probably accounted for the adoption of this system, rather than one of more easily identifiable simple tunes.

Finally, on May 6, to the great embarrassment of the governor, two steamboats arrived with supplies—the *Java* from Atkinson with emergency rations and the *William Wallace* from St. Louis with the regular consignment under Colonel March. Now, instead of having nothing to eat, the militia were loaded with double rations as they prepared for the ride to Rock Island. Disgusted and cursing, they dashed their extra food on the boat deck or heaved it into the river. Other than Governor Reynolds, perhaps the only cheerful Suckers at Yellow Banks were the 176 unmounted militia.[12] Thus far they had been treated with the

---

this route, because he had already arranged for supplies to be steamboated to Yellow Banks. On May 4 Atkinson received information (subsequently proved false) that Black Hawk was descending the Rock in the direction of Fort Armstrong. At once he dispatched a second express requesting the militia to hasten to Rock Island by way of Yellow Banks; Atkinson, of course, had no idea that Reynolds was already there. Thus, quite by error, the governor turned up in the right place.

12. Governor Reynolds had called for no unmounted volunteers, but when these men materialized at Beardstown, he deemed it poor politics

scorn that cavalry always reserved for infantry, which was even more pronounced in the West where horseless people were held in especially low regard. Now, however, these pedestrians had sweet revenge: They rode to Fort Armstrong in fine style aboard the steamboats. Hooting happily, they bid farewell to the cavalry as they glumly rode off into the wet wilderness.

The Reynolds anabasis ended on May 7, when the Sucker army met with Atkinson's regulars at the mouth of the Rock River. Finally General Atkinson was ready to push his army after Black Hawk, who had crossed the Mississippi more than a month before and who, by this time, had probably concluded that the Chemokemons would leave him in peace.

---

to turn them away. For the most part, these men were either too poor to own riding horses or too disreputable to be able to borrow them. Utterly useless in the campaigns to follow, they were attached to the U.S infantry as unwelcome tag-alongs or assigned garrison duties.

FIVE

The Battle of Stillman's Run

The yoke of oxen, slowly dragging
Two barrels of whisky in a wagon:
Three hundred men, with throats a-parching,
Through the woods and prairies marching;
The wagon in the quick-sand sinking,
The whisky must be saved by—drinking.

—ILLINOIS BARD

DURING HIS three-week wait for the Sucker army, General Atkinson had been busy dispatching letters in all directions in an effort to seal off the British Band from political allies. On April 14 he set off for Fort Crawford to look through that garrison for suitable reinforcements. From Galena he notified Henry Dodge, the war lord of the Lead Region, that the Sauk were "decidedly hostile" and reiterated the Davenport theory that they would "strike upon the frontier inhabitants as soon as they secure their women and children in the fastnesses of the Rock river swamps."

Dodge, who held a colonel's commission in the Michigan territorial militia and had helped Atkinson mop up the Winnebago five years before, ruled his diggin's at Dodgeville with an iron fist that brooked no interference from any man, white or red. Like Atkinson he knew that the slightest hint of Sauk success would unleash the Winnebago against the whites they hated; thus he took charge of mobilization in the Lead Region, even though most of the population resided outside his jurisdiction.

While at Galena, the general ordered Henry Gratiot, subagent of the Winnebago, to ascertain whether any members of that tribe living in the upper Rock River regions were disposed to join Black Hawk. And, complying with his original orders from the War Department, the general notified the commanders and Indian agents at forts Howard, Winnebago, and Crawford to prevent war parties of Sioux or Menominee from moving against the Sauk. Atkinson then steamed on to Prairie du Chien.

Conditions at Fort Crawford were appalling. For three years the garrison had been employed almost exclusively constructing a stone fort on high ground (the old log fort beside the river had rotted out) and the soldiers had become slovenly drunken Falstaffs for the most part. In their leader Colonel Zachary Taylor, however, they had a superb commander, an iron disciplinarian who was respected for his tough earthiness.[1] But the colonel had been on furlough for over a year and had left Major Gustavus Loomis in charge. (When he heard of the Sauk troubles, while in Louisville, Taylor boarded the first steamboat and, still clad in civilian clothes, reported to Atkinson at Rock Island in time to join the campaign.)

After instructing Loomis to block the mouth of the Wisconsin River two miles to the south with anchored mackinaw boats if Black Hawk attempted to break out of the projected encirclement, Atkinson returned to Rock Island, arriving April 18. On the following day there was a break in the deadlock when Keokuk's party arrived and handed over for trial three of the Sauk and Fox alleged to have murdered the Menominee the previous year. Here was proof—if confirmation of the obvious was required—that the majority of the tribe wished to avert a confrontation with the whites and had no intention of joining the British Band. At this point General Atkinson had accomplished what the War Department had ordered him to do. However he still had no instructions concerning the removal of Black Hawk.

1. Taylor was "ignorant of fear," said one of his sergeants, who related the following incident at Fort Crawford: Among a group of recruits was a German who spoke no English. Taylor bawled an order for him to stand at attention. When the man did not, the colonel, mistaking the cause, got hold of his ears and shook him violently. The German unleashed a blow that dropped Taylor like a log. Before the recruit could be lashed, Taylor shouted, "Let that man alone; he will make a good soldier."

Faced with a hopelessly snarled situation in which any decisive action on his part might be interpreted in Washington as the wrong one, the general played it safe by equivocating.

Since he adhered to the traditional army view that Indians backed down when confronted by a superior force, he over-stressed the current danger to both Reynolds and Dodge because he needed the men that only they could supply, without an embarrassing appeal to Washington. Writing to the Old Ranger on April 18—knowing nothing of the militia call-up—he admitted that the British Band had not yet committed any hostile actions; but he went on to say, ignoring the apparent contradiction, "they are so decidedly hostile that nothing short of punishment will bring them to a proper sense of their misconduct." A more rational Atkinson revealed himself in a letter to General Edmund P. Gaines on the same day. Alluding to the "strike-from-the-swamps" hypothesis, Atkinson noted, "I am rather of the opinion, however, that they will not, until an attempt is made to coerce them." [2]

As commander pro tempore in the absence of Gaines, Atkinson seemed to be so much in the shadow of his superior that his campaign was evolving as a carbon copy of Gaines's in the preceding year. This meant waiting until the militia came up, at which point it was assumed Black Hawk's defiance would dissolve. The greatest difference was that now the primary goal for the whites was no longer merely forcing the Sauk across the river, but rather to corral the Indians on the Illinois side and then forge a lasting peace out of their humiliation.

Not until April 24 did Atkinson send his first message to Black Hawk. [3] Two Sauk, a half-breed and a son of Chief Tama, car-

2. This opinion was echoed in the notes of Lieutenant A. S. Johnston and the published account of Captain Henry Smith, who served in the campaign as quartermaster. According to the latter, the officers believed that the Indians, "almost always more sinned against than sinning," would comply with the terms of an ultimatum once they saw the force assembled against them.

3. On April 15, presumably on St. Vrain's initiative, two Indians of Keokuk's party had been sent to persuade relatives of the Peace Party to return to Rock Island. On the day following the messengers returned with stories of how they had been threatened with whippings and how one brave implicated in the Menominee murders had boasted, as he brandished

ried his demand that the British Band return, concluding, "If your hearts are good I will send an officer to talk with you in three or four days." Two days later the messengers returned reporting that Neapope was now the principal chief and that he had said, "We have no bad feelings, why do they send to us to tell us to go back—we will not go back—we will go on." Black Hawk, on the other hand, had become much less confident. When asked for his opinion the old man had replied, "I do not command the Indians. The village belongs to the chiefs. . . . I have no bad feelings. My opinion goes with my chiefs." [4]

Much to the surprise of the whites, Henry Gratiot and a companion named Cubbage suddenly materialized at Rock Island on April 27 after a ten-day circuit through Winnebago territory. At Turtle's village (now Beloit, Wisconsin) Gratiot had found over three hundred Winnebago preparing for a religious ceremony and used the opportunity to vaccinate them (a smallpox epidemic had broken out in January) and to advise them to remain neutral. The agent reported that the British Band had indeed sent wampum to the Winnebago bands of the upper Rock, but that this had been rejected. Local chiefs had expressed alarm that the Prophet was encouraging Black Hawk and that there were uncontrollable members of their bands who might be induced to join in a move against the Chemokemons. The chiefs, wishing to separate the Prophet's band from the Sauk, decided to go to Prophetstown and to invite all non-Sauk to return and live with them. Gratiot approved this proposal; but, fearing that the hostiles might induce the chiefs to join the rebellion, he resolved to accompany them himself.

---

his lance that "he hoped to brake [sic] or wear it out on the Americans." St. Vrain's diary nowhere suggests that these envoys were dispatched as spokesmen for Atkinson.

4. In addition to Neapope these chiefs were Menakau ("The Seed"), Makatauauquat ("Black Cloud"), Pachetowart ("The Liar"), and Kinnekonesaut ("First Striker"). All prisoners interviewed after the war agreed that Black Hawk was their leader, which probably meant that he functioned as a general obliged to carry out decisions made by others, but influencing these decisions too. For instance, Neapope's comment. "I and others were principal chiefs, but Black Hawk was the head warrior and older than us and led us."

Reaching Prophetstown on April 24 with twenty-six Winne-bago, Gratiot found many members of the band disposed to join the upper Rock tribes. But the Prophet himself was "very sullen." The British Band, who were encamped a short distance below, came up the next morning, ripped down the white flag on the Chemokemon's tent, and hoisted the British flag in its place. Gratiot recorded the events in his diary: "I told them that the white flag was mine and demanded the reason for taking it down, —they replied that I might travel with a flag, but should not keep it up while here. I, nevertheless, ordered my Winnebagoes to raise it again.—they did so—and the Saukees raised theirs by the side of mine." [5] The Sauk then performed a war dance around the tent, exhibiting hostility especially toward Cubbage (maybe because they thought the poor vaccinator had "bad medicine"), until White Crow, a one-eyed Winnebago from Turtles' village gave them tobacco, at which they abruptly stopped. The next day the Sauk moved up the Rock. Originally Gratiot had planned to return directly to the Lead Region, but, concluding that it was dangerous to follow the Sauk toward Turtle's village, he went instead to Rock Island with most of his Winnebago escort, arriving there on April 27.

The arrival of Gratiot touched off such a complicated and contradictory chain of rumors and reports that it is impossible to account for them all. Keokuk, after hearing the agent's story, explained that by Sauk custom the two whites had actually been prisoners and had been freed by White Crow's gift of tobacco. Gratiot, who understood no Sauk, seemed uncertain about this; but on reflection he admitted that his Winnebago custodians had appeared alarmed about a situation he did not quite understand.[6]

5. Gratiot's entry may be compared with Lieutenant A. S. Johnston's rendering of the incident in his diary for April 27: "They at first would not permit the agent to hoist the *United States Flag* [his italics] and afterwards when he was allowed to hoist our flag, they ran up the British flag close to it!" Whether Gratiot changed his story or the young West Pointer misunderstood it cannot be ascertained, but it should be remembered that Johnston was keeping not a private diary but an official journal of the campaign.

6. As time went on, the Gratiot family fabricated the tale of "Colonel" Henry Gratiot's "escape" from the village, much of it reminiscent of James

Though he made no mention of the encounter in his diary, Gratiot told General Atkinson that before leaving Prophetstown Black Hawk showed him the general's letter, which the agent read to him. The Hawk then dictated a reply, which Gratiot paraphrased: "He returns you the letter, and in answer to it says, that his heart is bad—that he intends to go farther up Rock River—and that if you send your officers to him he will fight them." Did Gratiot, whose holdings in the Lead Region were second in size to Dodge's, lie to stir up a war which would inevitably eject another tribe of Indians west of the Mississippi? Had he misunderstood what Black Hawk had said? Or had the Hawk's attitude truly undergone such a change between the visit of the Sauk envoys and Gratiot's visit just twenty-four hours later? [7]

Contributing to the confusion, the Winnebago escort appears to have been playing a double-crossing role throughout. Although they repeatedly avowed neutrality, both to Gratiot and to Atkinson, Black Hawk's autobiography contains this jarring contention: "They [the Winnebago] said the object of his [Gratiot's] mission was, to persuade us to return. But they advised us to go on—assuring us, that the further we went up Rock River, the more friends we would meet, and our situation be bettered: that they were on our side. . . . They said they would go down with their agent, to ascertain the strength of the enemy, and then return and give us the news; that they had to use some stratagem to *deceive* their agent, in order to *help* us!" Whites later pounced on this

Fenimore Cooper: "Gratiot's men pulled for their lives, first losing then gaining. The maddened Sacs whooped and shrieked with anger at the possible miscarriage of their plans as they lent renewed vigor to their strokes, . . ." More than likely this tale was the creation of Gratiot's son-in-law, E. B. Washburne (U.S. senator, later appointed minister to France by President Ulysses Grant—a fellow Galenian), yet for several generations it was acceepted as gospel in Illinois.

7. Further complicating the puzzle is the note which John Dixon, the trader and innkeeper at Dixon's Ferry, said that Gratiot sent him from Prophetstown: *"War is declared, send out expresses."* This note was dated April 21 which meant that it was written three days before Gratiot arrived at Prophetstown. It was passed on by Dixon to Major Isaiah Stillman with results we will soon discuss.

statement as proof of Winnebago treachery. But, if treachery, toward whom? How is it reconcilable with the subsequent refusal of the Rock River Winnebago to provide the British Band with land to raise even a crop? Were the Winnebago actually deceiving not the whites but the Sauk (whom they hated for collaborating with Atkinson in the Winnebago War) by encouraging them to ascend the river, thereby provoking the whites? Or was Black Hawk, who had become permanently embittered by the failure of the Winnebago to help him significantly, coloring his narrative as revenge on the Winnebago? Unfortunately there exists no clear answer to any of these questions. Had the Indians, or Gratiot, deliberately sought to cover their tracks they could hardly have been more successful.

In any event, Gratiot's report convinced the regulars that the Sauk were indeed preparing to fight and goaded Atkinson into action. Writing to General Alexander Macomb, Atkinson described Sauk holding a war dance under the British flag, a deliberate attempt to stir up Old Hickory, and warned that "they must be checked at once, or the whole frontier will be in flame."

Black Hawk was then at Dixon's Ferry where, dining with the trader and his wife, he explained that he hoped to raise corn among the Potawatomie twelve miles up the river. At the same time Atkinson commenced his operation to cut off the Sauk at Dixon's. Having heard that the militia were mobilizing at Beardstown, he ordered Reynolds to march directly to Dixon's Ferry, while he began steamboating regulars to Galena, in preparation for an overland thrust from the northwest.

But the Battle of Dixon's Grocery never materialized. On May 4 a ragged Sauk named Poynekanesa came into Fort Armstrong bearing the startling information that the British Band had decided to return to Iowa and were then moving toward Rock Island. Just as the general finally began to close his pincers, the enemy unobligingly ran up the handle! Atkinson recalled the regulars from Galena and instructed Reynolds to move to Rock Island (which, as we have seen, the Old Ranger was doing already). By the time the general had stabilized his center it was discovered that Poynekanesa's report was absolutely without foundation. Whether the Indian had been motivated by a desire to help Black Hawk escape up the Rock or by a sense of humor, was never known.

On May 7 the first units of the Illinois militia appeared on the south bank of the Rock. Now, more than a month after the British Band had crossed the Mississippi, Atkinson finally felt bold enough to sally forth from the rotten logs of Fort Armstrong.[8] From the outset, relations between the regulars and the militia were marked by hostility and mutual contempt. The Suckers, who viewed themselves as "nature's noblemen" and "ring-tailed roarers," regarded Atkinson's blue coats as "hot-house lettuces" lacking the guts to perform the task of "smashing the Saukies to sky-blue fits." Officers, particularly West Pointers,[9] were "stuck ups" fit only for such dandyish activities as sipping tea with the ladies and "eating yellow-legged chickens" (for whatever reason, this typified Eastern degeneracy).

The regulars, on the other hand, scorned these undisciplined roughnecks who camped in "filthy nests" and whose bullying arrogance had all too often, in Indian fighting on the frontier, given way to precipitous flights to the rear. In the eyes of an urbane Virginian, Lieutenant Philip St. George Cooke (later a brevet major general during the Civil War), who brought a company from Fort Leavenworth to join Atkinson, the militia was composed of roughly equal parts villain and clown. Reflecting the skepticism the army professionals, he described the governor's camp as a bedlam of "citizen volunteers, who were as active as a swarming hive; catching horses, electioneering, drawing rations, asking questions, shooting at marks, electing officers, mustering in, issuing orders, disobeying orders, galloping about, 'cussing and discussing' the war, and the rumors thereof."

Knowing from experience the conflicts attendant upon a joint

8. Atkinson was still worried about possible censure for calling out militia. On May 3 he wrote to Gaines, "I did not call on the Governor for this force. It is fortunate, however, that he has been so prompt in taking the field." If the cost of the coming war proved exorbitant, it would be the fault of Governor Reynolds, not General Atkinson.

9. During his years in Congress, John Reynolds made a name for himself as an obstructionist of all bills designed to fund or to improve the military academy. Such an attitude was worth votes in Illinois.

expedition of this sort, Governor Reynolds explained that his job was "to harmonize and conciliate" (while, of course, being paid as a major general for performing this chore). But the antipathy between federal and state troops nevertheless marred the progress of the campaign.

After mustering the Illinois militia into the federal service on May 8, General Atkinson divided his newly begotten army into two autonomous, but presumably cooperating, wings with General Sam Whiteside commanding the 1,500 mounted volunteers and Colonel Zachary Taylor the 320 regular infantry, to which were appended the 150-odd pedestrian volunteers.

The march up the Rock after Black Hawk got under way on May 10. The orders called for Whiteside and Taylor to rendezvous at Prophetstown, but unfortunately they gave the former discretionary power to push further upstream if he deemed it prudent. The mounted volunteers promptly plunged into the wilderness and left the regulars leagues behind. To the regulars fell the dirty job of poling and cordelling upstream the supply boats—two keelboats, one ninety tons, the other thirty, and five mackinaw boats. By water it was twice as far to Prophetstown, the weather was unseasonably cold and rainy, and Taylor's rear guard was quickly left far behind. In addition, since the Rock had never been navigated by any vessel larger than a canoe, the men were in the water most of the time pulling the boats over bars and hacking at the undergrowth which overhung the river.

Midafternoon of the first day found Whiteside's horsemen at Prophetstown, where scouts—or spies, as they were called in that day—finding signs of the Sauk encampment, estimated that it had been abandoned more than a week before. After putting the village to the torch they pushed on, sweeping Reynolds and Whiteside along with them in their impatience to "take meat" (their term for battling with the Sauk). The spies brought in a senile Potawatomie who informed them that Black Hawk was at Pawpaw Grove, two days' march up the Rock.[10] The militia

10. Perhaps it was the appearance of this Indian which gave rise to another Lincoln story: It was said that a hungry Indian carrying a begging letter from Lewis Cass (then secretary of war, formerly territorial governor of Michigan) arrived in the militia camp. Suspecting that he was a spy,

stuffed two days' rations into their saddlebags and abandoned their quartermaster stores, which Taylor's force found, white with mildew, when he arrived there four days later.

The Sucker army rode into Dixon's clearing on May 12, their horses worn out and their supplies nearly depleted. John Dixon, proprietor of a ninety-foot log tavern, reported that the British Band, numbering about 500 warriors, had passed through two weeks before and were supposed to be camping near Old Man's Creek, about twenty-five miles further up the Rock. This information matched that from O. W. Kellogg, Dixon's brother-in-law, who owned the tavern on the Galena road and had counted 450 mounted braves. No one had reported any molestation by the Sauk. In the words of one local citizen many years later, "I never heard of Black Hawk's band, while passing up the Rock River, committing any depredation whatever, not even petty theft."

Whiteside reported his arrival at Dixon's to Atkinson, stating that he would not advance farther until the rear wing caught up. Without provisions, pursuit of Black Hawk was unthinkable. Atkinson begged Whiteside to send some men to assist him in pulling the flotilla upriver. None went; they were chevaliers, not keelboatmen or sutlers. Had the Suckers contented themselves with idling about the tavern until General Atkinson came up with supplies, they would have at least done some good by doing no harm. Unfortunately, however, two units insisted upon advancing while the others waited.

Since the end of April the battalions of Major Isaiah Stillman of Canton and Major David Bailey of Pekin had been ranging the frontier between the Rock and the Illinois rivers on special orders from the governor. Neither had reported to Beardstown nor been mustered into the federal service; therefore, the men argued,

___

some men decided to kill him, but Captain Lincoln forbade it. Charged with cowardice and squeamishness, Abe threw out a challenge: "If any man thinks I am a coward, let him test it." When a volunteer complained that Lincoln was "larger and heavier," Abe suggested that he select a weapon. The aggressor backed down. Such high-minded pomposity is wholly out of character with the real Lincoln, who, faced with this situation, would have cut down his opponent with a well-aimed quip or anecdote. The sole feature of this story that rings true is the eagerness of the militia to kill any Indian who chanced in their way.

these two battalions came under the jurisdiction of neither White-side nor Atkinson. The governor had hardly unsaddled his horse at Dixon's before men of these battalions besieged him, boasting that they would bring in the British Band "at the ends of their halter-straps." Their ringleader, Captain Abner Eads of Peoria, argued that, while the regulars were "crawling along, stuffing themselves with beef," a fistful of brave Suckers like himself could end the war. General Whiteside absolutely prohibited any such rash movement; but, as might be expected, the Old Ranger lacked the grit to deny his constituents what they wanted. On May 12 he issued the following famous order:

The troops under the command of Major Stillman, including the battalions of said Major Stillman, and Major Bailey will forthwith proceed with four day's rations to the head of Old Man's Creek, where it is supposed the hostile Sac Indians are assembled, for the purpose of taking all cautious measures to coerce said Indians into submission, and report themselves to this department as soon thereafter as practicable.

The order bore the signature of Brigade Major Nathan Buckmaster; Whiteside refused to sign it and Reynolds shrewdly avoided doing so. Exactly how the Sauk were to be coerced through the use of "cautious measures" was vague; but no one requested clarification, Stillman's hotspurs least of all.

Isaiah Stillman was the foremost son of Massachusetts to serve in the Black Hawk War. Born in 1793, he came to Illinois at some undetermined time and, as a Yankee trader, did a lively trade in pots, pans, and other notions at Copperas Creek Landing in Fulton County. Although political power among the Suckers was dominated by men of Southern extraction (fond of the quip "Is the gentleman in question a Yankee or a white man?"), Stillman applied himself to the militia ladder with plucky diligence. From a captaincy in 1827 he had, in just four years, ascended to the rank of brigadier general-elect, responsible for the defense of all that vast emptiness west of the Illinois River.[11]

11. Stillman's rank in the Black Hawk War was that of major because he was unable to recruit enough men to form more than a battalion. His election to brigadier in the statewide militia apparatus was confirmed in January 1833, despite his debacle in May 1832.

Burning to prove his mettle as cornfield marshal, Stillman had corresponded with Reynolds in January 1832 about a band of Potawatomie ranging about the bottoms between Spoon River and Copperas Creek "stealing hogs, burning hay, etc." Reynolds deterred him from "any lawless & violent mode of address . . . for the moment" in the Potawatomie crisis; but, when he learned of Black Hawk's invasion in April, he ordered Stillman to raise a command and to guard the northern settlements until the main Sucker army could be mobilized.

Like a prairie Paul Revere, the thirty-nine-year-old general-elect spread the alarm, appending to his dispatches such flourishes as, "Have your regiment in readiness—Warm work is expected." To his great disappointment no more than two hundred patriots (most of them recruited at his brother's grogshop in Peoria) rallied behind his standard. Further, his vanity took a drubbing at Dixon's when Major David Bailey, who had brought about threescore horsemen from Tazewell County, tried to assume overall command on the basis of service in the War of 1812. As a military man, Stillman was still a virgin, so to speak. When Reynolds confirmed his right to command it, of course, infuriated Bailey. The result was a cankerous hatred which sprouted between the two men and their commands.

As Major Stillman prepared to set off from Dixon's on May 13, Colonel James M. Strode, another backcountry Napoleon, made his bid for command of the battalion. He was the ranking officer at Galena, on his way home from court at Chicago. In argument the thin-ribbed Yankee Stillman was no match for the blowhard Kentuckian Strode, whose yeasty eloquence at bars and in taverns invariably drew an appreciative crowd. Governor Reynolds, however, rendered his verdict in favor of the little Yankee. Stuffing a volume of Chitty's *Pleadings* and an extra ruffled shirt in his saddlebag, the gargantuan colonel borrowed a fresh pony, little larger than a donkey, and attached himself to the column, "to see the fun," he explained to acquaintances. The disgruntled Bailey held his troopers far behind the others; but otherwise most officers raced each other to claim the honor of drawing first blood.

When later asked why he had sent this knockabout group of 275 men against Black Hawk when the whole of Whiteside's army would be provisioned within a few days, Governor Reynolds replied, "I thought they might discover the enemy." Such naïveté stands out even in the Old Ranger's well-stocked repertoire.

Meanwhile Black Hawk was submerging in an ever deepening gloom. Neapope and the Prophet, he had learned, were as dishonest as the Chemokemons. Neapope had promised that British support would come from Milwaukee, but it had not. The Prophet had assured him that the Winnebago and Potawatomie would welcome him to their country, but they had not. His people were nearing starvation, yet the tribes along the upper Rock rejected his plea for a plot of ground to raise some corn. Now a great army snaked up the river to destroy him, despite his careful avoidance of Saukenuk, which the Chemokemons wanted so badly, and his equal care in protecting the settlers and their property from molestation. His last hope lay with the Potawatomie bands scattered about the wooded region between the Rock and Lake Michigan, many of whom were long-time haters of the Americans and had been responsible for the Fort Dearborn massacre in 1812.

At the beginning of May Black Hawk established a temporary camp near the mouth of the Kishwaukee River (present Rockford)—called by the whites Sycamore Creek—and began discussions with headmen of the Potawatomie. He talked particularly with Waubonsee and Shabbona, both both old comrades-in-arms during the War of 1812. Initially Waubonsee, who hated whites and had two scalps at his belt to prove it, had encouraged Black Hawk; but the advance of Whiteside's army chilled his enthusiasm. Shabbona, on the other hand, consistently opposed complicity with the Sauk. Although he had fought beside Tecumseh until the great chief's death at the Battle of the Thames,[12] Shabbona had developed a singular affection for the whites and had become something of a pet among the settlements

12. He claimed to have killed the horse of Colonel Richard M. Johnson, who had struck down Tecumseh. After nightfall he returned to bury the body and found nearby the flayed corpse of a gaudily clad Potawatomie from which the Americans, mistaking it for Tecumseh, had cut long strips of skin, much prized as razor straps. Years later in Washington, however, Colonel "Tecumseh" Johnson gave Shabbona a gold ring, treasured by the old Potawatomie and buried with him.

about Ottawa. Like Keokuk he believed in the superiority of the white man's "medicine" and behaved on the premise that the existence of his band depended upon the largesse of the Chemokemon.

After several parleys, Black Hawk realized that the British had not arrived at Milwaukee to assist him. Viewing his situation as hopeless, he swallowed his pride and resolved to return to Iowa: "I concluded to tell my people, that if the White Beaver [Atkinson] came after us, we would go back—as it was useless to think of stopping or going on without provisions. I discovered that the Winnebagoes and Potawatomies were not disposed to render us any assistance."

That Black Hawk was not lying is supported by American reconnaissance. At Chicago, Colonel Thomas Owen, the Potawatomie agent, had been informed of Sauk movements and plans by loyal Indians with access to Black Hawk's camp. Because Fort Dearborn had been decommissioned and abandoned the year before, Chicago was extremely vulnerable to attack (the militia company there numbered only forty men) and Owen had done a superb job of dissuading his Indians from joining the Sauk. On May 12 the agent penned a dispatch to Atkinson which explained that headmen were trying to induce their bands to remove east of the Fox River in order to get beyond the reach of "exasperated militia" little interested in discriminating between friendlies and hostiles. Further, the Sauk were known to be starving and desired to cross the Mississippi, but dared not surrender to the militia.

It was too late for good sense and moderation, however. On the same day that Owen wrote his dispatch, Reynolds ordered Stillman forward. The heretofore bloodless misunderstanding between Sauk and Americans changed character irrevocably on May 14. At sunset on that day Stillman's rangers caught up with Black Hawk, forcing a fight.

In the early morning hours of May 15, Colonel James M. Strode dashed into Dixon's Ferry with the report that Stillman's command had been annihilated. His account of the battle was never forgotten by the swarms of open-mouthed Suckers crowding around the gasping fugitive: Just beyond Old Man's Creek the Indians had poured down a hillside in solid column and deployed in crescent formation with "such accuracy and precision of military movements never witnessed by man—equal to the best troops of Wellington in Spain." A handful of whites, including Stillman and Strode himself, tried to cover the retreat, but "in a short time all my companions fell, fighting hand to hand with the savage enemy, and I alone was left upon the field of battle." When a random ball whistled past his ear, the colonel broke for tall timber, "and the way I run was not a little."

Even allowing for Strode's reputation as one of the most inspired liars in the Northwest, it was perfectly clear that a disaster had taken place on Old Man's Creek. General Whiteside bugled his men awake, prepared to fight to the last man. On the heels of Strode came other mud-spattered and wild-eyed stragglers, each bringing similar lurid tales of mayhem and butchery. At dawn a head count showed that fifty-two men were missing and presumed dead. Participants were none too clear as to what had happened, but one conclusion was unmistakable: The Sauk had banged the Suckers to a smash.

Survivors of the battle at Old Man's Creek—or, as it was quickly renamed, "Stillman's Run"—narrated "such horrid and tragical stories of the disaster," wrote the governor in later years, that "no one knew what to believe." Indeed, reports vary so much as to the details of the fight that one is tempted to conclude that the participants must have been drunk, demented, or distant from the events they describe. In fact, only a few survivors were willing to talk about it. Because the affair was so humiliating, so shocking to their sense of manhood, a cloak of censorship dropped over the battle as effectively as though discussion of its detail had been declared punishable by death. Indicative of this psychic burial is the confessional of Lieutenant Asahel Gridley nearly half a century later: "I cannot say much about the fight, but this, and that is, we got most beautifully whipped in the fight with the Indians."

Reconstruction of the battle, then, can only be done by piecing together fragments. As we know, on May 13 Major Stillman marched out of Dixon's with the irascible Major Bailey tagging along well in the rear. It was a rainy Sunday, and after ten miles they made camp. When the night turned cold, the men dried out and warmed up by preparing an "anti-fogmatic" from the whiskey barrels in the commissary wagon. It was well into forenoon Monday before the column resumed its advance along the eastern bank of the Rock.

During the day two Indians were spotted—or imagined—on the skyline of the right flank which precipitated an impromptu cavalry charge that yielded no scalps but strung out the column for miles. Sometime during the afternoon the volunteers, disgusted by ox teams repeatedly mired in deep ooze, decided to leave behind their commissary wagon. Apparently without orders they grabbed whatever they wanted of both wet and dry groceries. Whiskey bungs were knocked open and the contents poured into canteens, bottles, coffee pots. A mood of camaraderie swept the column; recalled one volunteer a little nostalgically, "Everybody offered everybody a drink." By the time the advance reached Old Man's Creek, about an hour before sundown, many lagged far behind, as ill-disciplined as ever but considerably more cheerful. According to one volunteer the men were "corned pretty heavily."

Swollen by the heavy rains, Old Man's Creek had spilled over its meandering banks and formed a disagreeable slough. Beyond the creek, which could be traced in the boggy valley by tall willows hanging over bubbly water, lay a thicket of scrub oak and beyond this, half a mile away, rose a long ridge peppered with stumpy trees. Disregarding the military dictum not to engage an enemy with water at one's rear (assuming Stillman knew it at all), the major pushed across the slough to the thicket, which promised drier ground for bivouac. He had no inkling that Black Hawk's camp lay only five miles ahead, at the mouth of the Kishwaukee, although Sauk scouts had, of course, carefully watched Stillman's progress.

The British Band was at the time widely scattered throughout the region, making desperate efforts to bag game, grub edible roots, and beg food from neutral tribes. At his camp Black Hawk had that day been entertaining a Potawatomie delegation with a dog-feast. The ceremony was concluding when he heard that three or four hundred Americans had been seen just eight miles away. Knowing that his starving band was in no condition to resist, he decided to capitulate, no doubt somewhat relieved to have been forced into a decision which, however necessary, was repugnant to his nature. "I immediately started three young men, with a white flag, to meet them, and conduct them to our camp, that we might hold a council with them, and descend Rock river again. And directed them in case the whites had *encamped*, to return, and I would go and see *them*." [13] Distrustful of Chemokemons, he took the precaution of dispatching five warriors to observe the parley from a distance.

Major Stillman had posted sentries on the ridge to the north of his camp, but as the first wisps of smoke from campfires drifted up from the grove these men slipped back for their pork and whiskey suppers. The appearance of Black Hawk's envoys on the hillside was at first mistaken for these sentinels by Stillman who was promptly contradicted by a private who yelled, "No, the guard came in some time ago, General. It's Indians!" The information caused no universal alarm: Some men continued cooking, others saddled up and galloped toward the ridge. A grizzled old campaigner of 1812 called out cheerfully, "Get ready, boys, you'll have all the fighting now that you want!" Perhaps the majority of Stillman's force had not yet reached the creek and did not hear commotion in the bivouac area.

Captain Merritt Covell of Bloomington led a motley band of twenty volunteers to the ridge, where he found only two Indians, the rest having fled. Although Captain Abner Eads, who accompanied the group, was reputed to understand Sauk, he did not pause for a parley; instead he delegated himself leader of a shock force to pursue the fleeing Indians. Meanwhile, the two captives, doubtless seeing that their lives were in danger, exclaimed, "Me good Potawatomie!" and, pointing beyond the ridge, added, "Heap of Sauk!" Believing them, Covell said, "It's all nonsense; they're friendly Indians." In the failing light, small groups of whites galloped across the rolling prairie beyond the ridge in search of Indians. After another Indian had been seized, the three

13. Neapope's testimony confirms that the Sauk wished to negotiate: "I heard there were some Americans near us. I prepared a white flag to go and see them, and sent two or three young men on a hill to see what they were doing."

captives were led back to camp, where volunteers amused themselves by bartering with them for souvenirs and trying out their ponies.

The swarm of Suckers under Eads swept across the open country nearly to the Kishwaukee, killing two Sauk in the chase. When runners burst into Black Hawk's camp with news of what had happened, the old leader was preparing to meet the Chemokemon chief. Instead he gave the alarm and, collecting about forty braves (the others were on hunting parties), pushed south toward the shooting and shouting. At the first sign of Chemokemons, Black Hawk ordered a charge, expecting, he confessed later, "that we would all be killed!" The result was an absolute surprise to him. "The enemy *retreated!* in the utmost confusion and consternation, before my little, but brave, band of warriors!" According to Black Hawk only twenty-five Sauk pressed on toward the American camp. The old man himself was soon overwhelmed by excitement and exhaustion: "I found it useless to follow them, as they rode so fast, and returned to my encampment with a few of my braves."

No whites were killed during this attack, but their enthusiasm for Indian killing had been annihilated by this small group of Sauk who were unwilling to relinquish their scalps peaceably. The whites wheeled around and scampered back toward Old Man's Creek where, in the gathering darkness, they gave the alarm, punctuating their curses by shooting at all objects that moved and many that did not.

As the first wave of retreating volunteers stampeded past Major Stillman, he ordered an advance. Captain Eads then rode in on his lathered horse, and swore that only a fool would advance, that there were a thousand Indians in front.[14] Private A. H. Maxfield of Lewistown, who later wrote a spirited account of the battle, thought he saw Indians "on three sides like swarms of summer insects." The conviction grew that they had been led

14. Some men reported that the Sauk flew a red flag during the fight on the prairie. While it is possible that some volunteers got as far as Black Hawk's camp, which did fly the Union Jack, it is far more likely that the red flag was as much of an illusion as the thousand Indians.

into a trap and that a vast host of Indians was bearing down on them on both flanks. Hazel bushes turned into stealthy Indians.

War whoops sounded from all directions, fueling the impulse to run which swept the campground north of Old Man's Creek. Horses tethered to saplings reared up and plunged into the gloom, adding to the uproar. With a splendid sense of the psychological effect upon the panicky Suckers, advancing Sauk slammed their tomahawks against trees and simulated dying groans and screams. In the middle of the camp the three Indian captives began whooping in answer to their tribesmen hidden by the darkness. Private Maxfield heard somebody shout, "Kill those damned Indian prisoners!" He then heard a musket shot and saw an Indian tumbling over a campfire. Thomas B. Reed, of Eads's company, had killed the prisoner in cold blood. The other two escaped in the confusion. (One of them subsequently killed a volunteer and stole his horse and collaborated in the killing of another who had become mired in the slough. Unfortunately Private Reed got safely away.)

In the melee Major Stillman shouted an order for the men to fall back across the creek and form a line on line on the hilltop, one mile in the rear. The first part of this command the terrified militia obeyed with alacrity; but as one of them reported later, "our lines never again formed."

As the whites plunged through the slough, many lost their firearms. Those attempting to rally on the south bank discovered that their powder was wet. The empty snapping of flintlocks was just another powerful inducement to flee, hence the majority of the men decided for themselves that the most defensible hilltop was located at Dixon's Ferry, twenty-five miles south. Nor was Major Stillman at hand to beat his men back into line with the flat of his sword. Like nearly all his officers, the general-elect was also spurring for Dixon's.

A corporal in Eads's company, suspecting that wild shots in the dark were bringing down fewer Sauk than Suckers, warned his men not to discharge their rifles. This admonition was ignored until he added, "If you run into an Indian ambuscade, what will you do with empty guns?" He recalled that this argument had weight, for "the firing ceased but the flight kept up." It is indeed likely that many casualties were the result of frightened volunteers shooting one another in the dark.

What began as a disorderly retreat turned into a panicked rout. Voices bellowed in the dark, "Halt and fight!" Others screamed hysterically, "For God's sake! Don't leave us!" One story circulated of the chief surgeon mounting a horse tied to a stump and, unable to make his getaway, assuming that a Sauk had fastened himself to the halter strap. In a plea for his life, the doctor presented his sword to the stump, saying, "Mr. Indian, I surrender. Please accept my sword." After several terrible minutes he discovered his error, cut the strap, and took off after his companions.

Only Captain John G. Adams of Pekin seemed determined to make a stand. Nearly half a century earlier he had lost both parents in Indian wars and hoped to even the score in this campaign. From far over on the right came the sound of his voice, "Damn it! Stop and fight!" Though his horse had been shot from under him, Adams managed to maintain a one-man fight at the creek before being cut down.[15] In an effort to salvage some scrap of heroism from the debacle, Sucker publicists later would claim that Captain Adams had "prevented a perfect massacre." This was, of course, more nonsense.

Few Indians pursued the whites beyond Old Man's Creek, for the simple reason that the scattered plunder abandoned by them was more attractive than additional scalp locks. Those whites who carried tales of being pursued to Dixon's were followed not by screeching savages but by demons of their own imaginations. Like a collapsing concertina, waves of running men collided with the rangers who had not yet reached the battle area. Since the latter could only measure the fighting by its effect upon the "veterans," their own panic was even more acute. No hint of a second-line rally occurred. The rivalry between Stillman and Bailey suddenly became a contest to see who could

15. Since Adams was bald, his head was cut off and skinned rather than scalped. When news of this multilation reached his wife, it is said, she lost her mind permanently. She outlived her husband thirty-nine years, however.

first bear the tidings to Dixon's. Far out in front, and apparently determined to hold on to his lead, was Colonel James M. Strode.

Fugitives later recalled that the night was moonlit and balmy, with fleecy clouds in the sky. One volunteer remembered that it was a beautiful night for a ride, and regretted that he was on foot. Another compared the retreat to a game of blindman's buff "with our army to represent the blind man." For the most part, however, humor was retrospective. For twenty-five miles men, "hopelessly crazed," fled from shapes and shadows, tumbled into ruts and ravines, brush-whipped themselves in thickets of hawthorne and prickly pear. Few of them ever saw an Indian or fired a shot. The experience of Corporal Medad Comstock of Fulton County was typical, although as a long-distance runner he outclassed most of his comrades. Missing Dixon's in the dark, the corporal kept going all the way to Galena, where he reported that all the combatants "were as drunk as he was, got scared, and made the best time they could out of danger, but he didn't see a single Indian."

Early the following morning Black Hawk toured the battleground. After burying the Sauk dead, which he listed as three braves, the old Hawk picked over the Chemokemon camp, a litter of saddlebags, empty whiskey kegs, firearms, and cadavers. He could scarcely believe his victory. "I never was so much surprised, in all the fighting I have seen . . . as I was to see this army of several hundreds, *retreating!* WITHOUT SHOWING FIGHT!" He saw at once that, had the Chemokemons remained in the thicket during the Sauk onslaught, they would have had an impregnable position even had they been outnumbered. But to run "when they had *ten* to *one*" was unaccountable.

Despite his exhilaration at the victory, the wisdom of sixty-five years told him that the whites would come after him again. If they had killed three Sauk refusing to accept his white flag, what would they do now that their army had been thrashed and humiliated? The only apparent course still open to him was to lead his band up into the marshy wastes at the head of Rock River, known as the "trembling lands" where the enemy, with all his paraphernalia, would find it difficult to penetrate. Calling together his scattered foragers, Black Hawk departed at once.

Winnebago bands which had formerly avoided contact with the British Band now rejoiced at their success and offered them help. It was ironic that a Yankee trader and Sucker general-elect proved to be the most effective recruiter Black Hawk ever had.

Even before the survivors of Stillman's expedition had shaken the clods off their brogans at Dixon's, Governor Reynolds was dispatching letters designed to cope with the crisis. By candlelight he wrote General Atkinson, who was still struggling up the Rock, with news of the defeat: "It is impossible to inform you the number slain, but it is considerable enough so to be quite serious." At the same time the Old Ranger, in his nightshirt, dispatched three messengers to the south to call up two thousand additional volunteers.[16]

The fatuous Colonel Strode, now recovered from his midnight ride, was authorized to arrange the defense of the Lead Region. This carte blanche was just what Strode wanted, and he soon departed for Galena where he declared martial law and established himself as czar of the district.

A roll call at seven o'clock on Tuesday morning (May 15) showed the absence of fifty-two men from Stillman's original command. Assuming that clusters of men might yet be pinned down by the Indian hordes, General Whiteside started his whole army, without provisions, for Old Man's Creek "to cover the retreat." Left in charge of the camp at Dixon's was Major Stillman, already a pariah but not yet the scapegoat and laughingstock that he was later to become.[17] The Old Ranger, compelled to

16. One of the messengers, Private John A. Wakefield, bore the news through drenching rains to Kaskaskia. Drying out en route at an old woman's house, he was asked what bounty he received from his mission. "The honor of serving my country!" Wakefield proclaimed. "My friend," retorted the old woman, "you are in a poor business, and if that is all you get, I think you had best go home." Instead of heeding this sensible advice, the eager young volunteer hurried back to the theater of war and two years later published the only full-length, firsthand narrative of the Black Hawk War, *History of the War between the United States and the Sac and Fox Nations of Indians.*

17. In fairness to Stillman, it should be pointed out that some sources claim the major opposed the expedition to Old Man's Creek, but was

choose between remaining with Stillman or advancing with Whiteside, advanced.

For several hours after the departure of Whiteside, Major Stillman retained his self-possession; but, by three o'clock in the afternoon, assuming perhaps that the army had been gobbled up by the enemy, he began to lose it. A note to Atkinson betrayed his mounting hysteria: "You have been appraised [sic] of the defeat of the small party of men under my command by the Sac & other Indians. The whole force under General Whiteside has gone to meet them & apprehensions exist that the indians will leave the ground occupied yesterday, descend in canoes & attack this place. If they should do so our force is insufficient to maintain our ground, our men being fatigued & out of provisions & ammunition." A canoe attack! Having met the Sauk army, the major now braced himself for their navy. Atkinson replied that he believed it unlikely that the Sauk could overrun Dixon's with Whiteside's whole force in-between. Stillman mastered his emotions and composed no further exhortations or official reports. (Much to the annoyance of Atkinson and Whiteside, the major never submitted an account of his expedition for insertion in the records).[18]

With flintlocks primed and loaded, Whiteside's army, marching, one volunteer noted, "with more order and silence than they had ever done before," pushed toward the battleground. Expecting to find fifty of their comrades dead on the field, they were

---

pushed into it by Captain Eads and other hotheads (and by the knowledge that, if he refused to head it, Major Bailey would ascend to command). The fact that his commission as brigadier general was confirmed after the Black Hawk War suggests that Reynolds and others involved did not blame Stillman for the debacle.

18. Stung by jeering attacks in the newspapers of the West, Stillman briefly launched editorial counterattacks in the public press (for instance, *Missouri Republican* of July 10, 1832, and *Sangamo Journal* of June 21, 1832). He charged that "our sapient wiseacres and electioneering demagogues" were maligning the courage of his men, many of whom had fought at Tippecanoe, Bridgewater, and Fort Erie and had agreed that Old Man's Creek was a more desperate fight. He estimated the Indians at more than five hundred and claimed thirty-four kills.

mystified at first by their discovery of only eleven.[19] These, however, were horribly mutilated—scalped, genitals scooped out, entrails scattered about. (Many weeks later they learned that the Sauk had been told, probably by the Prophet, that the Americans would shortly castrate all Sauk males and import gangs of Negroes from the South to sire slaves on the females.)

Although Illinois folklore abounds with fanciful stories of how these fallen heroes were found lying next to strapping buck Indians whom they had slain after gladiatorial combat, the facts are otherwise: No Indian bodies were discovered on the battleground because Black Hawk had carried them off and buried them before the Americans arrived. The forty men of Stillman's command not accounted for had deserted. In their eagerness to get home, they had slipped past Dixon's Ferry and headed for the Illinois River settlements.[20] Few returned.

Governor Reynolds's entourage poked about the wreckage and bore witness to the empty whiskey kegs which, the chief executive wrote later, were "a partial cause of the disasters." He presided at the obsequies on the next morning for the nearest bodies which had been placed in a common grave on the hillside south of the creek. Four other bodies, discovered on the distant fringes of the battleground, were buried where they fell.[21] Probably apocryphal is the account that the obsequies con-

19. Some time later the body of a twelfth victim, Private Joseph Draper, was discovered south of the battleground. Draper had been fleeing on an unbridled horse when the animal turned and raced back into the melee.

20. Some fled all the way to Rock Island, which they reached before daylight on May 16. From the mainland they shouted to the island for a boat, proclaiming the presence of Indians so convincingly that the islanders dared not cross to ferry them over until daylight dispelled all nocturnal shadows.

21. In 1899, when the state decided to dedicate a monument to the deceased, the place of burial had been long forgotten and had to be located by excavation. Pick and shovel uncovered cavalry boots, buttons, and finally a headless skeleton, presumably that of Captain Adams. No others were exhumed. Attending the dedication ceremony in 1902 were eleven grandchildren of Captain Adams and a ninety-one-year-old veteran of the battle who told reporters that this was his first visit to the site since he had run off seven decades before. Buried in the ossuary with

cluded with the rousing war cry, "Remember Stillman's Run!" (In the years to come, however, most Suckers who had been involved did their best to forget, or to apologize for, their ignominious performance at Old Man's Creek.)

That night all was quiet on the front as Whiteside's army lay on their arms in watchful vigilance. Random shots were heard far to the north—the British Band discharging firearms to deter the Americans from pursuit. It worked. In the morning "General Sam" paraded his army on the open prairie—"doubtless by way of challenge to Black Hawk," wrote a sarcastic volunteer—and then retraced its way to Dixon's Ferry to await Atkinson's supply boats, which were still far down the Rock. A country editor who was serving in the ranks amused himself by comparing Governor Reynolds to Don Quixote, a marked similarity, even to the "horribly lengthened countenance" of each absurd warrior.

By sundown on May 16, Whiteside's force was again at Dixon's. Their frustrations were soon vented by the slaughter of "Father John" Dixon's cows, which also satisfied their hunger.

The Old Ranger busied himself trying to discover the reasons for the Stillman rout. According to one story, when he reprimanded one man for running away, the volunteer flew into a rage and swore that he feared Indian powder and lead as little as anyone in Illinois, "—but good God, Sir—who can stand their yells?"

At brigade headquarters Major Nathan Buckmaster used the respite to pen a doleful letter to his wife, "and I will make you one promise, I will stay with you in future, for this thing of being a soldier is not so comfortable as it might be."

Adams were Private David Kreeps, Private Isaac Perkins, Private Zadock Mendinall, of Captain Adams's company; Corporal James Milton of Captain James Johnson's company; Corporal Bird W. Ellis, Private Tyrus M. Childs, and Private Joseph B. Farris of Captain David Barnes's company; and Sergeant John Walters of Captain Asel Ball's company. Private James Doty of Eads's company was the only man slain north of the creek. Another man, Gideon Munson, a civilian presumed to have been a government scout, was killed half a mile east of the camp.

The present name of Old Man's Creek is Stillman's Run, but the pejorative nature of this name is little known in the region.

Messengers from the south shortly came in with, among other things, copies of the *Sangamo Journal*. In the issue for May 3, next to several columns given over to "Culture of Ruta Baga," there appeared the poetical overflow of a Springfield bard who celebrated the campaign in ringing rime:

> And to the very heaven of verse,
> Will I each sucker's deeds rehearse . . .
> And I will rear the lofty rhyme
> For this, and for all future time,
> That ages yet unborn may know
> The deeds achiev'd by Sangamo!

six

The Massacre at Indian Creek

> You have no idea, nor can I describe the panic
> & distress produced by this, & other murders. . . .
> The panic was not confined to women, & children,
> but prevailed among a large portion of the men
> of that part of the state, who fancied they saw
> an Indian in every bush, or behind every tree
> or stump, whenever they were out of sight of a
> fort.
>
> —Colonel Zachary Taylor

WHEN General Atkinson, with the regulars, finally reached Dixon's Ferry on May 17 he found the Sucker army hopelessly disorganized and demoralized: Mutinous, insulting militia besieged the governor's tent, demanding to be sent home. They argued that their thirty-day enlistment had nearly expired and whined that their families (whom they had abandoned readily enough three weeks before) needed them for spring planting. Although the Old Ranger begged them to remain for another twelve days and averred that the frontier would be overrun if they did not stay, bands of disgruntled, deserting Suckers tramped south along the Peoria trail in brazen defiance. Stillman's Run had removed all illusion of fun from fighting Redskins.

Recriminations bounced about Dixon's Ferry like buckshot fired into a steel drum: Atkinson blamed Whiteside, who blamed Reynolds, who blamed the rangers, who blamed Stillman, who stood mute.[1] Washing his hands of the debacle, Whiteside, who was genuinely shocked by the pusillanimous behavior of Stillman's men, leveled his accusing finger at the governor in a letter to Atkinson. Stating that he had absolutely refused to issue marching orders, he continued, "Contrary to my wish, however, his Excellency on the 12th gave Major Stillman an order to move against the hostile Indians." Having endured the gibes and boasts of the volunteers, the regular officers were not above twisting the knife. Colonel Taylor, alluding to "that disgraceful affair of Stillman's," charged that the Suckers "fled in the most shameful manner that every [sic] troops were known to do, in this or any other country."

Lieutenant Albert Johnston, who investigated the military aspects of the encounter, reached the conclusion that no battle had occurred at all, only a retreat. "Only one man was killed near the ground where they met the indians. The remainder of the dead were killed in flight." And a few days later, after examination of the battleground, Captain Henry Smith expressed the opinion that the bosky campsite, surrounded as it was by open prairie, afforded a defensive perimeter "where a hundred men ought to have repulsed ten times their number of an attacking force," almost exactly the opinion of Black Hawk.

To head off possible altercations between blue coats and Suckers and to safeguard his supplies from further waste, General Atkinson moved the regulars to the northern bank of the Rock, making the river, in effect, a *cordon sanitaire* sealing off the federal from the Illinois forces. Colonel Taylor threw up a turf fort around his depot, more to protect it from ravenous Suckers than marauding Sauk.

Atkinson was, of course, bitterly disappointed by the overwhelming stupidity of the Stillman fiasco, but he had to placate everyone in order to get on with the war. Writing to Henry Dodge on May 17, he expressed his regret that Stillman had

1. Contributing to the round robin privately (he was too good a soldier to criticize his commander publicly), Zachary Taylor expressed his opinion that Atkinson "ought to have prevented it," presumably by not allowing Whiteside's army to advance so far ahead of the regulars or by joining the militia in person to keep them in check.

ranged ahead of the army and his fear that the rout "has not only encouraged the Indians but closed the door against settling the difficulty without bloodshed." Having little or no confidence in Colonel James Strode, he pinned his hopes for the defense of the Lead Region on Dodge, who was bound to have his hands full if the Winnebago joined the war. Already he had arranged for citizens of the region to be armed from Fort Crawford if the war swept in that direction.

His next move was to scout the territory ahead so that Whiteside's army could pursue the British Band. Chosen to lead the scouting party was a thickset, swarthy man whose uniform was a dingy yellow blanket coat and mud-caked, unlaced brogans. "Colonel" William S. Hamilton drank and swore like the cattle drover he had in fact once been. At first glance "Uncle Billy," as he was familiarly called, seemed a living stereotype of the frontier ruffian limned in East Coast newspapers. Yet this moody, somewhat misanthropic and decidedly misogynous man of thirty-five owned and had read an edition of Voltaire printed in Paris. (It was his portion of the inheritance from the estate of his father, Alexander Hamilton, killed three decades earlier by Vice-President Aaron Burr. Uncle Billy was a prime example of the changes that could be wrought on a man of some cultivation and sensibility by the frontier milieu.

As the fifth son, he had had no opportunity for a Columbia degree and New York law practice. The family having fallen on hard times, William S. Hamilton had been sent to West Point more or less against his will. After a year or so he dropped out or was expelled (Academy records were destroyed in a fire in 1838) and went west as a surveyor. Despite a squeaky voice and an ill-disguised scorn for Western-style politics, Hamilton won election to the Illinois legislature in 1824, but was shelved during the Jackson period, having acquired the label "the little and degenerate son of a great father."

He squired Lafayette about Illinois in 1825, proving to be the only American with whom the ancient Republican could converse (the original French inhabitants of the state had been largely pushed aside and dispossessed by this time). He tried law, but his practice in Peoria was a failure. Once he defended an Indian charged with murdering a Frenchman. His client was convicted, but Hamilton, it was said, got him off by arranging for his escape from jail. Ever pursuing the Western bonanza that would allow him to return to New York wealthy enough to stand beside his distinguished brothers, he pinned his hopes for a short time on the much-talked-about Lake Michigan canal. But this came to naught. He got a government contract calling for the delivery of seven hundred head of cattle to Fort Howard at Green Bay. With a quickly collected gang of riffraff Hamilton whipped his lowing herd overland through barely charted regions and arrived having lost only a score of his charges. (When he had refused to sell a few steers to some squatters at Chicago, they drowned some animals to force a sale of the flesh.) His cattle drive was enjoyed by Western men elated to find the son of "General" Alexander Hamilton no better than themselves. As one of them told a visiting New Yorker, "He has none of y'r d—d foolish pride about him; but would just as soon drive any honest man's hogs over the prairie as his own."

By 1828 Uncle Billy was a familiar figure in the Lead Region, probably third in importance after Dodge and Gratiot. He had a double log cabin connected by lean-to at his smelting establishment, known as Hamilton's Diggin's (now Wiota, Wisconsin), for which he recruited laborers from the ranks of desperadoes and army deserters unwelcome elsewhere. There, among these roughnecks, William S. Hamilton found his bizarre pursuit of the American Dream steadily eroded by "the ravages of the Tiger"— hard liquor and hard gambling.

The Sauk war brought him forward, not because of a desire to kill Indians, but because repeated disruptions were destroying the lead industry and deterring settlement in the region. It was this man of better pedigree than promise who was given the job of finding Black Hawk. Because of dissension among the militia, two days passed before the column was ready to leave Dixon's Ferry and another two before it arrived at Old Man's Creek. En route reports came in that Indians—purportedly Potawatomie— had been running off cattle and burning out-buildings in the vicinity of Ottawa, a hamlet fifty miles south on the Illinois River. Since most of the settlers in that region had "forted up," Atkinson was not especially troubled by the news.

As Stillman's veterans were fit for nothing more than garrison duty in a peaceful sector, he dispatched them to Ottawa under their new commander, Colonel James Johnson of Decatur. Major Stillman continued to serve in this unit. Unfortunately these bruised volunteers were once again being dispatched into the eye of the storm, this time unwittingly.

Meanwhile Atkinson continued on toward Old Man's Creek. For the Sucker militia the landscape was at least becoming familiar. If Sauk scouts hung about their flanks, remarked a sardonic volunteer, "[they] must have thought we made visits of mourning over the names of the departed." General Atkinson had planned to keep the regulars and volunteers together so that another catastrophe could not develop. But on May 21, Hamilton and his scouts arrived at the camp at Old Man's Creek with disturbing information: Indian trails, though widely diverging, seemed to indicate that the British Band was bearing off to the east toward the "Big Woods," an unmapped wasteland spreading roughly toward Chicago. (This information was false, as we have noted.) Fearing that he might lose all communication with the outside if he entered the woods, Atkinson decided to drop back to Dixon's Ferry with his infantry (which was unable to keep up anyway) and allow Whiteside's horsemen to scour the region. Withdrawal of the regulars on the following day set off, among the militia, fresh mutterings and desertions that quickly reached mutinous proportions. Every possible argument was presented to halt the pursuit: Their period of enlistment had ended, they were nearing the Michigan line and lacked authority to cross it, the regulars had deserted them. But uppermost was the memory of Stillman's fate.

Inertia overcame the Sucker army on May 24, while they bivouacked at Black Hawk's old camp on the Kishwaukee. Browsing through the debris, men found scalps which some said had been taken "fresh from the bleeding heads of those who had been mercilessly slain," while others argued that "they were perfectly dry and seemed to have been taken years ago." General Samuel Whiteside became convinced that no large body of Sauk had ever occupied the camp and that it was fruitless to continue such a wild-goose chase. Governor Reynolds assembled all officers of the rank of captain and above to vote on the issue of pursuit versus retreat. Whiteside maintained that he would not order an advance no matter what the majority decided. Reynolds suggested building a fort on the spot to protect all skulkers, while braver souls advanced. The result was a tie.

In the meantime, the volunteers, completely fed up with everybody, continued to drift off, no longer only individually, but in whole companies as well. To stop them Reynolds published an order demanding that each man keep his place in the ranks; anyone attempting to pass out of the army on either flank would be taken into custody; officers failing to restrain them would be arrested. Because Whiteside refused to sign this order, Major Nathan Buckmaster issued it in Whiteside's name. (Buckmaster, a candidate for sheriff in St. Clair County, must have wondered how the Old Ranger could save him from this act of political suicide.) This was the last straw. Even men who might have gone on, railed against this gubernatorial tyranny. The army dissolved. Instead of returning along the Rock to Dixon's, where they would have to run the gauntlet of Atkinson's regulars, the erstwhile volunteers moved due south toward the mouth of the Fox River at Ottawa.

Atkinson, in his turf fort at Dixon's was left uninformed that the Sucker army had abandoned the field and continued dispatching messages to Whiteside for information as to the latter's whereabouts. Not until May 27 did he learn that the Suckers were disbanding their army some fifty miles to the southeast.

Meanwhile alarming reports had reached Dixon's Ferry: Indians had killed dispatch riders on the Galena road, cutting that town off from Dixon's. Worse, other bands had attacked the settlements along the Illinois River and massacred nearly a score of people on Indian Creek, just six miles north of Ottawa. Whether these attacks came from Sauk or from other tribes drawn into the war by Black Hawk's victory at Stillman's Run, no one could say. But the nature of the war had changed: The Indians had taken the offensive, just when the Sucker militia was disbanding for home.

Almost alone among inhabitants of Illinois, Shabbona comprehended the immediate danger of the Sauk victory over Stillman.

While the whites busied themselves sending out burial parties, quibbling over whose fault it was, and guessing where Black Hawk might have gone, the faithful old Potawatomie took upon himself the responsibility for alerting the white settlers between Bureau Creek and the Fox River.[2] With the help of his son and nephew, "Mister Shabbona," as he liked to be called, spread the alarm across a hundred-mile swath of bog, prairie, and clearing. Most settlers, frightened of Indians in the best of conditions, fled to Ottawa or to neighbors whose cabin walls were thicker.

One settler who chose to ignore Shabbona's warning was William Davis, a hulking Kentuckian who had arrived with his wife and five children along Indian Creek two years before. During the Sauk troubles in 1831 he had succumbed to the panic and taken refuge in Ottawa; but he had sworn never to run from an Indian again. Even by standards in Illinois Davis's hatred of Indians was preternatural. Ignoring the objections of Potawatomie living upstream from him, he dammed Indian Creek, blocking off the migration of fish to the Indian village. He invariably met any delegations of head men with a loaded shotgun on his arm. Finally, in the spring of 1832, when he caught a Potawatomie tearing an outlet in his dam, he thrashed the trespasser badly with a hickory stick. Whites in the neighborhood condemned such behavior, although not from humanitarian motives, but from apprehension that the local Indians would take revenge. As one of them remarked matter-of-factly later, "Had he *killed* the Indian it might have ended the affair."

So determined was William Davis not to be discomfited by a few Indians that, when the families of his nearest neighbors, the Halls and the Pettigrews, took refuge at Ottawa, he went there to convince them to return to his establishment. By May 20

2. Earlier Shabbona's nearly fanatical loyalty to the whites had almost cost him his life. He had ridden into Dixon's Ferry to warn the Americans of Black Hawk's parleys with the Potawatomie and arrived there before Whiteside's army. Some of Stillman's pot-valiants yanked him from his horse, accused him of being a spy, and "abused him in a shameful manner." John Dixon rescued him from a ring of drunks yelling "Tomahawk him" and saved his life by keeping him in his tavern for two days. How the Americans repaid him for his loyalty is treated in a later chapter.

he had gathered together a varied assortment of twenty-four whites and was carrying on business as usual at his farm. Late one afternoon, while the women were indoors with the elder Pettigrew and the other men were at the smithy or in the fields, about forty Indians burst out of the woods and commenced firing. The resistance showed no false heroics: At first sign of fire, the men in the shop dived through the windows (if they got the chance) and those in the fields took to their heels, leaving the people indoors to shift for themselves. John Hall, twenty-three-year-old son of William Hall, described what happened, some thirty-five years later:

The tomahawk soon ended the cries of those in the house, and as near this moment as possible they fired about twenty shots at our party of five, neither of us being hurt, that I know of. The next motion of the Indians was to pour some powder down their guns and drop a bullet out of their mouths and raise their guns and fire; this time I heard a short sentence of a prayer to my right and a little behind. On turning my eyes to the right I saw that my dear father was lying on the ground shot in the left breast and expiring in death. On looking around, I saw the last one of the company were gone or going, and the Indians had jumped the fence and were making towards me. Mr. Davis was running in a northeast direction for the timber. Looked back and said, "Take care," he having a gun in his hands. . . . I immediately turned toward the creek, which was fifteen or twenty steps from where I stood. The Indians by this time were within three paces of me, under full charge, with their guns in hand. I jumped down the bank of the creek, about 12 feet, which considerably stunned me. At this moment the third volley was fired, the balls passing over my head, killing Mr. Norris and George [hired hands] who were ahead of me, and who had crossed the creek to the opposite shore, one in the water and the other on the bank. I then passed as swiftly as possible down the stream, on the side next the Indians, the bank hiding me from them.

Young Hall joined three of Davis's sons and spread the news of the massacre to Ottawa.

The people indoors had been caught in a trap. Pettigrew, with a child in his arms, was shot as he tried to bar the door; the women were tomahawked as they ran screaming about the cabin.[3] Two of the Hall girls, Rachel, fifteen, and Sylvia, seventeen, were spared; but, because of shock, they could never describe how the others were killed. They themselves jumped on a bed and screamed. "We were trying to hide or get out of the way, while there was no place to get." Indians seized them and dragged them out of the cabin where the youngest Davis boy was being executed (two Indians held his hands while another shot him). Nearly petrified with shock and fear, the Hall girls were conducted to horses in the timber, forced to mount, and carried off into captivity.

How much time elapsed before the whites at Ottawa worked up sufficient courage to assemble a company of men and set out for the Davis cabin is unclear because of the contradictory reports. It is probable, however, that they did nothing until a small band of scouts from Joseph Naper's settlement on the DuPage River near Chicago arrived to goad them into it. In any event, they started out on May 22 and were barely out of Ottawa when they met units of Colonel James Johnson's battalion coming from Dixon's Ferry. Though these veterans of Stillman's Run had orders "to protect the settlements," they wanted no further contact with Indians. Instead of assisting the relief party they increased their pace toward Ottawa.

The relief party found that fifteen whites had been massacred on Indian Creek, many of them hung on shambles like butchered pigs. The women had been slung by their heels to the outer wall of the cabin, their dresses falling over their heads. In this position "their naked persons [were] exposed to the public gaze"—doubtless considerable. Davis's body was found in a nearby field. The Indians had smashed his head into a red pudding, using his own musket as a club, and had mutilated him in a fashion that discouraged the burial party from ever trying to describe it.

3. For years afterward Potawatomie in the war party talked, with some relish, of how the women had "squeaked like geese" when run through the body with spears or clubbed with tomahawks. Subsequently it became clear that the Indian Creek massacre was motivated solely by grievances against Davis. According to Black Hawk, only three Sauk accompanied this war party. None of the Potawatomie participating in the attack joined the British Band.

Reports of the Indian Creek massacre, amplified by fictive details and following the similarly exaggerated news of Stillman's rout, swept across the Northwest like a prairie fire. The panic was nearly universal and often wholly preposterous. Far down in Fulton County stragglers from Stillman's command fired at a pack of wolves and war whooped to disperse the pack. Settlers nearby heard them and assumed it was an Indian attack. One farmer leaped to his horse and rode off yelling, "Murder! Murder!" In his haste to escape he used a new beaver hat as saddle and deserted his crippled son, who he figured had no chance anyway. Another family fled to a creek, where the father carried ten children across and was prepared to lead his brood in flight when he heard another child crying on the far bank. He started across again, but was restrained by the homespun wisdom of his wife who cried out, "Never mind Susan. We have gotten ten over, which is more than we expected at first." Susan was found and cared for by a neighbor. In Putnam County a bedridden rheumatic was abandoned by his household. When a band of Potawatomie arrived at his cabin, the old man suffered exquisite mental torture until the Indians seated themselves quietly and ate the supper spread on the table. Instead of killing the invalid, against whom they held no grudge, they fed and visited him for a week. Rangers arriving later found the old man improved in health and full of praise for the enemy. But, to place him in safety, the rangers evacuated him to Chicago.

To the east of Ottawa the settlements were rolled back to Chicago almost overnight like falling dominoes. At Plainfield the Reverend Stephen Beggs resolved to meet the danger head on. Over one hundred settlers, most of them new arrivals from out East, turned his cabin into a fort and tore down his outbuildings for a log breastwork. Their armory consisted of four shotguns and an uncounted inventory of axes, mattocks, pitchforks, and clubs. These were successfully employed in driving off equally frightened friendly Potawatomie seeking haven at Fort Beggs. Their resolution failed them, however, when a company of militia from Chicago arrived with graphic stories of Indians lurking in the neighborhood. At this news, Beggs remembered, "Strong men turned pale, while women and children wept and fainted." They fled to Fort Dearborn, covering the forty miles in an astonishing one day.

Chicago was packed with refugees, most of them helpless. While shanties multiplied along the sand beach south of the Chicago River, empty Fort Dearborn became the city's first tenement, with two or three families packed into each fifteen-by-fifteen-foot room. By the end of May the fort, recorded a native, had become "a crowded caravansary of frightened fugitives numbering more than five hundred persons." Fifteen infants were born during their brief stay at the fort, and the Reverend Beggs was saved from death by the direct intercession of God: A bolt of lightening smashed open the wall of his dormitory and left a charred seam within inches of a gunpowder keg. But worse things than Indians or thunderbolts were yet to come.

The defenselessness of Chicago was apparent to anyone pushing through the masses of complaining and praying humanity in Fort Dearborn or fighting his way through the drunken mob at Beaubien's Tavern. By default, the Indian agent Colonel Thomas Owen took charge of defense. With the help of Billy Caldwell and Alexander Robinson, friendly Potawatomie who, in 1812, had prevented the famous massacre of the Fort Dearborn garrison from becoming worse than it was, he was able to deter the Potawatomie from rendering assistance to Black Hawk beyond giving haphazard supplies and horses.

Cut off from Whiteside's army (which was worthless in any case), Owen appealed to the governor of the Michigan Territory for arms and men. There was in truth cause for alarm because, with incredible stupidity, Whiteside's men had burned and sacked a peaceful Indian village at Pawpaw Grove on their march through the "Big Woods." [4] A scouting party under "Captain" Jean Baptiste Beaubien, gingerly searching for hostiles in the environs of Chicago, came under fire, but not from Indians. A trigger-nervous youth in the party had accidentally discharged his rifle three

4. Responsible officers with the Sucker army realized the enormity of this unprincipled and unpolitic destructiveness. On May 25 Major Nathan Buckmaster issued an order demanding that the volunteers surrender all items taken from the village. Whether this was obeyed is unknown, but highly doubtful.

times as they advanced, nearly killing some of his companions. After the fourth shot, Beaubien demanded that he give up his gun. When the youth refused, the captain collared him and yanked it from his hands by force. If there were Indians skulking about in the undergrowth this uproar frightened them off.

The hysterical behavior of the settlers living between Ottawa and Chicago belied the fact that the Indian Creek massacre was an isolated and aberrant event. Only one other white was killed at this time by Indians in the region. Adam Payne, an elder in the New Lights Church, was a stump preacher who had been seized by the Lord and ordered to spread the gospel to the Indian. Shortly after Stillman's Run he arrived in Chicago from one of his missionary junkets, bound for his brother's farm in Putnam County. From a box on the parade ground at the fort he harangued a crowd for two hours before setting off into the stricken zone. Near the Fox River he was ambushed by Potawatomie, whom he tried to beat off with his Bible. Rangers later found his head, putrifying on a pole, its features nearly pecked out by buzzards.[5] The death of this backwoods apostle who had spent two years trying to Christianize the Indians, obviously without much practical success, recharged the shock waves already pulsating through northern Illinois.

Simultaneously with the Indian Creek attack, bands of Indians cut the Galena road, leaving Atkinson's turf fort at Dixon's Ferry an enclave without open lines of communication in any direction. Awareness of his isolation dawned on the general only gradually. Six men traveling from Galena on May 19 had been ambushed near Buffalo Grove (west of present Polo). William Durley was killed instantly and the others galloped back to Galena sounding the alarm. Colonel James Strode responded to the emergency by declaring martial law, but made no effort to investigate the attack or to determine whether the road had indeed been cut.

5. Well-meaning folk carried the head to Ottawa, soaked it in lye to remove the fleshy parts, and sent the skull to his brother for burial. Though he, too, was a lay preacher, Aaron Payne was so shocked by the murder that he joined the Sucker army and was himself nearly killed at Bad Axe.

Atkinson did not learn of the ambush until three days later, and only then because some wayfarers chanced on the body and returned to Dixon's with the news. Without mounted scouts he was pinned down, dependent on the word of the militia and civilians. For instance, four days elapsed before news arrived of the Indian Creek massacre.

With six local men, Felix St. Vrain (the Sauk agent) set off on May 23 to bury the body at Buffalo Grove and to continue with dispatches to Galena. They laid the multilated corpse of Durley to rest, camped overnight nearby, and moved on up the Kellogg Trail the following morning. In the foothills near Kellogg's Grove (now in Kent township, Stephenson County) they spotted nine Indians ahead and, without checking further, wheeled their horses and fled, with the Indians in pursuit. In the chase, three whites were killed, including St. Vrain. Another, mounted on the fastest horse, disappeared in another direction without a trace (it was assumed that he had been killed). The remaining three took evasive action for two days before riding into Galena on the morning of May 26. With almost theatrical precision, the horse of one rider dropped dead while fording the Fever River on the edge of town. The consternation produced by the report of the survivors may be measured by the twelve-day delay in dispatching a company to bury the victims. Not until long after the war did the whites discover that Winnebago, not Sauk, had attacked the St. Vrain party.

Galena already resembled a town under siege. Under Colonel Strode's direction, the citizenry was erecting a stockade in the center of town. Oak timbers a foot thick and fourteen feet long, were being planted in a four-foot ditch as a defensive perimeter. (The single gate of this huge pen, it might be expected, conveniently faced the log residence of the military governor.) The steamboat *Dove* had been impressed for use by the town; guards paced the waterfront to prevent able-bodied men from fleeing the town. On the steep hilltop overlooking the stockade a fieldpiece was mounted by Lieutenant John R. B. Gardenier, a regular officer whose prior duties had been keeping squatters away from the Fox mines at Dubuque. All healthy males were required to work on the fortifications from nine to six daily. The sale of whiskey was prohibited until seven o'clock at night, a particularly onerous regulation. Discharge of firearms was forbidden except as signal of an Indian attack. From his command post in Swan's grogshop, Colonel Strode whipped the populace into fighting trim and reminded his auditors that he was a candidate for the state senate, with elections coming up in August.

Assisting Strode in apprising the citizenry of the public danger was Dr. Addison Philleo, editor of the *Galenian* (whose motto was, "Let us Support the Interest of Our Own Country, and She Will Support Ours"). Prior to the Sauk crisis, Philleo had carried the mail and set bones on kitchen tables; but the war brought him a once-in-a-lifetime journalistic opporunity. He launched his newspaper on May 2 and his editorials called for "a war of extermination until there shall be no Indian (with his scalp on) left in the north part of Illinois." Warming to his literary labors, the fire-eating doctor sounded just the right note for his readers in patriotic exhortations: "Our country and our country's cause call for revenge. Revenge! Revenge! Revenge! Let the blood of those heroes [Stillman's martyrs] be washed from the spot on which it so nobly flowed until it shall rise into the heavens, and call down the God of war, who shall inspire every man among us with venegeance, that every one may glut his steel, and dye his hunting shirt purple with those monster's blood." Thus Philleo did more to publicize this fraudulent war than any other man in the West. His tortured metaphors and spread-eagle rhetoric was even reprinted without expurgation in distinguished Eastern newspapers like *Nile's Weekly Register*, conveying at firsthand picture of Western folk beleaguered in extremis by hostile Indians.

While this saturnalia of terror raged across the northern frontier, General Atkinson struggled, without much help from those whom he was trying to save, to create order out of the general pandemonium. To the north Whiteside's army had vanished in the "Big Woods"; to the west Indians were cutting him off from his Mississippi artery; and to the south the Indian Creek attack had made the average frontiersman turn tail. He thus sought aid from an unexpected source: the Sioux and Menominee. On May 26, having just received a dispatch from Washington allowing him to broaden the war to chastise the Sauk, he sent William S. Hamilton to Prairie du Chien with authority to collect and enlist friendly tribes into the federal service. Further, the erstwhile New York aristocrat was ordered to command these mercenaries in the field, an assignment probably no other white man in Illinois would have relished.

On the same day a score of Galena rangers under Major James W. Stephenson rode into Dixon's Ferry to report the attack on St. Vrain and to summarize Colonel Strode's progress as military governor of Jo Daviess County. Every inch a bureaucrat, General Atkinson was more shocked by the latter than dismayed by the former. To his mind Strode's behaviour was tantamount to revoking constitutional rights and severing the county from the federal union. If a war against invisible Indians were not enough, he now had the additional burden of a situtation bordering on treason and nullification. He penned a blistering letter to Strode admonishing him for "declaring martial law, pressing individual property, coercing personal labor, hiring steamboats by the day, etc., etc." On a more personal level, the general was infuriated when he learned that the Galenians were saying that Strode had been boasting that "he could whip the United States troops with twenty-five squaws." [6] Some of the official wrath spilled over to Stephenson and his rangers who, as civilians immune from Atkinson's authority, paid it back with double interest.

Bickering over conditions in the Lead Region abruptly ended on the evening of May 27, when Atkinson got word that Whiteside's army was being disbanded at Ottawa, leaving Black Hawk in possession of whatever he wanted to possess in the Northwest. In a frantic effort to shore up the crumbling militia, Atkinson collected his staff and crossed the fifty-mile expanse of prairie the following day. One event of the trip has been rather gleefully recorded, with many variations, by local historians, although it

6. Strode was stunned by this letter; for a short time it appeared that he was going to challenge Atkinson to a duel. In the end he swallowed his pride, denied that he had ever cast aspersions on the courage of army officers, and, fearing that he would be held responsible legally and financially for his deeds, surrendered his powers to a defense committee on May 30.

is nowhere documented in official sources: Halfway to Ottawa they spied a body of horsemen. Having no weapons other than pistols and sabers and assuming the unknown party to be Indians, they turned tail, with the Indians in close pursuit. After many miles, the federal troops heard trumpets behind them and, looking back, saw raised blankets, a military signal calling for a halt. The pursuers proved to be the company of Captain George B. Willis of Hennepin, who, so it is said, rebuked the general on the spot for his cowardice.

There are strong grounds for crediting this tale, for during the day three messengers arrived at Dixon's Ferry and reported that the Atkinson party was "in great danger of being overcome by superior force of the enemy." Major John Bliss, in temporary command there, ordered Major Stephenson to proceed down the Ottawa Trace and assist Atkinson. But Stephenson, still rankled by the regulars' abuse of Colonel Strode, refused to obey, arguing that his command had not been mustered into federal service. He put his refusal in a letter to Bliss, "Should your order have been couched in the phraseology of a request, my reply would have been that a majority of my company have dispended [sic] their business opperations [sic] and enrolled." Later Stephenson carried back to Galena the information that Atkinson had been "probably slaughtered by Indians." (The *Galenian* spread the news without hint of remorse or regret.)

By the time Atkinson reached Ottawa, most of Whiteside's force had broken up and taken the Peoria road for home. Since no federal officer had been present to muster them out, Major Nathan Buckmaster had obligingly performed this service. Initially the Old Ranger had mounted stumps and barrels in the various campments himself begging the men to remain until his new levy arrived from the south, but to little effect. Only 250 chose to re-enlist for twenty days. Among them was Captain Abraham Lincoln, who cheerfully accepted demotion to private in a new company.[7]

7. Lincoln had drawn thirty muskets and bayonets for his company. Twenty-seven muskets were eventually returned but only twenty-one bayonets. (The latter were popular candleholders.) Explaining why he chose to remain in the army, Lincoln later told his law partner William Herndon,

At one point, the governor appealed to a group of Sangamon County men who had already resolved to stay on. This unnecessary harangue so outraged one of their number, Sheriff James D. Henry, a fearless man who had never backed off from a fight, that he jumped upon a facing barrel and "poured out a regular tirade of abuse upon His Excellency, calling him an old, incompetent ninnycompoop and other hard names." In the midst of this altercation, General Samuel Whiteside appeared on the scene and the sheriff shot the barbed question at the old Baptist warrior, "What part have *you* played in this contemptible drama?" [8] Like a fool, Whiteside drew his sword and challenged Henry to a duel, a response so ludicrous, considering the discrepancy in brawn and age between the two men, that Henry could not restrain a guffaw, setting off a chorus of laughter among the crowd. Later, to show that he was still game, the general enlisted as private in a twenty-day company.[9]

There was nothing General Atkinson could do except watch the first militia levy disappear down any route leading south and to await the arrival of the second levy (now increased to three thousand men) which Reynolds had promised by June 12–15. He used this unexpected hiatus in his campaign to call for reinforcements from the army garrisons of his department, to order provisions required in the operation ahead (a full inventory,

---

"I was out of work and there being no danger of more fighting, I could do nothing better than enlist again."

8. The Sucker psyche was badly bruised by the flagrant dissolution of its army in mid-campaign, which produced in the words of Governor Reynolds "deep feelings of mortification and . . . irratable [*sic*] and bad feelings also." John Wakefield, a particularly patriotic chronicler of the war, wrote that the army was disbanded for reasons "I am not able to lay before the public." Captain Henry Smith, USA, said that the army had been disbanded because of "some cause connected with the local politics of the State." Doubtless these hints of deeply hidden secrets merely covered up the obvious—that the volunteers had lost all faith in the capacity of their leaders to find Black Hawk, not to mention thrash him.

9. According to one story, General Whiteside created considerable embarrassment at Ottawa. Having been informed that a Potawatomie living in the vicinity had killed one of his comrades in the War of 1812, he wandered about offering rewards to anyone who could point the man out to him.

from haversacks and tin cups to reams of stationery), and to long pen reports to his superiors. "The whole country from the Mississippi to the Lakes is infested by the enemy," he wrote General Alexander Macomb, preparing Washington for the major Indian war that could be looming.

Indicative of the unhappy situation in which the general now found himself is his pathetic letter of June 4 to Colonel Thomas Owen at Chicago, in which he begged the agent to dispatch some loyal Potawatomie into the "Big Woods" to determine whether Black Hawk was there.

Bad news spreads rapidly. The panic unloosed in Illinois set off reverberations elsewhere in the West, especially in those areas where Indians still lived, no matter in what state of dilapidation and degeneracy. While no one has ever catalogued all the localized tremors produced by Stillman's Run and the Indian Creek massacre in Western communities, enough material is available concerning the Michigan Territory to give a good picture of the mass hysteria that was generated by secondhand reports combined with fertile imagination.[10] Moreover, the role which Michigan played in the war merits comment, if only because Black Hawk's retreat up the Rock carried him beyond the jurisdiction (legal if not moral) of Illinois. In fact, when it became apparent that the British Band had no intention of giving up in fright at the first advance of the Sucker militia, influential people in Illinois began to grumble that it was Michigan's war and that they had no business meddling with it any more. Governor Reynolds in particular had come under attack by one faction, led by the former governor Ninian Edwards, which complained that Illinois was being bled white while other states—Louisiana and Maine were specifically mentioned—escaped their fair share.[11]

10. As far east as Georgetown, Ohio, militia were placed on alert. The governor of Missouri called for 2,000 volunteers (and got 150) to repel a possible invasion by Keokuk, of all unlikely people. The governor of Indiana set in motion a column for the defense of Chicago. And so on.

11. Edwards was especially bitter that charitable societies in the East spent barrels of money on starving Egyptians, yet callously ignored Suckers starving in the northern counties.

There seems little doubt that had it not been for the strong possibility that Black Hawk would return to Illinois from his hideout, Reynold's second levy of volunteers would have died aborning.

As we have seen, the Indian agent at Chicago, Thomas Owen, on hearing of Stillman's stampede, begged assistance from the governor of Michigan, specifying that this force be "of some magnitude" since "all the frontiers are in the most imminent danger." As the dispatch rider bearing this letter to Detroit passed through the swath of lower Michigan containing most of the white inhabitants, the alarming news of "Injuns a'comin'" spread like an epidemic through the settlements. Thus, long before orders to mobilize were received, drillmasters and their troops began organizing themselves at Gull Prairie, Gourdneck, White Pigeon, and many other crossroad hamlets.

Governor George B. Porter was out of the state on personal business (he had been gone seven months), but he had left as acting governor his secretary, Stevens Thomson Mason. (Mason was sometimes called the stripling because he was not yet twenty-one years of age; he is probably the only governor in American history too young to cast a vote in a political election.) Though his greatest responsibility to date had been presiding over the St. Patrick's Day celebration in Detroit, Mason issued a call for volunteers on May 22. He placed in overall command General John R. Williams, whose military expertise had been acquired as a private in the War of 1812, enjoining him "not [to] return to this place, until every shadow of danger from hostile Indians on the frontier is removed."

Far fewer than the three hundred volunteers called for actually reported at Ten Eyck's Tavern (now Dearborn), their place of rendezvous. In fact, except for a handful of men eager for a fight or for land warrants, there was little public support for a war. A public meeting convened in Detroit, for example, to pass the resolution, "Resolved . . . an Indian hostile to the Whites, and in arms cannot be found within 450 miles of Detroit." A writer for the Detroit *Free Press* put it more caustically, "There is no danger—no more probability of an invasion by Black Hawk's party than there is from the Emperor of Rusia [*sic*]." To finance the war, which he claimed was diverting capital and immigrants to less troubled regions of the West, the governor was reduced to borrowing small sums of money from private banks, as there were insufficient funds in the territorial treasury earmarked for repelling invasions.

Williams, as a former mayor of Detroit, was thought to have influence where it was needed; but he too quickly ran into obstructions. For instance, ordnance and quartermaster officers of the United States Army in Detroit refused his requests for armaments and supplies. However, the greatest problem he faced was catching up with his archrival, General Joseph Brown of Tecumseh, who at the first news of the mobilization, had collected five companies from Lenawee County and hurtled down the Chicago road to intercept the enemy. Though he had been instructed to wait for the Detroit troops, Brown, having stolen a march on his competitor, ignored all messages that demanded—or begged—him to halt.[12]

Williams's cavalcade left Ten Eyck's Tavern on May 25 and was encamped at the Washtenaw salt lick (now Saline) on the following evening when an ambiguous note arrived from Governor Mason. The boy-governor, having received much criticism, had resolved to call off the campaign. He instructed Williams to overtake Brown and issue a recall in person and then to "quiet the fears of the timid" in the western counties.

By this time, however, General Brown had reached Niles (140 miles to the west). He there found the defense of the Michigan frontier preempted by several hundred mostly unarmed militia talking about "a right smart power" of hostile Indians nearby, though none had seen any.[13] Brown dismissed this rabble con-

12. General Brown is principally remembered in Michigan history as the hero of the Toledo War a few years later. He solved this complicated boundary dispute between Michigan and Ohio by kidnapping the Ohio commissioners and holding them in captivity, defying the Buckeye authorities and militia. Years later he volunteered for the Mexican War, but his services, unfortunately for the Mexicans, were declined.

13. Guns were in such short supply that many volunteers had to borrow them from neighbors or peaceful Potawatomie in the region. One prime mover in mobilizing the resistance dropped out, arguing that while "he was ready to meet death, he feared the effect on his wife and children." Another was in fine physical trim until the order came to march to Niles, at which he developed an unaccountable paralysis in his great toe.

temptuously, urging that "all the troops should be presed [*sic*] through to this place" because "there is no dought [*sic*] but our troops has some thing to do." (One thing his troops were doing was looting a general store and helping themselves to the chickens of the neighborhood.) He then ferried his men across the St. Joseph River, but he advanced only a short distance farther because, as he reported later, news arrived from Tecumseh that his children had gotten measles and Mrs. General Brown had gotten very nervous.

Having beaten his rival to Niles, he rested on his laurels, allowing General Williams to catch up. Then, just as Williams was about to assume command of the Lenawee companies, Brown delivered his master stroke of the campaign—he ordered his men home! Momentarily reeling from this blow, Williams countered by placing armed sentinels along the river to keep the Lenaweeans from crossing. Further, he considered placing Brown under arrest for insubordination and desertion, but in the end vented his outrage in letters denouncing the unaccountable conduct of his cantankerous rival. Again ignoring his commander, Brown brushed aside the sentinels and returned home accompanied by those of his original command who chose to leave. Whether General Williams then pressed on westward on his own authority or by gubernatorial directive is unclear; by June 7, however, he had inched out to the stockade at Door Prairie (La Porte, Indiana).

While at Door Prairie, he received a request from Chicago to hasten to their defense. Reduced to one hundred men, Williams's column crossed the sand dunes to Chicago on June 11. There they were billeted in and about the three taverns of the settlement and received a spiritous welcome. General Williams warned Detroit that eight hundred more men would be required if the British Band attempted to cross Michigan for Canada and requested two field guns to repel this expected attack. (The request was ignored.) The Michigan army remained at Chicago about a week, until the arrival of Major William Whistler's regular army detachment from Fort Niagara. Two casualties were reported: A regular soldier assigned to instruct the unit in rifle practice (it had been discovered that of the entire Michigan column only two men—a colonel and a private—knew the rudiments of drill) used a loaded musket inadvertently. Twice it snapped harmlessly, but the third time it went off, shooting one volunteer through the arm and another through the leg. Martial ardor was further dampened by this unfortunate accident and, by June 26, General Williams had returned to Niles carrying in his wallet a thank-you note from the citizenry at Chicago, a copy of which had already been sent to the Detroit *Free Press*.

It had been a campaign notable, reported one volunteer, for its "grand magnificent halts." The biggest task still lay ahead— the filing and processing of more than five hundred applications for land warrants by Michigan veterans of the war, none of whom had seen, much less fought, an Indian during their service.[14]

14. A private from Gull Prairie who got no farther than Niles later reported that he obtained, in addition to one month's pay, land warrants for 160 acres which he traded for a good watch.

SEVEN *The People's Army: Second Try*

> What a fuss there is in putting down about
> 500 Indians.
>
> —GEORGE DAVENPORT

‹‹

IT HAD TAKEN General Atkinson five weeks to advance his headquarters from Fort Armstrong to Dixon's Ferry. Now, marooned at Ottawa by the collapse of the Sucker army, he would require four weeks more to once again establish headquarters on the Rock. He was faced by a quandary: What remained of the militia was uncontrollable, seemingly incapable of destroying anything except victuals and provender. Yet without them his regulars could do nothing except vegetate in their turf fort at Dixon's Ferry, cursing their lack of horses. Thus the commanding general and his staff remained at Ottawa to await the second levy of volunteers. In the meantime, Lieutenant A. S. Johnston was sent to Jefferson Barracks to fetch summer uniforms and other gear (and he used the lull in the campaign to see a daughter born in his absence and to invest in slaves for his household).

About 250 of Whiteside's militia had not joined the ignominious flight, but had stayed on to defend the frontier for an additional twenty days, the time Reynolds estimated it would take to recruit and muster his second levy. These were considered the Hurrah-boys, the clear-grit men, the topping cream of the rabble. Colonel Jacob Fry of Carrollton [1] was

1. Thirty years later Fry led the Sixty-first Regiment of Illinois Volunteers to Shiloh, opposing in battle Atkinson's former assistant adjutant

elected regimental commander and Sheriff James D. Henry of Springfield second in command. Adam W. Snyder, who was running for re-election to the state senate from St. Clair County, was voted captain of one of the five companies. Elijah Iles, the state senator from Sangamon County and builder of the first general store at Springfield, captained another. The fourth private to sign up in Iles's company was Abraham Lincoln. In front of him was John Todd Stuart. Worlds apart socially, the two men were brought together by the Black Hawk War: Stuart would later edge Lincoln out in the race for the legislature in 1832, but he was also to become Lincoln's law partner and introduce him to Springfield high society. Mustering this twenty-day regiment into federal service was the job of Lieutenant Robert Anderson, Atkinson's assistant inspector general (who twenty-nine years later would surrender Fort Sumter to a comparable body of state militia).[2]

The first task of the interim regiment was to regain control of the Dixon's-Ottawa corridor and to re-establish communications with the Lead Region. On May 31 Captain Snyder's company moved out, escorting Colonel Zachary Taylor who, like Atkinson, had been stranded at Ottawa, and with explicit orders to avoid contact with superior numbers of the enemy (for Atkinson was haunted by the specter of another Stillman's Run). On the following day, from Dixon's, Taylor reported that Galena was "perfectly panic stricken" and that he would order

---

general, General Albert Sidney Johnston. His son, James Barnet Fry (West Point, Class of 1847) headed the Bureau of Provost Marshal during the Civil War with the rank of brevet major general.

2. Although Anderson did not recall it, in 1861 President Lincoln reminded him of their earlier meeting. However, for many years the story was told in Illinois that Lieutenant Jefferson Davis mustered Private Lincoln into the United States service on this occasion. While it makes a better story, unfortunately this was not true. Whether Davis, a company commander at Fort Crawford, even saw active service during the Black Hawk War is a nagging mystery. The records indicate that he went on furlough in March and reported back to duty on August 18, after Bad Axe; but these are contradicted by testimonials swearing that he was present during the campaign. The possibility exists that he returned from his furlough early, took part in some of the fighting, and officially reported in later.

Snyder to bury the bodies of the St. Vrain party which had been festering landmarks ahead along the Galena road for better than a week. Much to the colonel's disgust, however, Snyder's men refused to proceed. They argued that Atkinson had ordered them back to Ottawa after their reconnaissance and that his order had priority over Taylor's. Suspecting that cowardice rather than priorities lay uppermost in their minds, Taylor unburdened himself in a letter to Atkinson dated June 2: "The more I see of the militia the less confidence I have in their effecting anything of importance; I therefore tremble not only for the safety of the frontier, but for the reputation of those who command them, who have any reputation to lose." Snyder's men obligingly carried this salvo with them on their return to Ottawa.

Because of Atkinson's policy of barricading his regulars behind their sod fortifications, Colonel Taylor could do nothing except chafe and storm in moody silence. He had to wait for Atkinson to move, which the latter did with extreme reluctance.

Between the Wisconsin River on the north and the Rock on the south lived five thousand Winnebago. Keeping them sufficiently apprehensive so they would not be tempted to join the British Band became the self-delegated responsibility of Henry Dodge of Dodgeville (Michigan Territory). While Atkinson waited at Ottawa and Strode played military games at Galena, Dodge crisscrossed this region in search of troublemakers.

Henry Dodge was born at Vincennes, Indiana, in 1782 (the same year as Henry Atkinson), where his shiftless Connecticut Yankee father, a former seaman in the slave trade, had come in search of his main-chance. Five uncles had been killed in Indian wars, and young Henry was not allowed to forget it. When barely out of his teens, Dodge set off to join the Burr expedition, but at New Madrid (Missouri) he learned that it had been outlawed and he returned to Ste. Genevieve where previously he had been lead mining.

When indicted by a grand jury of the county for treasonous activities, he pulled off his coat and thrashed nine of the jurors, convincing them he was as loyal an American as anybody. Admirers recalled that he was six feet tall and "straight as an Indian." The charge was dismissed and, by 1806, Henry Dodge had been elected sheriff of Ste. Genevieve County. Though a lawman, he believed that the quickest way to settle a dispute was by arranging a duel; and, lest someone shoot him in the back, he always wore a horse pistol sticking out of his coat.

During the War of 1812 Dodge led various Indian hunts in Missouri. On one occasion some Miami surrendered to him on condition that their lives be spared. When a few of the whites cocked rifles to butcher the captives ("a pledge to an Injun ain't bindin' on a White man" went the frontier saw), Dodge shook the ringleader like a rag, stuck his swordpoint at the man's breast, and promised to skivver him if an Indian were harmed. According to Dodge's biographer, the Miami ever afterward regarded "Old Hairy Face," his Indian name, as a kind of savior. But he never liked or much trusted Indians.

When the lead mines in Missouri began to be worked out, Dodge emigrated to the Galena area, arriving there in 1827 with his family and two Negro slaves. Though slavery was prohibited by the 1818 constitution of Illinois, this bothered Dodge no more than it did other Suckers. (The salt mines outside of Shawneetown were worked by slave labor until just before the Civil War.) He assisted Atkinson in putting down the Winnebago uprising and, by November of that year, he had occupied, quite illegally, a vast domain across the line in Michigan Territory. This open defiance of both federal authority and Winnebago property launched a massive squatter surge into the region. Advice attributed to Dodge on how to deal with Indians was widely quoted in the West: "First give them presents—then give them lead." He killed no Indians, however, probably because none ever stood in his way.

By January 1828 "General" Joseph M. Street, the newly appointed Winnebago agent at Prairie du Chien, was complaining to Superintendent William Clark that Dodge had brazenly taken land guaranteed to the tribe by an 1816 treaty. Street sent John Marsh, his subagent, to investigate. After guiding Marsh through his establishment (twenty log houses behind a palisade, two furnaces, 130 men "completely armed with rifles and pistols"), Dodge explained that he would leave "as soon as he conveniently could." Street attempted to obtain authorization for the Fort

Black Hawk. Painting by George Catlin.

Black Hawk. Painting
by Robert M. Sully.

State Historical Society of Wisconsin

Keokuk in later years.

*Courtesy of Smithsonian Institution
National Anthropological Archives, Bureau of American Ethnology Collection*

Fort Armstrong. Lithograph of 1854 from *United States Illustrated*.

Governor John Reynolds,
of Illinois, 1830–34.

Captain Abraham Lincoln,
Illinois Militia.

General Samuel Whiteside,
Illinois Militia.

Major Isaiah Stillman,
Illinois Militia.

Colonel Henry Dodge,
Michigan Militia.

"Colonel" William S. Hamilton,
Michigan Militia.

Brevet Brigadier General
Henry Atkinson, USA.

Colonel Zachary Taylor, USA.

"Verdict of the People." Painting by George Caleb Bingham, 1855.

Crawford garrison to eject him by force, but the commander never received an order. Miners gleefully circulated the story—probably true—that Dodge had said that no "spindle-legged, sharp-shinned soldiers" dared try to evict him. Thereafter his primacy went unchallenged in the western Michigan Territory. By 1831 he had been elected to the Legislative Council, where he argued for separation of Wisconsin from Michigan, and he had been appointed a colonel in the Michigan militia. His biographer was absolutely correct in characterizing Henry Dodge as "the captain of an aggressive civilization," though some might quibble about the last word.

Dodge was too intent upon amassing a fortune and creating a dynasty to waste his time Indian hating, hunting, or killing. Indians to him were nuisances, vaguely picturesque anachronisms that had to be brushed aside from time to time if the real values of the workaday world were to take hold and root. He bore them no grudge whatsoever, so long as they kept out of his way. Never did he doubt that the whites would eventually remove Black Hawk and his company; but, as an entrepreneur who had lost a lost of money by the slackening tide of immigration after the Winnebago War, he wanted the Sauk transported across the Mississippi quietly and quickly. The longer Black Hawk remained in the marshy wastes of the upper Rock the more likely it was that bands of Winnebago would help him.

Fortunately for the whites, the Winnebago were natural anarchists wholly lacking the spartan cohesiveness of the Sauk tribal organization (at least in the beginning). Probably largely because their language was so different from those of surrounding tribes, they seemed incapable of joining pan-Indian alliances and adapted rather easily to the presence of the Chemokemons who, like themselves, were comparatively recent arrivals to the region.[3] Though their war with the Americans in 1827 had been almost entirely bloodless, it had left them badly demoralized

---

3. Because their guttural speech contrasted so markedly with that of their Algonquin neighbors and their folk traditions pointed to an original homeland to the southwest, amateur ethnologists of the nineteenth century speculated that the Winnebago were descendants of Aztecs who had drifted north. Less romantic French *voyageurs* called them *Puants* ("stinkards"), presumably because fish comprised the major portion of their diet.

and almost sycophantically disposed to promise to do whatever the whites demanded.

For administrative purposes the United States had divided them into three zones, each with its own agent. Those Winnebago living about Prairie du Chien remained neutral during the Sauk War. Agent Joseph M. Street convinced them that they should submit to voluntary quarantine near his agency in order to demonstrate their nonbelligerency. Though Street had earned their respect battling Superintendant Clark for their rights, the walls of Fort Crawford and the presence across the river of the warlike Sioux were also powerful persuaders.

Those bands residing in the vicinity of Four Lakes (present Madison) liked and trusted their agent John Kinzie,[4] whose base was located at Fort Winnebago, an unfortified depot which had been jerry-built by amateur army carpenters (such as Lieutenant Jefferson Davis who had shown more ingenuity designing pilasters and pediments than in constructing sturdy closets and thresholds) following the Winnebago War. As the British Band advanced up the Rock, fifty lodges of "our Indians" (as Kinzie's bride called them) came to the fort and camped around the agent's dwelling, promising that if the Sauk attacked the fort they would have to kill Winnebago first. At first the garrison under Captain Joseph Plympton viewed the Sauk invasion with open contempt, one officer remarking to Mrs. Kinzie, "I do not think I would even take the trouble to fasten the blinds to my quarters." But, after Stillman's fiasco, the Winnebago grew restive and even Mrs. Kinzie packed two pistols to bed. Her sister-in-law, a lady who had witnessed the Fort Dearborn massacre, unsettled everyone with her fatalistic remarks, such as "This is

4. John Kinzie, the son of one of the first white traders at Chicago, was experienced in Indian affairs and widely respected by Indians of the Northwest. During the Fort Dearborn massacre of 1812 his family had been protected by friendly Potawatomie while other civilians and soldiers were being slaughtered on the beach.

His wife, Juliette Magill Kinzie was a twenty-six-year-old Connecticut woman newly arrived in the West. Though she had established affectionate relationships with many of the Winnebago, she sensed their hostility under the surface. "They did not love the Americans—why should they?" she wrote; in the question she tellingly indicted the whites.

the third Indian war I have gone through, and now, I suppose, it will be the last."

The most dangerous element among the Winnebago, however, was the bands inhabiting the swampy country around Lake Koshkonong, a great pond formed by the spillover of the Rock River. No American forts, agencies, or settlements existed in that region to deter the bands from assisting Black Hawk, and the influence of the Winnebago Prophet was thought to be powerful. Their agent Henry Gratiot, who lived more than fifty miles away, had found them cooperative and friendly during his visit to Turtle's village late in April, but this had been before Stillman's Run. To reassert Chemokemon dominance in the region Dodge and Gratiot rode to Four Lakes for a powwow with Winnebago headmen on May 26. At a time when whites elsewhere were putting the greatest possible distance between themselves and Indians of any sort, Dodge showed the cool courage which Indians most admired. Old Hairy Face warned that the American Father was "mild in peace but terrible in war," and minimized Stillman's defeat by adding that "when the main body of our arm[y] appeared the Sauks run." The tribal representatives pledged their neutrality, Little Black declaring, "When we look towards you, the weather is clear, and the wind does not blow." On their way back to the Lead Region, Dodge held a similar conference with other headmen at Blue Mound, some of whom expressed a willingness to fight the Sauk if the White Father provided powder and lead. Fearing treachery, Dodge did not respond to this offer.

It was at this conference at Blue Mound on May 28 that Gratiot learned that two white women were being held captive in the camp of the British Band. He knew nothing about the abduction of the Hall girls, but sent a message to White Crow and Little Priest, two Winnebago living near Koshkonong, promising "the highest reward that should be offered" if the women were brought to him unhurt. On June 2 a group of Indians appeared at the edge of the timber, three miles east of the Blue Mound. Notable trepidation was produced among the whites until a Frenchman went out to see what they wanted. He found White Crow, Little Priest, and twenty others with the Hall girls. Though "half famished, half naked" and psychically wrenched by their two-week capitivity and two-hundred-mile odyssey, neither had been molested physically. News of their recovery sped to Galena, inspiring the second "extra" (the first dealt with Stillman's Run) in the publishing history of that community. The saga of the Hall girls quickly became the Sucker version of the rape of the Sabine women, though the prurient dimension had to be imagined by the listener.[5]

After the slaughter at the Davis cabin, Rachel and Sylvia were mounted on horses and hurried off to the Sauk camp, where they had to watch Indians dressing, on small hoops, the scalps of the victims, including that of their mother. Their most terrifying experience came at a scalp dance which they feared would be terminated by their torture, murder, or worse. Three decades later they described this ceremony:

The Indians cleared off a piece of ground about 90 feet in circumference, and placed a pole about 25 feet high in the center, and 15 or 20 spears set up around this pole, and on top of the spears were placed the scalps of our murdered friends. Father's, mother's, and Mr. Pettigrew's were recognized by us. There were also two or three hearts placed upon separate spears; then squaws . . . painted one side of our faces and heads red and the other black, we being seated on the blankets near the center pole. . . . Then the warriors commenced to dance around us with their spears in their hands, and occasionally sticking them in the ground. And now we expected at every round the

5. Such tales provided the puritanic backwoodsman with the only pornography available to him. For instance, it was not what the Hall girls said had happened to them that intrigued, but rather what might have been left out. The fantasies of what Indian bucks did to white female captives was inspired by what white men thought they would like to do with a squaw given the opportunity. George Catlin, whose knowledge of Indian life was as extensive as anyone's, concluded that Indian males never dishonored female captives because such an act was degrading to them. Instead of being oversexed (for instance, Twain's Injun-Joe with Becky Thatcher in the cave), the Indian probably leaned to the other extreme because copulation was to him no deep mystery hedged about with taboo and guilt. Count Francesco Arese, an Italian visitor among the Sauk and other tribes during the 1830s, found Indian women disappointing as sexual objects when compared with European peasants or aristocrats. Copulation with them was too bluntly animal, too lacking in mystery.

spears would be thrust through us and our troubles brought to an end, yet no hostile demonstration was made by them toward us.

After this ceremony their fears abated somewhat.

Each day the Sauk camps moved five or six miles, always up the Rock River. Near Koshkonong, White Crow and Little Priest came to the camp to purchase the sisters with ten horses, along with wampum and corn. Though both girls were quite homely, one young brave refused to let Rachel be ransomed until White Crow threw in another horse. (Whether this Sauk planned to subject Rachel to his carnal pleasures was a titillating speculation much discussed by backwoodsmen, especially since he cut off two locks of her hair before she departed.) Fearing that the Sauk might change their minds, White Crow traveled all night to deposit the girls safely at his village. To allay their fears he let them sleep together, with squaws lying on each side. "I tryed to please and comfort them, but they were not accustomed to our mode of living and could not eat," he explained to Dodge later. (Hungry as they were the girls would not eat embryonic ducks cooked in the shell.) Though White Crow, who spoke English, expressed some misgivings about conducting them to the settlements for fear that the whites would blame him for their captivity, he collected a large escort and started west for Blue Mound, borrowing Rachel's white handkerchief to announce his peaceful mission to the fort. Before turning them over to the whites, he promised each of them a Sauk squaw as servant; but the Hall girls, who had doubtless seen enough members of that tribe to last them a lifetime, declined the offer.

With great fanfare they were escorted to Galena, fitted out in fine silk dresses, and steamboated to St. Louis as guests of William Clark. For a brief period Rachel and Sylvia Hall were the most sought-after and celebrated young ladies in Illinois.[6]

6. Clark took up a subscription which netted them about $500 and was administered by the Reverend Major Reddick Horn of Morgan County. Horn, an evangelical preacher, oversaw the depot at Fort Wilbourn during the Sauk War. Later the Hall girls received 160 acres along the tract reserved for the Illinois and Michigan Canal by legislative enactment. Then, as now, public notoriety was regarded as a positive virtue by most Americans, and many a young Sucker cast an admiring eye upon the Hall sisters,

One unversed in the Western ways of the whites might suppose that these Winnebago would have earned fulsome praise and gratitude for the rescue. Instead, they were shut up in a cabin overnight, and when they complained of this treatment were accused of acting suspicious. When Gratiot and Dodge arrived at Blue Mound for a conference with the prisoners, they were told that a Winnebago had alluded to Old Hairy Face as "soft-shelled" like Stillman. Dodge, pressed by his men, took a hard line. While he praised White Crow for his treatment of the girls—"No man, either civilized or savage could have acted with more delicacy of feeling"—he nevertheless retained five Winnebago (including White Crow's son) as hostages to guarantee the future good conduct of the tribe.

During the two-day discussion which followed, the Winnebago had ample time to regret having gotten involved with the Misses Hall. In his pocket Henry Gratiot had Atkinson's note authorizing a ransom payment of up to $1,000 for each of the Hall girls. How much of this was paid, if anything at all, is not indicated by his private journal or the official minutes of the conference. What is revealed, however, is Dodge's anger when he learned that White Crow had given ten horses to the Sauk; this was trafficking with the enemy, proof that the Winnebago were providing aid and comfort to the British Band. Even worse was White Crow's inadvertent confession that a Winnebago had sold a horse to a Sauk earlier. Dodge demanded and got the $40 that had exchanged hands during this transaction.

To prove his lack of complicity with the Sauk, White Crow, during the two-day parley, pin-pointed the exact location of the British Band at the Whitewater River on the east bank of the

---

and their property. In one Indiana town William Munson read about the famous abduction and vowed to a companion that he would marry one of the girls. In 1833 he moved to their neighborhood and after a six-week courtship carried off Rachel as his bride. Shortly thereafter, William Horn, son of the Reverend Major, won Sylvia. Rachel, who ever afterward suffered from nervousneses, remained in La Salle County, Illinois, and bore four living children before her death in 1870. Sylvia, the more delicate one, moved to Nebraska, where her husband was a bulwark in the Methodist Episcopal Church. She bore eleven little Horns and died in 1899.

Rock, twenty miles above Turtle's village. He also reported their number at 380 Sauk braves and 100 Kickapoo. The few Potawatomie, Dodge learned, who had joined Black Hawk after Stillman's battle had returned to their homes. Further, White Crow expressed his willingness to double-cross the Sauk by offering them cornfields and then lead the Chemokemons against them in a surprise attack.

Two days after the conference broke up, James Aubrey, the commander of the fort at Blue Mound, was ambushed and killed. The attackers were never identified, but they were probably some of these same Winnebago, bruised from their encounter with Chemokemon justice.

Although Colonel Dodge's bold forays were eventually to restore some semblance of order in the Lead Region, Colonel James Strode's bravado still set the tone for Galena, which endured its siege with poor grace. As the stockade neared completion, the community was so racked by internecine squabbling that the defense committee issued mournful appeals for unity: "It is but too true . . . that the flame of patriotism does not burn alike in every bosom." On one memorable occasion, as a scouting expedition prepared to leave town, a drunkard named Kelsey bombarded militia captain Charles McCoy with ribald remarks; the captain replied with pistol shots that stretched Kelsey dead in the street. Taken before Strode, the defendant was acquitted, causing a Michigan surveyor stranded in Galena to record dryly, "In the midst of all this fright, the good people of Galena found time for revelry and for homicide."

A major reason for dissension in the Fever River valley was the unwillingness of the townspeople to permit the refugees, estimated at one thousand homeless souls, to set up camps in town or to take refuge in the stockade in the event of attack. The fortifications appeared to exist not to protect good Galenians from the Indians, but rather from the horde of fugitives.

What was needed to unite the community, opined Strode and others of the military leadership, was a scare. Accordingly, on June 4, he fired off the cannon at midnight, the signal announcing an Indian attack. The results exceeded his expectations. One townsman writing his brother in Massachusetts a few days later graphically rendered the alarm: "The scene was horrid beyond description; men, women and children flying to the stockade. I calculated seven hundred women and children were there within fifteen minutes after the alarm gun was fired—some with dresses on and some with none. . . . Sick persons were transported on other's shoulders; women and children screaming from one end of the town to another. It was a false alarm." The local postmaster raced to the stockade, wrapped in a sheet and shouting for his trousers only to be met by a beldam who shoved a musket into his hands and said, "Take this gun and don't be scared to death." When the truth got out, tar brushes appeared among the mob which had gathered at Swan's Tavern to call for an investigation. Colonel Strode promptly skipped town until the excitement subsided and his martial ambition stagnated for the time being.

Galena was overrun by Indians, however, four days later (June 8), when Colonel Billy Hamilton arrived with 170 warriors, most of them Sioux, from Prairie du Chien. With feathers waving and drums beating they were an impressive spectacle, so impressive in fact that the city fathers placed a ten o'clock curfew on their war dancing and kept them away from the stockade. Coleader with Hamilton of this aboriginal shock force was another morbid Easterner. John Marsh, who had been an instigator of the Great Rebellion at Harvard College in the 1820s and who later, as rancher-millionnaire, would earn the title of "the meanest man in California," had acquired, from his Sioux "wife," a phobia of the Sauk. He eagerly recruited for Hamilton and joined the expedition.

These mercenaries had set off for Dixon's Ferry on June 10, but were shunted to Hamilton's Diggin's (renamed Fort Hamilton) by Zachary Taylor because the second militia army had not yet been formed and he disliked having Indians hanging about his fort. In this irrational war it seemed that only the so called lazy Redskins could be depended on to meet a timetable.

Just before the Indians left Galena, the company of Captain Elijah Iles arrived to liberate the beleaguered town. Had the Sioux unexpectedly encountered the Suckers on the road there is no guessing what might have developed. As it was, however, the peppery captain from Sangamon had had his hands full for the past three days. On reaching Dixon's Ferry from Ottawa, Iles had rejected Taylor's invitation to camp on the north bank of the Rock, knowing of the colonel's contempt for citizens masquerading as soldiers. "I told him," he wrote fifty years afterward, "we felt just as safe as if quartered in his one-horse fort."

Ordered to find and bury St. Vrain's group and to open the Galena road, the captain set off on June 8 with Colonel James D. Henry, an experienced militiaman, attached to the company as an adviser. At sundown of the first day, spies dashed in with reports of a large body of Indians sweeping toward them, dead ahead. A tremor struck the column and Iles offered the command to Henry who refused, but walked behind the line of men talking in a calm voice. The Indians turned out to be Colonel Dodge at the head of a hundred rangers en route to Atkinson's headquarters to report the release of the Hall sisters and the whereabouts of the British Band. They had already found and buried the St. Vrain bodies. On the day following there was another brief alarm when spies mistook one of their own group for an Indian because he was wearing a red shirt. No genuine Indians were sighted during their march.

At Galena they received a tumultuous welcome from citizens who expressed their conviction that the British Band would shortly try to escape to Iowa by a forced march through the Lead Region. Yet when Henry inquired what they planned to do to assist in blocking such a move, the defense committee informed him that it would not take the field "even were they to pass in sight of their doors." This craven admission was passed on to Colonel Taylor on the return of Iles's company to Dixon's Ferry on June 13, providing "Old Rough and Ready" with fresh fuel for his already considerable contempt of Suckers. In his opinion, the militia of Jo Daviess County was the worst of a universally sorry lot. Colonel Dodge of Michigan was a war horse, but Colonel Strode was useless.

As the time drew near for the mobilization of the second volunteer army in mid-June, hawks and doves alike added their piping and cooing to the hullabaloo. Hawks now called for, not merely the removal of the Sauk, but rather the extermination of them. Editorials became filled with jingoistic rhetoric, as this one from the *Galenian,* headed "To Arms! To Arms!": "Now is the time that every man should buckle on his armour and be prepared for action. . . . If one would show that his steel had been dyed with human blood, let him boast that it came from the heart of a Sac." The editor became so inflamed by his own propaganda that he turned over his newspaper to an assistant and joined Henry Dodge's band as surgeon.[7] Even Colonel Dodge, usually as emotionless as a granite statue, let himself go in a letter printed in the *Galenian:* "We are not to have peace with the banditti collection of Indians until they are killed up in their dens."

Nor was this genocidal lust restricted to frontier ruffians. Refined gentlemen such as Dr. Horatio Newhall of Galena, Salem-born and Harvard-bred, wallowed in it too, as soon as his economic interests were threatened. Before Black Hawk crossed the Mississippi the doctor had written that the Sauk "are not blamable"; afterward, "I hope no vestige of those scoundrels will be left." This craving for murder, not justice, even characterized William Clark's (the superintendent of Indian affairs in the West) letter to the secretary of war on June 8: "as they [Black Hawk's band] have afforded sufficient evidence not only of their entire disregard of Treaties, but also of their deep-rooted hostility in shedding the blood of our women & children, a War of *extermination* [his italics] should be waged against them." Remember that, at the time Clark wrote this letter, the only blood spilled by the Sauk was that of the Suckers at Old Man's Creek, and that only because the whites had refused to accept their surrender. Clark, like the other hotheads, had jumped to the

7. This assistant, J. B. Patterson, a Virginian stranded in Galena during the war, in 1833 put in literary form the Black Hawk autobiography dictated to Antoine LeClaire, the Rock Island interpreter. Later he published the *Spectator* at Oquawka (formerly Yellow Banks), where his son Edward projected, with Edgar Allan Poe, the publication of *Stylus,* a literary magazine designed to make Oquawka the literary capital of the American republic. Poe died before details could be arranged.

conclusion that the Sauk were responsible for the Indian Creek and St. Vrain massacres.

Not everyone in Illinois succumbed to this collective insanity. At Jacksonville a faculty-student group from Illinois College infuriated the townsfolk by marching through the streets with cornstalks in demonstration against the war. Some editors, like J. Y. Sawyer of Edwardsville, refused to rouse the rabble in either the name of God or the governor. For instance, the June 19 issue of the *Illinois Advocate* lambasted Governor Reynolds for announcing that these were "stirring times": "It must be 'stirring times' indeed," wrote Sawyer, "when with 30,000 military at his command, the Governor cannot *control* or *expell* 600 'poor Indians' without taking every civil officer from his post." After enduring in silence sarcastic missiles of this sort, the governor finally answered his critics in a letter to the ex-governor Ninian Edwards: "I wish you to inform my friends that I am 'bullet proof.' I have done right, and care not for slander; that I go in for nothing; that as soon as the storm settles in my favor, which it is compelled to do, I will bid a long farewell to public life and live at home in peace." Proof that the Old Ranger had no intention of "going in for nothing" is found in his letter of the next day to the secretary of war Lewis Cass in which he requested payment for his military services in both 1831 and 1832. Cass replied that he appreciated "the laudable motives which led you to devote yourself to the duty" but that Congress had authorized nothing for civilian commanders in chief.

For the most part, however, the people of Illinois simply acquiesced in the approaching purge of the Sauk nation. If they thought of it at all, they did so trying to figure out how to turn a dollar from it. At Rock Island, for example, George Davenport, whose business was booming, wrote his partner Russell Farnham on June 8, "What a fuss there is in putting down about 500 Indians." Davenport certainly spoke words that history cannot gainsay.

If the first muster in April had faced cold, wet, and disagreeable weather, the second in June was equally discomforted by the heat. From all corners of Illinois, volunteers trooped to

Ottawa, gagging on the dust raised by their mounts and swatting the green-headed prairie flies that descended in iridescent clouds. William Cullen Bryant, editor of the New York *Evening Post*, traveling in Illinois that summer, recorded in his journal the intolerable emptiness of the prairie north of Springfield, the "dirt and discomfort" of villages where barefoot women cracked lice from the heads of children "brown with dirt," and the hopeless squalor and ignorance of the settlers. Every few miles he fell in with bodies of the militia, "their way marked by trees barked and girdled," and listened to the complaints of settlers who had lost pigs and chickens to the drepradations of these "hard-looking" men, "unkempt and unshaved, wearing shirts of dark calico, and sometimes calico capotes." [8]

Near Hennepin gangs of volunteers infested the countryside like river pirates and terrorized the local inhabitants by holding raucous shout-downs beside camp meetings, kicking over beehives, shooting sheep, and pulling up potatoes. When the governor arrived from downstate he patiently listened to complaints about his soldiers, passed around his plug of tobacco, and urged the sufferers to petition the United States government for compensation.

Because the Illinois River was drying up, General Atkinson transferred his headquarters to Fort Wilbourn, supply depot for the new army, twelve miles downstream from Ottawa. Here he began to organize his second force, christened in the official records as the Army of the Frontier. Only a few of these recruits had served in the ill-starred Whiteside campaign; and though they were untrained and unruly, at least they were not yet frightened or disillusioned. Gangs of them brushed aside orderlies to gawk at General Atkinson in his quarters (and on one

8. According to Parke Godwin, Bryant later claimed that he first met Abraham Lincoln among a group of these volunteers. This is utterly false, as a charting of the itinerary of each proves; Bryant turned back long before Ottawa. Three decades later, as a prime mover within the Republican party, he did push the candidacy of Lincoln, however.

Bryant's meditative poem "The Prairies" (1833) was inspired by his travels in Illinois during the Black Hawk War.

occasion to gawk at Lieutenant A. S. Johnston, whom they mis-took for the general), much as though he had been caged ex-pressly for such purpose. By June 12 bombastic oratory had become the order of the day in the campments about Fort Wil-bourn, as three brigades took form from the great mass of fer-menting human dough.

Still smarting from criticism of his earlier campaign, Gover-nor Reynolds permitted his volunteers to elect all their officers, even their generals. Elected general of the First Brigade, re-cruited from the southernmost tier of Illinois counties, was Dr. Alexander Posey, from Shawneetown. What his qualifications were, besides a reptuation for never pushing aside a convivial glass, history has not clarified, but most likely one influence was the family name, for the lower Wabash Valley was known as "Posey country." [9] The new general was something of a Sucker variety of the Renaissance man. Having mastered theology (he was said to have been an ordained minister of some unspecified faith) and medicine, he developed an interest in military glory and therefore attached himself to the staff of his brother-in-law Brigadier General Joseph M. Street, who in the 1820s com-manded the Gallatin County militia brigade.

His most distinguished service came during the visit of Gen-eral Lafayette to Shawneetown in May 1825, an event pro-claimed by a rhapsodic local historian as "the greatest public event that the young city-metropolis had ever experienced." At the town landing bolts of calico were unwound as a path for the ailing general to the banquet awaiting him at Rawlings Tavern, an edifice distinguished on two counts—it had two stories, and it was brick. Major Posey's talent for handling emer-gencies came to the fore when the departing steamboat bearing

9. When Abraham Lincoln's father emigrated from Kentucky to Indi-ana, his family was ferried across the Ohio River by a Posey. The first political speech young Abe heard in Illinois was delivered by a Posey. The adjacent county in Indiana was named for a Posey. In sum, the Poseys were the first family in the oozy wastes of southern Illinois, a domain unkindly described by Charles Dickens as a place where "the waters of the Deluge might have left it but a week before" (*Martin Chuzzlewit*).

Lafayette up the Ohio struck a snag barely out of sight of Shaw-neetown. Posey, and some other officers, arranged for the rescue of the luggage from the stricken vessel.

In any case, the newly elected general was innocent of any serious military experience. Doubtless he was elected because he would not be apt to hamstring his men with bothersome regulations. Within two days of his election to brigade command, he was rebuked by Atkinson for failing to eject from his camp "unauthorized persons vending ardent spirits" and for allowing his men to discharge firearms without authorization or just cause. The 962 men of Posey's brigade (not counting their private servants, known as nigger boys) were mustered into the United States service on June 15.

The general-elect of the Second Brigade, most of whom came from eastern counties, was a man so colorless that not even his exalted rank in the Black Hawk War sufficed to save him from historical oblivion. Born in the piney-woods country of north Georgia in 1796, Milton K. Alexander claimed that he had commanded a company during the War of 1812 and fought Seminoles under Old Hickory. Because he was cross-eyed, he appeared more furtive than in fact he was. In the 1820s he drifted into Edgar County, where he opened a store and cultivated a farm.

By the time of the Black Hawk War, Alexander had proven his prowess as a small-town politician by achieving such posts as regimental militia colonel, clerk of the Edgar County court, and postmaster of Paris, Illinois. He and Governor Reynolds were old friends, though the friendship was marred by the fact that Alexander's political ambition never soared higher than a perch among the backbenchers at Vandalia. He did serve one term in the state senate just after the Sauk War.

During the aborted 1831 campaign against Black Hawk, he served on the governor's staff, and doubtless the Old Ranger pressed hard for his election to command the Second Brigade. In the campaign getting under way, General Alexander proved to be a capable officer, never happier than when obeying some superior's order. The 959 men of his brigade were mustered into service on June 16.

The Third Brigade, which drew from the western counties (particularly from Sangamon and Morgan), was the last to be formed, but always first in the field.[10] The men elected Sheriff James Dougherty Henry of Springfield to command them, a decision which proves that not everything the militia did was wrong. Henry was a no-nonsense man's man of sinew and bone. He was rough, but not a roughneck. At a time when the legendary frontier virtues were degenerating into a grubby pursuit of land and dollars, Henry refurbished the image. He was a tough, fearless fighter who could endure hardships without a whine or whimper, just as was recounted of the early pioneers of the nineties. No man or woman seems ever to have known him intimately, or to have spoken ill of him.

Since General Henry was the man most responsible for terminating the Black Hawk War, it is important to convey something of his background. Henry was born somewhere in Pennsylvania in 1797. He was illegitimate, and knowledge of this fact, or his knowledge of other people's awareness of it, shaped and twisted his life. It was rumored that his father was an officer in the regular army, but he seems to have borne his mother's surname. As a boy he was so poor that he never went to school; at fifteen he ran off to fight in the War of 1812 and never returned home. Six feet tall, Henry had a powerful build; but he was gentle until angered, at which time he lost all control of his temper. He settled in Delaware, Ohio, as apprentice in the cobbler's trade, but within a year had to leave town after he thrashed three shoemakers, presumably because they called him a bastard.

Henry keelboated on the Ohio for a time, and in 1820 turned up in Edwardsville, Illinois, as a shoemaker.

His Edwardsville interlude ended with an act of violence more shocking than the Delaware episode. When a Negro slave named Jarrett insulted him, Henry became enraged "to a fiendish

10. Indicative of the want of confidence in Governor Reynolds is the complete absence of militia companies from his home county of St. Clair enrolled in the second army. In April four companies from St. Clair had joined him at Beardstown.

degree." Dragging the black into the street, he ripped off all
the man's clothes except his trousers, tied him to a hitching rock,
and thrashed him with five hickory withes. When Jarrett begged
for mercy, Henry drew a knife across his belly and threatened
to gut him if he complained. Since it was court day, a crowd of
over a hundred people gathered to witness this shocking performance, but not one dared to stop it. Finally a woman, hearing
Jarrett's screams, pushed Henry aside and let the victim escape.
Though the townspeople were inured to public whippings, especially of "hard-headed niggers," Henry's nearly psychotic attack
alarmed them. Personally they liked him, but they feared him
and, in the end, unintentionally ostracized him.

In 1826 James Henry moved on to Springfield, where he engaged in business. One of the first men to enlist for the Winnebago War, he failed to reach Prairie du Chien, to his great disappointment, because his commanding officer got lost beyond
Galena. A year later he was elected sheriff of Sangamon County
and there earned a reputation for humanity and justice. In the
1831 campaign he commanded a regiment, and in the following
year a battalion in Whiteside's army. He enlisted as private in
the interim regiment, but was elevated to lieutenant colonel. At
Fort Wilbourn he again enlisted as a private and was elected
general by unanimous vote. His Third Brigade—the largest with
1,275 men—was mustered into federal service on June 20. Almost
alone among the Sucker officers, Henry commanded respect from
regulars as well as militia.

All told, General Atkinson now had at his command about
thirty-two hundred mounted militia and five hundred regulars,
in addition to the Indian detachments pulled together by Colonel
Billy Hamilton. Colonel Henry Dodge's force of several hundred
mounted rangers cooperated with the Army of the Frontier by
scouring the region north of the Rock River, watching for a
possible breakout by Black Hawk. And, thanks to Winnebago
and Potawatomie spies, working with Indian agents Henry Gratiot, John Kinzie, and Thomas Owen, the American commander
had at his disposal an extraordinary intelligence network which

pin-pointed the British Band at Lake Koshkonong, fifty miles
north of Stillman's run.[11]

All that remained was for Atkinson to march his vast host to
the enemy and root him out. Unfortunately for the Chemokemons, Black Hawk suddenly played his own cards, making havoc
with the general's plan.

11. Weeks before the second army began to move, Atkinson had been
informed of the whereabouts of Black Hawk by the following: Captain
Joseph Plympton of Fort Winnebago (June 5), John Kinzie (June 7),
Thomas Owen (June 11), Colonel Henry Dodge (June 11). Moreover, in
mid-June Henry Gratiot employed a white man, Oliver Emmell, to disguise
himself as a Winnebago and to spy upon the Sauk. Assisted by White
Crow, Emmell reported on June 27 that the Sauk camps extended "from
lake Kashkenon along cat-fish river to its mouth, a distance of six or seven
miles."

EIGHT *The Sauk Counterattack*

> Blood flows here on a small scale tolerably fast.
> —JOHN REYNOLDS

<<<<<<<<<<<<<<<<<<<<<<<<<<<<<<<<<<<<<<<<<<<<<<<<<<<<<<

BLACK HAWK'S surprise at the pusillanimous behavior of the whites at Old Man's Creek did not engender in him or his band any overconfidence in his power. Undertaking a pitched battle against Atkinson's entire force did not form any part of the Sauk strategy.

As for other tribes, except for the settling of specific grudges, the Potawatomie took no part at all in the Black Hawk War. The Winnebago involvement, however, manifested itself almost at once, commencing with the sortie which netted them the scalps of William Durley and Felix St. Vrain's party and continuing until the second Atkinson army massed in the Rock valley. However, the presence of the feared Sauk in the heart of their territory placed a strain upon the Winnebago economy out of all proportion to the gratification afforded by Chemokemon embarrassment. Altercations between hot bloods in both tribes kept up a volatile atmosphere, particularly the rampant horse-stealing forays of the Sauk. No real Winnebago-Sauk entente ever existed, or was possible. Winnebago war parties never included more than a dozen warriors eager to avenge a particular wrong or to take an easy coup, and they always went alone. Accusations by whites that Winnebago functioned as guides for the British Band are doubtless true; but, for the most part, such guides primarily wished to lead the Sauk out of their territory and onto lands belonging to some other unfortunate band.

Lulled into a false sense of security after Stillman's Run, Black Hawk made no move against the whites until mid-June, when he learned that a second army was being mobilized at Ottawa—an army obviously intended to chastise him. To distract the whites from a direct assault upon his main camp around Lake Koshkonong, he decided to harass the settlements in the Lead Region. Accordingly, he held a dog-feast, collected the Sauk medicine bags, and launched war parties to the west, to convince the enemy that his band had begun its move to Iowa. There were two assault waves, the first making contact with the enemy on June 14, the second on June 24. The first consisted primarily of horse-stealing and marauding bands of no more than twoscore Indians bumping into an approximately equal number of whites; the second consisted of a series of premeditated attacks upon specific targets, led by the Hawk himself.

Most of the Sauk braves remained at Koshkonong to hunt for and protect the noncombatants who were rapidly reaching a condition of semistarvation. Judging from the reactions among the whites of the Lead Region, one might think that hundreds of Indians had been loosed upon the settlements.[1] Although with characteristic bombast and exaggeration, frontier folk subsequently alluded to the Battle of Pecatonica and the First Battle of Kellogg's Grove quite as though the combat had been considerable, these fights were at most tragicomic affairs, of significance primarily because the whites would have it so.

A band of Kickapoo struck first. On June 14, six miles southeast of Fort Hamilton (now Wiota) they ambushed six men working at the Spafford farm. In the melee Bennett Million, a hired hand, leaped into the Pecatonica River and made his escape, by keeping the embankment between himself and his pursuers until he had a three hundred yard start. He then swam underwater fifty yards to the opposite shore, clawed up an em-

---

1. The regulars understood the Indian tactic. Lieutenant A. S. Johnston wrote in his field journal on May 29, "Their mode of warfare is such that while you keep a sufficient force in motion against them to contend with their main body you must necessarily keep troops at every available point on the frontier to hold in check small parties which it is their custom to detach to a great distance."

bankment twelve feet high (it is hard to credit the story that "at one bound he sprang from slippery shore to the top of the perpendicular bank," even allowing for his considerable motivation at the moment), and set off "at full lope" for the fort. As Colonel Billy Hamilton was absent enlisting Indians, the temporary commander sent to Fort Defiance (five miles southeast of present Mineral Point) for assistance. Fort Defiance, in turn, sent an express to Henry Dodge calling for more assistance; a dozen men rode over to Fort Hamilton that evening.

Before setting off for Spafford's farm the next morning, a noisy row developed over who had the right to command. Once this was settled by voice vote, the rangers rode out. They nosed about the battleground and buried four bodies, all of them horribly mutilated. (The body of John Bull, said to be an army deserter, was fished out of the Pecatonica; the discovery that his watch was still running made a profound impression on the rescuers.) The burial party made no attempt to scout for the enemy or to find a man named Spencer, who had absolutely vanished. On returning to Fort Hamilton another row developed because the locals refused to feed the Defiance crowd, arguing that their supplies were low.

Early in the morning of June 16, Henry Dodge and two rangers rode to Fort Hamilton from Dodgeville to assume command. A quarter of a mile from the fort they passed a terrified German named Henry Appel and pressed him to join them. Appel agreed, but said he had to fetch a blanket from his cabin. As soon as Dodge passed out of sight, Appel headed for Dodgeville, only to be shot to pieces by some Kickapoo. The arrival of his bloodstained horse at Fort Hamilton a short time later caused "wild excitement and disorder," remembered one witness. Some wished to dash after the Indians, others to dash away from them. Dodge made them all form a line; and, after a short speech containing the exhortation, "charge them sword in hand," he ordered all cowards to remain behind (about half of them) and the rest to follow him. Leaving four men to bury Appel, twenty-nine others pursued the Indians through a thicket of prickly ash and brier, with Dodge in the advance.

The trail wound around the outside of a horseshoe bend in

the Pecatonica, an easily fordable stream at this season, and to the peninsula formed by the loop. Posting four men on high ground to watch for an Indian breakout, Dodge forded the stream to the neck of the loop where he left four men to tend the horses and proceeded with twenty-one men on foot.

The Kickapoo, concealed in the underbrush and behind an embankment, loosed "most terrific yells" and a masked volley that dropped three whites. "Charge 'em, boys! Damn 'em! Charge 'em!" yelled Dodge, his voice propelling the men forward before the Indians could reload. The Kickapoo loomed up with stone mallets as the whites gained the edge of the embankment and poured down a volley from six feet away. A white coming in from the left heard Dodge shout at him, "There's an Indian! Kill him!" But before he could turn he heard a shot followed by Dodge's outcry, "There, by God! I've killed him myself." Nine Kickapoo lay dead in the ditch and two were killed attempting to flee. It was an ecstatic moment for men who "had never heard a hostile gun or burned powder at a foe," that they had known by a kind of instinct what to do. With knives they hacked off the scalps. One scuffle broke out between two whites reaching an Indian body at the same time; "That's my hair!" one shouted.

The Battle of Pecatonica came to an official close several hours later when Colonel Hamilton arrived at the ground with a handful of his Indian mercenaries, who, enraged at having missed the fight, hacked the Kickapoo bodies into pieces and scattered the remains about the peninsula (where the whitened bones marked the site for three decades). Four whites had been wounded, three of them mortally.[2]

Weeks later, rangers searching a farm near the Pecatonica were thrown into consternation when a figure rushed out of a corncrib toward them. It was Spencer, the missing victim of the

2. The death of Samuel Wells, wrote an early Wisconsin chronicler, "would have been a theme for the song of the minstrel, had it occurred in the days of chivalry." Told that he would die, Wells called for Henry Dodge and asked, "General, have I behaved like a soldier?"

"Yes, Wells, like a brave one."

"Send that word to my old father."

The old father was Rennah Wells of Rock Island, the foremost trouble-maker among the squatters who had ousted Black Hawk from Saukenuk.

Spafford's farm attack. He had outrun a Kickapoo riding a captured plow horse and had then lain hidden for two days. The distant firing of Dodge's rangers at Pecatonica he mistook for an attack on Fort Hamilton and assumed that the Sauk had overrun the Lead Region. Spencer never recovered from his shock. The following winter he went crazy, wandered about the region, and finally vanished for good.

The report of the battle that Dodge prepared for Atkinson on June 18 must have provided that harassed officer with the most cheering news of his Illinois campaign to date. In the Lead Region, Dodge found the populace nearly prepared to fall on their knees before their deliverer.[3] Jo Daviess County talked of running him as the next governor of Illinois, obligingly ignoring the fact that he was a citizen of Michigan. In Prairie du Chien the people chipped in to buy him a double-barreled shotgun. And in Galena the Daughters of the Lead Mines, by far the most prestigious of the ladies' sewing circles, presented him with a homespun and hand-stitched Star-Spangled Banner as emblem of their veneration.

Dodge's victory at the Pecatonica stands as the whites' finest hour in the Black Hawk War. With odds only two-to-one in their favor a band of settlers stood up against an Indian volley, endured war whoops, and attacked the enemy with spirit. Because this was the first American battle to take place on Wisconsin soil, it has assumed an importance in that region not fully acknowledged in the nation at large. In later years the participants, many eager to claim credit for the heroic exploits of the attack, would refight the battle many times in passionate letters to the editor.[4]

3. A day before the battle Congress had authorized the recruitment of six companies of United States rangers for the defense of the frontier and had designated Henry Dodge as their commander.

4. The literature dealing with the Pecatonica fight is astonishingly vast, considering that it was in fact a minor affair. Two of the participants, Peter Parkinson and "General" Charles Bracken held such a bitter controversy in Wisconsin newspapers over details of the fight that they developed an underlying hatred for each other. Although they lived on adjoining farms, each man erected his own fence on contiguous land, and for more than thirty years refused to speak to or about the other. The nub of their disagreement was that there seemed to be an insufficient amount of heroism to go around.

Only a native son could agree with the summation of one of these veterans who wrote, "the annals of border warfare furnish no parallel to this battle."

While Colonel Dodge was thrashing the Kickapoo at Pecatonica, however, a small band of Sauk was buffeting Captain Adam Snyder's company near Kellogg's Grove, twenty miles to the south. Snyder, it will be recalled, led the interim company which had earlier refused Colonel Zachary Taylor's order to patrol the Galena road and bury the St. Vrain party. After Elijah Iles had opened the road a week previously, Snyder took his company over it on June 13. One of his men had murdered a comrade-in-arms and the captain wanted to hand him over to the civil authorities in Galena.

By June 15 he had returned to Kellogg's Grove and established camp in the log and bark huts of the former inn. The night was stormy and a sentinel lying under a tree fired his gun in the air after seeing an Indian creeping through the grove illuminated by a flash of lightning. In the morning a missing horse supported the sentry's tale. Snyder started in pursuit with forty men, after picking up a trail leading to the southwest. Brevet Major Bennet Riley, with two companies of regulars and no horses, remained at Kellogg's Grove with twenty volunteers who had lost interest in hunting Indians.[5]

After a twenty-mile chase, Snyder's men came upon the place where the Indians had breakfasted (a kettle still boiled on the fire). Tethered nearby was the horse they had stolen. After milling about for an hour, they discovered, to their great frustration, the Indians' tracks which led back toward Kellogg's Grove. After another ten-mile pursuit they overtook four Indians, who offered to surrender, but ex-General Whiteside signaled that they should fight it out. The Indians jumped into a ravine and the whites opened fire from surrounding trees.[6] Eager for glory,

5. Riley later distinguished himself in the Seminole War and in the Mexican War, where he was brevetted to major general for gallant conduct at the Battle of Contreras. The present Fort Riley, Kansas, was named in his honor.

6. When cornered, the Sauk often used this tactic. They used the lip of the ravine as parapet as long as they could, then stood in the bottom with guns raised at the skyline to shoot their assailants as they looked in.

Private William Makemson of St. Clair County stepped from behind a tree and said, "Let me give them a pop." He fired a shot and reeled back with two bullets in his belly. Whiteside shouted, "Rush 'em, boys! Their guns are empty!" Minutes later the Indians were dead and scalped.

Their elation at having taken four scalps, however, was soon dampened by the sweat that rolled off their bodies as, on foot, they tried to carry the two-hundred-pound Makemson to Kellogg's Grove. The bearers became separated from the main body, which had spread out to find water for the wounded man. As they dragged him down a hillside, Indians opened fire from an ambush only two miles from base. Two bearers were hit and the others disappeared through the undergrowth to catch the men leading their horses, who, at first fire, had galloped back to find the main body. In this confusion Snyder and Whiteside formed a line and opened fire when a few Indians got within a hundred yards. Private Whiteside was credited with having fired the half-ounce ball that hit the leader, the same Indian who had wounded Makemson during the initial attack. No trace of the latter was ever found, however. The Indians immediately withdrew, probably having no more stomach for the fight than the Chemokemons. Captain Snyder retreated with due dispatch to Kellogg's, meeting on the way Major Riley with a company of regulars alerted by the sound of distant gunshots.

They slept on their rifles that night, and in the morning returned in force to bury the three whites. No evidence of further Indian kills could be found. Presumably the Indians had been Sauk, although none of the participants troubled to report this— a scalp was a scalp.

As a result of his victory at Kellogg's Grove Captain Snyder found the citizenry of St. Clair County sufficiently proud of the martial glory of their native son to re-elect him to the state senate in 1832. Only his untimely death in 1842 prevented him from occupying the governor's chair in that year. If this seems too much

---

Black Hawk was expert in this technique. In 1815 he held a Missouri company at bay after taking refuge in a sinkhole and made his escape at nightfall.

fame for so minuscule a victory, it is consistent at least with most historical frontier accounts and their inflated catalogues of nature's noblemen. In his history of Illinois (1854), Governor Thomas Ford took the real measure of the Suckers when he explained that he wrote perforce about "small events and little men" for the simple reason that "there was nothing else in the history of Illinois to write about." For all that, midgets deserve study.

Even as the First Brigade of Atkinson's army began to move from the base camp to Dixon's Ferry on June 20, news of fresh Indian attacks arrived to shake the general's equanimity. On Bureau Creek, just fifteen miles from Fort Wilbourn, an unidentified band of Indians killed a settler at his cabin door (June 18). To parry this thrust, Alexander Posey's spy battalion under Major John Dement [7] was diverted from the march to scour the threatened sector. They found only some ragged Potawatomie, professing love and loyalty to the Great American Father, but one of whom had doubtless settled a personal grudge. Meanwhile Posey's brigade, stiffened by two companies of the Sixth Infantry, just arrived from Fort Leavenworth, lumbered across the undulating prairie to Dixon's Ferry. On the second morning these volunteers raised the cry "Indians!" and scattered over the prairie. They shortly returned in triumph, having used this ruse to rid themselves of government-issue incumbrances, including rations for fifteen days. They were fine fellows, much appreciated by the beaming Posey. General Milton Alexander moved off on June 21, and General J. D. Henry, with Atkinson's staff, two days later.

At Dixon's Ferry Colonel Taylor was again stewing about the irresponsibility of the militia. After the fight near Kellogg's,

7. John Dement (1804–83) was a native of Tennessee who settled in Franklin County as a youth. By the age of twenty-four, he represented his district in the legislature. After the war he married the daughter of Henry Dodge and settled near Dixon's Ferry. On his visit to America during the Civil War, the British novelist Anthony Trollope watched the mustering in, at Dixon, Illinois, of a volunteer regiment sponsored by John Dement.

Captain Snyder brought his company to Dixon's to be disbanded, because their twenty-day enlistment had expired. Whether the Galena road remained open was anyone's guess. That Indians infested the whole region northwest of the Rock was known, however. On June 18 Captain J. W. Stephenson of the Galena militia, in pursuing a small party of Indians who had captured some horses at Apple River Fort (present Elizabeth), had been routed, with the loss of three men, at Waddam's Grove, twelve miles north of Kellogg's Grove. Taylor had earlier been forced to recall Major Riley's companies from Kellogg's because no scouts were available to them. Nearly bursting with impatience, Colonel Taylor now waited for Posey's meandering brigade.

The first to arrive at Dixon's tavern were the volunteers of Major Dement's spy battalion, all of them exhausted and irritable after a three-day hunt for hostiles along Bureau Creek. On the morning of June 23, having given them one night's rest, Taylor poled across to their camp and personally ordered them to Kellogg's Grove immediately, spicing his address with allusions to his past experience with cowardly, skulking citizen-soldiers. By the time the colonel had concluded his lecture, Dement later reported, the men "were almost ready to fight Taylor rather than obey him." They regarded themselves as an elite corps, representing the finest blood of southern Illinois. (Dement was state treasurer; Zadock Casey, of his staff, was lieutenant governor; another aide, Stinson H. Anderson, was to become lieutenant governor.) Major Dement salvaged the pride of his battalion (and deftly proved that he could not be bottled with Taylor's label) by calling out, "Men! You need not obey his orders. Obey mine and follow me." He then swam his horse across the Rock and his battalion followed. Taylor greatly relished John Dement and enjoyed telling brother officers how the volunteer major gave him his comeuppance.

The Dement battalion of about 120 men rattled into Kellogg's Grove on Saturday evening (June 23) and, finding no spoor of Indian, passed Sunday in hunting and idling about the oak grove. Had they scouted the Galena road toward Apple River twenty miles west, they might have picked up the sound of distant firing, for at that moment Black Hawk in person was providing the defenders of the Apple River Fort with his own form of Sunday sermon.

Exactly when Black Hawk, with his war parties, estimated by the old war chief at two hundred braves, left their base camps at Koshkonong to attack the Lead Region is not known; but it appears to have been after the encounters with Dodge and Snyder.[8] His purpose was to lead the Chemokemon army on a goose chase far to the west, picking up whatever booty, particularly horses, he could lay his hands on. He selected Apple River for his first attack because a figure in a dream instructed him to go there. This force presumably did not move en bloc, but followed the traditional pattern of Indians on a war journey, fanned out across the countryside; they knew exactly where and when they were expected to rendezvous.

On Wednesday morning (June 20), a hidden party of Indians (presumably Sauk) ambushed two men within rifle shot of Blue Mound fort, ending at one swoop any sense of security which had been generated by Dodge's victory at Pecatonica. An express rider was immediately dispatched for Dodgeville twenty miles to the west with an urgent request for aid in repelling fifty or one hundred Indians. The Colonel, however, was so involved with last-minute plans for the coming campaign with Atkinson that four days passed before he collected a force to investigate the incident. He found the defenders at Blue Mound so petrified with fear that they had sallied forth to bury only the nearer victim, leaving the more distant one bloating in the sunshine.[9]

8. Since Black Hawk never alluded to either the Pecatonica battle or the first fight at Kellogg's Grove it is likely that the Indians involved operated independently. White Crow, who had visited the Sauk camp at some date between June 16 and 25, told Henry Gratiot on June 27 that war parties had been sent "for the purpose of making an attack on some part of the mining region" and were due back at Koshkonong on June 28. Though this information arrived too late for the whites to counter the move, it was nevertheless meticulously accurate.

9. The victims were Emerson Green, a miner from Helena, and George Force, who took over command of the fort after Aubrey's death on June 6. According to one resident, Force's body was left on the prairie deliberately because Force had refused to help retrieve Aubrey's earlier. The gold watch which the Indians took from Force's pocket was later found on a Sauk killed at Four Lakes on July 21.

The fort had not been attacked and the Indians had vanished days before. Ebeneezer Brigham, the first settler of the district, reflecting the state of mind of his fellows, penned in his notebook at this time, "Our situation is a delicate one. I expect an attack from the Indians. We cannot stand a siege." This entry was followed by the names and addresses of his next of kin. And as a result of this fruitless reconnaissance, Dodge was far off the scent of the Sauk when they struck Apple River that same day.

The Apple River settlement lay in the "knobs" country twelve miles east of Galena. It is characterized by deeply pitted valleys and timbered hillsides, resembling Pennsylvania or Tennessee, whence most of the settlers had come. They had hacked out a crude stockade in the hollow beside the creek, without considering that this was a poor site for detecting or defending against hostile Indians. By first light on June 24, Black Hawk's war party had infiltrated the bosky hillocks around the fort and were waiting with infinite patience for an opportunity to strike. It was a wet Sunday and only a few whortleberry pickers animated the quiet scene.

Late in the morning three horsemen, loud-mouthed fellows, entered the fort from Galena. They were carrying dispatches to Dixon's and paused long enough to refresh themselves. When they resumed their journey they were near-drunk and rode off "whooping and halloing." A quarter of a mile from the fort a shot dropped the leading man from his horse with a thigh wound. The other two spurred to his aid and opened fire at the invisible enemy, only to discover that their guns had not been loaded. Somehow they retrieved the wounded man and retreated to the fort. The leader of the trio, "Captain" Fred Dixon unwisely covered the retreat of his fellows, careening about and brandishing his empty rifle at enemies still unseen. As soon as the Indians unleashed a rattle of shots at the pot-valiant horseman, Dixon galloped back to the fort, but found the gates barred, the settlers inside, anticipating a frontal assault by the Indians, and deaf to his entreaties and immune to his profanity. He soon gave up and set out headlong for Galena. On the road he ran smack into several Sauk rushing toward the uproar. He so startled them that they leaped aside and, before they could collect their wits,

Dixon was gone. At Galena he reported the fort besieged by 150 Indians, a figure canonized by subsequent reiteration. A few hardy Galenians urged the formation of a relief column, but Colonel James Strode vetoed the proposal on ground that the fort must have already capitulated. The parlous times required that Galenians serve Galena; therefore, the colonel strengthened the guard, posted an alert, and prepared for the worst.

While a token force of Sauk peppered the fort at Apple River with rifle balls, others plundered the cabins in the environs, collected horses, and drove off hogs and cattle. Within the log pen children bawled, women wrung their hands, and men prayed. Concerted resistance was nearly nonexistent until a virago named Mrs. Armstrong injected some spirit into the caterwauling mob.[10] A coarse-tongued, tobacco-spitting female, she "drove round the fort like a fury, cursing and swearing like a pirate," forcing the women to load muskets and the men to return the fire. To prevent the children from crying and thereby revealing to the Indians that they were frightened, she herded all of them into one room and kept them there, posting a female guard at the door with a club. One man, hiding in an empty flour barrel, found himself pulled out and shoved to a loophole by Mrs. Armstrong. She was so successful in invigorating the defense that a youth named Harkelrode stuck his head over the palisade for a clearer view (or perhaps to taunt the attackers) and was killed by a ball through his neck. He was the sole fatality on either side during the seige that lasted anywhere from three-quarters of an hour to three hours.[11]

Though some of his warriors wanted to fire the fort with flaming arrows, Black Hawk refused because he feared that a

10. A British traveler, Charles J. Latrobe, who passed through this community one year later discovered that it was impossible "to get two honest men to concur in the same account of any given event." But he suspected that if the truth were ever known, it would amount to "a chronicle of shame." By this time Apple River folk were estimating that the Indians had numbered 270.

11. Black Hawk recalled this hyperactive youth vividly: "One of their braves, who seemed more valiant than the rest, raised his head above the picketing to fire at us, when one of my braves, with a well-directed shot, put an end to his bravery!" *Sic transit gloria illini.*

conflagration would attract reinforcements. Some time in the afternoon he then withdrew from Apple River and quickly moved toward Kellogg's Grove, where the rangers of John Dement's command were lazing away a rainy Sunday afternoon.

On Sunday night a chance wayfarer from Galena brought Dement news that he had seen signs of Indians en route; but he had apparently learned nothing of the Apple River fight. On Monday morning (June 25) Dement ordered out a company to reconnoiter and to seek some horses that had strayed off during the night. The men spotted four Indians on the prairie, hooted the alarm, and chased them into a stand of timber where Black Hawk lay in ambush. The major and his staff, fearing a second Stillman's Run, dashed after the men, ordering them to come back. When they were a quarter of a mile from the timber, the Sauk opened fire, cutting down two rangers and driving the others back in a "tumultous retreat." The Indians, stripped to the skin and well mounted, charged the whites, converging from three directions. Major Dement and a handful of stalwarts loosed a volley that temporarily halted the first wave of the attack and gave the company time to take refuge in the buildings of Kellogg's Grove.[12] Over to one side, however, three whites on foot looking for their horses were chased and slaughtered by the onrushing Sauk. Dement's small group narrowly escaped being cut off. The major himself was said to have been so angry at the pandemonium which seized his force that he strode up and down outside the buildings until a bullet put a hole through his hat and drove him inside.

Whether with or without orders, at least five rangers sped for Dixon's to sound the alarm while the rest fired from doors and

12. Black Hawk's account of the battle praised Dement's conduct highly: "The chief (who seemed to be a small man) addressed his warriors in a loud voice; but they soon retreated, leaving him and a few braves on the battle-field. . . . The chief and his braves were unwilling to leave the field. I ordered my braves to rush upon them, and had the mortification of seeing two of my *chiefs* killed, before the enemy retreated. This young chief deserves great praise for his courage and bravery; but fortunately for us, his army was not all composed of such brave men." Pukquawa, a Sauk interviewed in August, confirmed the loss of two principal warriors in the fight. In addition, Black Hawk confessed that seven others were killed.

windows whenever an Indian exposed himself, which was not often. Oddly enough, the buildings were worthless as block-houses, for, despite the many military units that had camped in them, no one had troubled to cut loopholes or remove chinking. Most of the men might as well have been shut up in log crates, for all the fighting they could do from the buildings. Neverthe-less, seeing that a frontal attack would be suicidal, Black Hawk convinced his war party to withdraw at once to Koshkonong, "as we had run the bear into his hole, we would leave him, and return to our camp." Within two hours after the opening attack, the Sauk had disappeared.

Like the men, the horses had huddled about the buildings. Knowing how difficult horses were to come by in that part of Illinois, the Sauk mowed them down in order to hamper the Chemokemon ability to fight as much as possible. Dement's men had to listen impotently as their mounts whinnied, reared, kicked, and galloped off to join the Indian ponies. When Dement's bat-talion reappeared blinking in the light of day, a horrible sight greeted them. The whole grove appeared to be covered with dead, dying, and bleeding horseflesh. In all twenty-six horses had been killed, twelve disabled and eighteen run off. (This is the official count; some sources place the number of missing horses as high as fifty-seven. Half of Dement's battalion had been ren-dered horseless by the battle.) And the five dead rangers, all of them shockingly mutilated, lay among the carnage where they had fallen like broken dolls.

Two hours before nightfall General Alexander Posey's brigade reached the grove. An express had found them near Buffalo Grove. They had dropped their paraphernalia and left commis-sary wagons to rush to Dement's relief. Posey dispatched a regi-ment after the Sauk, but signs of Indians in a woods half a mile north made them return to gather reinforcements. Although many officers, including Dement, urged an immediate advance, Gen-eral Posey postponed operations till morning. "It was not within my power to go in immediate pursuit," he wrote Atkinson. When the martial ardor of the First Brigade returned with daybreak, Black Hawk had gotten away.

On the morning of June 26 an odd company under Captain

Jacob Early, a Springfield circuit rider and physician, reached Kellogg's Grove. The impressions of Private Abraham Lincoln, who had enlisted in this company after Elijah Iles's twenty-day company had been disbanded, are worth recording: "I remember just how those men looked as we rode up the little hill where their camp was. The red light of the morning sun was streaming upon them as they lay heads toward us on the ground. And every man had a round red spot on the top of his head about as big as a dollar, where the redskins had taken his scalp. It was frightful, but it was grotesque; and the red sunlight seemed to paint everything all over. [pause] I remember that one man had buckskin breeches on." It is a singularly groping and hollow recollection, though somehow appropriate for a soldier who, for the second time, had arrived at the battlefield only in time to pick up the dead. Anticlimactic as Lincoln's service was, it was nevertheless thrilling when placed beside that of the average Black Hawk War volunteer who seemed either to be dashing after imaginary Indians or slapping gallinippers in camp. Lincoln at least saw out-and-out corpses. Few of the volunteers ever could boast of that.

NINE *The "Trembling Lands" Campaign*

This, as I have before observed to you,
is the most difficult country to operate in
immaginable [*sic*] and the enemy the most
uncertain to find.

—GENERAL HENRY ATKINSON

THE INDIAN attacks in the Lead Region, which left nineteen whites dead between June 14 and 25, failed to convince General Atkinson that the British Band was truly attempting to break for Iowa. But they did compel him to deflect half of his army into the region to make certain. He had scarcely returned to the turf fort at Dixon's Ferry (after a necessary absence of nearly a month) before his carefully laid plan to march directly to Lake Koshkonong began to crumble. General Milton Alexander's Second Brigade had to be dispatched immediately to scour the woods between Kellogg's Grove and Plum River (present Savanna) with orders to rejoin the main column on the march up the Rock. Alexander Posey was already en route to Fort Hamilton to join with Henry Dodge's rangers and William Hamilton's mercenaries.

James Henry's brigade arrived at Dixon's Ferry during the afternoon of June 25. At nine in the evening a ferocious rattle of musketry broke out in the militia camp, which sounded as though they were being assaulted by thousands of Indians. Atkinson immediately dispatched a company of regulars in a mackinaw boat to ascertain the cause of the commotion. Lieutenant Philip Cooke discovered, to his great astonishment, the entire militia brigade firing joyously into the air, with General Henry atop a stump bellowing for them to quit. Because of the wet weather he had allowed his men to test their priming by firing their muskets. This, however, had gotten out of hand as they reloaded and fired just for the fun of it. The noisy festivity next spread to the horses, which broke their tethers and stampeded through John Dixon's worm fence. Cooke estimated that nearly one thousand horses broke loose, many of which were permanently crippled or lost. After he had "damned all to posterity," Henry jumped down and resigned his commission in disgust. But the next day, after officers had promised to keep their men in tighter rein, Henry resumed his command. Moreover, he staggered Atkinson and Taylor by offering a manly apology in writing for the behavior of his men.

Bad news then came in from Colonel Hamilton. Most of the Indians he had collected from Prairie du Chien had gotten tired of waiting for the army to move and had trickled back home, leaving him with only twenty-five Menominee. The Sioux harshly criticized Hamilton, whom they called a "little man," for having starved and ill-used them. Some returned home by way of Galena, where they were held for a time as deserters; others went to Prairie du Chien, where "General" Joseph Street gave them a tongue lashing for cowardly conduct and turned a deaf ear to their complaints of hunger and worn-out moccasins. The whites were encountering ill will from Indians all along the frontier, even from so-called friendlies. Though Atkinson encouraged the Potawatomie and Winnebago to prove their neutrality by camping near the settlements, he also aroused their resentment by feeding them spoilage from his commissary and only half-rations of that. (Children received quater-rations!) The Indians would have fared better had they closely followed the army and feasted on the rations which the volunteers tossed away.

General Posey, who had advanced his brigade a total of only ten miles in three days, became embroiled in a bitter hassle that assumed mutinous proportions over thirteen barrels of pork. The trouble started when Colonel Hamilton, with a rag-bag assortment of miners and Menominee arrived to guide Posey to Fort Hamilton. Posey repaid Hamilton by ordering him to Buffalo Grove to fetch the baggage and pork left there four days before when he had dashed to the relief of Major John Dement at Kellogg's Grove. Hamilton, of course, told Posey to go to hell, or something to that effect. Outraged by this act of insubordination, Posey placed Hamilton under arrest. But he was released when Colonel Dodge joined the column and protested that Illinois officers had no authority over citizens of Michigan. By this time many of Posey's men had become disgusted with the sluggishness of their commander and urged Dodge to take command of the First Brigade.

Seeing that he was about to be erased from Command, the Shawneetown physician called for an election. Standing in a hollow square, he sounded an appeal for his old neighbors not to desert and disgrace him. The story goes that tears rolled down his cheeks as he begged for this vote of confidence. Moved, it is said, by pity, the First Brigade rallied round their local son and reinstated him, though the vote was close. Major Dement, disgusted with Posey for allowing the Sauk to escape, promptly resigned his command of the spy battalion. Posey dropped his charge against Hamilton to placate the mutineers. (Presumably the thirteen pork barrels at Buffalo Grove were allowed to rot where they were.) Confidence in General Posey was never completely restored. Dodge, for instance, demanded and obtained permission to cooperate with Alexander's brigade when they made their junction with General Atkinson's army a few days later.[1]

By June 28 the Army of the Frontier, substantial enough to do battle with a Central American republic, began its march up the Rock toward the putative peat-bog fortress of Black Hawk. The table of organization listed two divisions: the First, consisting of the First and Second brigades, with Posey in nominal command as senior brigadier (he had been elected to that rank one

1. Posey's assistant quartermaster, twenty-year-old John A. McClernand, must have observed all this politicking with great interest. Thirty years later, as one of Lincoln's political generals, he earned a nasty reputation as master of the intrigue against George B. McClellan in the East and Ulysses S. Grant in the West. A wheelhorse in state and national politics, Posey's former aide narrowly missed election as speaker of the House of Representatives in 1860 and, in 1876, served as chairman of the Democratic national convention which nominated Samuel J. Tilden.

day earlier than Alexander); and the Second, consisting of the Third Brigade and Taylor's four hundred-odd regulars, with Brevet Brigadier General Hugh Brady as divisional commander. Crowning this force was an artillery unit under Lieutenant Washington Wheelwright which dragged two field pieces through terrain barely passable by horses. (This was the first campaign for Wheelwright, a brilliant West Pointer whose assignments proved so impossible that he threw up his military career the following year and spent the remaining four decades of his life as a quiet notary public in New York City.)

The sixty-four-year-old Brady was a splendid-looking man with silky white hair, a keen eye for good horses and beautiful women, and vivid, albeit tedious, recollections of active service with Mad Anthony Wayne four decades earlier. Born of Pennsylvania squatter stock, Brady was probably the only man still in the United States Army with firsthand knowledge of frontier depredations by Indians during the Revolutionary War. Ever game for a bloody round, he had left Detroit where he had commanded a subdepartment on hearing of the Sauk disturbances in April. With a single aide, he had ridden to Fort Winnebago with stoic disregard for the dangers as he passed through regions infested with hostile or vacillating Indians. He arrived in time to bolster the confidence of a garrison badly in need of a grandfatherly hand. In the first week of June, at the height of the unseemly panic in the Lead Region, General Brady led two companies of Fort Winnebago regulars through the wilds to Galena and on to Dixon's Ferry. Asked what he thought about the war, Brady's reply was widely quoted: "Give me two infantry companies mounted, and I will . . . whip the Sauks out of the country in one week." Brady was surely among the bravest men in the West (or the most senile). Given his choice of divisions, the flinty old man, upon a cursory examination of the Posey-Alexander brigades, chose the other.

Progress up the east bank of the Rock was rapid—by Black Hawk War standards. In seven days the army covered one hundred miles as the crow flies, although they did not proceed so directly. The wake of the expedition was quickly marked by the litter of unused pork and corn, powder and shot, and other items dispensed by the government, except, of course, whiskey.

On June 29 they camped on Stillman's Run, slapped mosquitoes, and meandered over the battleground like pilgrims at a shrine. Wooden battens jammed into the earth marked the graves of the dead; down by the creek "dead horses, burnt wagons, saddle bags, and remnants of clothing [lay] scattered over the ground." A few miles on, at the Kishwaukee River, they picked up ninety-five Potawatomie, of which twenty were chiefs, headed by Billy Caldwell. (The names of some of them so confused Lieutenant Robert Anderson, the assistant inspector general, that they were listed twice and presumably paid a double rate at the end of the campaign.) The Indians joined the spy battalion looking for signs of the enemy—unaware that their worst enemies were not Sauk but Chemokemons, who would absorb the tribal lands of the Potawatomie during the year to follow.

The first day of July found the army at Turtle's village (present Beloit), deserted by its Winnebago inhabitants. Spies brought in information that Sauk had been fishing in the river that very day, causing Atkinson to issue orders to prepare to resist a possible night attack. Skittish sentries fired warning shots several times after nightfall and buglers turned out the army; but all were false alarms. In the morning, Atkinson prudently threw up a breastwork in some nearby timber—"a precaution which he was always after famous for," a volunteer scoffed—and ordered General Henry's spy battalion to advance in battle formation. Shots far ahead announceed the beginning of battle; Atkinson's camp braced to attack or defend. A rider galloped back to announce that no Sauk had been found, the shots had been half a dozen Potawatomie firing at a deer. By now cursing the Potawatomie as well as the Sauk, the Second Division pushed forward twenty miles, camping near the mouth of the Yahara River, the stream which drains Four Lakes. They were four miles from Lake Koshkonong.

Lake Koshkonong, sometimes aptly called Mud Lake, was a bewilderingly complicated body of water, oozing across the flattish landscape like a glob of ink across a sheet of paper. Although only eight miles long and three wide, the lake had an involuted shoreline that, if stretched out, would have extended fifty miles. Somewhere in that amorphous waste of marsh and hummock, hidden by dog willow and sedgy aquatic growth, Black Hawk was believed to be hiding. Scouts on July 3 reported that the Indian trail was becoming warm. Captain Jacob Early sent back word that he had seen, with a borrowed telescope, three Indians in canoes on the farm shore on the lake. (A journalist wryly noted that "Capt. Early seemed always a little too *early* in finding Indian trails.") Major William L. D. Ewing of Vandalia, commander of Henry's spy battalion, swore that he had found a Sauk trail only two days old. But, as might have been expected, it was a band of Potawatomie, under Captain George Walker of Chicago, who discovered the main Sauk camp on a fishhook peninsula. Although abandoned, the area was replete with five fresh graves, scalps taken from members of the St. Vrain party, artifacts attributed to the Hall sisters, and even wisps of hay tauntingly pointing in the direction the Indians had taken. Atkinson set up camp on open ground southeast of the lake to await reinforcements from the First Division, which had been futilely scouting the Lead Region and were hourly expected.

The Fourth of July passed quietly, with but a few curses directed toward the invisible Black Hawk. Governor Reynolds, who required frequent injections of political pomp, confessed later that his Fourth at Koshkonong brought him "a melancholy and sadness of feeling indescribable." He would surely have preferred the celebration in Galena, where the leading lights drank wine in the offices, above the print shop, toasting the principals of the war. ("To Colonel W. S. Hamilton—may he prove a chip off the old block." "To General Black Hawk—may a propitious heaven grant us the scalp of this bird as a precious treasure.") The rigors of the campaign had begun to penetrate the governor's veneer of optimism. "We were almost hunting a shadow," he wrote.

For three nights Atkinson squatted among the hazel brush, prickly ash, and chokecherry in his bivouac while scouts combed the territory ahead for the spoor of Black Hawk. Rangers came in, their horses caked with mud and their faces brushwhipped, to report such discoveries as a gutted white dog with tobacco tied to its tail or potshards picked up in a swamp. Major Ewing's scouts brought in the biggest prize of all: an ancient Sauk, nearly blind and half-starved. Atkinson had him fed and threatened him with death if he lied. "The old fellow told all he knew, which was not very much," reported a volunteer. He had been falling behind the others and had been abandoned. The chiefs had never informed him of their plans, but he guessed that Black Hawk had retreated up the far side of the lake. Since he was "foolish, blind, and a skeleton," the whites released him. "To shorten his days we concluded the best plan would be to give him plenty to eat, and leave him to kill himself in that pleasant way," John Wakefield recorded. His actual death was less merciful, however. A few days later, some of Posey's men found the poor creature, shot him after a sadistic round of taunts and torture, and carried his scalp triumphantly back to southern Illinois.

Patrols ranging the western bank failed to detect any human beings other than the advance scouts of Posey's brigade, which had arrived on the far shore of the Rock on July 5, the day after Alexander joined the army. Having at last regathered his scattered legions, Atkinson planned a massive advance up both sides of the Rock on July 6. If Black Hawk were to be subdued, the blow had to be struck promptly, for both Alexander's and Posey's brigades had arrived with utterly empty commissary wagons. Looming before General Atkinson was the specter of a long retreat because of lack of provisions. He issued an order that each volunteer conserve his food "as a contrary course will certainly subject him to suffering and want, detached as we all are at a distance from our depots."

Because of the feud between Dodge and Henry, he had to order Alexander's brigade to exchange position with Posey's. This transfer averted possible duels, but left the divisional organization in a shambles and caused further bungling and embarrassment. Captain Charles Dunn, one of Posey's company commanders, went out on the morning of the transfer to inform his sentinels, one of whom mistook him for an Indian and shot him in the groin. Surgeons despaired of his life for a time, but he pulled through. Dunn was an important man in Illinois politics, a commissioner of a nonexistent canal, thus a whole battalion was required to escort him back to Dixon's Ferry.[2] Two days after this

2. Dunn survived to become a shirt-sleeve judge in the Lead Region after the war. G. W. Featherstonhaugh, a British traveler, attended one of

incident, which prompted a regular officer to write that the militia were "generally more dangerous to their friends than to their enemies," Atkinson promulgated an order demanding that Posey's men stop stealing horses from Henry's brigade.

As a final aggravation to Atkinson, news arrived from Dixon's Ferry by an express that Brigadier General Winfield Scott was en route from the East to assume command of the Army of the Frontier. If Atkinson wished to salvage what remained of his military reputation, he had to find and thrash the British Band before Scott arrived. On July 6 the army lumbered north on both sides of the Rock River.

Five miles north of Lake Koshkonong the right wing of the army encountered the Bark River as it ran into the Rock after a sinuous passage from the east. Since it was not conveniently fordable, Atkinson moved along its south bank seeking a place to cross. After four miles he discovered another obstacle, the Whitewater River, which joined the Bark from the south. Horsemen could cross but infantry could not, nor could packhorses, commissary wagons, or fieldpieces. Yet, if they continued along the Whitewater in search of a ford, they would be turning back southward toward Illinois. While scouts sought a crossing place, the army bivouacked at the neck of the Y, across from an abandoned Winnebago camp called Burnt Village.

On the morning of July 7, a spasm swept through the army when some soldiers fishing in the Bark were fired on from the far shore. A regular of the First Infantry was badly wounded.[3] The army saddled up hurriedly to join battle; it ap-

---

his trials in 1837. On the day of the verdict Dunn staggered into the courtroom so drunk he could barely gain his seat without falling. He ordered a miner convicted of killing Henry Dodge's nephew to pay a fine of $300. Dunn further impressed the Briton by using a toothbrush to stir his brandy sling and a tablefork to clean his nails.

3. A few days later he died and his grave became the first location of Fort Atkinson, Wisconsin. A miniature palisade surrounded a barrel head with the inscription:

LIEUT. DANIEL DOBBS
SHOT BY INDIANS IN THE YEAR
1832

The rank of lieutenant was a posthumous, and erroneous, promotion.

peared that their bayonets might soon be required for something other than roasting bacon over a campfire. Lieutenant Meriwether Lewis Clark of the Sixth Infantry, son of the Indian superintendent, was writing to his father when the firing broke out; he penned, "My horse cannot be found and I fear the poor fellow is sacrificed. Well it will only make me add one to the few scalps I am going to take from Black Hawk, Napope, etc." [4] However, before scalps could be taken, it was necessary to find the heads on which they fit. Search parties found nothing. (After the war some friendly Winnebago confessed that members of their group had swum across to Burnt Village, fired on the fishermen, and swum back unnoticed in thick fog.)

A mile south the army forded the Whitewater and entered a region called by the Indians the "trembling lands," a quaking bog of muddy pools, stunted tamarisk, sedgy hummocks. Horses stepped on what appeared to be sod and plunged to their bellies in yellow water. It was a hog wallow beyond description and almost beyond belief. By noon the advance had reached the south bank of the Bark without finding a place to cross. Someone gave out the word that the ford was nine miles farther upstream; but after four miles they wore out and camped. The next morning (July 8), after a council in which Indian guides swore that it was impossible to get over the Bark by proceeding upstream, Atkinson gave it up and returned to the former campside opposite Burnt Village. Here he planned to throw across a light bridge in the morning. The drinking water was foul and full of "wrigglers"; dysentery struck the army. It put General Brady out of combat for the remainder of the campaign. The old general was returned to Detroit lying upon a bed of straw in a farm wagon; but, by the following year, he had recovered sufficient strength to put down a Negro insurrection in that city.

With shovels they dug up sod and threw it in the river, along with brush, to fashion a crude causeway across the Bark. Abra-

4. Lieutenant Clark never took a scalp, and a year later he resigned from the army. During the Mexican War he served in California with the Missouri Volunteers and during the Civil War joined the Confederacy. In his declining years he was commandant at the Kentucky Military Institute and architect of the Kentucky State buildings in Frankfort.

ham Lincoln was doubtless among the men of Captain Early's company which half-rode, half-swam to Burnt Village on the morning of July 9. When Early reported signs of Indians in the morass beyond the Bark, Colonel Billy Hamilton crossed with his Menominee and made a wide circuit of the area. In the evening he brought back the information, accepted by Atkinson, that the Sauk had gone farther north beyond their daily range. But, once again Captain Early had seen imaginary signs.

Atkinson nevertheless abandoned pursuit and led his army back to the Rock River, where he established the base camp that became Fort Koshkonong (now Fort Atkinson), a few hundred yards south of the mouth of Bark River. Provisions had dwindled to practically nothing. Ordnance officers had caissons full of ammunition, including one hundred burnished cannon balls, but quartermaster personnel were doling out a handful of corn per man from the bottoms of the barrels. A lieutenant in Henry's brigade spoke for everyone when he wrote in his journal, "becoming quite discontented." Nearly one month had passed since the first volunteers of the second levy assembled at Fort Wilbourn, yet the only Sauk taken had been a foolish, blind old man.

On July 10 Atkinson had to disperse his army to avoid starvation. And on this same day General Scott landed with the first of his relief force in Chicago. The brigades of generals Henry and Alexander, accompanied by Colonel Dodge's rangers, were dispatched to Fort Winnebago so they could draw twelve days' rations and return to Koshkonong. Although the distance was thought to be thirty-six miles, it proved to be nearly twice that far. General Posey's brigade received marching orders for Fort Hamilton sixty miles west, with instructions to "remain there till further orders," in effect, placing the Shawneetown physician so far from rest of the army that his capacity for doing further harm was severely hampered.[5] Governor Reynolds's entourage slipped away to Fort Hamilton on the first leg of their homeward journey.

5. From Fort Hamilton, General Posey wrote Atkinson bitterly complaining that his provisions were inadequate, that his horses had broken down, and that his men wished to know whether their pay would be continued if they had to remain longer than their ninety-day enlistment. He had already lost half of his brigade through unauthorized departures.

Worried because the Illinois militia might walk off with muskets belonging to the State of Illinois, the Old Ranger wrote a letter advising Atkinson to attend to their collection at the end of the campaign. He then pushed on to Galena where, during a pause for refreshment at Swan's Tavern, he assured critics that Black Hawk was finished and that General Atkinson would accomplish the mission he was paid for "or leave his bones on the field of his labors." 6

Dwindling supplies gave Atkinson an excuse to discharge out-right large numbers of volunteers, who immediately departed for home. Among these was Private Abraham Lincoln, whose last official duty in the Black Hawk War was to write out Jacob Early's company roll for Lieutenant Robert Anderson. Lincoln traveled on foot with his messmate George Harrison because their horses had been stolen the night before. By hitching rides whenever they could find them, Harrison and Lincoln covered the two hundred miles to Peoria in five days. There they pooled their resources and bought a canoe. Lincoln carved a paddle from a plank, and they drifted down to Havana. Harrison later recalled that travel by canoe was slower than by foot. "We let her float all night and in the morning always found objects still visible that were beside us the previous evening." After selling the canoe in Havana, they crossed the burning prairie to New Salem. On July 19 the *Sangamo Journal* welcomed home Dr. Early's troops ("They have borne the heat and burthen of the day") and apologized to A. Lincoln for having failed to list him among the legislative candidates some weeks before. The mistake was a natural one—few people in the county had ever heard of him.

With the three brigades of ravenous and unruly volunteers no longer hanging about his neck, Atkinson could turn to those mili-

6. Within a few days of his return to Belleville, Reynolds had re-opened his correspondence with Secretary of War Lewis Cass, the princi-pal purpose of which was to obtain remuneration for his service in the war. "The privations and sufferings of the citizens I know as I have been nearly all the time on the frontier, or marching the Army since the middle part of April last." In order to squeeze the federal government for every possible penny, he listed July 16 as the date of his departure from Atkin-son's camp, an error in his favor by six days.

tary duties more natural to him—writing letters and building forts. Fort Koshkonong shot up like a toadstool in a five-acre clearing. The burr-oak stockade, eight feet in height, flanked by four blockhouses, and surrounded by a brush corral, required but five days to construct. The general, whose optimism had long since waned, ordered thirty days' provisions for three thousand men to be shipped to Fort Hamilton. Having abandoned his role as peacemaker among the Indian tribes, he sent Colonel Billy Hamilton to Green Bay with instructions to recruit two hundred Menominee, specifying however that these Indians were to operate in front of the army and "not throw themselves upon me in the rear." He informed General Winfield Scott that the enemy had probably withdrawn up the Rock "some thirty or forty miles" and warned that "the greatest difficulty in subduing him will be to come up with him, which is extremely doubtful unless he should stop to give us battle." Of the militia he wrote, "I have too many militia in the field to get along without great difficulty. They must be fed and supplies are difficult to be carried to the remote points we have to traverse." [7] He recommended dropping "at least a third or one half of them." Among other advice to General Scott, was to leave the artillery at Chicago.

One of the dispatches which arrived at Ford Koshkonong was an issue of the *National Intelligencer* that reprinted the speech of a Western senator who branded the regulars as the "sweepings of cities" and extolled the militia for being able to make fifty miles a day and subsist off the country. In the face of such a monumental lie, Atkinson's officers barely knew whether to laugh or rage.

Lacking stockade, blockhouses, and artillery, Fort Winnebago (Portage, Wisconsin) was less a military installation than an agency house and depot. Though it had been built after the

7. Feeding the militia proved to be as difficult as plugging a rathole. In the report on the war which he wrote for the Department of War in November, Atkinson blamed the militia for the breakup of his army: "but for the waste of provisions by the volunteers, and unavoidable losses in swimming rivers and the miring down of horses in creeks and swamps the supply would have been ample 'till the train of wagons arrived, although they were delayed, several days."

Winnebago War to intimidate the Indians of the region, the presence of dozens of bands, most of them Winnebago trying to get out of Black Hawk's path, camping round the whitewashed buildings had been intimidating the whites for several months. There were so many Indians about that Captain Joseph Plympton barely had room to hoist the Stars and Stripes in the morning; the best the whites could do by way of defense was to barricade themselves behind "venetian blinds and panel doors." Had the Winnebago so desired, they could have overrun the token garrison with little effort. The potential danger had begun to loom so great that, on July 4, all the women and children had been evacuated by boat to Fort Howard (Green Bay). All reports indicated that Black Hawk was moving toward Fort Winnebago, presumably intending to seek refuge in Chippeway country near the Canadian border.

Meanwhile, among the militia units bound for Fort Winnebago, a meaningless but nonetheless fierce competition developed to see which could arrive first. Henry Dodge's rangers won the race handily; but the brutal pace took its toll of the horses, already in poor condition after two weeks of hard campaigning and indifferent fodder. Dodge arrived on the evening of June 11; the next morning he set his men to baking bread for the brigades of James Henry and Milton Alexander, which arrived in late afternoon.

The horses, numbering as many as a thousand, were turned out to graze in the tall grass and wild peas near the portage.[8] The militia camped nearby. During the march from Koshkonong the horses had showed signs of skittishness, probably because they resented being driven so hard. In any case, after the militia turned in on the evening of July 12, the herd took alarm at something and stampeded through the campground. Lieutenant James Justice of Henry's brigade described what happened in his diary: "We were soon roused from our slumbers by the runing of the

8. There was a three-mile log causeway connecting the Wisconsin and Fox rivers (not to be confused with the Fox River at Ottawa, Illinois) over which small boats could be pulled. At this time the causeway provided the only water link between the Mississippi and the Great Lakes. Only when the rivers were swollen was the causeway not required.

horses which had taken a fright and were runing through our encampment with a nois equal to thinder and appearantly without regard to what should be before them and we were evidently in great danger of being run over and killed but fortuneately the horses passed through the encampment without hurting any person." Some of the animals dashed against the causeway and were killed; others doubled back and bore down on the camp a second time, scattering the Suckers like dry leaves in a gale. Great numbers galloped back down the trail toward Koshkonong. At first light a massive roundup began, which required two days to complete and entended over a thirty-mile area. Ninety horses were never found, and those recovered were in even worse condition than before. With surely unintended humor, Major W. L. D. Ewing of Henry's spy battalion informed Atkinson that the only horses not joining in the stampede were worthless nags "generally unfit anyway." The whites at the fort blamed the Winnebago for inciting the stampede. Nothing was ever proven, but it was certainly true that the Indians (and the regulars at Koshkonong, when they learned of it) enjoyed the Chemokemons' discomfiture enormously.

Every scrap of information collected at the Portage indicated that the British Band had set up camps near the Rock Rapids (present Hustisford), forty miles to the east. Pierre Paquette confirmed this and offered to guide the troops. Paquette was a strapping Winnebago entrepreneur with a fair share of French blood who traded with his people and hauled boats across the causeway. His strength was legendary in the Northwest (he had been known to put his own shoulder on the yoke when one of his oxen broke down). And his prosperity guaranteed his reliability to the whites. Moreover, Colonel Billy Hamilton, who was on his way to Green Bay, had done some investigating and guessed that the rumored location of the Sauk was about right. Either Dodge or Henry, the true instigator is yet in doubt, hit on the idea of returning to Fort Koshkonong by way of the Rock Rapids.[9] It

9. Wisconsin chroniclers say that Dodge engineered the plan; those of Illinois push Henry. The fullest account supports the Wisconsin claim. Charles Bracken, one of Dodge's rangers, wrote that Major James W. Stephenson of the Galena militia was employed to win Henry over to the

was even suggested that it might be possible to get above the Sauk and drive them to the south or west.

On July 14, the day before starting back to Koshkonong, a council of all officers captain and above, debated the plan. General Alexander absolutely refused to go on what was called "a wild goose chase after a Jack-o-lantern," adding that the expedition had not been authorized in Order No. 51, which had instructed the brigades to "draw twelve days' rations of provisions (exclusive of the subsistence of their respective commands during their stay at the fort) and return to these headquarters without delay." General Henry, on the other hand, swore that he would hunt the Sauk alone if he could recruit fifty men to follow him, and the caucus of Henry's brigade ratified his plan. Unmounted or backsliding men could accompany Alexander's brigade back to Fort Koshkonong. Then Lieutenant Colonel Jeremiah Smith of James Fry's regiment circulated a petition declaring their unwillingness to hunt Black Hawk among Henry's officers. This was submitted to Henry, who ordered every officer whose name appeared on the paper placed under arrest and escorted to Koshkonong for trial. Since the general himself was the mutineer, this order was a preposterous bluff, but it worked. Within a quarter of an hour the petition had been withdrawn. Some of the officers apologized personally, their eyes streaming with tears. The general reinstated everyone, even Colonel Smith, who argued somewhat implausibly that he had not known what the petition contained when he signed it.

On Sunday afternoon (July 15) the militia broke camp at Fort Winnebago. Alexander's brigade, with the castoffs from Henry's set off to rejoin Atkinson. Their horses were packed so high with rations that they bore a vague resemblance to camels. At the same time General Henry, with about 600 hand-picked men, and Colonel Dodge with 150 struck out for the rapids of the

---

plan. ("Between Henry and Stephenson the closest intimacy existed; they had been arraigned together at Edwardsville for a high crime [whipping the slave Jarrett?], of which, however, they had been honorably acquitted.") My guess is that Henry (a man of small imagination) had to be convinced, but, once convinced, nothing could swerve him from pursuing that route back to Atkinson.

Rock. This elite corps, guided by Pierre Paquette and a dozen Winnebago, had vowed to give the Sauk the very Jessee. They were barely out of sight before the Negro servants belonging to the regular officers at Fort Winnebago began to sprinkle drops of cologne water about the mess room and quarters "to sweeten up after them milish officers" who had converted the barracks into a pigsty.

More potent disinfectants would shortly be required in Wisconsin and Illinois. A portent of what was to come is found in a headline in the *Sangamo Journal* for July 5 which read, "Cholera in Canada!" Immediately above was printed an announcement that an expedition under General Winfield Scott had been organized to terminate the Sauk War. But now Scott's army was battling for its life against an enemy more deadly than Black Hawk.

TEN *The Plague*

The dead bodies of deserters are literally strewed
along the road, between here and Detroit.
No one dares give them relief, not even a cup of
water. A person on his way from Detroit here,
passed six lying groaning with the agonies
of the cholera, under one tree, and saw one corpse
by the road side, half eaten up by the hogs.
        —*Niles' Weekly Register*

❮❮❮

IN WASHINGTON, President Andrew Jackson had lost, by mid-June, all confidence in the capacity of General Atkinson to end the war with the Sauk. At best the "Hero of Horseshoe Bend" had an undisguised contempt for Indians (his Indian policy was probably the most tyrannical in American history); but 1832 was an especially bad year, an election year. Pressed as he was by such "snarling partisans" as Henry Clay and John C. Calhoun (Henry Atkinson was a Calhoun protégé), Jackson could ill afford the embarrassments of bungled frontier squabbles. From the perspective of nearly a thousand miles, Atkinson seemed to be doing nothing except spend money. Over $150,000 had already been spent to bring Black Hawk to his knees; yet it appeared twice that amount would be required in the coming weeks to compel the old Hawk to release his grip. Unable to account for Atkinson's backwardness (several dispatches, including a report on the Stillman debacle, had failed to reach Washington), General Alexander Macomb prepared to throw his Western general to the political wolves.

The culmination came on June 12 when the *National Intelligencer,* an opposition sheet, announced ominously that "the whole frontier was in a complete state of alarm and confusion." Within hours a decision had been reached to replace General Atkinson. On that day John Robb, acting secretary of war, sent a hectoring letter to Atkinson, who was at that moment gathering militia at Ottawa for a second attempt, which said, among other things, "someone is to blame in this matter, but upon whom it is to fall, is at present unknown." Lest his innuendo be unclear, Robb enclosed a note which he had just received:

You will by way of postscript say to Genl Atkinson, that the Black Hawk & his party must be chastized and a speedy & honorable termination put to this war. . . .

Yrs.
A.J.

The letter was less an ultimatum than a document for the file, for three days later General Winfield Scott received orders to assume command of all troops in the field, although Atkinson, of course, remained in command until Scott arrived. Secretary Lewis Cass, who had resumed his desk at the War Department, gave the new commander extraordinary powers: He could enter any department for troops and call upon whatever militia resources he required. One sentence in Cass's letter to Scott made the government's attitude toward the Indian perfectly clear: "It is very desirable that the whole country between Lake Michigan and the Mississippi, and south of the Ouisconsin, should be freed from the Indians." This included not just Sauk, but allies such as the Potawatomie and Winnebago as well.

Though Andrew Jackson had little patience with the Whiggish politics and the prissy mannerisms of Winfield Scott, he was said at the moment to be even more out of sorts with General Edmund P. Gaines, the head of the Western Department, because that general disagreed with his policy of removing all Indians west of the Mississippi. Jackson's and Scott's was the natural antipathy that existed between Tennessee hill-country men and Virginia quasigentlemen: The one looked forward to what would be, the other back to what never was, but ought to have been. Jackson was suspicious of generals who required, even during a hard campaign, a hot bath every other day. And there was also an ugly story circulating in the army that Scott had once dismissed an aide-de-camp for failing to identify a quotation from Dryden. Such airs were intolerable. On his side, Scott looked with ill-concealed contempt upon the antics of a president who, in response to a mild French request beginning, "je demande . . ," shouted irritably, "No Frenchman tells *me* what to do!" Democracy, to Scott, meant backwoods rowdies and Tammany mobs. It had come almost as a personal affront to each that the other had emerged from the War of 1812 revered by his men and acclaimed by the nation as a hero.

The natural antipathy between them had come to a head in 1817 when Scott commented to DeWitt Clinton that Jackson's controversial campaign in West Florida, a filibustering raid, really, had so exceeded instructions that it was "mutinous." Jackson challenged Scott to a duel, but the Virginian begged off by pleading religious scruples against dueling. A lively exchange of letters, characterized by Scott's rhetoric on the one side and Jackson's illiteracies on the other, ended with a long period of strained silence between the two. (In the long run, Old Hickory came off somewhat better, for Scott was lambasted in the press as a hypocrite after he issued a challenge, in defiance of his scruples, to Clinton for having promulgated a deliberate falsehood.) For all this, no one doubted, least of all Jackson, that beneath the fuss and feathers there was a soldier's soldier. In the words of his biographer, the forty-six year old general, solidly molded on a six-foot frame, could be depended on "to handle regulars, volunteers, settlers, and Indians with satisfaction to all concerned—except possibly the Indians."

With astonishing efficiency General Scott collected in New York nine companies of coastal artillery, outfitted as infantry, drawn from the harbor installations at Hampton Roads, Baltimore, and New York. In what soon proved to be a serious mistake, he also assimilated a motley gang of 208 recruits undergoing training at Fort Columbus, New York; among these was a disproportionate share of petty thieves, drunkards, country-bred rustics, and immigrants, gathered together by recruiting sergeants more concerned with filling quotas than with finding suitable men. Already a contingent from Fort Niagara was in transit to Chicago,[1] and Scott was to pick up the remaining companies from that fort as he passed through Detroit. The whole garrison at Baton Rouge, except one company, received orders to move immediately to the assistance of Atkinson. In all, General Scott planned to transfer about one thousand regulars to the scene of the hostilities. These were to be joined by six companies of mounted rangers, a mobile assault force authorized by Congress on June 15 for "the defense of the frontier," as soon as they could be recruited in the Western states. This was a battalion funded by the federal government in lieu of cavalry; Henry Dodge became its first commanding officer.

Before departing from New York, Scott received a warning from an army surgeon that an epidemic of Asiatic cholera was expected in the United States. Originating in the Ganges area in 1826, the disease had reached Western Europe by 1831, and it was feared that emigrants would carry it to North America, probably by way of Canada. Physicians believed that cholera was an aerial poison like malaria, though many had observed that it was not necessarily transmitted by contact with or proximity to the diseased. That the disease was spread through contaminated water and food had not yet been discovered. General Scott was told that only dissolute persons needed to fear the disease, a folk belief so solidly welded to the prevailing work ethic that, when cholera struck New York City, the citizenry demanded that grogshops and whorehouses be shut down in order to arrest

1. The force consisted of two companies under Major William Whistler, proceeding under an order issued in February to reactivate Fort Dearborn, which had been abandoned the year before. On June 17 Whistler's force arrived at Fort Dearborn and expelled John R. Williams's Michigan militia. (General Scott would absorb this garrison, even though they were not part of his call up.) Major Whistler, a thirty-year veteran of Western service, had assisted his father, Captain John Whistler, in the construction of Fort Dearborn in 1803. Major Whistler retired from the army in 1861 after sixty years of service, believed to be a record.

His nephew (son of George Washington Whistler, a West Pointer who later supervised construction of the St. Petersburg-Moscow Railroad), James McNeill Whistler doubtless shares with Edgar Allan Poe the distinction of being West Point's most famous dropout.

the epidemic. Further, Scott was briefed on the accepted methods of treating the disease: tartar emetic to counter vomiting, opium to control diarrhea, calomel to increase the flow of bile.[2] What he was not told, because the board of health was suppressing the information, was that the plague had already appeared in New York.[3] In all likelihood, his contingent of Fort Columbus recruits had already been exposed and would spread it among the regulars.

Within a week of the mobilization order the newly created Northwestern Army was steaming up the Hudson on its way to the Black Hawk War. Scott stopped at West Point to pick up twenty-nine cadets of the mediocre Class of 1832 who had volunteered for the expedition, delighted by the opportunity to step from parade ground to field of battle. Among these were: John Macomb, son of the commanding general; Jacob Brown, son of a former general in chief; George Crittenden, a future Confederate general from Kentucky; and Randolph Marcy, a career officer later overshadowed by his son-in-law George B. McClellan. The most distinguished career officer of the class, Erasmus Keys, chose to remain behind with fifteen other pariahs.

After a gallant farewell to his wife and daughters, whom he had sent to the Point for their safety, Scott's expedition, numbering between 700 to 850 men, steamed on to Albany and crossed

2. During the epidemic, "specifics" for combatting the disease proliferated. The following was tried at West Point: "3 drachms oyster shells, 2 drachms pulverized gum arabic, 2 drachms white sugar, 4 drops of oil of cinnamon, ½ oz. paragoric, 1 drachm lavender compound, 4 oz. water. Dose—Tablespoon every hour or so. Shake well before using, and will not keep more than a few days in hot weather." Among the poor, powdered rhubarb was the usual nostrum.

3. After eleven deaths had announced the presence of the disease on July 5, a member of the board resigned and denounced his fellows for withholding information about earlier cases for fear that business might suffer. Forty years later, when an official investigation of the epidemic was undertaken, it was found that the pertinent records for April, May, and June of 1832 had vanished from the files. An estimated one-third of the population fled New York City in July and August. The situation was so grave that President Jackson called for a day of prayer. By October about thirty-five hundred had died, a high percentage of which were inmates of hospitals and almshouses.

to the Great Lakes by the Erie Canal. Though few knew it, cholera was seeping through the entire region. At Plattsburgh emigrants had been turned back into Canada at gunpoint; Scott's boats were among the last to pass through the canal before it was shut down in a futile effort to prevent the epidemic from spreading westward.

Upon reaching Buffalo on June 26, Scott required only a week to locate and charter, for $5,500 apiece, four lake steamers to transport his army to Chicago. The *Henry Clay* had recently been used in transporting emigrants to the West, but the captain had had the vessel disinfected with chloride of lime. Scott boldly (or ignorantly) chose the *Clay* as his flagship and set off with the *Sheldon Thompson* on July 2. The other boats, the *Superior* and the *William Penn* were scheduled to sail a few days later carrying provisions, munitions, and equipment. Somewhere on Lake Erie the general posted his first order, a breezy prohibition of "all mutilating and scalping of prisoners, or the bodies of the enemy who may be killed in action." Winfield Scott believed in fighting a clean war and had no time for frontier barbarities.

The *Henry Clay* won the inevitable steamboat race to Detroit, tying up at the wharf in the evening of July 4. Ashore were two companies from Fort Niagara waiting to be picked up. They had been quartered in a brick warehouse along the river, a district abounding in grogshops, and nearly all were drunk. Meanwhile two recruits on the *Clay* had developed unmistakable cholera symptoms—vomiting, diarrhea, blackened features. Horrified, the port authorities demanded that the boat anchor offshore and refused permission for anyone to come ashore. But they were too late. Messengers from the Fort Niagara companies had already inadvertently carried the plague back to the warehouse from which it later spread to the city.[4]

4. Or so it was alleged. By July 6 the messengers had been stricken and were dead; the city authorities demanded that the companies leave Detroit. On July 9 they boarded the *William Penn,* despite the obvious ravages of the disease among them, but were dropped off at Fort Gratiot to prevent contamination of the boat. (The Fort Niagara surgeon deserted his men and took to his room at Woodward's Hotel.) One quarter of them (twenty-one men) died of the disease. According to a Detroit physician of

When the *Sheldon Thompson* arrived off Detroit a few hours later, Captain Augustus Walker found, to his surprise, the *Clay* anchored near Hog Island (present Belle Isle). Since Walker reported no illness aboard his boat, other than seasickness, Scott transferred his staff, a crack artillery company, and about half of the West Pointers to the *Thompson*. This relieved the crowding aboard the *Clay*, a smaller boat, but it might be argued that Scott had left the recruits to their fate. It smacked of elitism, and doubtless was. Both boats got under way for Mackinac on the morning of July 5. A discretionary order permitted the *Clay* to make an emergency landing on deserted Bois Blanc Island in Lake Huron, should the epidemic get out of hand. By that time two victims had died and had been thrown overboard.

Conditions in both boats were wretched. The July sun beat down on glazed water, and the boilers, located above decks, were as hot as furnaces. Sanitary facilities were primitive: Men drank water from open hogsheads out of a communal tin cup. To catch a gulp of fresh air, they queued up at the bow. Queasy men vomited and defecated wherever they could. Even the officers' deck, was "crowded almost to suffocation," recalled one sufferer. Since the *Thompson* sat so low in the water that the skipper feared the boat would swamp when they reached Lake Huron, he insisted that some companies be dropped off at Fort Gratiot,[5] a post at the head of the St. Clair River, seventy miles from

that time, sixteen cholera cases were ferried ashore from the *Clay*, of which eleven died before morning. It is more likely that these patients were among the Fort Niagara group, for other sources state that the city quarantined Scott's flagship.

By July 18 there were fifty-eight cases of cholera at Detroit and the upper story of the capitol had been converted into a hospital. After passing a law dealing with sanitation and quarantine, the city council fled.

5. The fort was built by and named for Charles Gratiot, brother of the Winnebago agent. The sixteenth graduate of West Point (Class of 1806), the Missouri-born Gratiot rose rapidly in the Corps of Engineers until he had become brevet brigadier general and chief engineer of the U.S. Army in 1828. In 1838 he was dismissed from service by order of President Martin Van Buren on a charge of mishandling public funds. For the remaining seventeen years of his life, Gratiot sought to clear his name and to become reinstated, but without success. At the time of his death he was a clerk in the General Land Office at Washington.

Detroit. Scott landed two companies there, then plunged ahead to Mackinac without checking on the *Clay*, which lagged far behind.

The situation aboard the *Henry Clay* worsened by the hour. So many soldiers were falling ill that the crew demanded that they turn back and could barely be compelled to perform their duties. Dr. Josiah Everett, head surgeon of the Northwestern Army, warned the military commander, Lieutenant Colonel David Twiggs, that the epidemic would sweep away everyone unless they landed and isolated the stricken; but Twiggs, a literal-minded Georgian, regarded in the army as a brutal disciplinarian, insisted upon making Bois Blanc Island.[6] For reasons never explained, the steamer required two days to reach the St. Clair River. (Perhaps Twiggs stopped each time one of the recruits jumped overboard and attempted to swim to land.) The captain of the *Clay* subsequently noted that "the disease had become so violent and alarming on board of her that nothing like discipline could be observed." Under these deteriorating circumstances, Twiggs decided to disembark his men at Fort Gratiot, though it hurt him to do so.

A drenching rain had begun to fall as the *Clay* edged toward the dock at Fort Gratiot on July 7. Even before the steamer had come to rest, the recruits spilled ashore, deaf to shouted commands which many of them, through ignorance of English, did not understand anyway. In the rain, great numbers fled to nearby woods and fields in a desperate race to put the cholera behind them. Those already weakened by the disease crawled along the river bank seeking a place to die. Leaving these "traitors" where they dropped, Colonel Twiggs moved his three seasoned com-

6. As commander of Fort Winnebago two years earlier, Twiggs acquired an unsavory reputation as martinet. To punish a soldier who threatened his life, Twiggs trussed him is chains and hauled him about as though he were a piece of luggage. Yet in battle he was a tiger. Congress voted him a sword for his role in storming Monterey in 1846. A Southerner to the core, General Twiggs surrendered his force and stores to the State of Texas prior to the outbreak of the Civil War and was cashiered from the army. Unfazed, Twiggs accepted the rank of major general in the Confederate Army. Had he not died in 1862, he would probably have been tried for treason after the war.

panies and those recruits still within his command to a sandy bluff south of the fort. In order to avert contamination of the log fort, he set up camp in the open. For half a century the tongue of land on which Twigg's men at out the epidemic would be called locally Cholera Point. Before the *Clay* had been unloaded, two crew members were stricken by the disease. Eventually three died before the captain reached Buffalo where the boat was thoroughly disinfected.

For two days it rained, and the men lay under soggy blankets because field equipment had been stored on the supply boats bringing up the rear of the expedition. Cases of cholera broke out among otherwise healthy soldiers, contradicting the widely held notion that only profligates succumbed to the disease. Panic swept even the seasoned troops after Lieutenant Joseph Clay collapsed and died within six hours on July 8. Desertion became so rampant that Twiggs ringed the camp with armed guards, who also vanished. Men seemed to be drowning in rain, vomit, and defecation. Dr. Everett induced Twiggs to appropriate a log shed near the barracks as a hospital, but the colonel refused to occupy the fort, fearing the place might be contaminated permanently.

The garrison and the two companies that Scott had disembarked meanwhile moved down the St. Clair River thirteen miles and escaped the epidemic.

By July 10, out of a command originally numbering 360 men, Twiggs had lost 175 through desertion and about 55 from cholera. The loss was greatest among the raw recruits, of whom only 23 out of 208 remained on duty at Cholera Point. How many of the deserters eventually returned to duty is not known. A letter from Detroit printed in *Niles' Weekly Register* recounted all that is known: "Of the deserters, scattered all over the country, some have died in the woods, and their bodies have been devoured by the wolves. . . . Straggling survivors are occasionally seen marching, some of them know not whither, with their knapsacks on their backs, shunned by the terrified inhabitants." For years after hunters of the region came upon bits of bone, straps and belts, and buttons marked "USA," in woods and ditches.

With shotguns, settlers kept the fugitives at bay and denied them food or water lest the contagion spread to them. Sick men would have received scant sympathy among a population terrorized by the epidemic. In southern Michigan, those militia units called out in May to halt the advance of Black Hawk from the West threw up barricades on the roads to turn back stages and travelers from the East. Even Governor Stevens Thomson Mason was apprehended by a sheriff as he tried to sneak past a village while on an official journey to the western regions of the territory. The inexplicable behavior of the epidemic added to its terrible effect upon those who believed it a visitation by an inscrutable deity. The plague skipped over Ypsilanti and Ann Arbor, but decimated the village of Marshall nearby.

Dr. Everett contracted the disease and died. Twiggs himself came down with it, but recovered. His last order at Cholera Point authorized the sixteen West Pointers on duty with him to flee for their lives. They commandeered a boat, returned to Detroit, and dispersed for home. This option, however, was not available to the other soldiers who were victims both of the cholera and Colonel Twiggs's maniacal rage for obedience. Two-thirds of his command was finally wiped out by death or desertion.

Oblivious to the desolation behind him, General Winfield Scott steamed on to Fort Mackinac where, during a brief fueling stop, three soldiers and two crewmen came down with the vomiting and diarrhea. After dropping them off at the steamboat agency (three of them later died), the *Sheldon Thompson* set off again for Chicago on July 8. At dawn of the next day, as they passed the Manitou Islands in Lake Michigan, six violent cases had developed among the troops. The symptoms, ever the same, were described by an officer who survived an attack of the disease:

I was thrown down on the deck almost as suddenly as if shot. As I was walking on the lower deck I felt my legs growing stiff from my knees downward. I went on the upper deck and walked violently to keep up a circulation of the blood. I felt suddenly a rush of blood from my feet upwards, and as it rose, my veins grew cold and my blood curdled. I was seized with a nausea at the stomach and a desire to vomit. My legs and hands were cramped with violent pain. The doctor gave me 8 grains of opium and made me rub my legs as fast as I could; he also made me drink a tumbler and a half of raw brandy, and told me if I did not throw up the opium I would certainly be relieved. I did not throw it up and was relieved, but not until I had had a violent spasm. The pain is excruciating.

Except for prescribing opium, the surgeon proved useless for he was as frightened as everyone else. Instead of ministering to the sick he "gulped down half a bottle of wine, went to bed sick, and ought to have died," Scott wrote later.[7]

With safety valve wedged shut, the *Sheldon Thompson* pounded and plunged toward Chicago in a race against death. Beyond Mackinac there was nothing but woods and water, a three-hundred-mile virgin emptiness without town, clearing, or woodpile. Packed and stinking of hot metal, blistered paint, and human offal, the *Sheldon Thompson* rattled into a watery void where no other steamboat had ventured before. With his usual scorn for physical danger, General Scott tried to calm his men by exposing himself everywhere on the boat. And when opium and calomel failed to arrest the disease, the general bent over the victims and commanded them to recover. He vanquished the panic that surged barely under control, but the plague spread furiously throughout the boat. Thirteen men, wrapped in their weighted blankets and lashed with cordage went overboard. The sergeant who supervised the first burial was himself heaved over six hours later.

During the evening of July 10 (the day Atkinson dispersed his militia brigades at Koshkonong), the lighthouse at Chicago came into view, then a fleet of schooners, and finally the low bulk of Fort Dearborn beyond the sandspit blocking the Chicago River. It was a flat, desolate, and cheerless place. Beyond the dunes, backlighted by the glaring western sky, lay a dozen log hutments and two frame houses. The populace crowded down to the beach (there was no dock), but scattered when Captain Walker shouted

7. The names of the surgeons accompanying the expedition are known; but, since at least four of them resigned or were forced to resign after the Black Hawk War, the identity of the one execrated by General Scott cannot be ascertained. This was the second instance of a surgeon with the expedition being charged with dereliction in the performance of his duties.

that there was cholera aboard. The schooners at anchor promptly hoisted sail and stood out to sea. Lieutenant Edwin Sumner went ashore in the yawl [8] and ordered the evacuation of the fort by sunrise in order to set up his hospital. Before Scott could disembark his troops, three more died and were dropped overboard during the night. In the morning the unwholesome sight of the dead men, plainly visible in three fathoms of pellucid water, obliged Captain Walker to shift anchor.

Although his crew had become mutinous, it took the master of the *Sheldon Thompson* four days to get off from Chicago because no fuel could be found. Eventually he bought a roofless log barn and three-acre fence which his men chopped up and loaded on board to fire the boilers. The captain recalled that, when he issued the order to hoist anchor, the crew "seemed almost frantic with joy."

Within a week of their arrival at Chicago 55 of the 190 men who landed were dead and 65 others were convalescent. Fort Dearborn had become a stinking charnel house. The dead were dragged out and buried on a dune near the lighthouse (today the northwest corner of Lake Street and Wabash Avenue) with the sand shoveled out to cover one body providing a hole for the next. Men seized with the initial symptoms begged comrades not to allow them to be buried alive, but many were. Lieutenant Humphrey Marshall of Kentucky, one of the recent cadets, wrote a classmate at West Point that he had witnessed scenes "as are sufficient to rack the senses of a devil." Three of Scott's aides, among them Captain James Monroe, nephew of the former president, showed symptoms of the disease and were ordered to the East for safety. All the recent cadets in Scott's charge were sent home; but release came too late for Lieutenant Franklin McDuffee of New Hampshire, the only member of the class of 1832 to die in the Black Hawk War. Aboard the *Thompson*,

8. Twenty-eight years later, after Twiggs had defected, Sumner succeeded him as one of the three regular army brigadiers. During the Civil War he became the oldest, at sixty-five, corps commander in the Union Army. Another young lieutenant aboard the *Thompson* was Joseph E. Johnston, a West Point-trained artillerist who rose to the rank of general in the Confederate Army.

McDuffee had run up a bill and the steward drew in his account book a coffin, on the lid which was written, "Account settled by Death." [9]

Within two days of Scott's arrival, Chicago had become a ghost town. All the back-country folk who had stampeded to the security of Fort Dearborn during the Sauk panic now fled into the wilderness "with more precipitate haste and terror from the deadly pestilence," recorded the Reverend Stephen Beggs. The Indian agent Colonel Thomas Owen left so hurriedly with his family that dinner dishes remained neatly arranged on the table. This thorough evacuation of the town allowed Major Whistler's garrison, many of whom had families with them, to occupy Beaubien's Tavern and other vacant edifices. Less fortunate than most was Lieutenant James W. Penrose who had brought with him from Fort Niagara his mother, two sisters, his wife, and their four-month-old son. The Penrose ménage had to camp in the corner of a rail fence with carpets spread over them to keep off the wind and rain. Mrs. Penrose never forgave General Scott, not for evicting them, she understood that, but because each day he rode by, looked in, and observed that they were more comfortable than his own family, exiled to the rigors of West Point. (The infant at her breast, William H. Penrose, later became a brigadier general under Sheridan during the Civil War.) Scott's quarantine, however, prevented the epidemic from spreading to the Dearborn garrison, which camped along the beach eight miles away.

The official report on the Black Hawk War prepared by General Alexander Macomb in November puffily noted that only eighteen days had been required to transport the Northwestern Army a distance of eighteen hundred miles, "a rapidity which is believed to be unprecedented in military movements." But Scott

9. Only one other officer, Lieutenant Gustavus Brown (West Point, class of 1829), died at Chicago. The master of the steamboat later wrote, "There was one singular fact—not one of the officers of the army was attacked by the disease, while on board my boat, with such violence as to result in death." This was not singular at all. The officers were billeted apart from the soldiers, drank from their own containers, and ate at the captain's table food from a separate commissary. Death was not very democratic, in this instance.

himself felt no elation at the brilliance of his maneuver. Out of the more than 700 men sailing from Buffalo, only 135 were on duty in Chicago. The epidemic proved to be the most formidable enemy "Old Fuss and Feathers" ever met. Years later he told a Chicagoan that "he had never felt his entire helplessness and need of Divine Providence as he did upon the lakes in the midst of the Asiatic cholera" because he could not "storm his works, fortify against him, nor cut his way out, nor make terms of capitulation."

Although Scott was anxious to cross the eighty-mile swath of prairie and join Atkinson at Koshkonong, he felt morally bound to remain with his men, even though he could do little for them. On July 12 he informed Atkinson of the catastrophe and conjectured that he would not be able to set off from Chicago for ten days at the earliest. Even were his soldiers fit, they would have to wait for the other vessels bringing up their field equipment. What had happened to them, he could not say.[10] For the moment, he wrote, "Our prospects are deplorable."

In the meantime, it was up to Atkinson to continue the war against Black Hawk. Through a grisly irony, the cholera provided that doomed commander with a last chance to redeem himself by an eleventh-hour victory. His task in the days ahead was not just to overtake Black Hawk but to keep General Scott from overtaking him.

Weeks later, when the Sauk learned of the plague raging among the Chemokemons, they expressed neither surprise nor satisfaction. Long before, the Prophet had told them that, if the white man dared make war against the Sauk nation, they would be struck dead by the arm of the Great Spirit. Clearly, this had happened, according to prophecy.

10. The *William Penn* reached Chicago about a week later with the two companies that had been dropped off by Scott at Fort Gratiot. No cases of cholera had developed. The *Henry Clay* and the *Superior* had turned back, the latter without explanation or apology. Fearing that the Illinois militia would run off when they learned of the epidemic, Scott wrote Governor Reynolds on July 15 to assure him that the quarantine at Chicago would be maintained until the disease had spent itself.

> . . . the battles of "Ouisconsin Heights" and the
> "Bad Axe River" will never be forgotten, until the
> present generation should have passed away, and
> the memory of traditionary tales be dead among them.
> Those two battles . . . secured lasting renown
> to the whole army, and exalted the character
> of the state.
> —Governor Reynolds's address to the legislature, 1832

◄◄◄

GENERAL ATKINSON received Scott's letter announcing the cholera epidemic on July 16. On the same day, thirty-six wagons piled high with provisions arrived at Fort Koshkonong. Once again the general was obliged to launch some sort of campaign against Black Hawk, but he had only befogged notions of what to do and where to go. He had lost his last remaining shreds of confidence in the militia to do much of anything besides cram their gullets with pork and whiskey. The bold and resourceful frontiersmen pictured in Western folklore and Eastern penny novels were unfortunately not much in evidence among his troops. Even the independent spirit of the frontiersman seemed to have degenerated into nothing more positive than a snarling anarchy. The Jacksonian revolution had perverted the frontier ideal of democracy into a search for personal gain at public expense.

Within hours after the wagon train reached the fort, the first pack horses from the Portage also began to come in. There were now so many provisions that they had to be stacked in the fort, exposed to the elements; there most remained, rotting and picked over by Winnebago bands, long after the whites had vanished from the region.

For the next two days General Alexander's rag-bag column straggled in. They could easily have been the models for a lithograph entitled "The Forlorn Hope: Return from Moscow." With horses lame, men exhausted, muskets missing, clothes tattered, they looked as though they had been thrashed by a vastly superior army. They, in fact, had seen no hostile Indians. Great droves of them tramped past the fort on their way home, having decided that fighting Black Hawk was futile.

Whether General Atkinson was distressed by the information that Henry and Dodge had struck out on their own for the Rock Rapids is not known. There was certainly nothing in his instructions to either commander to authorize this foray, which might easily culminate in a second Stillman's Run.[1] Yet there was little that he himself could do except push up the Rock to join them. Leaving a company of regulars under Captain Gideon Low in charge of his depot (with instructions for militia units in the vicinity to remain outside the fort unless it came under attack), Atkinson rode off with Zachary Taylor's regiment and Milton Alexander's brigade on July 19, following, for reasons no one ever fathomed, the same route up the south bank of the Bark River which had bogged them down two weeks before.

Their objective was to break into the marshy wedge of land lying between the Rock and the Bark rivers, the "muddy triangle," as the regulars called it. The "trembling lands" were as quaky and bottomless as ever. After proceeding only ten miles in the rain, they made camp. The men were soaked and campfires barely smoldered. A tempest blew during the night; it turned tents inside out and stampeded the horses. Lieutenant

1. In his official report on the war, Atkinson foxily wrote that the brigades dispatched to Fort Winnebago had been "instructed to pursue the enemy should they fall upon his trail in either going or returning." Thereby he took part of the credit for Henry's discovery and pursuit of the British Band. This ignores a more important question, however: Were the militia authorized to search for Black Hawk or merely to pursue him if found?

Philip Cooke, who shared Atkinson's tent, was aroused by a "rushing, rumbling sound as of an earthquake" and saw on all sides the "glaring eyeballs and arched necks of hundreds of horses" as they galloped through the campground. A messmate leaped into a tree as the animals rushed under him, brushing his legs. For General Alexander's brigade this was the second stampede within a week; many of his men were foot soldiers thereafter. It was universally believed that the Winnebago scouts provoked the stampede, which must have made Atkinson wonder whether they were in fact leading him away from the supposed Sauk camp.

Based upon a compilation of notes from White Crow and other Winnebago, the staff had prepared a sketch which purported to show the exact position of Black Hawk's stronghold, although, to the eyes of at least one officer, it more nearly resembled "the schoolboy puzzle of the walls of Troy." Nevertheless, on the morning of July 20, two expresses from Henry and Dodge burst into camp with electrifying news. The trail of the British Band had been discovered. They were breaking out of the swamp and moving westward toward the Mississippi, with Henry and Dodge in close pursuit. The dispatch from the Sangamon general concluded, with his customary peroration, "This movement I hope will meet your entire approbation." Here was the stroke of luck that Atkinson had been praying for. Back he rushed to Koshkonong.

After a three-day swing to the north, to comb the tributaries of the Fox River, General Henry's column dropped down to the Rock Rapids, logged by a militia diarist as "a very barrony place." Here they found some Indian families who claimed to be good Winnebago, but who aroused suspicion. Each had a different story as to the whereabouts of the Sauk, and one of the squaws was wearing the dress of a white woman, with a hole in it, which some suggested was a bullet hole, near the waist seam. Whether this dress had been stripped from a victim of the Indian Creek massacre they never learned. In any case, General Henry decided, even though it might be an absolute fabrication, to investigate their report that Black Hawk was at Cranberry Lake, twenty miles farther up the Rock.

Colonel Dodge immediately wrote Atkinson, suggesting the propriety of moving the army to the rapids. At two o'clock in the afternoon of July 18 this letter was sent off in the care of W. W. Woodbridge, a Pecatonica veteran, and Dr. E. H. Merryman of Springfield.[2] Guided by Little Thunder, a Winnebago scout, they expected to cover the twenty-five miles to Fort Koshkonong by nightfall. About ten miles from the rapids, the messengers chanced upon a fresh trail in the brush, which the whites assumed had been made by scouts from Fort Koshkonong. Two miles further on Little Thunder whirled his hores around and, without a word of explanation, headed back toward the rapids as though the devil were after him. Gripped by the same fear, although without knowing the cause, Merryman and Wood-bridge spurred after him, but fell far behind. Badly brush-whipped by hawthorne and prickly ash, the whites burst into Henry's camp at dusk, and were nearly killed by a rattled sentry who fortunately happened to be a poor shot. Little Thunder had already arrived and was explaining to Pierre Paquette that he had found the trail of the British Band making to the southwest. Great quantities of edible bark had been stripped from trees, evidence of large parties suffering from hunger.

General Henry prepared to take up the pursuit at daylight, ordering that vehicles and encumbrances be left behind. The men ransacked the five supply wagons, each taking what he would need for a forced march. News of the fresh trail, a participant remembered, "seemed to give new life to every heart." The same three messengers again set off for Fort Koshkonong on July 19 (the day that Atkinson began his march into the "trem-

2. An epidemic of dueling swept Illinois in the early 1840s. In June 1842 Abraham Lincoln chose Dr. Merryman to serve as his second when challenged by James Shields, a long-time political adversary offended by a lampoon. The altercation was settled peacefully, however, and the two men became friends. But Merryman quarreled with Shields's second, General Sam Whiteside. In October Whiteside challenged Merryman to meet him in St. Louis to resolve the affair, and the doctor selected Lincoln as his second. This spat, too, was settled without recourse to pistol or cutlass.

bling lands"), carrying, in addition to Dodge's letter, Henry's account of their discovery and his declaration of intent to pursue the enemy. Henry was a man who acted when necessary, straightening out the interlocking chain of responsibility later.

Pushed from their camps on Lake Koshkonong, which abounded in pike, bass, and catfish, the British Band found splendid hiding places in the mucky wilderness east of the Rock River, but almost nothing to eat.[3] Black Hawk described their worsening situation: "We were forced to dig *roots* and *bark trees,* to obtain something to satisfy hunger and keep us alive! Several of our old people became so much reduced, as actually to *die with hunger!* And, finding that the army had commenced moving, and fearing that they might come upon and surround our encampment, I concluded to remove my women and children across the Mississippi." Many of his followers, particularly those with familial links to the Winnebago, had already slipped away. Surrender was out of the question—Stillman's Run had proven that. What probably alarmed the war chief most of all, however, was the movement of the militia to Fort Winnebago, which he doubtless interpreted as a maneuver to encircle him. With his enemy the Menominee to the north, the blue coats to the south, Lake Michigan to the east, and the militia to the west, Black Hawk resolved to break out of the box before the lid could be clamped shut. He intended to cross to Four Lakes and descend the Wisconsin River to the Mississippi; with luck he could dodge the Prairie du Chien garrison and the Sioux-infested territory on the far shore of the great river. In a brilliantly scouted movement, the British Band emerged from the swamp just before Atkinson and Henry closed the gap between them, at some point crossing the trace that Alexander had followed, only hours before, on his way back to Koshkonong from the Portage. Had his people not stripped bark from the trees in their passage, the

3. The location of his last hideaway in Wisconsin has never been ascertained, but the lakes near present Oconomowoc would be a reasonable guess. It is likely that the main body crossed the Rock near Watertown during their breakout. With ditching, damming, and draining, the hydrography of the region has been drastically altered since Black Hawk's day.

Chemokemons might have continued wallowing in the swamp for days.

General Henry's order on Thursday morning (July 19) to take up pursuit of the Sauk met with whoops of jubilation among the militia. All gloom and grumbling disappeared. Men who had been complaining about their broken-down nags now boasted of what splendid steeds they had, so that they would not be debarred from the hunt. Lieutenant James Justice summarized the mood in his diary: "The soldiers had begun to dispair of ever seeming [*sic*] an Indian without a white knapkin on his head and the word good Winebago or Potawatamie in his mouth but on the Inteligence [*sic*] of the express finding the trail and that we were to follow on in pursuit the soldiers were seen gathering their horses and sadling [*sic*] them with as much cheerfulness as if at home." Twelve miles to the southwest they picked up the Sauk trail, sometimes a single path through scrub willow and marsh grass so wide that a city dandy could have followed it and at others breaking into as many as seven parallel tracks. Scouts figured that the Indians were a day and a half ahead and were bearing toward Four Lakes. Oblivious to creature comforts, the militia waded their horses through bogs and, when the animals became mired in quicksand, dismounted men chased the others on foot. A hammering rain slowed them down in the afternoon, but by nightfall they had narrowed the gap to a single day. After wolfing down chunks of raw bacon and handfuls of wet cornmeal, they bedded down without tents, many without blankets, as well, on spongy turf near Rock Lake (twenty miles east of present Madison). The same prairie storm that disrupted Atkinson's camp in the "trembling lands" lashed Henry's brigade during the night, but the horses were too waterlogged and weary to run away.

Friday morning dawned, clearing but cold. The troops gulped down more cold rations and resumed the chase at seven, leaving behind hundreds of puddles marking the spots where they had slept. Following the line of what later became the Chicago and Northwestern Railroad, they had already formed a tentative line of battle when spies brought in a Winnebago prisoner who divulged that the Sauk were only two miles ahead. They actually spotted no Indians, however, until within sight of Third Lake (Monona), although holes in the ground indicated where the Band had dug out wild potatoes. There was a distant glimpse of Indians passing along the narrow isthmus between Fourth (Mendota) and Third lakes; but, by the time the whites had tightened their formation, the enemy had disappeared. Although it was getting dark, General Henry wanted to continue pursuit, but was dissuaded by Pierre Paquette, who warned that the undergrowth on the isthmus favored the defenders. It was later learned that the Sauk had prepared against a night attack and, when it did not come, withdrew about midnight. The militia threw out a cordon of sentinels, cooked a hot meal, and slept on their muskets.

July 21, a cool Saturday, would be remembered by most of these militiamen. A faint festive atmosphere showed in the cheerful zest of the men rising at the morning bugle call, toasting bacon over campfires, and saddling up for the chase. The sodden wastes of eastern Wisconsin had been left behind. This was wooded, rolling country, with crystalline lakes on both sides of the isthmus. Men who would gut an Indian without batting an eye waxed poetical about the sylvan landscape. Lieutenant Justice praised the "delightful view" and regretted that he "had only time to take a passing view of the Romantic beauties of the wilderness." And even that most dour chronicler of the Sauk War, John Wakefield, found himself momentarily bewitched by the setting. "If those lakes were any where else," he wrote, "they would be considered among the wonders of the world. But the country they are situated in is not fit for any civilized nation of people to inhabit." (Wakefield's prediction proved to be a poor one—the hills over which he rode are today largely buried under tons of brick, steel, and concrete in downtown Madison.)

The Sauk made no attempt to delay the whites' advance, but the undergrowth was so dense in places that progress was slow. The only Indians on the isthmus were those too weak or despairing to maintain the stiff pace of retreat. Dr. Addison Philleo gained the distinction of taking the first scalp. Ranging with scouts near Third Lake he came upon an aged Sauk huddling in a thicket and "popped him on the spot," as he told some admirers later. To fetch the scalp, he used the Indian's own knife, but the blade was so dull that strenuous effort was required to tear it loose. Rangers crowding around heard the Sauk groaning, to which the doctor replied, "If you don't like being scalped with a dull knife, why don't you keep a better one?" This retort quickly became established as the bon mot of the campaign. A little later another Sauk was spotted near a fresh grave (presumably a member of his family who had died during the retreat). As the whites lunged toward him, the Indian fired his musket, which contained six balls, leaving a Galenian with a multiple wound in his leg. The Sauk "was shot to pieces" and Dr. Philleo was quickly at work sawing off the scalp. The third victim, an Indian bayoneted to death (and repeatedly after), lost his scalp to someone quicker than the good doctor.

Philleo promptly dispatched his scalps to Galena, where they were exhibited for at least four decades. With them he sent a squib for his newspaper: "It is not common for *editors* to fight with weapons more potent than the *goose quill!*—and when they do, it is the duty of the press . . . to note them." Further, he promised to provide his subscribers, in a few days with "a lecture on *Indian killing.*" Within a few weeks stories about the Scalping Editor were being reprinted in newspapers throughout the country.[4] The Black Hawk War had found its hero.

This unrestrained scalp-hunt led over the hill which would later be the site of the state capitol and through the burr-oak which would become the state university. Three Indians were killed, all in cold blood, and one white wounded. The greatest toll, however, was of the horses of the pursuers, many of them literally ridden into the ground, where they lay foaming and dying.

4. These were not always flattering to Philleo. The Cincinnati *Chronicle* commented, "We trust that the Galenian is the only paper in the Union that could boast of such a feat, and that its editor is the only one of the fraternity capable of perpetrating so disgusting and cruel an act." This was probably written by Benjamin Drake, an atypical Westerner who went against prevailing attitudes in 1838 with his controversial compilation *The Life and Adventures of Black Hawk*, which took the side of the Sauk in discussing the war.

Philleo remained Dodge's trusty factotum, and was recommended by him to General Scott for an appointment as surgeon in the army.

Despite frenzied efforts to overtake the main body of the Sauk, the ambush-nervous whites failed. Each time they narrowed the gap, mounted parties of Indians displayed themselves on the flanks, compelling Henry to halt and tighten his column. The Sauk then vanished. West of Fourth Lake the terrain became broken up by wooded knolls. The path of the main body was easy to follow—peeled oak bark, edible weeds like spikenard grubbed from the earth, bundles dropped or thrown away —but the militia commanders worried about war parties which could pop up anywhere. Only rarely did any Sauk exchange lead with the whites; they held back the pursuers just enough by their menacing ubiquity. At one point Major W. L. D. Ewing's spy battalion, assigned the advance, moved ahead so cautiously that Colonel Dodge's miners swept around his flanks, forcing Ewing to push his men forward "with blows and curses," to maintain the center for the honor of Illinois. To make things worse, early in the afternoon a chilling rain began to fall, blurring the features of the knobby landscape.

Keeping a mobile wall of mounted warriors between the pursuing Chemokemons and his women and children, Black Hawk fell back toward the ancient Sauk village on the north bank of the Wisconsin River (near the present Sauk City), twenty-five miles northwest of Fourth Lake. Even though no one in his band had ever lived there (the village had been abandoned more than fifty years before) he doubtless felt that if the Great Spirit intended to assist them, the intervention would come at that hallowed place. He planned to make a stand among the serrated ridges and scarred ravines on the outer fringe of the Wisconsin Valley, giving his noncombatants time to drop into the wide river bottom and cross. The Wisconsin was a wide but shallow river, dotted with islands and sandbars.

By early afternoon the Band had reached the sandy river bank and had begun the crossing when a rider came from Neapope (who, with some twenty braves, had been responsible for the feints that had been causing the pursuers so much trepidation and lost time) with word that the Chemokemons had reached the heights not more than a mile behind. Collecting fifty warriors, Black Hawk returned to assist the rear guard. He climbed a high knoll out of musket range, to overlook the developing battle and direct the Sauk defensive counterattacks with yelled command. Nothing more than a holding action was contemplated.

At about three in the afternoon Captain Joseph Dickson, in the lead with some of Dodge's spies, came under head-on attack by a band of mounted Sauk. The whites fled and sounded the alarm. Colonel Dodge dismounted his men and led them forward to a grassy slope where they squatted down until the Indians got within thirty yards. They then fired a volley that turned the attackers back after a brief exchange of shots. "The heads of the Indians above the grass," Dr. Philleo communicated to the *Galenian*, "resembled *stumps* in *a newly cleared forest*." Hearing the firing in front, General Henry brought his brigade to the site within ten minutes. Leaving every tenth man to tend the horses, he prepared to repel another charge. (Lieutenant Colonel Jeremiah Smith, ringleader of the mutiny at Fort Winnebago, was made chief corralmaster.) Dead ahead, about a mile away on lower ground, lay the gloomy reaches of the river, barely visible in the drizzle and haze. To their left was a ravine leading down to the river bottom, a wide and open expanse of grass and cane. Beyond the ravine rose a complicated network of heavily timbered knolls, from which the Sauk began to pour down a raking fire at the whites.

Henry's men were strung out a quarter of a mile waiting for a mounted attack from their front when the shots began to drill into their left flank. A quarter-turn was all that was needed to put the face in position to withstand an assault from the woods beyond the ravine; but, after taking the galling fire for half an hour, it became clear that the Indians planned to remain where they were. The chanting voice of Black Hawk on a knoll behind and above the Indian line added to the whites' conviction that the enemy planned a suicidal frontal attack. During the shooting, Colonel Gabriel Jones had a horse shot from under him and one of his privates, Thomas J. Short of Randolph County, was killed. Half a dozen others received their red badges of courage. Meanwhile the mounted Sauk disappeared, reappearing in an attack on the far right wing under Colonel Jacob Fry, in command of what was rather pretentiously called the reserve. A company armed with no more than rocks could probably have held off this feint, for the Sauk hoped only that their whooping hullabaloo would prevent the whites from descending to the river bank and slaughtering their people. "Our men stood firmly," reported Dr. Philleo, naïvely unaware that that was exactly what the Indians wanted.

Under the fire from the ridge, Henry's brigade took half a dozen more casualties, none of them serious, before the general ordered an attack. Colonel Gabriel Jones of Randolph County and Colonel James Collins of Sangamon were instructed to storm the heights while Dodge and Ewing (still competing for honors) requested, and got, permission to dislodge at bayonet point the Sauk who lurked at the bottom of the ravine. The Suckers cleared both places without serious opposition, as the Sauk fled to the lowlands near the river where they prepared for another attack.

Badly scared by the tales he had heard of Stillman's Run, General Henry withheld close pursuit until he had scoured neighboring ridges and hollows for concealed Indians. By this time darkness was coming and, after viewing the labyrinth of marsh grass and willows along the riverbank, which had to be approached across open dunes, he postponed further attack until morning. The brigade set up camp on the high ground where they had first come under fire, set out a double line of pickets, and fortified for a night attack.

This delay gave the British Band ample time to escape over the Wisconsin. Black Hawk had followed the crossing closely and, when he learned that his people were safe, he ordered his harriers to disperse in different directions and to join him, by separate routes, at the river. He later noted that the Sauk were "astonished to find that the enemy were not disposed to pursue us," and estimated his losses at six warriors. The whites could only guess that thirty or forty had been killed, for an examination of the ground in the morning revealed that the departing braves had apparently carried off their casualties as well.[5] Of much less

5. Dodge's report to Atkinson (July 22) claimed that thirty-five scalps had been taken in the battle, in addition to the three at Four Lakes; Henry's report (July 23) gave "between thirty and forty" as the number. Only a short time was required to increase this figure to sixty-eight, a

importance than the body count to the Americans, who even then took statistics as the true measure of a battle, was the tactical victory that belonged to Black Hawk. He had conducted a twenty-five mile retreat, protecting his noncombatants and escorting them safely over the river by coolly conducting a battle against a force at least ten times that of his, and then slipped out of reach at the proper time. Half a century later Jefferson Davis, who heard about the battle countless times while at Fort Crawford, called it "a feat of most consummate management and bravery, in the face of an enemy of greatly superior numbers. I never read of anything that could be compared with it. Had it been performed by white men, it would have been immortalized as one of the most splendid achievements in military history." [6] When one considers the behavior of the whites at Stillman's Run, Apple River, Galena Fort, or Kellogg's Grove the assessment seems less glaringly overstated.

On Sunday morning (July 22) the militia marched on foot to the river bank "where we expected to find the residue of the enemy's force," Henry wrote Atkinson. They found detritus of all sorts abandoned during the crossing, but no trace of Indians. They then wasted a day at the river, drying clothes and exploring the undergrowth in search of lurking Indians. John Wakefield recalled a glow of satisfaction at having "destroyed a number of the very same monsters that had so lately been imbuing their hands with the blood of our fair sex." A few volunteers, still intoxicated from their first encounter with Indians, badgered the Winnebago guides, trying to provoke them into a fight. One strapping Sucker gave Pierre Paquette's dog a gratuitous kick,

---

number that became official through repetition. Speaking for the Sauk, Chief Weesheet, interrogated after the war, stated that five warriors had been killed in the battle, but confessed that many more died afterward, on their trek west. Everyone agreed that hunger was a more effective killer of the Sauk than the Chemokemons.

6. According to the interviewer, an Iowa historian named Charles Aldrich, Davis said that he had witnessed the battle, clearly an error on Aldrich's part. The only regular officer observing the fight was Lieutenant Alexander Hooe of the Fort Winnebago garrison, who accompanied Pierre Paquette and the other Winnebago guides.

responding, when Paquette objected, "I'll kick you, if you say much." The Sucker then lunged at Paquette, who peeled the skin from his cheek with his fist, lifted him up by the throat, and shook him "like an aspen leaf." When asked whether he thought he was a man, the Sucker choked out, "I was where I come from, but I see I ain't here." Within a few hours Paquette and the Winnebago guides left the camp to return to the Portage.

Respect for the prowess of the Sauk remained so high that, when the Americans went into camp for the night, General Henry built a ring of bonfires forty yards from the sleeping zone so that any Indian approaching would be silhouetted against the light. Moreover, he ordered that the men sleep at their firing positions with loaded muskets within reach. Before midnight they were roused up by the sound of their horses stampeding away. Shouts of "Indians!" jarred the men awake, as they "prepared for the worst," recorded John Wakefield. Nothing further happened until an hour or so before sunup, when an Indian voice wailed from a knoll somewhere above them. To Lieutenant James Justice the eerie sound came from "a voice that I never heard equaled by any voice in the course of my life." Henry assumed it to be a Sauk call to battle. Because Paquette and the Winnebago guides had gone, there was no one in camp who could interpret what the Indian was saying.[7]

To counter what he had decided was an attempt by the Sauk to frighten his men, General Henry "harangueed [*sic*] the soldiers in a very beautiful and spirited speech," as one soldier put it. Judging from what has been recorded of his exhortation, it must rank as one of the most eclectic and inane in frontier history. Thus the general drowned out the voice coming down from above, "Remember! You are fighting a set of demons! Stand firm, my brave Suckers, until you can see the whites of their eyes before you dis-

7. Individual volunteers later disputed this. Lieutenant D. S. Harrison of Dodge's battalion said that he understood enough to know that the voice pleaded for peace and for permission to cross the Mississippi without being molested. P. J. Pilcher of Ewing's battalion claimed that he plainly heard the Sauk words for "Friends, we fight no more." He said that when he reported this to Henry he was told, "Pay no attention to anything they say or do, but form in line of battle."

charge your muskets! And then meet them with a charge as you have before done, and that too with great success!" Putting on bold faces, the troops began caterwauling and yelping to show the Sauk they were ready for a fight. Some yelled, "Stillman is not here!" Near daybreak the voice died away. Scouts ranging over the knoll (the same one used by Black Hawk directing the battle) found only horse tracks and a buried tomahawk, a sign of peace. After the war, it was learned that Neapope had called from the hilltop, issuing a plea for peace. When this overture failed, the young chief deserted the British Band and fled to the protection of Winnebago on the Rock River.

On Monday morning (July 23) Henry and Dodge called off further pursuit of the Sauk because, once again, their food and whiskey supplies had been exhausted. During the previous night the Indians had returned to the battlefield to butcher the dead horses for meat, but the whites were too finicky for such fare. The campaign had to be postponed still further while the volunteers backtracked to the depot at Blue Mound, twenty miles south through rough country, to replenish their supplies of side meat, cornmeal mush, and whiskey.

After returning to Fort Koshkonong from the spongy margins of the "trembling lands" and dropping off the dregs of Milton Alexander's militia with Captain Gideon Low, General Henry Atkinson struck off on July 21 (the day of the fight at Wisconsin Heights) to overtake the Indians. Failing that, he hoped at least to catch up with Henry and Dodge. As he headed around Lake Koshkonong to the south, he sent word to General William Posey at Blue Mound requesting him to intercept the Sauk—although he must have realized by then that the First Brigade of Illinois volunteers would do little, if anything.[8]

The ironies of fate most surely must have occured to General Atkinson during his four-day, eight-mile march to Blue Mound:

8. Beginning with this letter, Atkinson used the heading "The North-west Army" instead of "The Army of the Frontier." His adoption of General Winfield Scott's heading suggests that he conceived of his own role henceforth as a subordinate one. No doubt he was glad to be relieved of the responsibility for terminating the war.

The feckless militiamen who had been virtual millstones around his neck had, by disobeying his orders, found and (he had by then learned) thrashed the enemy which he had been hunting for more than a quarter of a year, yet had never seen. At Blue Mound, however, he discovered that reports of the victory at Wisconsin Heights had been grossly exaggerated. Despite exhilerated reports that the militia had "slapped the Sauks all to flinders" and "crowded Black Hawk mighty hard," the British Band still ranged at large somewhere north of the Wisconsin; no one knew exactly where.

To the regulars it seemed hardly possible that the militia, having caught up with the enemy, had allowed him to escape. Lieutenant Philip Cooke, for example, listened almost in disbelief as these Sucker gumps told of their cool under fire and re-enacted the battle, as though it had been an event "before which Tippecanoe, etc. might hang its head." The ultimate absurdity, however, came during the next three decades as Henry's partisans waged a relentless campaign in newspapers from Milwaukee to St. Louis to establish who was truly responsible for the victory at Wisconsin Heights.[9] The last word was had in the 1880s by an Illinois legislator who outraged both Suckers and Badgers when he curtly wrote, "Let Dodge have it. Instead of a victory, it was a most inglorious defeat." The honors, he continued, went to fifty Sauk "barely able to stand up due to hunger" who held back an army.

Realizing that haste was essential if the British Band was to

9. The most dramatic episode occurred in the spring of 1847 when Governor Thomas Ford read before the Illinois legislature a draft chapter of his history of Illinois bearing on the Black Hawk War. Much to the satisfaction of his auditors, he argued that credit for ending the war belonged to Henry, not Dodge. Garbled newspaper accounts made it appear that the governor had disparaged Colonel Dodge, who at once wrote a letter demanding to know whether Ford was responsible for the phraseology of certain quasi-insulting paragraphs. The suggestion of a possible duel wafted through the region, with the odds favoring Dodge heavily. Though the governor was a spunky little man, he would have had little chance unless he chose rocks for his weapon and induced the colonel to fight him from the bottom of a well. The governor provided the colonel with a full account of what he had written, and there the matter rested.

be captured before they escaped across the Mississippi (where, of course, the army intended to put them anyway, if it caught them), General Atkinson collected the best-looking nine hundred of the militia gorging themselves at Blue Mound and, with his four hundred regular infantry, set off on July 25 for the Wisconsin River.

Once Black Hawk had moved north of the Wisconsin, the frontier folk of the Northwest, many of whom had been forted up for two and even three months emerged from the dozens of log pens which had sprouted throughout the territory. And the names of most of these forts would soon be forgotten—Defiance, Union, Beggs, Johnson, Nonsense, Naper, Jackson, Apple River, Hamilton, Vinegar Hill, White Oak Springs, New Digs, Funk, Deposit, Door Prairie, to name only a few. Galena, however, was unique. On Tuesday night, July 24, fire broke out in Dr. Jim Crow's stable in the stockade. The populace fought the blaze bravely until someone remembered the stored powder kegs. There was one fatality in the rush to evacuate the fort: Old Amos Farrar, Galena's first citizen and a former associate of George Davenport in the fur trade, clutched his heart and died. For weeks he had been babbling about "George Davenport's War."

TWELVE *Bad Axe*

Kill the nits, and you'll have no lice.
                                —"Big Tooth John"

◄◄

ONCE he had recovered from his surprise at the failure of the Chemokemon to pursue him across the Wisconsin, Black Hawk altered his plan to use the river as a barricade and moved thirty miles downstream to the Pine River Valley (present Gotham). The Sauk had collected enough rafts and shallops for eighty people, most of them women and children, to use the Wisconsin as an escape route; the remainder joined Black Hawk on an inland trek through the Ocooch Mountains, heading for the Mississippi River above Fort Crawford. Presumably they aimed for the mouth of the Bad Axe River, which emptied into the Mississippi about thirty miles above Prairie du Chien. There the great river shoaled and mats of islands in the channel made a crossing feasible. The rough terrain between was expected to make rapid pursuit by the Chemokemons impossible, since horses were useless in such country save as beasts of burden. As guides the Sauk had a few Winnebago, the only tribe acquainted with that remote and wild region.

Information that the British Band had crossed the Wisconsin River and might be moving downstream toward Prairie du Chien had already been conveyed by Henry Dodge to Major Gustavus Loomis, commandant of Fort Crawford in the absence of Colonel Taylor. Loomis anchored a flatboat, manned by twenty-five regulars and armed with a six-pounder at the mouth of the Wisconsin to block that escape route.

The fear now was that Winnebago bands upstream from Prairie du Chien might help the Sauk across the Mississippi by lending or giving them canoes. Joseph Street, the Winnebago agent, had already induced many bands to camp near his agency to insure their absolute neutrality. Now, on his recommendation, Major Loomis agreed to round up the bands farther upriver and to alert the Sioux to the Sauk approach. As the *Enterprise* had just arrived with two companies of the Fourth Infantry from the south, Loomis hired it to carry the subagent, Thomas P. Burnett, up to the Winnebago villages. The message Burnett carried was that, if the so-called friendlies did not report to General Street at once, their canoes would be broken up and they would be denied their annuities. In such manner, by July 25, the whites had spread a net along forty miles of the great river which they hoped the British Band could not slip through.

General Atkinson reached the Wisconsin on the afternoon of July 26. There Alexander Posey's brigade awaited them. Although Posey had been instructed to tear down the huts in the settlement of Helena (present Tower Hill) and prepare rafts, his men had accomplished little. Because of the torpidity of "the Dr. Mr. General" (as Lieutenant A. S. Johnston called him in his journal), Atkinson's army failed to cross to the north bank of the river until July 28, which gave Black Hawk a five-day lead. Few believe that he could now be overtaken, and complaining among the militia once again became rampant. Not even the discovery of a waterlogged Sauk corpse, which must have floated down from the battleground, could restore their enthusiasm for the job ahead. John Wakefield remembered "more dissatisfaction prevailing than I observed during the whole campaign"—if that were possible. Accustomed to bogs and flat prairies, these volunteers from southern and central Illinois looked at the rugged ridges of foggy blue mountains ahead with deep uneasiness. The landscape, so wild and unfamiliar, spooked them. They dubbed it "the alps" and, with their farmers' eyes, saw that it was unfit for the plow, therefore worthless. The men of Henry's brigade were especially disgruntled: They had been assigned to bring up the rear and care for the baggage wagons, which they always swore was Atkinson's punishment of General James Henry for having whipped the Indians.

About noon on Saturday (July 28) spies found what they

thought was the trail. General Atkinson and Colonel Dodge rode forward together to examine the signs. After riding about in circles for a time, Dodge suddenly drew his sword as if about to resist an enemy attack and began to utter what Lieutenant Philip Cooke later described as "unintelligible exclamations," primarily blasphemous. Atkinson, who was no woodsman, appeared to follow the colonel in "blind sympathy." (Both men were portly and their antics resembled those of an aged pointer "searching for the hole of a ground-squirrel" with a baffled city dog following in imperfect imitation.) The trail led them parallel to the river, to the intense relief of the militia, who were beginning to crack sardonic jokes about how they might have to "eat their horses" if they entered the sawtooth mountains to the north. However, after a few miles, the trail veered up the Pine River and into the gloomy forest. It was fine country for a nature poet but rough going for an army. If whites had ever visited this region at all, they had certainly not charted it. Ten years later the region was still so wild and untracked that one wayfarer spent six months wandering about lost before stumbling into a woodcutter's camp near the Wisconsin River.

After a single day of toiling through this natural obstacle course in which perpendicular bluffs alternated with swampy ravines, there was scarcely a man who did not wish himself back among the sloughs of the "trembling lands." Horses were useless in such country, but the frontiermen's attachment to horses prevented the militia from sending them to the rear. There was so little forage for the animals that at night the men had to feed them saplings. The first time the wheeled vehicles became enmired, half the army halted to prepare a dike with pick and shovel; the second time, they were left behind or intentionally broken. Marching by unit became impossible and eventually the troops were spread out across a ten-mile swath, each group seeking the easiest route through what even Atkinson admitted was "the most difficult country imaginable." At times it was even impossible to find level places on which to roll up into a blanket; and one morning they woke in a deep hollow to find frost on the ground. The walnut trees were so high, wrote a volunteer from Clark County, that the best marksmen would have their work cut out for them in "shooting a squirrel at the top." Even Colonel Zachary Taylor, a spartan campaigner, thought it a hard march, occupied as they were "in wading swamps & marshes & passing over a number of hills that in Europe would be termed mountains which before had never been passed by a white man even a trader, much less an army."

The Ocooch Mountains seemed like a region of the dead. From time to time they skirted moldering fortifications, the work of who knows what long-gone tribes. And, beginning on the third day, the trail of the Sauk could be followed by carrion birds hovering above "the corpses, not of warriors only, but of poor women." In default of fresh scalps, Some men remove putrescent ones.

To the regulars it was a mystery why Black Hawk made no effort to impede them. A few snipers skillfully concealed could have delayed the advance for days. Horses could have been stampeded at night. Packhorses driven ahead by what Lieutenant Cooke called "these gallant knights of the whip" could have been ambushed. Although officers approached each new obstacle— fallen tree, mountain stream, peat bog—with apprehension, they saw no Indians except the dead; a few had wounds, but most were apparent victims of starvation and exhaustion. Officers on Atkinson's staff whispered among themselves that the general was in such distress about the endless possibilities of an ambush that he deliberately held back the pursuit.

By the end of the third day, men had begun to be less concerned with overtaking the Sauk than with whether they would get clear of the ghastly region without broken bones or snake bites. No one seemed to know where they were beyond the vaguely defined triangle between the Wisconsin and the Mississippi. Lieutenant Cooke freely confessed later that "all were in profound ignorance of our whereabouts—we were certainly all 'lost.'" In fact they were less than thirty miles from Colonel Taylor's home garrison of Fort Crawford, but he, like everyone else was so baffled by the miserable country that they might as well have been marching on the back side of the moon.

While General Atkinson's army scrambled that through the Ocooch Mountains, the center of the campaign shifted to Prairie du Chien. Two hours after midnight on Sunday, July 29, the village was jarred awake by the boom of the six-pounder at the mouth of the Wisconsin three miles to the south. Lieutenant Joseph Ritner, a young West Pointer who commanded the barge, had made contact with the Sauk seeking to escape along the Wisconsin River. Three canoes had gotten within a few feet of the barge before being detected and fended off. At this point-blank range grapeshot had tumbled the Indians in the first canoe into the river. The Lieutenant thought the others had been disabled, since after two rounds the scene had become obliterated by smoke and darkness. At daylight Winnebago parties, supervised by citizens and soldiers at Prairie du Chien, began a search for the survivors who had scattered south of the river. Most of the Indians eluded pursuit until Colonel Billy Hamilton and some Menominee from Green Bay found them the following Saturday and slaughtered them.[1]

Excitement of a different sort occurred on the following day when the citizenry of Prairie du Chien crowded to the wharf to watch the landing of the spanking new steamboat *Warrior,* launched that summer in Pittsburgh and on its maiden run, captained by Joseph Throckmorton, to ports of call between St. Louis and Fort Snelling. The *Warrior* was a streamlined barge with three great boilers sitting in the open like teakettles and a pilot house nailed to the deck like a fancy chicken coop. Protruding from her bow was a life-sized wooden Indian, the principal feature of the boat.

Major Loomis promptly chartered it to reconnoiter the river as far north as Waubasha's village (near LaCrosse) and to again alert the Sioux to the impending Sauk incursion. Lieutenant

1. George Boyd, the Menominee agent at Green Bay enlisted about three hundred of that tribe for Atkinson, most of whom arrived at Prairie du Chien after the war had ended. He also tried to recruit the Stockbridge Indians, who had been transplanted from New York state to Green Bay a decade before. These were one of the civilized tribes of Iroquois who had been converted to Christianity. Much to the disgust of the citizenry at Green Bay, the Stockbridge group refused to join, arguing that war was incompatible with the tenets of their adopted faith. This proved to most whites in the region that it was impossible to turn an Indian into a decent, responsible citizen.

James W. Kingsbury and a platoon of infantry hauled a six-pounder aboard the 115-foot steamboat and, after collecting a motley crowd of curiosity seekers, self-appointed Indian experts, and some Winnebago, Throckmorton's vessel hammered up to Waubasha's village. A few miles upstream they came upon a soldier in a canoe. He had recently been discharged at Fort Snelling, and had seen no Sauk on his voyage through this danger zone. He joined Throckmorton's expedition, infected by the enthusiasm of the whole company, all of whom were "anxious to get a pop at the Indians," in the words of one participant.

While returning to Prairie du Chien on Wednesday, August 1, Throckmorton met a Sioux on the river who said that the Sauk, four hundred strong, were on the Bad Axe River. After stopping to gather wood for the boilers, the captain steamed down to investigate. At four in the afternoon, they sighted Indians just south of the mouth of the Bad Axe River. Moving in closer, the Americans saw that they were constructing rafts and shallops at the water's edge. Women and children helped the men at this task. They had arrived at the great river earlier in the day, confident for the first time since their breakout two weeks earlier that they were within reach of sanctuary on the far shore.

The approach of the *Warrior* did not distress Black Hawk. Though the boat was unfamiliar to him, he recognized Throckmorton's pennant; he knew the captain, believed him to be a fair-minded man, and expected him to accept their surrender. It is also likely that he hoped to barter with the captain to ferry his people across the river. Black Hawk told some women, "Run and get me the white flag. I will go on board that boat." He ordered his warriors to put down their guns and told the women, "I will save you and the children by going on board and giving myself up." When the women failed to locate the white flag, Black Hawk put a small piece of white cotton cloth on a pole and called to request the captain to send his small boat ashore and allow him to board. This request was imperfectly translated; the whites on the *Warrior* thought that the Indians were attempting to lure the steamboat itself to shore. A Winnebago voice on the *Warrior* called across the water, "Is there any chief there, or is Black Hawk there?" Through his Winnebago interpreter Black Hawk replied, "I am Black Hawk—and I wish to come and shake hands with you."

There was a brief period of quiet during the hot afternoon, with both sides unwilling to do anything except watch the other. This was suddenly broken by a piercing shout from the steamboat, in Winnebago, "Run and hide! The Chemokemons are going to shoot!" A load of canister from the six-pounder in the bow "mowed a swath clean through them," recalled one of the gunners. The Indians scrambled up the river bank into the protection of trees and hollows in the ground, but not before two more loads had been fired on them. Captain Throckmorton's account of the fight reveals the man in its sportsman's tone:

As we neared them, they raised a white flag, and endeavored to decoy us; but we were a little too old for them; for instead of landing, we ordered them to send a boat on board, which they declined. After about fifteen minutes' delay, giving them time to remove a few of their women and children, we let slip a six-pounder, loaded with canister, followed by a severe fire of musketry; and if ever you saw straight blankets, you would have seen them there. I fought them at anchor most of the time, and we were all very much exposed. I have a ball which came in close by where I was standing, and passed through the bulkhead of the wheel-room. We fought them for about an hour or more, until our wood began to fail, and the night coming on, we left and went on to the prairie. This little fight cost them twenty-three killed, and of course a great many wounded. We never lost a man, and had but one man wounded (shot through the leg).[2]

After the first mangling blast from the *Warrior* no other Sauk were injured (Throckmorton's casualty estimate is somewhat exaggerated), but the presence of the vessel delayed until nightfall further preparations to convoy the band across the river.

2. In his autobiography, Black Hawk spoke of this incident, crediting Throckmorton with more humanity than he possessed: "The Winnebago, on the steam boat, must either have misunderstood what was told, or did not tell it to the captain correctly; because I am confident that he would not have fired upon us, if he had known my wishes. I have always considered him a good man, and too great a brave to fire upon an enemy when sueing for quarters."

The wounded white man was the recently discharged soldier picked up on the river.

Having outgeneraled and outrun the Chemokemon army for nearly four months, Black Hawk had now to contend with their navy. Among the Sauk there was great apprehension that the steamboat would reappear in the morning. However, no Indian accounts emanating from the band make any reference to the approach of Atkinson's legions from the east.

On the fifth day of their wilderness trek (August 1), General Atkinson's army emerged from the heavy timber onto a high plateau broken by grassy valleys and scattered oak groves. After crossing a small stream (later identified as the Kickapoo River), they became aware of the presence of the Mississippi not far ahead. At last assured that they would not "starve in this dreary waste," the men increased their pace in their eagerness to reach the great river. Half a dozen dead Indians lay along their line of march,[3] along with the clean-picked skeletons of horses.

At sundown they came upon a campground which the Sauk rear guard, or, more probably, a band lagging behind, had occupied as recently as that morning; embers were still smouldering. Nearby was the improvised grave of a chief. He lay in a reclining position against a tree, arms folded and body painted red. A crude log frame covered with bark served as sepulcher. He seemed, Lieutenant Cooke wrote, "in grim defiance, even in death." The volunteers were delighted with the discovery, taking the scalp, disfiguring the corpse, and then kicking the tomb to pieces.

The greatest trophy found at this camp, however, was an old Sauk so feeble that he could not rise from the ground. He told his interrogators that Black Hawk planned to cross the river in the morning. The "maganimous volunteers," as Lieutenant Cooke called them, amused themselves with the invalid for a time before killing him. Sixty-six years later one of the participants tersely recounted to a "small but highly appreciative audience," "The query was what was best to do; leave him to starve or kill him. We decided it better to kill him. Shot him." [4] This act of

3. The approximate route of their march from the Wisconsin to the Mississippi passed through Gotham, Richland Center, Boaz, Soldiers Grove, Rising Sun, Retreat, Victory.

4. The speaker was H. S. Townsend, a former Dodge ranger; the occasion was the sixty-sixth anniversary of the Battle of Bad Axe cele-

mercy accomplished, they slaughtered some beeves and fried steaks for supper. By ten o'clock the camp was quiet, with each chevalier mustering his strength to do battle in the morning.

As the old Sauk had told the whites where they were, General Atkinson dictated and dispatched a note to Major Loomis at Fort Crawford, announcing that the army would move out at two in the morning to engage the enemy at the riverbank. He did not expect to meet a very formidable enemy: "They have been hard pressed by the troops. Their route from the Ouisconsin is strewed with dead, generally from wounds received in the battle . . , and they suffer much for provisions. They subsist entirely on horse flesh." The ever-prudent Atkinson also asked that a steamboat be sent up the river to block off any Sauk escape, being unaware of the *Warrior* bombardment earlier that afternoon. On board he wanted sixty barrels of flour and thirty of pork for the Suckers, and a six-pounder with five thousand rounds of ammunition for the Sauk.

Bugles roused the camp at two on Thursday, August 2. The three Illinois brigades were delayed for hours chasing down their horses in the foggy darkness, but Colonel Dodge's battalion moved out promptly with Taylor's regulars. Atkinson's plan was to hit the main body of the Sauk at the river. Posey and Alexander, neither of whom had won any laurels or seen any enemy thus far in the war, were to cut off those Indians who fled north. Henry was to leave his pack horses after the battle had begun and intercept any Sauk retreating southward. The general's plan seemed elaborate for whipping a crippled band of semistarved Indians: It was as though he feared they might have suddenly been reinforced by something like a crack British regiment. In fact, he had a four-to-one edge in manpower.

The vanguard crossed high grassy slopes which descended into and then climbed above a great bank of morning fog. After they had marched three miles, the mist had burned off except for a

---

brated at Victory, Wisconsin. Between two and three thousand people attended this historical fair which was housed in twenty tents beside the river. Shortly after Townsend's speech a pelting rain set hundreds of the audience dashing to their carriages and homes. Plans to establish a Bad Axe Battle Island Assembly Ground, to be given over to an annual eight-day session of "historical, literary, and religious work" dissolved in rain.

long fleecy cloud marking the bed of the great river below them. Ahead of them were rolling terraces of high grass and parklike woods descending to the foggy bottoms where the Sauk were supposed to be. Above them, Lieutenant Cooke recalled, stretched a rosy summer sky, "as quiet and as peaceful as if man had never been there." A staff officer rode in to report that Sauk had been spotted in a woods ahead. Leaving their knapsacks with a guard, the regulars advanced in a battle line, with Dodge's rangers plunging ahead through grass high as a horse's back. Firing broke out from a woods to the right. Assuming that this came from the Sauk rear guard, Colonel Taylor swung his line to the north. When more shots came from a grove yet farther to their right, the whole white advance drifted in that direction. Posey's brigade caught up and moved into position next to the regulars, with Alexander's beyond Posey's to the far north. Henry moved straight ahead into the vacuum created by this shift. The Sauk had deliberately employed this diversionary tactic to draw the whites away from their main camp.

By eight o'clock "there was pretty hot work." Dodge's spies under Captain Joseph Dickson ferreted out and killed fourteen Indians at the first outpost; these "kills" precipitated a pell-mell dash toward the river. Atkinson sent out an order for the rangers not to break ranks, but the advance was by then uncontrollable. When Dodge shouted to the courier, "Tell Atkinson I'll not obey his order!" his men cheered him and pressed forward. Overhanging the riverbank was a limestone cliff, down which the rangers slithered to pursue the Sauk snipers into the dark timber and thickets. Once in the high brush they were lashed by fire from an ambush; they staggered back to regroup, then hurtled on. One volunteer, who received a bullet through his whiskers and another through his hat, seemed "dazed and wild after that," remembered a companion. Coming upon an Indian woman with a child strapped to her back he lifted his musket, saying "See me kill that damn squaw." His shot broke the child's arm and buried itself in the woman's back. Lieutenant Robert Anderson rescued the infant from further harm, later bringing it to headquarters. Dr. Addison Philleo also had some sport from the incident when he amputated the maimed arm (some said unnecessarily) in front of an appreciative gathering after having given his patient a biscuit to chew on for an anesthetic.

So long a farce, the Black Hawk War now became a brutal slaughter. Other than the ruse to draw the whites up the river, the Sauk had no defensive plan. Their only aim was to convey as many of their people over the river as possible. While Dodge's rangers were pursuing the thirty-odd Sauk skirmishers, Henry's brigade struck the main camp on the river—which was open and defenseless. What ensued was more cold-blooded murder than a battle. One soldier in Henry's spy battalion wrote triumphantly, "We were by this time fast getting rid of those demons in human shape. . . . They are much frightened when they see death stare them in the face; which was the case at this time. When we came upon the squaws and children, they raised a scream and cry loud enough to affect the stoutest man upon earth." All contemporary narratives confess that noncombatants were shot down by the score. John Wakefield admitted that many of them were killed by accident; proof that remorse did not overwhelm him, however, appears in his indifferent remark, "but such was their fate." Volunteers dashed wild-eyed through the camp, frantic not to miss a scalp and forfeit such a chance to attain manhood—Western style. Firing at any object that moved, they rat shot Indians hiding in the rubbish of the camp, burrowing into holes along the beach, or fleeing to the river. They often nearly shot each other in their eagerness to capture those supreme frontier fireside ornaments, human scalplocks.

John House, known to his companions as "Big Tooth John" (because of eyeteeth which protruded like tusks), arrived too late to carry home any worthwhile plunder. Ranging the riverbank, however, he found an infant tied to a piece of cottonwood bark. Its mother had apparently launched it on the river, but the current had pulled it back to the shore. House took deliberate aim and fired. Reproached by men who thought this a bit excessive, House replied, "Kill the nits, and you'll have no lice."

Men of Alexander's brigade, which had missed the liveliest action of the massacre, continued to hunt desperately for stray Sauk; some were finally rewarded for their perseverance when, under the riverbank, they found a group of squaws who had burrowed so deeply in the sand that only their noses were exposed. Bayoneting and shooting these women was particularly amusing because of their muffled writhings which resembled miniature earthquakes.

Along the riverbank many women had stripped off their clothes as they prepared to swim the river. One woman named Namesa seized a horse's tail and was pulled safely across holding her baby by the teeth, although volunteers sprinkled the water around her with shots. Few of the others were so lucky; the sight of the naked women inflamed these frontiersmen of rigid Methodist and Baptist background with a sexual excitement that took various outlets. Some merely shot their victims, while others dragged their captives into the undergrowth. Arriving on the scene, one young army lieutenant rescued a young girl from what he euphemistically called "very uncomfortable circumstances." For a fleeting moment he, too, felt the stirrings of certain "symptoms of romance," but got hold of himself and sent the girl under guard to the rear. Nearly seventy years later a Sucker describing Dodge's advance toward the Sauk camp revealed how erotic fancy sweetened the act of killing: "Three squaws were shot on that race; they were naked." Then he burst out with, "We have been accused of inhumanity to those Indians. It is false as hell, we never did it. With Henry's men we killed in three-fourths of a mile, 82 Indians. We lost three men."

The whites saw themselves as engaged in a holy war that exempted them from responsibility for the slaughter at Bad Axe. They were ridding the earth of hateful varmints, characterized by John Wakefield as "wretched wanderers [who] are most like the wild beasts than man—wandering from forest to forest, and not making any improvement in the natural mind." Indians were nomadic outlaws who refused to heed the Puritan God's commands to squat and to work. Wakefield continued, "The Ruler of the Universe, he who takes vengeance on the guilty, did not design those guilty wretches to escape His vengeance for the horrid deeds they had done, which were of the most appalling nature." The most unforgivable sin of the Sauk, of course, was their illumination, over the previous four months, of white cowardice, incompetence, and selfishness. Rather than face the moral consequences of what he knew was murder, Wakefield spoke for the others when he proposed that the Almighty had decreed the slaughter and that the whites were but obedient agents of His vengeance. A two-hundred-year heritage of Indian hating had been passed down to the bloodletters at Bad Axe, who were as devoid of guilt as they were of mercy.

By the time Colonel Zachary Taylor arrived at the Sauk camp with his infantry, the massacre on the mainland was ending— through want of further victims. Volunteers were yelping and dancing with scalps in their hands or rooting through plunder wrested from the Indians. A few shots still came from a willowed island separated from the mainland by a stagnant slough. To oust the enemy would have required a frontal assault with full exposure to their fire. The militia balked at this work, claiming that as taxpayers they supported the army, that the regulars were trained for such operations, and so on. Colonel Taylor was by this time so accustomed to the excuses of the Sucker militia, that he did not even trouble to remind them of their duty. Three companies of infantry moved into the slough and, with muskets and cartridge boxes held above their heads, began to wade across. The first soldier in the water was hit and floundered. Two others waded toward him, one of whom was struck in the head and killed instantly. They fell back to the mainland with five dead. Taking cover, they opened fire on a colored object barely visible in a thicket on the island. After a number of devastating volleys, Colonel Taylor ordered his men across the bayou again. This time they made it without a shot being fired against them. The colored object turned out to be a blanket, shot to shreds, hanging on a tree. Nearby was a wounded infant wailing beside its dead mother. The warriors, if any had been there, had crossed to another low island.

Probably those Indians moving from island to island would have eventually escaped across the Mississippi had not the *Warrior* appeared at the Bad Axe at two in the afternoon. Jubilant at the sight of this unexpected assistance, one army captain tried to flag the boat, but received in reply a shot from the six-pounder which smashed into the trees and brought a shower of leaves and limbs down on his head. On the previous evening, the village of

Prairie du Chien had turned out to load cordwood aboard the *Warrior*, which then had set off at crack of day. Heavy fog on the river held Throckmorton back as they poked through channels without being certain where they were. At last they heard the battle, before they saw it, and the captain shouted "Dodge is giving them hell!" The Menominee scouts aboard began whooping for a fight.

The *Warrior* drove up and down the channels between the islands, raking the undergrowth with the six-pounder and running down those Sauk attempting to swim or raft across the river. Some Sauk dived under the water and lay with only their mouths and nostrils above the surface. But, by steaming in close to shore, the *Warrior* ran these down as well. Any Indians who appeared on the surface of the water were ground under the paddlewheel or shot by the Menominee hanging on the guards. The presence of the *Warrior* allowed the regulars to root out pockets of Sauk hiding on the islands. At one point Throckmorton himself grew so excited that he snatched up a rifle and drilled an Indian trying to crawl to shore. Writing to a friend that night the Captain related, "Before we could get back again, on account of a heavy fog, they had the whole army upon them. We found them at it, walked in, and took a hand ourselves. The first shot from the Warrior *laid out three. . . .* I tell you what, *Sam,* there is no fun in fighting Indians, particularly at this season, when the grass is so very bright. Every man, and even my cabin-boy, fought well."

During the fighting, John Fonda, a volunteer gunner on the *Warrior* and in later years sheriff at Prairie du Chien, reported watching an Indian and his five sons, all of whom he knew personally, take a stand behind a fallen log on the mainland. The old man loaded for his sons who, with each shot dropped a sucker assailant until volunteers poured over the bluff behind them and scalped them instantly. They also cut two parallel gashes down the backs of each victim and ripped off the skin. These strips were in great vogue as razor straps. Fonda himself was later the proud owner of one of these.

By midafternoon the battle had ended on the mainland, and the *Warrior* conveyed a mixed force of regulars and militia to the thickly wooded islands, from which occasional shots were still coming. After a lunch of crackers and whiskey, the whites advanced and found only a few women and children, although they spotted two men high up in trees. The volunteers opened fire, without command, and the Sauk plummeted like wounded squirrels, grabbing at limbs but jerked loose by their momentum, smashing to the earth. A Menominee warrior who bounded ahead to take a scalp was shot in the back by a militiaman, who doubtless had resolved to bag an Indian and cared little whether his target was friendly or hostile. Later the regulars carried the body of the Menominee to the mainland and buried it with military honors beside their own five dead.

Black Hawk and the Prophet had disappeared. General Atkinson ordered a search among the bodies for anyone answering their descriptions. Two men of Dodge's battalion thought they had found something: Earlier they had come upon two Sauk hiding behind a log in the slough. They killed one; but the other, an old man, jumped up and tried to surrender. The whites reloaded and loosed a volley that tore off a finger of his outstretched hand. They fired repeatedly but the old Sauk dodged their bullets by diving into the murky water. It was too shallow to conceal his legs; after shooting him in the legs several times, they ran out of ammunition and, on their return, the Sauk had vanished. After hearing this story, Atkinson sent twenty men to find him. Following a trail of blood, they found him in a thicket. A pint of whiskey made him talkative; it became clear that he was not Black Hawk. He knew enough English to cry out, "White man, white man, have mercy on me!" He died.

Though the battle was over, the gloating and looting continued. Of the British Band which had crossed the Mississippi in April one thousand strong, there now remained about forty Sauk prisoners, most of them women and children. Less than one hundred had escaped across the river; interrogation of the prisoners suggested that Black Hawk and the Prophet had gone north with about forty more the night before. No one really knew how many Sauk had been killed at Bad Axe. On August 5, Atkinson put the Indian dead at 150; three weeks later he doubled the figure to include those who had drowned and those killed on the far shore by Waubasha's Sioux, who took sixty-eight scalps in a single attack.[5] However computed, the loss was staggering and the British Band had been eliminated as a factor in tribal politics. Henceforth Keokuk would reign without strong opposition, passing on his position to his son.

The victory had been easily won. Zachary Taylor reported five regulars dead and five wounded; James Henry, seven wounded; Milton Alexander, one wounded; Alexander Posey, one wounded; Henry Dodge, six wounded. Among the gentlemen volunteers two, perhaps three, of the wounded later died at Prairie du Chien. The statistics reveal the true nature of the Battle at Bad Axe.

Lieutenant Philip Cooke of the Fourth Infantry registered his disgust at the militia's looting the pitiful detritus of the Sauk camp. Indian ponies were considered the most valuable trophies, next to scalps. They were auctioned off from one volunteer to another and, in turn, auctioned again to the citizens at Prairie du Chien. Copper kettles, blankets, war clubs, pieces of Indian hide oozy with gore, scared war gourds in which rattled the teeth of drumhead fish, beads and bracelets, were all carried off. One Sucker gave off a whoop, waving five hundred dollars in the air, which he had found on an Indian corpse. A Winnebago decorated his forehead with the finger of a Sauk fastened in place with a headband of human skin. Throughout this ghoulish carnival, the Sauk women and children huddled together, seeming not to hear or see anything, their eyes glazed. It must have been during this time that the "Scalping Editor," Dr. Addison Philleo, amputated the infant's arm, a spectacle which nearly all eyewitness accounts of the battle allude to. Lieutenant Cooke recalled that the operation was regarded as a joke because the wound was not that severe.

5. On August 18 the acting Sauk and Fox agent at Fort Armstrong reported 114 prisoners of war incarcerated there, but of this number only 8 were braves, many of them old men. About 8 more were subsequently picked up, bringing the number of survivors to approximately 200. Some Sauk with Winnebago family connections doubtless remained hidden permanently or until the roundup was discontinued. Some Kickapoo are said to have returned to the Wabash Valley from Koshkonong.

To protect the lives of the prisoners—for the volunteers were beginning to likker it up—General Atkinson sent them down to Prairie du Chien with the wounded men. One captive aboard the *Warrior* was an old Sauk who attracted great attention during the passage when "he attempted to destroy himself," wrote John Fonda, "by pounding his own head with a rock, much to the amusement of the soldiers."

If a historical marker is ever constructed at the present hamlet of Victory, Wisconsin, to commemorate the achievement and sacrifice of American soldiery at the Battle of Bad Axe, it should be large enough to admit three tableaux in bronze: a militiaman shooting a baby in the river; a physician sawing off a child's arm; and an Indian hammering his own head with a rock.

For two more days following the battle at Bad Axe, Atkinson's legions luxuriated in the rank river bottom. Ushering in an era of good feelings, the general published a ringing note congratulating the volunteers on their hard-won victory. Brigade commanders prepared reports chronicling the activities of their respective forces in the battle.

General Posey had swung too far to the north to engage in any real fighting, but he had captured eight Sauk children and three squaws. The inactivity of the First Brigade came as no surprise to anyone, for the feeling generally in the army might have been expressed, "keep close to Posey and you'll never get hurt."

The case of General Alexander was more unfortunate. Placed north of Posey, none of his command had seen action except for two companies who slipped off, presumably without orders, to join General Henry. For nearly two months the plodding general from Edgar County had obeyed every order with trusting loyalty, and he had missed out on every kill. Doubless sympathetic, Atkinson gave Alexander's brigade the privilege of crossing the river in two mackinaw boats to pursue the remnant of the British Band. Major William Archer, Alexander's aide-de-camp, took 130 men of the Second Brigade on this expedition which bagged only a small Sauk boy nearly eaten up by mosquitos. Archer had wanted to take fifty stalwarts and pursue the Sauk trail which led farther south, but the men refused to continue. It made no difference, however, since the Sioux caught the Sauk fugitives, and Archer was easily re-elected to the Sucker senate anyhow.

By the time Atkinson prepared to transfer his headquarters to Prairie du Chien on August 4, each arriving steamboat was disgorging its load of tourists and carrion seekers. One Eastern dentist harvested the teeth of dead Sauk. But thirty years later the bones of the dead still remained strewn about the battle area. Volunteers regaled visitors with extraordinary tales of heroism, pointed out the salient sites with names like Battle Valley, Battle Bluff, Battle Slough, and Battle Island.

News of the victory trickled back to the settlements of northern Illinois, occasioning wild rejoicing. At Apple River Fort the people loaded a cannon they had molded out of lead ignots and fired it joyously. It exploded, killing an amateur artillerist. Downstate the enthusiasm was less marked. At Edwardsville the *Illinois Advocate* reported the termination of the war in a smalltype, five-inch column on page three! In these sectors of the state, where Governor Reynolds was abhorred, jubilant announcements that the war was over were likely to be received with the reply, "What war?" The advance of the cholera was of much greater concern.

Leaving the militia behind to move by horseback, Atkinson's regulars embarked on the *Warrior* for Fort Crawford on August 4. For forty miles the steamboat churned past floating bodies of Sauk. The Menominee on board used them for target practice until a musket blew out a patch blistering an officer's face. The general showed some inclination to have the euphoric Indians thrown overboard, but contented himself with prohibiting further shooting. At Prairie du Chien the boat was met by canoes paddled by Winnebago squaws offering to sell "the sodden scalps of corpses four [*sic*] days in the water." The village had a festive air. For several days relatives of the Menominee killed by the Fox in 1831 had been dancing in the street. While warriors stood two in a row shaking gourds and beating drums, squaws in the middle kept time by grunting and shaking Sauk scalps dangling from long poles. The militia enjoyed it. John Wakefield found it "a very novel scene," and noted that "from their countenances, they appeared to be perfectly happy."

Only one problem marred the celebration of victory—Black Hawk and the Prophet remained at large; otherwise the war had ended. General Winfield Scott had arrived at Galena, whence he dispatched congratulations to General Atkinson. The volunteers soon forgot their cowardly behavior in the Black Hawk War and began to bask in the satisfaction of a job well and valiantly performed. No doubt John Wakefield spoke for most of them, summing up his feelings about the war: "It filled my heart with gratitude and joy, to think that I had been instrumental, with many others, in delivering my country of those merciless savages and restoring those people [the settlers] again to their peaceful homes and firesides, there to enjoy in safety the sweets of a retired life." The shocking feature of this pastoral fantasy is the speaker's absolute conviction, untainted by any moral ambilalence, that justice had been done.

> I do not permit the criers of our village or camps
> to proclaim any bad news against the Whites—
> not even the truth.
>
> —KEOKUK

THERE WAS A STORY popular in the Northwest for many years that, when General Winfield Scott arrived at Prairie du Chien on August 7, he arranged a victory banquet aboard the *Warrior*. General James D. Henry arrived last, a bit sheepish, and as he took his seat Scott boomed out, "Well, General Henry, it appears you are disposed to reverse the old maxim." "How, Sir?" responded the embarrassed Henry. "Why, Sir," Scott explained, the rule has been to be first at the feast and last at the fray." Not to be outdone by the Suckers from downstate, the Lead Region had its own story certifying that Colonel Henry Dodge was acknowledged as the foremost chieftain of the war. It declared that Atkinson, meeting Dodge at some Prairie du Chien festivity, hugged him and cried, "Dodge, you have saved me! You have dragged me on to victory!" Both these improbable dialogues suggested that the militia had been held back by the bungling incompetence of the regular army, instead of the other way round. Closer to the truth was that Atkinson had found the presence of the militia a necessary liability: Without them he could do nothing, with them he could do only a little more.

He hung about Scott's headquarters for another month, very much the number-two man, before resuming his paper work at Jefferson Barracks. His final order of the Black Hawk War, dated September 3, instructed Zachary Taylor to expel from Dubuque's mines a horde of squatters which had moved over there, though the Fox inhabitants had had nothing whatever to do with the

British Band. The sordid problem of Squatter Sovereignty was being renewed, though this time with a new cast.[1]

General Scott had arrived overland from Fort Dearborn with only three members of his staff. While en route he had slashed bloated militia rolls wherever the excess was most noticeable, as at Ottawa, Fort Wilbourn, and Dixon's Ferry. Wholesale mustering out of the three militia brigades commenced in earnest under Lieutenant Robert Anderson. Those men ailing or without horses were, at their option, steamboated to St. Louis for a few rounds at the grogshops and whorehouses (though not at government expense) before trudging back to their respective homes. Those with horses trooped overland by way of Dixon's Ferry.

Governor Reynolds, having already pushed the Department of War hard for remuneration for himself and his staff, shortly began to press for prompt payment to what he called "the brave volunteers" who left their plows to rush to the defense of their country.[2] As it happened, the war ended just as payments were being disbursed throughout the state to veterans of the 1831 expedition to Rock Island, and many of these soldiers were complaining that they had gotten only $19 for fighting in the earlier Sauk war. Editors blistered Congress for placing such a niggardly valuation on patriotism. The *Sangamo Journal* demanded

1. In later years Taylor characterized his battles with the squatters as "worse to manage than the Seminoles or even the Mexicans." No loyal Democrat, he startled some Washington circles when he recommended that the army be allowed "to burn and destroy the establishments of all squatters . . . and to remove them and all other whites who may attempt to trespass . . . upon the Indian territory without being legally authorized to do so." This sensible proposal, which would have accorded the Indians genuine contractual rights, was regarded by the Jacksonists as entirely reprehensible.

2. Though the government balked at paying Reynolds at the going rate for major general, eventually Secretary of War Lewis Cass arranged the matter to the satisfaction of His Excellency. On December 6 the governor penned a thank-you note to Cass that pretended the request had been motivated by a sense of personal honor, not by cold cash: "And as to myself the pecuniary consideration, altho' I am not wealthy is to me not so grateful, as the decided approbation of the Government, on my course, in the late war." Moreover, Reynolds got extra pay for serving as a commissioner in treaty negotiations with the Sauk.

that Sucker volunteers "receive the SAME PAY AS MOUNTED TROOPS of the United States." Eventually these stalwarts were well compensated by payment in land warrants and in cash for per diem service, transportation, rations, and loss of property. Six months later the same newspaper, cheered by reports that the United States would soon pay out $700,000 worth of war claims, flippantly editorialized, "Uncle Sam can't do better with his loose change than to send it here for distribution." The Black Hawk War was the best cash bonanza in Illinois history.[3]

The indirect costs of the war were staggering. The cholera epidemic failed to be checked at Chicago. Doubtless General Scott himself carried the disease to Galena, which by August 19 had reported sixteen cases and one death. Having assumed that it had run its course among his troops at Chicago, Scott prematurely ordered them to Fort Armstrong under Lieutenant Colonel Abram Eustis. Four days after the column reached Rock Island, the scourge exploded in the camps occupied by Atkinson's force, even though Eustis tried to keep his men bivouacked at a distance. Cramped together and sharing the same drinking water, circumstances were ideal for the spread of the disease. Within a week, fifty-six men had died. Men who had borne the hardships of the recent campaign without complaint now deserted at the rate of fourteen per day. Three Galena physicians came down to assist; one of them, Dr. Philleo, took one look at the stinking ward at Fort Armstrong and refused his services unless he received a higher compensation. Once again, Scott assumed the duties of chief surgeon and head nurse, boldly exposing himself to the disease.

3. The number of men who fought in the Black Hawk War has not been determined. Perry Armstrong, a historian of the war in the 1880s, after counting the names appearing on the muster rolls of 177 volunteer companies recruited in Illinois, came up with the figure of 7,787 men, excluding field officers, teamsters, surgeons, guards, and the like. Add to these approximately 1,500 regulars, the Michigan volunteers, armed civilians, and Indian mercenaries, and the figure of 12,000 is quickly reached. The number of white fatalities stood at 72, of which only 33 were known to have been killed by the Sauk; Winnebago, Kickapoo, and Potawatomie probably accounted for the remaining 39.

Still convinced that cleanliness and temperance were necessary to fend off the disease, General Scott posted the following famous order on August 28, at the peak of the epidemic: "[The commanding general] peremptorily commands that every soldier or Ranger who shall be found drunk or sensibly intoxicated . . . be compelled, as soon as his strength will permit, to dig a grave at a suitable burying place large enough for his own reception, as such grave cannot fail soon to be wanted for the drunken man himself or some drunken companion. This order is given as well to serve for the punishment of drunkenness as to spare good and temperate men the labor of digging graves for their worthless companions." The order failed to stop the cholera, but it is said to have brought temporary sobriety to the camps.

Fearing that cholera would spread to the three Sauk hostages imprisoned at Fort Armstrong since early April, Scott allowed them to seek safety in the woods, after taking their pledge that they would return after the epidemic had ended. Though warned that they would probably be hanged for their part in the Menominee murders, the Sauk promised to surrender themselves when a signal flag was hung in a dead tree on the island. After the disease had run its course and the signal given, all three paddled back to the fort. Impressed by this behavior, Scott paroled them pending an appeal and later secured their pardon.

Travelers on the Mississippi could have found Rock Island simply by following the nauseous stench reaching across the river as hundreds of men "puked and purged all night." One doctor reported that during the convulsive spasms preceding the death of a patient, the screech was so unearthly that he involuntarily covered his ears with his hands. The disease continued to spread south and west until the first frost. By November it was raging as far south as New Orleans, where five hundred deaths per day were reported and great bonfires of tar and pitch burned to purify what was thought of as poisoned air. In the spring of 1833 the epidemic again emerged and struck with increased fury. Among these victims was that Indian nemesis, the ex-governor, Ninian Edwards, who drowned in his own vomit and defecation at Belleville.

Had it not been for Joseph Street's tough tactics with the Winnebago of his agency, Black Hawk might have remained at large in the wilds of Wisconsin indefinitely. But Street warned some headmen of the tribe that they, too, were under suspicion for having possibly assisted the British Band during the late war. To prove their good will, they were ordered to fetch in Black Hawk; to make the order less bitter, Street offered $200 and twenty horses as reward. Hunting bands had no difficulty in tracking both Black Hawk and the Prophet (in all likelihood both were being sheltered by the Winnebago all along), who had drifted northwest with their few remaining followers to the vicinity of La Crosse.

Both leaders had left Bad Axe after the initial attack of the *Warrior* and had, therefore, missed the battle entirely. According to the testimony of two Sauk prisoners of war, Black Hawk stated that his intention was to take refuge among the Ottawa tribe far to the north. While they did not admire him for skipping out on the battle, neither did they deplore this move, for anyone wishing to depart with him was free to do so. Once he saw that the Winnebago would not protect him or assist in conducting his party through Menominee country, he surrendered without a struggle.[4] Winnebago women made him a hunting dress of fine white deerskin; and two headmen, One-Eyed Decori and Chaeter, escorted Black Hawk's party to Prairie du Chien, less as prisoners of war than as honored guests. Fortunately for the honor of the victors, the militia riffraff had disappeared from the Prairie by the time the canoe bearing the Sauk captives landed on August 27. Whatever their faults, Colonel Zachary Taylor and "General" Joseph Street adhered to the code of the gentleman, which did not sanction abusive treatment of a defeated foe.

In the ceremony which followed, the Winnebago appeared

4. According to Black Hawk, he entered the lodge of a Winnebago chief and announced that he intended to give himself up to the American war chief "and *die,* if the Great Spirit saw proper." This does not quite square with Winnebago reports that he had to be induced to surrender and told them, "You want us to be killed by the Whites; as you so wish it, we will go."

more unnerved than Black Hawk, who sat as stoic as ever, a wizened old man barely more formidable than a sack of dry bones. One-Eyed Decori appeared to believe that unspeakable tortures lay ahead for the prisoners and spoke to them, "My father, we have done what you told us to do. We always do what you tell us, because we know it is for our good. . . . You told us to bring them to you alive. We have done so. If you had told us to bring their heads alone, we would have done so, and it would have been less difficult than what we have done. . . . We want you to keep them safe. If they are to be hurt, we do not wish to see it. Wait until we are gone before it is done." Then, to allay white suspicions that the Winnebago had assisted the British Band during the war, he continued, "My Father, many little birds have been flying about our ears of late, and we thought they whispered to us that there was evil intended for us, but now we hope these evil birds will let our ears alone. We know you are our friend, because you take our part, and that is the reason we do what you tell us to do." After both Taylor and Street had assured the envoys that the prisoners would be treated well, Chaeter rose to reiterate what Decori had said, concluding his speech with a flash of grim realism: "My Father, soldiers sometimes stick the ends of their guns into the back of Indian prisoners when they are going about in the hands of the guard. I hope this will not be done to these men."

Black Hawk never regarded himself as an able speaker. His address to his captors, recorded in the *Galenian* (in which he alluded to himself in third person as though caught and ground up in Chemokemon machinery), included no hypocritical note of apology: "Black Hawk is an Indian. He has done nothing of which an Indian need be ashamed. He has fought the battles of his country against the white man, who came year after year to cheat his people and take away their lands. You know the cause of our making war. It is known to all white men. They ought to be ashamed of it. The white men despise the Indians and drive them from their homes. But the Indians are not deceitful. Indians do not steal. Black Hawk is satisfied. He will go to the world of spirits contented. He has done his duty. . . . Farewell to my nation! Farewell to Black Hawk!" Another version has him say,

"An Indian who is as bad as the white man could not live in our nation. *He* would be put to death and eat up by the wolves." Other than to recite the customary homilies of Indian affairs, there was very little that the whites could say in effective rebuttal.

Neither torture nor execution lay ahead for Black Hawk. In rare moments of candor even the crudest frontiersman was aware that the war had been foisted on the Sauk. And, while there is a certain amount of truth in the notion that the frontiersman's favorite Indian was a dead one, it was also true that, if he had not done the killing himself, he did not want anyone else to do it. The government had made no plans to deal with the leaders of the British Band, should these be taken alive, so as soon as they came within his jurisdiction, General Scott resolved to ship them to Jefferson Barracks where Atkinson could take over the problem. Accordingly, he sent Lieutenant Robert Anderson, with a squad of soldiers, on board the faithful *Warrior,* to fetch the prisoners.

Almost immediately cholera began to spread through the steamboat. Throckmorton had to drop off some of the soldiers at Galena and, by the time he docked at the Prairie, Anderson himself had developed the initial symptoms of the disease—nausea and acute diarrhea. When the lieutenant insisted upon continuing, Colonel Taylor assigned his favorite company commander, Lieutenant Jefferson F. Davis,[5] who had just reported in from leave, to accompany the prisoners to Jefferson Barracks. On September 4 they got under way aboard the *Winnebago,* which had thus far escaped contagion. Anderson had requisitioned from the Fort Crawford armorer such items as handcuffs and shackles; but it is unlikely that Davis, who soon took charge, subjected his prisoners to this sort of degradation. Black Hawk liked Davis,

5. A favorite until Davis began to court Taylor's daughter Knox later that year. Transferred to a dragoon regiment in 1833, Davis continued his courtship by mail and married Knox two years later in Kentucky. Taylor refused to attend the wedding. Within three months Knox Davis died in a yellow fever epidemic. Taylor's objections to Davis as a son-in-law were variously given. In the Lead Region it was believed that having once watched the lieutenant dancing obscenely with an Indian girl at a tavern, Taylor became outraged when he began to show attention to his daughter.

whom he called "the young war chief who treated us all with much kindness." During a stopover at Galena, where a wharf-side mob gathered to ogle the captives, the lieutenant secured his prisoners in their cabin. At Rock Island the master of the *Winnebago* refused to land because of the epidemic. General Scott was rowed out in a small boat to contest this point, but the captain would not let him aboard. Scott had learned that Black Hawk had important disclosures to make, presumably about Winnebago collaboration in the war, and wanted to talk to him, for the government wished to expropriate valuable Winnebago lands as quickly as possible. Failing to make contact, Scott ordered Atkinson to interrogate Black Hawk, and the *Winnebago* steamed on to St. Louis.

General Atkinson's reception of Black Hawk's party was less than gracious. He put all of them in ball and chain, doubtless resolving that the old war chief would never again lead him on a chase through bog and over mountain. Several weeks later Neapope and half a dozen others arrived in a mackinaw boat, bringing the number of captives to twenty. During the waning weeks of the summer, the citizenry of St. Louis flocked down to the barracks in such numbers that Atkinson had to post visiting hours. He became, in effect, the custodian of a museum with live specimens walking and airing themselves. The public ex-pressed great disappointment in Black Hawk, described by the St. Louis *Republican* as "infirm of body, and an imbecile in mind. Neither his physiognomy nor his actions give any indica-tion of talent or of tact." The Prophet, on the other hand, made the excursion worthwhile. His massive body and sulky moods corresponded to the preconception of a savage Indian. "A fine-looking fellow—free and fearless," noted the *Republican*. Some-times he would glare balefully at the spectators and rattle his chains. Once, when the artist George Catlin started to draw his portrait, the Prophet picked up his ball and chain and exclaimed, "Make me so, and show to the Great Father!"

Black Hawk expressed his mortification at being locked up and chained: "Was the White Beaver afraid that I would break out of his barracks, and run away?" he later wrote. "If I had taken him prisoner on the field of battle, I would not have wounded his feelings so much, by such treatment—knowing that a brave war chief would prefer *death* to *dishonor*." Such confinement was worse than any torture he had ever envisioned. Perhaps because of this treatment he never revealed to Atkinson the nature of his disclosures promised to Scott. Because of a mild outbreak of cholera among them in December, Atkinson removed the chains from all hostages except Neapope and the Prophet. And by this time they were permitted to manufacture little pipes as a reward for not trying to run away.

Not even a cholera epidemic could keep Governor John Reynolds away from Rock Island in mid-September, when the time came to inflict a treaty on the Sauk and Fox nation for their "unprovoked war upon unsuspecting and defenceless citizens of the United States"—to quote from the final text. It might seem that eliminating three-quarters of the British Band during the late war had inflicted suffering enough on them. Moreover, one might wonder with whom the Americans expected to negotiate a treaty, since Black Hawk, the Prophet, and Neapope were incarcerated in St. Louis. But such assumes that the treaties aimed to achieve reasonable and just goals. The United States had no more interest in the British Band as such; the Black Hawk War was now so much dead history. The proclaimed object of the treaty was to force the Sauk and Fox to cede lands west of the Mississippi—as reparations for the barbarities perpetrated by the followers of Black Hawk, none of whom were even allowed near the treaty grounds. That this land had to come from the holdings of the nation as a whole, the majority of whom had adhered to the Peace party led by Keokuk, was regarded as immaterial and irrelevant. The Chemokemons reasoned that some of the Sauk had gone on the warpath, and the fact that most of them were dead merely simplified the argument: One could not seek damages from a dead Indian.

Because of lingering vestiges of cholera at Fort Armstrong, the opening session on September 19 was held across the river (present Davenport, Iowa). Appointed U.S. commissioners, Winfield Scott and John Reynolds lined up against Keokuk. General Scott appeared in stunning regalia, his large frame festooned with medals and gold braid.[6] In contrast, Governor Reynolds presented an unimposing picture. Hovering in the background was George Davenport, who had been assured by Reynolds that his $40,000 claim against the Sauk and Fox would be included on the agenda. Scott opened the conference with a stern reproach: Since the Sauk chiefs had failed to prevent Black Hawk from "making an unjust war upon the unoffending white settlers . . . the whole confederacy had forfeited as much of their territory as the conquerors might choose as an indemnity." And that, as the negotiations proved, was considerable.

The only dissenter to the whites' case was Joshua Pilcher, appointed acting Sauk and Fox agent after Felix St. Vrain's death. Originally Pilcher seemed a safe appointee—he had once run a lottery, directed a bank in Kentucky, and as an agent of the American Fur Company at Council Bluffs was attuned to the whites' perspective in dealing with Indians. But once this able bureaucrat and opportunist had been installed as Sauk agent he initiated an investigation of George Davenport's books and generally used his post as Indian agent to look after the interests of the Sauk rather than to rubberstamp decisions of the whites who had installed him. Early in the war he had written Superintendent William Clark that Missourians who had claimed that Keokuk's band was planning to join Black Hawk were liars. He had later written Clark that Davenport had been cheating the Indians at his trading post. Shaken by such inexplicable behavior, Davenport branded Pilcher "an evill Genious equel to the Cholra if he had the same pour [power] to scourge mankind." Whether Pilcher could have successfully withstood the rhetoric of Scott and the jingoism of Reynolds is questionable. In any case, he did not have the chance. Whether by accident or machination, he was called downriver during the negotiations to fetch the Sauk and Fox annuities, making sure that the only person who could have

6. Scott's costumery was often so imaginative that it bordered upon the ridiculous and laid him open for caricature. Thirty years later a Confederate lampoonist, George Washington Harris, described Old Fuss and Feathers entering a room: First a gigantic plume appeared through the doorway, and far to the rear an immense sword fitted with a small wheel attached to the tip of the scabbard.

stood up for the interests of the tribe missed the negotiations altogether. A few weeks later he had been replaced by a more reasonable agent, Marmaduke Davenport.[7]

The massacre at Bad Axe showed how Americans dealt with hostile Indians; the treaty at Fort Armstrong, what they did to friendlies. In the end, the Sauk were forced to cede a strip of land fifty miles wide along the west bank of the Mississippi, extending from Missouri almost to the present state of Minnesota. This tract, which comprised about six million acres of choice farmland, was obtained for less than ten cents an acre. Commissioner Reynolds, reporting to Secretary of War Cass, glowingly calculated that the ceded territory "will be worth more . . . in thirty years, than seven millions of dollars, & for which, deducting the expenses of the war, the U. S. will only have to pay, in the same term of years, about $660,000." [8] Payment (without interest) would be made on the annuity principle of $20,000 each year for thirty years, which amounted to about $4 per year for each Sauk. There was, however, a catch. The first two annuities were to go to George Davenport and his partner Russell Farnham to settle their account. What this ultimately meant was that the tribe would have to go so deeply in debt for advances against their credit that the traders would end up with their entire annuity.

In time this cession became known as the Black Hawk Purchase, intimating Black Hawk had willingly negotiated it. The Indians pledged to vacate the area by June 1, 1833, except for a four-hundred-square-mile tract on the Iowa River which was set off as a reservation (and later reclaimed by the government when the land became valuable). The Fox bands working Dubuque's mines found themselves evicted as well, although they had had

7. Time vindicated Pilcher, for after William Clark's death, he became superintendent of the Western tribes although he quit the job after two years.

The former Sauk and Fox agent, Thomas Forsyth, raged when he learned of the imprisonment of the Sauk leaders "for no other fault than defending themselves like men when attacked by a worthless drunken set of fellows under Major Stillman." In his judgment William Clark was directly responsible for the war.

8. Reynolds underestimated the period of time required to settle Iowa. By 1838 it had entered territorial status; by 1846 it had acquired statehood.

nothing to do with the Black Hawk War. The few other items which the tribe received are quickly enumerated: a blacksmith shop for a thirty-year period plus forty kegs of tobacco and forty barrels of salt for the same period.

To salve their consciences, Americans gave outright to the surviving members of the British Band thirty barrels of pork, twelve bushels of salt, and thirty-five beef cattle, all war surplus. None of Black Hawk's people and only a few of Keokuk's had been able to plant a crop. Those who did not starve during the following winter looked forward to a special gift of six thousand bushels of corn in April. All prisoners of war were released, except the twelve hostages at Jefferson Barracks. How long these men would be held, none could say. General Scott guessed that they would receive ten-year sentences.

Though it hardly seems possible, the whites felt that this treaty was unusually generous on their part. In his memoirs, General Scott noted that "the spirit of forbearance and liberality on the part of the United States, were the prominent features in these settlements." Secretary Cass ("Big Belly" as the Indians called him), in a letter to Scott a month later, commended his "spirit of proper liberality towards the Indians." And governor Reynolds soon had to defend himself against disgruntled Suckers who accused him of selling out to the Indians: "Give 'em lead, not corn!" was their general attitude. One citizen of Illinois, however, expressed his illiterate delight at the treaty: In a letter ominously marked "private," George Davenport wrote Pierre Chouteau Jr., czar of the St. Louis fur trade, "They have sceded to the United States the west Bank of the Mississippi fifty miles deep and have staplated to pay us our claim of forty thousand dollars. it will no doubt pass the Cenate." That viper Pilcher had been "verrey unfriendley to our claim, but he could do nothing. the Commissionr [Reynolds] was genrley at my house." Though Davenport was a poor hand at spelling, there was nothing wrong with his arithmetic beyond a habit of multiplying figures that he was supposed to add. This master confidence man was so skillful that Keokuk's people had called on him to represent their interests in the negotiations.

After signing the treaty on September 21, General Scott

treated the headmen and their families to a dinner on Rock Island. The festivities featured that sort of entertainment at which the army excelled—a massive display of pyrotechnics. Rockets, mortars, and cannon erupted with crash and roll. Fireballs and thunder caused "much shouting of delight from the Indians . . . notwithstanding their usual *nil admirari,* or phlegm," wrote General Scott, pleased to be giving the Indians some pleasure in exchange for their seven million acres. On the turf near Fort Armstrong, a dance followed. Since Indian custom forbade their women from participating, the blue coats seized Sauk warriors instead. Keokuk, who earlier that day had been designated "chief, in the name of the President of the United States," enacted a pantomime depicting how on a war party long ago, he had taken a scalp. Finally the music died, the dancing ceased, and the crowds drifted off. For the last time the Sauk slept at Rock Island. Everybody seemed "contented and cheerful," Scott reported; and, doubtless, even among the Indians there existed a pleasant afterglow. Chemokemons could be generous and charming people, so long as they got what they wanted. Officially the Black Hawk War had ended.

The question as to what to do with the dozen hostages at Jefferson Barracks became, as winter came on, a frequently raised one in official correspondence. Washington Irving, who visited them in December, found "a forlorn crew—emaciated and dejected—the redoubtable chieftain himself, a meagre old man upwards of seventy." It seemed preposterous to pretend that they posed a serious threat to the life of the Republic. General Scott suggested that they be sent to Fort Monroe, at the mouth of the Chesapeake, where no guard would be required. General Atkinson urged that they be escorted on a tour of the East, in order to see something of the great strength of the United States, and then returned to the tribe with Keokuk as their parole officer. Ultimately Secretary Cass adopted both proposals.

As soon as the ice broke up on the river, the delegation set off for Washington by steamboat. Among the captives were Black Hawk, the Prophet, Pamaho ("Fast Swimming Fish"), Neapope, the Prophet's adopted son, and Black Hawk's son Nasheaskuk ("Whirling Thunder"). Escorting them were a lieutenant, two guards, and the interpreter, Charles St. Vrain. At Wheeling they transferred to a stage coach before a gaping but friendly crowd and traveled the National Road to Frederick, Maryland. Here they boarded a railroad, a phenomenon which Black Hawk praised as an extravagant contrivance, though he noted, "I prefer riding on horseback, however, to any other way."

Arriving at Washington on April 22, they had to wait three days for an audience with President Jackson. Black Hawk wore a clean buckskin hunting dress with a bright blanket tossed about his shoulders. At his side he carried his medicine bag, fabricated from the skin and feathers of the sparrow hawk. In token of his peaceful mission, his hair was shaved except for a tuft on top. Jingling baubles hung from ears deeply pierced. In his arms he carried a Sauk war bonnet as gift to the Great Father. Jackson, who had little use for Indian palaver or ceremony, bluntly demanded to know why the British Band had gone to war against the whites. Black Hawk was stunned by the inquiry; as he explained later, "I thought he ought to have known this before; and, consequently, said but little to him about it—as I expected he knew as well as I could tell him." Until this point the captives had supposed that their tour was merely a ceremony, at the conclusion of which they would be permitted to return to their people. To their great surprise, the president informed them that they must stay awhile at Fort Monroe. The Prophet argued with mounting anger: The war had not been the fault of the Indians, for they had had a right to plant crops; their families were endangered by raids from the Sioux and Menominee and they wished to return and take care of them. Jackson assured them that he intended to prevent future warfare among the various tribes and dismissed them. Alone with his cronies later, Old Hickory donned the headdress; shook his head till the quills rattled; and, alluding to his political enemies, remarked, "I don't think those fellows would like to meet me in this."

The dejected captives arrived at Fort Monroe on April 26, where they were treated more like celebrities than prisoners by the artillery regiment of Colonel Abram Eustis.[9] So long as they remained within the ramparts they were free to do as they pleased. The most onerous feature of their captivity was having to answer the questions of the throngs of visitors who came for a view of the Great Chief Black Hawk. Officers' wives gave them baubles and cooked them dainties, which the Indians received with punctilious courtesy. Black Hawk later confessed, however, that the only enjoyable food he had during his entire captivity was a strip of dried venison sent to Jefferson Barracks by George Davenport. Artists proved to be nearly as importunate as the curiosity seekers. Robert M. Sully, the romantic portraitist, portrayed the severe lines of Black Hawk's wizened face as those of a senior Southern statesman. George Catlin had earlier painted Black Hawk in his Sauk garb; but Sully and other Eastern artists like John Wesley Jarvis and Charles Bird King rendered the war chief in the quasiregimental costume provided by Andrew Jackson. Whatever ferocity had once lain deep within these men seemed to have been drained; from objects of fear, they had been transformed into subjects for pity.

After six weeks at Fort Monroe, the hostages commenced the tour planned to impress them with the hopelessness of defying the will of white America. After inspecting a seventy-four-gun ship of the line in the navy yard at Gosport, even the Prophet showed signs of moderating. From the balcony of their Norfolk hotel, he addressed a throng, promising all of his white friends hospitality in the West. June 6 found them installed in a Baltimore hotel, but the stifling heat and the endless visitors necessitated their removal to the tranquility of Fort McHenry in the harbor. Quite by accident their itinerary began to overlap that of President Jackson, then starting out on a tour through the Northeast. At one theater journalists were hard put to decide whether the audience craned their heads to view Old Hickory or Black Hawk.

At a parley the following day, Jackson did not mince words as he told the old man, "What can you do against us? You may

9. Black Hawk was certainly accorded better treatment than his friend Jefferson Davis, who was shackled in a gloomy casemate of Fort Monroe following his capture after the Civil War. These two rebels most likely shared many areas of mutual interest and common sympathy.

kill a few women and children but such a force would soon be sent against you as would destroy your whole tribe. . . . If you again plunge your knives into the breasts of our people, I shall send a force which will severely punish you for all your cruelties." The words of the great Democrat penetrated. In Philadelphia, after touring the mint and watching a crack drill team perform in front of the Congress Hall Hotel, Black Hawk told a journalist, "I see the strength of the white man. They are many, very many. The Indians are but few. They are not cowards, they are brave, but they are few." The journalist thought the old man was "depressed in spirits" but noted that his head "would excite the envy of a phrenologist—one of the finest that Heaven ever let fall on the shoulders of an Indian." [10]

New York came as the climax of their tour. As they crossed to Manhattan by ferry, they were informed that a man would ascend in a balloon from Castle Garden. "We watched with anxiety to see if it could be true," recalled Black Hawk, "and to our utter astonishment, saw him ascend in the air until the eye could no longer perceive him. Our people were all surprised, and one of our young men asked the *prophet* if he was going up to see the Great Spirit." The Prophet, however, was finding many questions beyond his capacity for cogent reply. Barely on land, the Sauk were mobbed by a crowd demanding a view of "General Black Hawk." Fearing a riot, the authorities provided a police cordon that ushered the Indians through back streets to the Exchange Hotel and cancelled reservations in the hotel where they had been booked. There were more fireworks, more soirees, more interviews, more presents. Society ladies singled out Nasheaskuk (or "Tommy Hawk" as he was often called in the press) for special attention; they "warmly kissed him" and thrilled at the preposterous story that he had become enamoured of one of the Hall sisters. At one point, a gentleman hoping to engage in a religious conversation with one of "our sons of the forest," pur-

10. The *American Phrenological Journal* published an analysis of his head based upon a plaster of Paris cast taken in New York during Black Hawk's second Eastern journey in 1837. Among the resulting data were: individuality—very large; self-esteem—very large; destructiveness—very large; hope—small.

sued Nasheaskuk into the hotel; but when he explained his mission, the Sauk smiled and replied in English, "I la-zee, I la-zee." Pulling a blanket over his head, he fell fast asleep.

The New York diarist Philip Hone wrote on June 12, the date Old Hickory arrived in town, "with the exception of LaFayette's arrival, we have never witnessed such a scene." Three days later, after Jackson had gone, he wrote, "The celebrated Indian chief Black Hawk and his companions . . . now occupy the place in the public curiosity which Gen. Jackson so recently filled." But honest journalists observed that the Sauk visitors made rather poor copy; they spent most of their time sleeping and hiding. To supply the public with the drivel it craved, reporters began to manufacture such catchpenny columns as "Black Hawkiana" and "Black Hawkisms." Here was some real Indian lore: Black Hawk patting a lady on the head and remarking, "What a beautiful head for scalping." Or Black Hawk saying after a fireworks display, "It is nothing to burning up a Long-Knife town." Or Black Hawk trying to drink a bottle of cologne that a lady had given him and hurling it away as he called out, "Give me some firewater." Or Black Hawk giving another lady the scalp of a white woman and asking her to wear it for his sake. Or Black Hawk chasing a temperance fanatic from his room with his tomahawk. Even in the East, whites demanded their stereotypes.

The fact was that the prisoners were exhausted and bored. When their custodian Major John Garland prepared to move on to Boston, they objected; out of respect for their feelings, the major cancelled this leg of their tour. On June 22 they left by steamboat for home. At the Albany landing there were so many curiosity seekers that Major Garland feared for the safety of his charges. This was no genteel assemblage, content with a discreet peek at "noble savages," this was a mob, Garland reported, of "ruffian like appearance." Recruiting some gentlemen from the steamboat, the major led a spirited charge to a getaway carriage. They escaped, but in the melee Garland's pocket was picked of $100 and their driver bloodied by brickbats hurled by the irate mob. After dark he had the prisoners don Chemokemon clothing so that they could all slip away to Schenectady unobserved. After the nasty Albany incident, they traveled as rapidly and as inconspicuously as possible. A little guiltily, Garland explained his decision to the secretary of war, "The people of the towns and villages do not appear satisfied with the rapidity of my movement. The fact is, both the Indians and myself are heartily tired of crowds."

Black Hawk bore up poorly during the grueling tour. An editor who met him on the Lake Erie packet said the old man worried lest his hat blow off and complained of being unable to sleep in the suffocating cabin.

As they steamed up the Detroit River, Black Hawk must have observed the Union Jack flying over Fort Malden on the Ontario shore and remembered the better days when he had a British Father. At Detroit the crowds seemed surly; and it was reported that a mob there burned the Sauk in effigy. They hurried to Green Bay by steamboat and to Prairie du Chien by way of the Fort Winnebago portage. Since it had been decided that the Prophet would live among the Winnebago, he was dropped off at Fort Crawford; the others continued to Rock Island. Passing Dubuque's mines, Black Hawk learned for the first time that the west bank of the Mississippi had been seized by the Chemoke-mons. "I am very much afraid," he predicted, "that in a few years, they will begin to drive and abuse our people, as they have formerly done. I may not live to *see* it, but I feel certain that the day is not distant."

On August 2, 1833, the first anniversary of Bad Axe, Black Hawk was reunited with his tribe at Fort Armstrong. But there were still more unpleasant surprises in store for him. Major Garland explained that the Great Father now acknowledged Keokuk as principal chief and that Black Hawk was obliged to obey and respect him. Hearing this, Black Hawk sprang to his feet "so deeply excited," reported a white observer, "as to be almost unable to utter a word." Again he had been tricked by the Chemoke-mons. He had thought himself free, only to find himself paroled to what to him was a contemptible creature. Finally he exclaimed angrily, "I am a man—an old man—I will not conform to the counsels of any one. I will act for myself—no one shall govern me. I am old—my hair is gray—I once gave counsels to my young men—Am I to conform to others? I shall soon go to the

Great Spirit, when I shall be at rest. What I said to our Great Father, I say again—I will always listen to him. I am done."

Both whites and Indians present listened with horror to this outburst from a tired old man who seemed possessed by some devil to speak his mind, when to say nothing guaranteed his freedom. All wanted to obliterate or excuse this last defiance. Keokuk smoothed it over. The presence of Keokuk was the price which Black Hawk had to pay for his freedom. Black Hawk was done.

Epilogue

Our education seems to consist in knowing how
most effectually to cheat them; our civilization
in knowing how to pander to the worst propensities
of nature, and then beholding the criminal
and inhuman results with a cold indifference . . ,
while our religion is readily summed up in the
consideration of dollars and cents.
        —JOHN BEACH, Sauk and Fox agent (1842)

WITH THE INDIANS hurled back apparently forever from the
legislative halls and grogshops of Vandalia, the time had come
for the Suckers to exchange their muskets for plowshares and put
in a crop of corn. However, the last shots at Bad Axe had barely
died away when Governor John Reynolds began to once again
show an interest in new battles. Perhaps he had discovered that
his constituency showed more enthusiasm for a leader actively
astride a saddle than for one apparently lounging in the gubernatorial chair. In any case, in his address at the opening session
of the legislature in December 1832, the governor sounded them
out about his latest plan, removal of the few remaining tribes
from the sacred soil of Illinois. According to reliable sources in
the Lead Region (Editor Addison Philleo), the Sauk and Fox
had allied themselves with the Potawatomie and the Winnebago
and planned to attack settlements in the spring. No less an authority on Indian plots than General Sam Whiteside had been
dispatched by the governor to investigate these rumors; he had
confirmed them. As it happened, Reynolds's war fever coincided
perfectly with announcements in early December that federal
paymasters were en route to Illinois to pay veterans for their
services in the recent war.

His constituents, however, had had enough of John Reynolds's saber rattling. In the Lead Region, Uncle Billy Hamilton, making his own investigations, found that a few Indians begging and stealing food had ignited the war rumors.[1] In a letter to the *Galenian,* he denied that any Northwestern tribe planned any aggression: The Winnebago, he reported, had no love for the white man; but they retained enough fear to remain peaceful. Talk of another war so frightened Indians of the region that several headmen came into the settlements in January to offer themselves as hostages. King Keokuk I, as he was now being called in the press, reiterated his great affection for the white man.

In time, the cries of the hawks were hushed, as it became clear that no enemy threatened. The editor of the *Sangamo Journal,* aiming at Reynolds, warned, "If we have another war, the Whites alone will be at fault." This view prevailed. The State of Illinois launched no more wars against Indians within its boundaries. Instead, its erstwhile allies, the Potawatomie and the Rock River Winnebago, were ejected by treaties dictated in late 1833.

On the far side of the great river, the Sauk and Fox nation rapidly deteriorated. With lands and pride wrested from them, they succumbed to Chemokemon whiskey. Perhaps because they now perceived that their Iowa lands would soon pass from their control also, they made no particular effort to break up the matted prairie sod and build a new trans-Mississippi Saukenuk. Those few land-hungry squatters who began pushing into the Sauk domain met no resistance. Bad Axe had left deep, uphealing

1. The Winnebago, particularly those bands around Portage, suffered terribly during the winter of 1832–33. Few of them had been able to harvest a crop, and the passage of the army through their district had driven off the game. Their annuities had been delayed by bureaucratic errors in Detroit, and Agent John Kinzie had not been able to provide emergency relief because quartermaster stores at Green Bay and Portage had been emptied by the recent war. Great numbers crawled into Fort Winnebago, perishing of starvation under the eyes of their agent who was powerless to help them.

wounds which no tribesman wished to open again. The time had come for the Sauk and Fox to open their hearts to Jesus.

In 1834, a pious young missionary, working within the auspices of the Society for Propagation of Christian Knowledge, arrived at Rock Island. He startled George Davenport with the information that he had come to Christianize the Sauk. Although the trader, who was convinced that the appointed role of the Indian on the earth was to take pelts not to get religion, objected on grounds that "missionaries would only make them worse," Cutting Marsh recruited a guide and plunged unafraid into the Sauk preserve. "Often when looking at their condition," wrote this graduate of Dartmouth College and Andover Theological Seminary, "I felt somewhat of that stirring of spirit which Paul felt at Athens."

At the principal Sauk village on the lower Iowa River Keokuk greeted the young missionary with abusive language, saying that he knew why Marsh had come and wished to hear nothing about it. Marsh remained anyhow and, while mooning about the village, stumbled upon the lodge of Black Hawk. Behind a neat sapling fence, festooned with vines of melon and pumpkin, stood a bark structure surrounded by a garden with no trace of weeds. Black Hawk was absent, but entering anyway, the preacher received a polite reception from other members of the family. Dining room chairs of Chemokemon manufacture graced the well-brushed clay floor. "Such a specimen of neatness and good order I never before witnessed in any Indian lodge," he reported. Marsh learned that, despite the Hawk's political eclipse, the old man still had loyal supporters within the tribe and retained as much respect, though of a different order, as "haughty Keokuk."

Passing on to other Sauk and Fox villages, Marsh encountered only a sense of defeat and discouragement. As a tonic for Indian ailments, it was obvious that demon rum offered more than sacramental wine. Prowess among the Indians had now come to be measured by a warrior's capacity for consuming huge quantities of whiskey. Chief Poweshiek gave the preacher a hearing and expressed his willingness to permit a few braves to receive English instruction, but nothing more. When Marsh outlined how

Jesus would alter their lives, Poweshiek countered, "But our way is best. The Great Spirit has made us to fight and kill one another whenever we are a mind to. If we should now change our life it would displease the Great Spirit and we should all be sick and die off." On one occasion, the preacher was briefly encouraged when an elderly warrior expressed interest in the Bible he carried; but he was soon disappointed when he learned that his questioner hoped that it was strong medicine, useful in killing Sioux. His efforts to expound ideas of sin and atonement were met with laughter. But his blessing of the food proved to be more comprehensible; as one Indian told him, "Why that is just like the Indians. I thought the white people never did it but were like the hogs because they thought themselves God." It seemed hopeless. Marsh began to retire privately into the woods to commune with God and to escape the drunken screeching of the Sauk at their nightly revels. After a few months, the preacher slipped out of the country, despairing of Christian propagation and carrying back with him only a bad case of dysentery.

By 1836 the Sauk and Fox had become so dependent on annuities from the government and credits from their traders that Keokuk's proposal to sell his four-hundred-square-mile preserve met with no resistance from the tribe. Whites were crowding into this tract anyway. Therefore, in September, headmen assembled on the riverbank opposite Rock Island to negotiate with Henry Dodge, who just weeks before had shaved four million acres from Menominee holdings in Wisconsin for $.10 an acre (sum payable in twenty years without interest). Mounted on a $300 horse aglitter with silver bridle and saddle, Keokuk made a startling contrast with Black Hawk, who was dressed in simple buckskin breeches and an old blue frock coat. George Catlin, foremost Indian artist of that period, attended the conference and noted, "The poor dethroned monarch, old Black Hawk, was present, and looked an object of pity. . . . He stood the whole time outside the group, and in dumb and dismal silence, with his sons by the side of him, and also his quondam aide-de-camp, Nah-pope, and the Prophet." These renegades were not permitted to speak out. When Neapope rose to complain about the whiskey traders, Dodge declared him out of order and Keokuk gave the young warrior a baleful look "that the Devil himself might have shrunk from."

Very quickly Keokuk disposed of his preserve. He asked $1.25 an acre, Dodge offered $.75, and they struck a bargain. Old Hairy Face was a bit miffed by the high price (compared with the Menominee the Sauk and Fox were Yankee traders), but he consoled Washington with his hunch that the land could be sold at $3.00 an acre. Naturally the treaty was filled with un-read fine print. Claims outstanding were payable at once and $100,000 of the settlement would be withheld for distribution over a ten-year period, an arrangement providing white traders with the opportunity to grab it all in time. Pushing even harder, Dodge offered to purchase all the remaining lands north of the Missouri River and to arrange for the removal of the nation to new lands in the Southwest. Although Keokuk turned his back on this offer then, the idea had been sown in his mind.

During the fall of 1837 a large delegation of Sauk and Fox journeyed to Washington for a conference called by Secretary of War Joel R. Poinsett. The ostensible purpose of this powwow was to patch up their quarrel with the Sioux; but, when the dele-gation left Washington they had signed away 1.25 million more acres. Those unfamiliar with Indian affairs must surely have wondered how it was possible for so small a tribe to accumulate nearly $100,000 in fresh debts in a single year—the amount the government paid the traders. It further gave Keokuk the sum of $28,500 for distribution to his people, which would have amounted to about three-quarters of a cotton blanket for each tribe member had the chief distributed it equally, which he did not; and it arranged to invest $200,000 of the balance in "safe state stocks" that would guarantee the tribe 5 percent interest annually. The present location of this trust fund cannot be traced.

In the years that followed, there would be other sordid trea-ties and shady deals, until by 1846 the Sauk and Fox had been removed to a reservation near the headwaters of the Osage River in Kansas. There their history ends, except for one faction which, finding conditions intolerable, returned to Iowa and established a home in Tama County.

Mercifully Black Hawk was spared further wrenchings. He

had accompanied the delegation to Washington in 1837 (Keokuk liked to have the old man along), but showed little interest in the proceedings. At each steamboat landing and crossroad grocery he upstaged Keokuk, of whom most whites had never heard. But for the most part he sat moody and uncommunicative as Chemokemons milled about trying to establish which Indian was Black Hawk. Sauk pranksters amused themselves by pointing to the interpreter Antoine LeClair, a balloon-shaped man, so obese that he could barely move. The joke always moved LeClair into a paroxysm of rage, while Black Hawk sat completely impassive and immobile. Although the delegation toured several Eastern cities, seeing such wonders as Catlin's Indian gallery in New York and Faneuil Hall in Boston, Black Hawk preferred the dim solitude of his hotel rooms.

Back in Iowa, Black Hawk found himself gradually elevated to a patriarchal level among the better class of whites in the region. Often when he appeared in the streets of Burlington, the territorial capital, he was invited to dinner or to listen to debates in the assembly. Though he understood few words of English, he would sit stoically through slang-whanging legislative arguments, the sense of which few whites could even follow. The editor of the Fort Madison *Patriot* urged Iowa people to adopt the nickname "Hawkeyes" in honor of its most famous Indian. Whites settling in the vicinity of his village (near Eldon, Iowa) reported him a good neighbor; although, on the other hand, a generation of frontier mothers in northern Illinois hushed their children with the admonition, "Be quiet or Black Hawk will get you." His dignity and pride never eroded. Dining at a white acquaintance's house, Black Hawk was once told he must wait until a captain of dragoons seated at the table had finished before he could be served. The Sauk responded, "I know the white man is a chief, but *I* was a chief long before his mother knew him. *Your meat— my dogs should not eat it!*" With this, he stalked grandly away. The whites used Keokuk; Black Hawk they respected.

His last public appearance took place at the Fourth of July celebration at Fort Madison in 1838. Seated as an honored guest at a great table overlooking the great river, Black Hawk received a toast and rose to make a short speech: "A few summers ago I was fighting against you. I did wrong, perhaps, but that is past. It is buried. Let it be forgotten. Rock River was a beautiful country. I loved my towns, my cornfields, and the home of my people. I fought for it. It is now yours. Keep it as we did. It will produce you good crops." In spite of the generous thoughts, whites noticed that he often muttered to himself, "*Nesso Chemokemon. Nesso Chemokemon.*" Whether the accurate translation of this was "Kill White man" or "White man kills," no one could quite say.

In September 1838, when departing for Rock Island to receive his annuity, Black Hawk was stricken by an attack of "bilious fever." His last request was for a white doctor. None came and he died at his bark home on October 3. His body, dressed in his military coat, was wrapped in four blankets and placed on a plank sunk fifteen inches into the ground. His top hat, decorated with tinted feathers, was placed on his head, which lay on a pillow. Three commemorative medals, the brightest one a present from the city of Boston, hung from his neck. At his left side was a sword presented to him by President Jackson; at his right, two canes, gifts of Henry Clay and the Saganash colonel Robert Dickson. An A-frame canopy of puncheons and turf was constructed over the body to keep off wild animals and water. A thirty-foot pole flying a silk American flag stood at the head of the grave and a peeled oaken post bearing totemic inscriptions at the foot. To ward off souvenir hunters, the family erected an eight-foot paling fence around the site; but whites soon forced it apart and dug out both ends of the tomb to look.

Even in death Black Hawk was hounded by white men. Within nine months of his burial, a local physician named James Turner stole the corpse, convinced that he could make a fortune by exhibiting it in the East. Using a hog-scalding kettle, Turner cooked off the flesh and fled with the bones to Warsaw, Illinois, to place himself beyond Iowa law. He had the skeleton wired together; but, before he could realize his dream, Governor Robert Lucas succeeded in having the bones returned to Burlington. Black Hawk's wife arrived to view the bones, examined each one "with the apparent curiosity of a child," and convinced that they were in a safe, dry place, she left them with the governor. On leaving office in 1840, Lucas put the bones in the care of a physician who occupied rooms next to the Geological and Historical Insitute. There they remained until 1853, when a fire consumed the Institute and the doctor's office. Black Hawk was at last beyond the reach of meddlesome Chemokemons.

Keokuk endured. He led the remnants of his tribe to a bitter exile in Kansas and died at the agency in 1847, murdered it was said by a political enemy named Hardfish. His son, Moses Keokuk, a Baptist minister, succeeded him and ruled unsurely for nearly half a century. In the 1880s the bones of Keokuk were exhumed and returned for reburial to the Iowa city that bore his name (formerly the village of Puceshetuck). Stuffed in the sepulcher with him was an odd assortment of trash, which included a Keokuk city directory, an issue of the *Weekly Gate City,* a $10 Confederate bill, and some low-denomination postage stamps. What interpretation some archaeologist of the future will make of this cache it is difficult to imagine. Perhaps it will be as preposterous as the prediction of a local editor of that day that Keokuk "may in time be idolized as a saint."

With the conclusion of the Black Hawk War, the victors, for the most part, dispersed to their homes and garrisons and began the long process of forgetting. For a short time both Governor Reynolds and General Atkinson remained together in an uneasy alliance, presumably because each had lurking fears and doubts about his role in the instigation and conduct of the war. Fearing ridicule and exposé, they quickly tried to find a sympathetic and trustworthy son of Illinois to write a history of the war flattering to themselves. As it turned out, the governor selected for this task a local bard named John Russell, whose literary fame extended throughout the Western country from the American Bottom to Shawneetown. Russell, who had authored a treatise on the Vermont state prison and an antiwhiskey tract entitled "The Venomous Worm," commenced a history of the Black Hawk War. But despite the offer of a $100 subsidy from Atkinson and the promise of a clerical post at Jefferson Barracks, the manuscript was never completed. Apparently he himself succumbed to the venomous worm.

John Reynolds need not have worried; his political career was perfectly safe. In 1834 he surrendered his governor's chair to the former militia general Joseph Duncan and assumed Duncan's congressional desk in Washington. During his seven years in the Capitol, the Old Ranger supported the annexation of Texas, worked to establish a federal armory on Western waters (specifically at Rock Island), and acquired the reputation of never turning away from his door anyone claiming damages sustained in the Black Hawk War, so long as the claimant was a white man. In 1843 he returned to Belleville intending, as he recounts in his memoirs, to devote his declining years "to science and to literature." Disappointed by the public response to his semiautobiographical tract, *John Kelly*, written to "enforce morality and virtue" among the younger generation, he found his métier in *My Own Times*, a memoir full of the blundering banalities that adequately describe the author. Following an unsuccessful bid for the post of state superintendent of schools, the Old Ranger died at Belleville in 1865.

None of the militia generals participating in the 1832 campaign made any indelible mark on Sucker history following the war. The mysterious General James Henry found a gala celebration awaiting him at Springfield when he returned home from Bad Axe. Prominent citizens crowded into Miller's Hotel to lionize the hero of the war and to talk about running him for governor. Henry, however, catching a glimpse of fine ladies in the reception hall waiting to meet him, refused to enter and remained in the bar. By the spring of 1834 there was a statewide clamor for Henry to run for governor, but during this hullabaloo he suddenly vanished from Illinois. On March 5 his body was discovered in a hotel room in New Orleans, a derelict of such little consequence that no one in that city was aware that he was a hero of the Black Hawk War or that his admirers in Illinois were calling noisily for his candidacy. Later the story circulated that he had gone south because of poor health; but the death of James D. Henry remains as obscure and mysterious as his life.

Other veterans showed none of Henry's shyness in redeeming war credits, at inflated value, for political preferment. Three governors in a row, after Reynolds, were veterans of the campaign against Black Hawk. Legislators, judges, canal commissioners, postmasters, scribes, and doorkeepers who acquired their posts on the basis of fighting Sauk, are uncountable.[2]

Among the militia generals, Samuel Whiteside is an exception: He belonged to an older school of frontiersmen who battled Indians for the pleasure of it, rather than for a chance at the pork barrel. As for the others, Milton Alexander took but a single term in the legislature before returning to the Paris post office where he died in 1856. William Posey resumed his duties as physician and druggist at Shawneetown where he died in 1842. Ill-starred Major Isaiah Stillman cheerfully courted anonymity at his general store in Canton, where he passed away just as Lincoln issued his call for volunteers in 1861. Colonel James M. Strode, having parlayed his militia service into a state senatorial seat, subsequently moved on to Chicago, where he continued his career as barroom raconteur.

Of the Lead Region veterans, Henry Dodge soared highest in the years that followed. For four years he commanded the first regiment of dragoons in the Western army, a unit composed largely of rough frontier types like himself, but laced with regular officers, few of whom found their colonel either admirable or congenial. One officer characterized Old Hairy Face as "a thorough backwoodsman, very fond of talking over his own exploits . . . not much of a soldier." But, in his reports, Dodge alluded to treachery among his officers and made an inveterate enemy in particular of Lieutenant Jefferson Davis. By 1836 he had returned to Dodgeville and served two terms as governor of the Wisconsin Territory and nine years in the United States Senate. At the time of his death in 1867 towns and counties throughout the West bore his name.

Failure continued to dog the footsteps of Dodge's neighbor and political rival, William S. Hamilton, who took up the Whig banner when Jacksonian Democracy blew through the Western country. His war service carried him to the territorial legislature

2. Governors were Joseph Duncan, Thomas Carlin, and Thomas Ford. Members of congress included Zadock Casey, Adam Snyder, John T. Stuart, Samuel McRoberts, James Semple, Sidney Breese, John McClernand, Orlando Ficklin, Abraham Lincoln, and Orville Browning.

in 1836, where he led a movement to make Cassville the permanent capital, bought up land in that vicinity, and was wiped out when Four Lakes was chosen as the site. Bitterly disappointed by political and financial failure, Hamilton lingered in Wisconsin until 1849 when news of the gold discoveries in California lured him further west. Accompanied by his ubiquitous mulatto companion, he set off in a new wagon for Sacramento, promising neighbors he would return in two years a rich man. Panning gold on Weaver Creek, he cleared $12,000 during his first year, and opened a general store. Records indicate that he died of cholera in 1850, although a stubborn rumor persisted in the region that he had been murdered. One of his wealthy New York brothers traveled to California to make certain that this wayward Hamilton had a suitable gravestone.

The trader George Davenport continued to amass a fortune, but his wealth proved to be his undoing. On July 4, 1845, six river pirates broke into his house on Rock Island and seized the old man while his family was attending a patriotic fair on the mainland. When he refused to give them the combination to his safe, they tied him up, applied hot pokers to his feet, and finally flailed him to death. Three of the murderers were caught and hanged.[3] Davenport's interpreter, Antoine LeClair, also accumulated a great fortune and became a founding father of Davenport, Iowa. Shortly after the Black Hawk War, William Clark gave up his position as superintendent, but held on to his remarkable collection of Indian artifacts. He amused himself by electrifying doorknobs in his house and requesting Indian visitors to open doors for him. The Royal Geographical Society failed to note his death in 1838, although it did attend to the lapse fourteen years later, after prodding from Americans.

The Black Hawk War proved to be the climax, and anti-

3. According to local accounts, the body of one culprit was packed into a barrel of whiskey marked "Pure Gin" and shipped by steamboat to a medical college in St. Louis. The barrel arrived drained of its liquid, and on interrogation the captain admitted that he and his crew had tapped and drunk it. As punishment, he was then told what else the barrel contained. The skeleton of another murderer today dangles as a popular exhibit in the museum of the Black Hawk State Park in Rock Island.

climax, of General Henry Atkinson's career. During the late 1830s the Seminole Wars in Florida drained Jefferson Barracks of its soldiers and, despite the general's protests, the Department of War refused to return his men. In 1838 the Senate confirmed his appointment as territorial governor of Iowa. Suspecting that this was a ruse to remove him from the army, Atkinson declined the post. When he died at Jefferson Barracks in 1842, his command numbered only four officers and thirty-one enlisted men, a force too small for even a decent military burial. Two companies of St. Louis militia were steamboated to the barracks as reinforcements; rifle volleys from citizen soldiers announced the entrance of the spirit of White Beaver into the next world.

The officer of Atkinson's army most distinguished in later years was Colonel Zachary Taylor, whose victories in the Mexican War elevated him to the White House as the Whig candidate in 1848. As president, the crusty Taylor showed a greater interest in cattle fairs and horse shows than in affairs of state. After a tenure of only eighteen months, he died in office, killed, it has been said, by an overdore of iced milk and cherries after a Fourth of July celebration. His subaltern, Lieutenant Jefferson Davis, subsequently became secretary of war under Franklin Pierce and the chief executive of the Confederacy. General Winfield Scott failed to be elected president, as the Whig nominee in 1852, but he remained commander in chief of the army until the Civil War. Atkinson's assistant adjutant general in the Black Hawk War, Lieutenant Albert S. Johnston, distinguished himself in wars against the Mexicans, the Mormons, and the United States.

Among the Indians allied with the whites, none deserved more gratitude than Shabbona, the Potawatomie who alerted the settlements just before the Indian Creek massacre. Yet in 1836 he was ordered beyond the Mississippi with others of his tribe. Following the murder of his son and nephew by rancorous Sauk (Shabbona claimed Neapope engineered this vendetta), he returned to Illinois and occupied his old village at Shabbona Grove in Henry County until 1849. Leaving his land in the charge of a white neighbor, he went off to visit his tribesmen in Kansas. On his return he found that his land had been sold. When he began cutting tent poles in the grove, the new white proprietor ejected him by force. For years Shabbona's family ranged the settlements between Ottawa and Joliet, camping in fence corners and subsisting on gratuities and garbage. Finally citizens took up a collection and bought him twenty acres of marshy land near the village of Morris. Shabbona lived among the whites as beggar, drunkard, and clown until 1859 when he died and was buried with martial pomp in the Morris cemetery.

The twentieth century has obliterated most traces of the war from the face of Illinois. Here and there one may find curiosities tucked away in museums, a stone tomahawk dropped by a Kickapoo at Pecatonica (Wisconsin Historical Society); a corroded musket fished out of the Whitewater River (Fort Atkinson Historical Society); or the kettle Dr. Turner used to boil down Black Hawk's bones (Black Hawk State Park). But such relics are almost as rare as are Sauk warriors in Illinois and Wisconsin today. Not even Dr. Philleo's prized scalplocks, a side-show feature at Galena for more than a generation, have survived the passage of time. Nor have any striking emblems or mottoes survived the Black Hawk War. And, in the end, the frontier culture that won the war proved as envanescent as the Indian culture that lost it. In fact, names like Reynolds, Atkinson, Posey, or Henry are completely lost today, while Black Hawk is memorialized in a Chicago hotel and hockey team.

The most visible legacy of the Black Hawk War is the present city of Rock Island, a grubby monument to the white man's almost mystical belief in quantity as the best index of a civilization. The cornfields of Black Hawk lie beneath the concrete and asphalt of shopping centers and shabby blocks of houses. Black Hawk now works for the local chamber of commerce, as does any other local American celebrity of the past. Among the enterprises capitalizing on his name are an archery shop, a window pane company, a frozen food locker, an antique shop, a state bank, a world travel agency, a golf range, a motel, and a pest exterminator. Bumper decals bear the inscription "Support Black Hawk," which refers to the local college. Asked about Black Hawk, a white gas pump attendant may explain that the old war chief fought with Lincoln in the Civil War. The brochure published by the Black Hawk State Park, a 207-acre preserve on a wooded bluff overlooking the Rock River, highlights the war: "On one side was a native race fighting for its ancestral lands; on the other, settlers and soldiers, our own forebears, determined to banish fear of the scalping knife from their cabins and clearings." The text concludes sweetly, "Now a spirit of peace seems to brood over the valley."

This peace is interrupted every Labor Day weekend when Sauk and Fox stage an Indian Powwow at a stockade within the park. On this occasion warriors and squaws, outfitted in un-authentic grab that must surely come from a Hollywood ware-house, shuffle and jump to the rhythm of beaten tomtoms and rattled chains allowing hundreds of Chemokemons, armed with American flags and Japanese cameras, to participate vicariously in a segment of their heritage. Though billed as "descendants of Black Hawk," it is most likely that the dancers trace their line back to Keokuk. Most of them are middle-aged, for younger, more militant, members of the tribe regard the Powwow as a de-grading circus.

Although the local white traders continue to make money from the Indians, nowadays the Chemokemons are the ones to snap up the gewgaws and trinkets. The reservoir of racial hatred is now focused between black and white; no Rock Islander hates Indians any more, there are too few left to hate.

A state highway winds up the Rock Valley through a mag-nificent pastoral landscape with carbon-black soil in its river bot-toms. The willow-fringed Rock River is lyrically beautiful. It is easy to understand why the squatters from the knob regions of Kentucky and Tennessee coveted this country and also why the Sauk courted extermination to keep it. The highway department has installed markers informing travelers that this is a portion of the bogus "Hiawatha Pioneer Trail." The markers are overlapping profiles of an idealized pioneer and an Indian facing the same direction, as though gazing together across America.

A mile beyond the town of Oregon, the immense figure of an Indian stands on the south bluff of the river. Swathed in a blan-ket, it gazes down the river toward Rock Island. When Lorado Taft's forty-two-foot statue was dedicated in 1911, the audience hissed Hamlin Garland for alluding to the Black Hawk War as an "unjustified assault of white settlers and squatters upon peaceably inclined Indians." Today the Hawk has been completely incorporated into the American pantheon. Even the postage machine at the local courthouse automatically stamps its outgoing mail, "Blackhawk—Ogle County." Illinois has much veneration for the Sauk now that they are gone and with them their claim. Taft's statue, floodlit and a ghostly white after sundown, looms larger than any other monument commemorating that dirty little war.

A few miles to the north, the village of Stillman Valley has grown up around the well-tended gravesite marking the fight at Old Man's Creek. On top of a fifty-foot granite shaft stands a shirt-sleeve militiaman, reminiscent of a minuteman. The figure, inappropriately immobile and confident, gazes northward across the creek toward the hills beyond as though watching for the Sauk. Marble headstones list the names of the nine volunteers buried at the site. Fifty miles northwest, a truncated obelisk, crowned with imitation cannon balls, commemorates the freedom fighters of Kellogg's Grove. The mecca for pilgrims visiting the shrines of the Black Hawk War, however, should be Galena; but nearly all vestiges of its ignominious era have been erased, except for an occasional pit in uncultivated hillsides where miners once dug for ore. Fragments of the oak stockade may be seen in the basement of the Amos Farrar house, but everything else has changed. Even the headstones in the old burial ground on the bluff have crumbled; the river has silted up; and the lead industry is nearly gone. Tourism has replaced mining as the way to wealth in Jo Daviess County. Galena is now a stunning, nineteenth-century museum town, peppered with eclectic Victorian mansions clinging in picturesque disarray to steep hillsides. These architectural outcroppings are the last remaining by-products of the rage for wealth which led to the Winnebago and Black Hawk wars. There seems to be little else.

Brief Biographies

<<<<<<<<<<<<<<<<<<<<<<<<<<<<<<<<<<<<<<<<<<<<<<<<<<

ALEXANDER, MILTON K. Resident of Paris, Illinois. Governor Reynolds's aide in the 1831 campaign. Elected brigadier general of the Second Brigade (Second Army).

ATKINSON, HENRY. Brevet brigadier general. Commander of the Right Wing of the Western Department, with headquarters at Jefferson Barracks below St. Louis. Charged with the prosecution of the Black Hawk War.

BLACK HAWK (Sauk). War chief of the British Band.

BLISS, JOHN. Major of the First Infantry. Commander at Fort Armstrong.

BRADY, HUGH. Brevet brigadier general. Commander at Detroit who joined Atkinson on the Rock River and assumed command of the regular troops during the campaign until incapacitated near Lake Koshkonong.

DAVENPORT, GEORGE. American Fur Company agent at Rock Island and principal Sauk and Fox trader.

DIXON, JOHN. Trader and innkeeper at Dixon's Ferry, upper Rock River.

DODGE, HENRY. Resident of Dodgeville, Michigan Territory. Veteran of Winnebago War. Colonel of the Michigan militia and a principal war leader of the Lead Region.

FRY, JACOB. Resident of Carrollton, Illinois. Veteran of the 1831 campaign. Commander of interim regiment, May–June 1832.

GAINES, EDMUND PENDLETON. Brevet major general. In charge of the force which forced Black Hawk west of the Mississippi in 1831. His absence on leave in 1832 resulted in Atkinson's assuming command.

GRATIOT, HENRY. Farmer and miner, Gratiot's Grove, Michigan Territory. Winnebago subagent.

HAMILTON, WILLIAM S. Son of Alexander Hamilton, miner at Hamilton's Diggin's (Wiota), Michigan Territory. Scout and recruiter of a friendly Indian force (Sioux and Menominee).

HENRY, JAMES D. Sheriff of Springfield. Governor Reynolds's aide in the 1831 campaign. Commander of the spy battalion, Whiteside's Army. Elected brigadier general of the Third Brigade (Second Army).

JOHNSTON, ALBERT SIDNEY. Second lieutenant of the Sixth Infantry at Jefferson Barracks. Served at Atkinson's assistant adjutant and kept an official log during the campaign.

KEOKUK (Sauk). Headman of the Peace party, opposed to Black Hawk.

LINCOLN, ABRAHAM. Resident of New Salem. Company captain in the First Army; private in the interim regiment; private in the Second Army (Henry's Brigade).

LOOMIS, GUSTAVUS. Brevet major of the First Infantry. Temporary commander at Fort Crawford in the absence of Colonel Zachary Taylor.

NEAPOPE (Sauk). Influential younger chief of the British Band.

OWEN, THOMAS. Potawatomie agent at Chicago.

PLYMPTON, JOSEPH. Captain of the Fifth Infantry. Commander at Fort Winnebago.

POSEY, WILLIAM A. Resident of Shawneetown. Brigadier general of the First Brigade (Second Army).

PROPHET (Winnebago). Adviser and shaman attached to British Band.

REYNOLDS, JOHN. Governor of Illinois, 1830–34.

ST. VRAIN, FELIX. Sauk and Fox agent at Rock Island.

SCOTT, WINFIELD. Brigadier general. Commander of the Eastern Department. In mid-June 1832 dispatched to Illinois to assume command of the Northwestern Army created to defeat Black Hawk.

SHABBONA (Potawatomie). Prowhite spokesman of the Potawatomie tribe.

STILLMAN, ISAIAH. Resident of Canton, Illinois. Major of an unattached battalion routed at Stillman's Run, the first battle of the war.

STREET, JOSEPH M. Winnebago agent at Prairie du Chien.

STRODE, JAMES M. Resident of Galena. Colonel of the Jo Daviess County militia and military autocrat of the Galena area.

TAYLOR, ZACHARY. Colonel of First Infantry, commander of Fort Crawford. Returned from leave to join Atkinson at Rock Island and assume command of regulars in the expedition up the river. Afterward commander of Fort Dixon.

THROCKMORTON, JOSEPH. Captain of the steamboat *Warrior*.

WHITE CROW (Winnebago). Guide attached to the Dodge-Henry column.

WHISTLER, WILLIAM. Major of the Second Infantry. Took command of Fort Dearborn in mid-June 1832.

Bibliography

‹‹

General References

The first book-length treatment of the Black Hawk War (and the only one by a participant) is John A. Wakefield's extremely rare *History of the War between the United States and the Sac and Fox Nations of Indians* (Jacksonville, Ill., 1834), which is generally reliable as a fleshed-out log of the campaign, except for occasional lapses in chronology. His rabid hatred of the Sauk reflects the stock response among the Illinois volunteers. The Indian perspective on the war is conveyed by Black Hawk's autobiography, published as *Life of Ma-ka-tai-me-she-kia-kiak, or Black Hawk* (Cincinnati, Ohio, 1833). It was dictated to the Rock Island interpreter Antoine LeClair and published by John B. Patterson, a sympathetic Illinois editor. Although the phraseology is Patterson's, the narrative is clearly Black Hawk's. The most accessible edition is Donald Jackson's *Black Hawk: An Autobiography* (Urbana, Ill., 1954), which contains a superb introduction and notes. The most widely read account of the war during the nineteenth century was Benjamin Drake's *The Life and Adventures of Black Hawk* (Cincinnati, Ohio, 1838). It is largely an anthology of documents and clippings favorable to the Sauk which went through seven printings by 1849.

For the next half-century interest in the war languished until Perry A. Armstrong published his *The Sauks and the Black Hawk War* (Springfield, Ill., 1887). Siding with Drake against Wakefield, the author reawakened interest in the nearly forgotten war by lambasting the whites for their incompetence, inhumanity, and cowardice. Despite his flamboyant rendering, Armstrong collected many recollections and anecdotes from participants just before they began to die. A native of the Illinois Valley, he was saturated with Black Hawkiana and could not be wholly objective with his materials. Though brief, Reuben G. Thwaites's *The Story of the Black Hawk War* (Madison, Wisc., 1892) presented for the first time a systematic, balanced account of the war utilizing historical method.

The last important book on the subject, Frank E. Stevens's *The Black Hawk War* (Chicago, 1903), is marred by the author's anti-Sauk bias. Meticulously researched but wretchedly structured, it provides the best foundation on which to build one's own scaffolding. Essentially Stevens was a collector and compiler rather than historian or writer. Cyrenus Cole's *I Am a Man: The Indian Black Hawk* (Iowa City, 1938) is a readable but superficial account of the war. William T. Hagan's *The Sac and Fox Indians* (Norman, Okla., 1958) is unique because it encompasses the history of the tribe from its historical beginnings to the modern period.

The most important autobiography bearing upon the war is John Reynolds's turgid *My Own Times* (Belleville, Ill., 1855), which gives away more than the author intends. Governor Thomas Ford's *A History of Illinois* (Chicago, 1945; originally published, 1854) includes an account of the 1831 war and is indispensable for establishing the social and political background of the period. John W. Spencer's *Reminiscences of Pioneer Life* (Davenport, Iowa, 1872) describes the first white settlement at Saukenuk. Mrs. John H. Kinzie's *Wau-bun: The "Early Day" in the North-west* (New York, 1856) recounts the progress of the war as experienced by a white woman of fine sensibility at Fort Winnebago.

The regular army perspective on the war in devastatingly chronicled in Philip St. George Cooke's sardonic *Scenes and Adventures in the Army* (Philadelphia, 1857). George A. McCall's *Letters from the Frontier* (Philadelphia, 1868) is written in a similar vein, but unfortunately treats only the 1831 campaign. Henry Smith's "Indian Campaign of 1832" (*Wisconsin Historical Collections,* vol. 10) outlines the campaign as viewed by one of Henry Atkinson's company commanders; this is a reprinting of his report published originally in 1833.

Important compilations of documents include: Evarts Green and Clarence Alvord, eds., *The Governors' Letter Books 1818–1834* (Springfield, Ill., 1909), for Reynolds's correspondence; Charles J. Kappler, ed., *Indian Affairs: Laws and Treaties* (Washington, D.C., 1903), for texts of treaties; Clarence Edwin Carter, ed., *The Territorial Papers of the United States,* vol. 13 (Washington, D.C., 1948), for early conflicts between the tribe and the federal government; and U.S. Congress, *American State Papers* (Military Affairs) (vol. 5, Washington, D.C., 1860), for the official report on the war.

Files of Illinois newspapers on microfilm at the Illinois State Historical Library provide details available nowhere else and evoke the war as a contemporary event. The most valuable are the Edwardsville

Illinois Advocate (1831–32), *the Galenian* (1832–33), and the Springfield *Sangamo Journal* (1832–33). *Niles' Weekly Register* (Baltimore, Md., 1831–33) covers the war as a national event. Ransacking back volumes of Illinois, Wisconsin, and Iowa historical magazines proved to be a disappointing enterprise; but the first fifteen volumes of the old *Wisconsin Historical Collections* (1855–1900) contained all sorts of useful lumber written by participants and observers of the war. The *Michigan Pioneer Collections* provided materials about the activities of the Michigan militia.

The acquisition of knowledge owes more to osmotic function than rational process; to itemize those significant secondary works is to point to individual raindrops in a downpour. Among the regional studies of more than passing interest were: Henry Brown, *The History of Illinois* (New York, 1844); William R. Smith, *The History of Wisconsin* (Madison, 1854); H. F. Kett, *The History of Jo Daviess County* (Chicago, 1878); John Wentworth, *Early Chicago* (Chicago, 1876); and Alfred T. Andreas, *History of Cook County, Illinois* (Chicago, 1884). Later studies include: Milo M. Quaife, *Chicago and the Old Northwest* (Chicago, 1913); Theodore C. Pease, *The Frontier State* (Chicago, 1922); Bruce E. Mahan, *Old Fort Crawford and the Frontier* (Iowa City, 1926); Henry P. Beers, *The Western Military Frontier* (Philadelphia, 1935); and Peter L. Scanlin, *Prairie du Chien* (Menasha, Wis., 1937).

Biographical studies containing important treatment of the war are: Louis Pelzer, *Henry Dodge* (Iowa City, 1911); Charles W. Elliott, *Winfield Scott* (New York, 1937); Brainerd Dyer, *Zachary Taylor* (Baton Rouge, La., 1946); Charles P. Roland, *Albert Sidney Johnston* (Austin, Tex., 1964); and Roger L. Nichols, *General Henry Atkinson* (Norman, Okla., 1965).

Other sources used will be cited in the Chapter References.

The Black Hawk War Collection

The most important repository of Black Hawk War materials is the Illinois State Historical Library in Springfield. Mrs. Ellen M. Whitney of the library staff has devoted nearly twenty years to the task of assembling the Black Hawk War Collection and publishing a three-volume documentary history of the war. The first volume, a compilation of militia rolls, titled *The Black Hawk War, 1831–1832*, appeared in 1970. When her project is completed, the student of the Black

Hawk War will have easy access to every important document and letter bearing on this subject. The resources of the collection have formed the basis of my book. Among the more indispensable holdings are Atkinson's letter book, his file of letters received, and his order book; Reynolds's order and letter books; and A. S. Johnston's field journal. Also housed in the collection are copies of relevant letters from the National Archives and transcripts of evidence and exhibits presented before the Indian Claims Commission (Dockets 83 and 158) during the 1950s by the Sauk and Fox tribe in their attempt to gain reparations for early land seizures by the United States.

The State Historical Society of Wisconsin possesses a smaller collection of materials bearing on the war which includes manuscripts (cited in the chapter notes, when used) and a file of newspaper clippings not available elsewhere.

Chapter References

The purpose of these notes is not to attach a source to every assertion but to indicate the materials used in each chapter. Wherever relevant the core of the Black Hawk War Collection (Atkinson's letter books, the Johnston journal, etc.) carries the main burden of my narrative. Use of this material ought to be clear from the context, as should quotations from Black Hawk's autobiography. Working on the assumption that nearly two decades of collecting by the staff of the Illinois State Historical Library has brought into its net every item of consequence, I have not burrowed in the National Archives. Perhaps my trust is without foundation; but, having worked through the Black Hawk War Collection, I find it easier to imagine that fresh discoveries, if they are made, will come from attics in Illinois rather than from file cabinets in Washington.

Abbreviations used are as follows:

ISL   Illinois State Historical Library
ISHS   *Journal of the Illinois State Historical Society*
MPC   *Michigan Pioneer Collections*
WHC   *Wisconsin Historical Collections*
WHS   State Historical Society of Wisconsin

A full bibliographical citation appears only when the source has not been listed previously.

ONE *Upriver with the General*

MASSACRES AT PRAIRIE DU CHIEN   Sac and Fox agency file (film), Iowa State Historical Society; James H. Lockwood, "Early Times and Events in Wisconsin," *WHC*, vol. 2; George D. Lyman, *John Marsh, Pioneer* (New York, 1931); John Fonda, "Early Reminiscences of Wisconsin," *WHC*, vol. 5; Mrs. H. S. Baird, "Indian Customs and Early Recollections," *WHC*, vol. 9; Scanlin, *Prairie du Chien.*

ATKINSON BIOGRAPHY   Nichols, *General Henry Atkinson.*

WINNEBAGO WAR   Mahan, *Old Fort Crawford;* Thomas McKenny, "The Winnebago War of 1827," *WHC*, vol. 5; William J. Snelling, "Early Days at Prairie du Chien," *WHC*, vol. 5; Scanlin, *Prairie du Chien;* Nichols, *General Henry Atkinson;* Lockwood, "Early Times and Events in Wisconsin."

TWO *The Sauk and Fox: The Rise*

SAUK CREATION MYTH   John E. Chapin, "Sketch of Cutting Marsh," *WHC*, vol. 15.

ETHNOLOGY   Anthony F. C. Wallace, "Prelude to Disaster," in Whitney, *Black Hawk War;* Thomas Forsyth's report in Emma H. Blair, *The Indian Tribes of the Upper Mississippi Valley*, vol. 2 (Cleveland, Ohio, 1912). Jonathan Carver's observations come from his *Travels Through the Interior Part of North America* (London, 1781).

U.S. INDIAN POLICY OF THE PERIOD   Annie H. Abel, "The History of Events Resulting in Indian Consolidation West of the Mississippi," *Annual Report of the American Historical Society* (Washington, D.C., 1908).

CONFRONTATION OF THE AMERICANS AND THE INDIANS AT ST. LOUIS   Carter, *Territorial Papers;* Logan Esarey, ed., *Messages and Letters of William Henry Harrison*, vol. 1 (Indianapolis, Ind., 1922).

QUASHQUAME'S DRUNKENNESS   Isaac Galland, *Chronicles of the North American Savage* 1 (1835).

TEXT OF THE 1804 TREATY   Kappler, *Indian Affairs.*

TRIBAL VERSION OF THE TREATY NEGOTATIONS   William Jones, comp., "Notes on the Fox Indians," *Iowa Journal of History and Politics* 10.

AGRICULTURE STATION   Donald Jackson, "William Ewing, Agricultural Agent to the Indians," *Agricultural History* 31.

Bibliography

Pɪᴋᴇ ᴇxᴘᴇᴅɪᴛɪᴏɴ   Donald Jackson, ed., *The Journals of Zebulon Montgomery Pike*, vol. 1 (Norman, Okla. 1966).

Aᴍᴇʀɪᴄᴀɴ ᴘᴇɴᴇᴛʀᴀᴛɪᴏɴ ᴏꜰ ᴛʜᴇ ᴜᴘᴘᴇʀ Mɪssɪssɪᴘᴘɪ   Mahan, *Old Fort Crawford*.

Bʀɪᴛɪsʜ Bᴀɴᴅ ɪɴ ᴛʜᴇ Wᴀʀ ᴏꜰ 1812   Hagan, *Sac and Fox Indians*.

Pʀᴀɪʀɪᴇ ᴅᴜ Cʜɪᴇɴ ᴀɴᴅ Sᴀᴜᴋᴇɴᴜᴋ ᴄᴀᴍᴘᴀɪɢɴs   Scanlin, *Prairie du Chien;* Mahan, *Old Fort Crawford*.

Bʀɪᴛɪsʜ ɢᴜɴɴᴇʀ's ʀᴇᴘᴏʀᴛ   "Captain T. G. Anderson's Journal, 1814," *WHC*, vol. 9. An interesting account of Taylor's repulse is John Shaw, "Personal Narrative," *WHC*, vol. 2.

ᴛʜʀᴇᴇ *The Sauk and Fox: The Fall*

Comprehensive accounts of the Sauk and Fox between 1815 and 1832 may be found in Hagan, *Sac and Fox Indians*, and in Wallace, "Prelude to Disaster."

Sᴘᴇᴇᴄʜᴇs ᴏꜰ Bʟᴀᴄᴋ Hᴀᴡᴋ ᴀꜰᴛᴇʀ ᴛʜᴇ ᴡᴀʀ   "Papers of Dominion Archives at Ottawa," *MPC*, vol. 16, and "The Bulger Papers," *WHC*, vol. 13.

Nᴇɢᴏᴛɪᴀᴛɪᴏɴ ʙʏ ᴄᴀɴɴᴏɴ   Timothy Flint, *Recollections of the Past Ten Years* (Boston, 1826).

White expansion up the Mississippi: Beers, *Western Military Frontier;* Major Stephen H. Long, "Voyage in a Six-Oared Skiff . . . in 1817," *Collections of the Minnesota Historical Society*, vol. 2.

Lɪꜰᴇ ᴀɴᴅ ᴄʜᴀʀᴀᴄᴛᴇʀ ᴏꜰ Kᴇᴏᴋᴜᴋ   Drake, *Life and Adventures of Black Hawk;* Vertical file, Keokuk (Iowa) Public Library; George Catlin, *Letters and Notes on the Manners, Customs and Conditions of the North American Indians*, vol. 2 (New York, 1841).

Wʜɪᴛᴇs sᴇᴛᴛʟᴇ ᴀᴛ Gᴀʟᴇɴᴀ   Moses Meeker, "Early History of the Lead Region of Wisconsin," *WHC*, vol. 6, and Kett, *History of Jo Daviess County*.

Accounts of the white settlement at Saukenuk are hopelessly snarled as to time and events. Wallace brilliantly summarizes the controversy as it is reflected in extant documents. Spencer's *Reminiscences of Pioneer Life* gives the squatters' viewpoint as Black Hawk's autobiography gives the Indians'. Texts of the squatters' petitions are published in Stevens's *Black Hawk War*.

Tʜᴇ 1830 ɴᴇɢᴏᴛɪᴀᴛɪᴏɴs   Sac and Fox Agency File.

Kᴇɴɴᴇʀʟʏ ʟᴇᴛᴛᴇʀ   Governor Reynolds's correspondence, Archives Department, State of Illinois.

THE 1831 CAMPAIGN   McCall, *Letters from the Frontier;* Ford, *History of Illinois;* Reynolds, *My Own Times;* Spencer. Text of capitulation articles is in Reynolds.

FOUR *The People's Army*

From this point on, the mass of correspondence in the Black Hawk War Collection forms the backbone of my narrative. For the most part, the following notes refer to materials outside the collection.

PANIC AT ROCK ISLAND   Armstrong, *Sauks and the Black Hawk War.*

DEMORALIZATION OF THE WESTERN GARRISONS   George Croghan, *Army Life on the Western Frontier* (Norman, Okla., 1958).

ATKINSON'S DELAY AT ROCK ISLAND   [Felix St. Vrain], "A Diary of the Black Hawk War," *Iowa Journal of History and Politics* 8.

TEXT OF REYNOLDS'S CALL FOR VOLUNTEERS   Reynolds, *My Own Times.*

ILLINOIS MILITIA ORGANIZATION   Pease, *Frontier State;* Isabel Jamison, "Independent Military Companies of Sangamon County," *ISHS* 3.

INDIAN HATING   John Woods, *Two Years Residence in the Settlement on the English Prairie* (London, 1822).

REYNOLDS'S EFFORTS TO OBTAIN MILITIA FUNDS   Greene and Alvord, eds., *Governors' Letter Books.*

THE WAR AS A LUCRATIVE JOKE   Charles F. Hoffman, *A Winter in the Far West* (London, 1835).

RATES OF MILITIA PAY   "A Black Hawk War Payroll," *ISHS* 47.

LINCOLN IN THE WAR   William H. Herndon, *Herndon's Lincoln,* vol. 1 (Springfield, Ill., 1921); William E. Baringer, ed., *Lincoln Day by Day* vol. 1 (Washington, D.C., 1960); Alfred A. Jackson, "Lincoln in the Black Hawk War," *WHC,* vol. 14.

REYNOLD'S BIOGRAPHY   Pease, *Frontier State;* Ford, *History of Illinois; My Own Times.*

BEARDSTOWN MUSTER   Browning diary, Frank E. Stevens papers, ISL; J. N. Gridley et al., *Historical Sketches,* vol. 1 (1907).

WHISKEY AND RECRUITS   Charles Ballew to Ninevah Shaw, Shaw papers, ISL; *History of Pike County Illinois* (Chicago, 1880).

LINCOLN AT BEARDSTOWN   Risdon M. Moore, "Lincoln as a Wrestler," *Transactions of the Illinois State Historical Society* 9 (1904); John Snyder to Frank Stevens, Stevens papers, ISL.

YELLOW BANKS MARCH AND INTERLUDE Browning diary; Governor Reynolds, Order and Letter Book, ISL; *My Own Times.*

FIVE *The Battle of Stillman's Run*

ZACHARY TAYLOR IN THE WAR Dyer, *Zachary Taylor;* Holman
Hamilton, ed., Taylor letter, *Wisconsin Magazine of History* 24;
Fonda, "Early Reminiscences of Wisconsin."

ENVOYS TO BLACK HAWK AND THE GRATIOT MISSION M. M.
Quaife, ed., "Journals and Reports of the Black Hawk War," *Mississippi Valley Historical Review* 12; St. Vrain diary.

GRATIOT BIOGRAPHY E. B. Washburne, "Col. Henry Gratiot,"
WHC, vol. 10.

REGULARS VIEW MILITIA CAMP Cooke, *Scenes and Adventures in
the Army;* Robert Anderson, "Reminiscences of the Black Hawk War,"
WHC, vol. 10.

THE DAILY MOVEMENTS OF THE ARMY FROM ROCK ISLAND TO BAD
AXE A. S. Johnston field journal; Wakefield, *History of the War;*
supplemented by Smith, "Indian Campaign of 1832."

WHITESIDE BIOGRAPHY John T. Kingston, "Early Western Days,"
WHC, vol. 7.

STILLMAN BIOGRAPHY Biographical file, Archives Department
State of Illinois; Greene and Alvord, eds., *Governors' Letter Books.*

No definitive account of STILLMAN'S RUN exists. My composite
account is based on the following sources: Reynolds, *My Own Times;*
E. Davis, *The Good Old Times in McLean County, Illinois* (Blooming-
ton, Ill., 1874); *History of Peoria County, Illinois* (Chicago, 1880);
A. H. Maxfield letter, *Sangamo Journal* (June 14, 1832); *History of
Jo Daviess County;* Stillman letter, *Sangamo Journal* (July 19, 1832);
R. H. McGoon letter (1854), WHS.

STRODE'S ESCAPE Ford, *History of Illinois.* A hysterical account of
the battle appeared in *The Galenian* (May 23, 1832).

THE SAUK VERSION Black Hawk's autobiography; Neapope's testimony, "Minutes of Examination of the Indian Prisoners" (August 20,
1832), ISL.

SECONDARY ACCOUNTS Frank E. Stevens, "Stillman's Defeat,"
Transactions of the Illinois State Historical Society (1902); J. A.
Atwood, *The Story of the Battle of Stillman's Run* (Mt. Morris, Ill.,
1904), primarily useful for the excavations. Buckmaster to wife, Buckmaster-Curran papers, ISL.

SIX *The Massacre at Indian Creek*

WHITESIDE ARMY MARCHES AFTER BLACK HAWK William Orr, "The Indian War," *ISHS* 5; Reynolds, *My Own Times;* Armstrong, *Sauks and the Black Hawk War.*

REGULAR OFFICERS' CRITIQUE OF THE DEBACLE Johnston field journal; Smith, "Indian Campaign of 1832."

HAMILTON BIOGRAPHY Sylvia J. Muldoon, *Alexander Hamilton's Pioneer Son* (Harrisburg, Pa., 1930); Larry Gara, "William S. Hamilton," *Wisconsin Magazine of History* 41; Kinzie, *Wau-bun.*

SHABBONA BIOGRAPHY Nehemiah Matson, *Memories of Shabena* (Chicago, 1878); Alta P. Walters, "Shabonee," *ISHS* 17.

INDIAN CREEK MASSACRE Stevens, *Black Hawk War;* Armstrong, *Sauks and the Black Hawk War;* Ford, *History of Illinois;* Charles Scanlan, *Indian Creek Massacre* (Milwaukee, Wisc., 1915).

TESTIMONIES BY THE HALL GIRLS and their brother appear in Stevens, *Black Hawk War,* and in Brown, *History of Illinois.*

CONDITIONS IN CHICAGO Wentworth, *Early Chicago;* Andreas, *History of Cook County, Illinois.*

ST. VRAIN MASSACRE Smith, *History of Wisconsin,* vol. 1, part 1; *Galenian* (May 30 and June 12, 1832). Wakefield and nearly all the Illinois county histories recount anecdotes of the panic following the massacres. Atkinson pursued by "Indians": Matson, *Shabena.*

MICHIGAN'S WAR *Sangamo Journal* (June 21, 1832).

SERVICE OF THE MICHIGAN MILITIA "Papers of Gen. John R. Williams," *MPC,* vol. 31; J. Sharpless Fox, ed., "Territorial Papers, 1831–1836," *MPC,* vol. 37; Henry Little, "A History of the Black Hawk War," *MPC,* vol. 5; E. Lakin Brown, "Autobiographical Notes," *MPC,* vol. 30; Lawton T. Hemans, *Life and Times of Stevens Thomson Mason* (Lansing, Mich., 1920); Ralph Ballard, *Tales of Early Niles* (Ft. St. Joseph Historical Society, n.d.); George Hoffman letter, Andreas, *History of Cook County, Illinois.*

SEVEN *The People's Army: Second Try*

DODGE BIOGRAPHY Louis Pelzer, *Henry Dodge.*

CONFERENCES WITH WINNEBAGO Quaife, ed., "Journals and Reports," *MVHR 12;* Peter Parkinson, "Notes on the Black Hawk War," *WHC,* vol. 10; Daniel M. Parkinson, "Pioneer Life in Wisconsin," *WHC,* vol. 2; Smith, *History of Wisconsin,* vol. 3; *Galenian* (May 30 and June 7, 1832).

HALL GIRLS SEQUEL   Scanlan, *Indian Creek Massacre.*

GALENA UNDER SIEGE   *Galenian* file; *History of Jo Daviess County;* Newhall papers, ISL; Elijah Iles, *Sketches of Early Life and Times* (Springfield, Ill., 1883).

ILLINOIS COLLEGE DEMONSTRATION   *Illinois Advocate* (June 12, 1832) and Newhall papers.

REYNOLDS TO EDWARDS   E. B. Washburne, ed., *The Edwards Papers,* vol. 3 (Chicago Historical Society).

REYNOLDS TO CASS   Greene and Alvord, *Governors' Letter Books.*

BRYANT IN ILLINOIS   Parke Godwin, ed., "Illinois Fifty Years Ago," *Prose Writings of William Cullen Bryant* (New York, 1884).

TERRORISM AT HENNEPIN   *Sangamo Journal* (July 5, 1832).

POSEY BIOGRAPHY   Personal file, Illinois Archives; *History of Gallatin, Saline, Hamilton, Franklin, and Williamson Counties* (Chicago, 1887).

ALEXANDER BIOGRAPHY   Armstrong, *Sauks and the Black Hawk War.*

HENRY BIOGRAPHY   Frank E. Stevens, "A Forgotten Hero: General James D. Henry," *Transactions of the Illinois State Historical Society* (1934); Reynolds, *My Own Times.*

EIGHT *The Sauk Counterattack*

PECATONICA FIGHT   Dodge's dispatch to Z. Taylor, June 18, 1832, ISL; Charles Bracken and Peter Parkinson, "Pecatonica Battle Controversy," *WHC,* vol. 2; Parkinson, "Pioneer Life"; Albert Salisbury, "Green County Pioneers," *WHC,* vol. 6; Smith, *History of Wisconsin; Galenian* file.

ADAM SNYDER'S FIGHT NEAR KELLOGG'S GROVE   *Illinois Advocate* (June 26, 1832); Spencer, *Reminiscences of Pioneer Life.*

WADDAM'S GROVE FIGHT   Jeanne Lebron, "Colonel James W. Stephenson," *ISHS* 35.

BLUE MOUND SKIRMISH   Ebenezer Brigham memo (1832), WHS; Brigham interview, "Early Times in Wisconsin," *WHC,* vol. 1; "Edward D. Beouchard's Vindication," *WHC,* vol. 7.

APPLE RIVER FIGHT: Emilie (pseud.), "A Reminiscence of the Black Hawk War," *WHC,* vol. 5; Alfred Brunson," "A Methodist Circuit Rider . . . ," *WHC,* vol. 15. Aftereffects: Charles J. Latrobe, *The Rambler in North America,* vol. 2 (New York, 1835).

DEMENT BIOGRAPHY   Armstrong, *Sauks and the Black Hawk War.*

KELLOGG'S GROVE FIGHT Reynolds, *My Own Times;* miscellaneous reports in Atkinson's file of letters received, ISL.

NINE *The "Trembling Lands" Campaign*

HENRY'S BRIGADE AT DIXON'S FERRY Cooke, *Scenes and Adventures in the Army.*

POSEY QUARREL WITH DODGE Moses M. Strong, "The Indian Wars of Wisconsin," *WHC,* vol. 8.

BRADY BIOGRAPHY "General Hugh Brady," *MPC,* vol. 3.

THE ARMY'S MOVEMENTS UP TO AND WITHIN THE "TREMBLING LANDS" Johnston field journal; Smith, "Indian Campaign of 1832"; Reynolds, *My Own Times;* Wakefield, *History of the War;* Lt. Col. E. Bruckner, "A Brief History of the War with the Sac and Fox Indians," *MPC,* vol. 12; James J. Justice, "Black Hawk War Diary," ISL; C. N. Shaw, "Journal of a Campaign against the Hostile Indians," ISL. The difficulties of campaigning in the region are summarized in Atkinson's letters to Scott and Macomb, ISL.

"LIEUTENANT" DOBBS *The History of Jefferson County, Wisconsin* (Chicago, 1879).

GALENA CELEBRATES THE FOURTH *Galenian* (July 11, 1832).

A useful collection of documents dealing with the KOSHKONONG CAMPAIGN is Mrs. George Swart's, *Footsteps of Our Founding Fathers* (Fort Atkinson Historical Society, n.d.).

FORT WINNEBAGO EXCURSION Justice diary; Reynolds, *My Own Times;* Ford, *History of Illinois;* Parkinson, "Pioneer Life"; Wakefield, *History of the War.*

PURIFICATION OF THE FORT Kinzie, *Wau-bun.*

TEN *The Plague*

CALL-UP OF SCOTT'S ARMY Cass to Scott, June 15, 1832, ISL; Adjutant General's Order No. 51, June 16, 1832, ISL.

SCOTT BIOGRAPHY Elliott, *Winfield Scott; Memoirs of Lieut.-General Scott by Himself* (New York, 1864).

CHOLERA EPIDEMIC OF 1832 J. S. Chambers, *The Conquest of Cholera* (New York, 1938), which includes an account of the epidemic in Scott's army.

OTHER ACCOUNTS OF THE CONTAGION *Niles' Weekly Register*

(June 23, July 7, July 14, July 28, August 11, 1832); William Chapman letters of July 17 and September 6, 1832, USMA Library, West Point. The skipper of the *Sheldon Thompson*, Captain Augustus Walker, wrote two accounts of the epidemic, "Early Days on the Lakes," *Publications of the Buffalo Historical Society* 5, and appendix to John Wentworth, "Fort Dearborn," *Fergus Historical Series* (1881).

EPIDEMIC AT FORT GRATIOT AND IN MICHIGAN   "History of Fort Gratiot," *MPC,* vol. 18; C. B. Burr, ed., *Medical History of Michigan,* vol. 1 (Minneapolis, Minn., 1930).

THE PROPHET'S PREDICTION   *Sangamo Journal* (August 2, 1832).

ELEVEN *The So-Called Battle of Wisconsin Heights*

ATKINSON'S DELAY AT KOSHKONONG   Cooke, *Scenes and Adventures in the Army;* Smith, "Indian Campaign of 1832"; Bruckner, "A Brief History of the War."

HENRY AND DODGE PURSUE BLACK HAWK   Wakefield, *History of the War;* Justice diary; Parkinson, "Pioneer Life."

WISCONSIN HEIGHTS   Wakefield, *History of the War;* Justice diary; Parkinson, "Pioneer Life"; *History of Grant County, Wisconsin* (Chicago, 1881); Satterlee Clark, "Early Times at Ft. Winnebago," *WHC,* vol. 8; Charles Bracken, "Further Strictures," *WHC,* vol. 2. Though not participants, Reynolds and Ford treat the battle extensively. Henry's report to Atkinson was published in an "extra" of the *Sangamo Journal* (August 3, 1832). Dodge's report appeared in *Niles' Weekly Register* (August 18, 1832). Dr. Philleo's report appeared in the *Galenian* (July 25, 1832). Jefferson Davis's alleged praise of Black Hawk's escape, Charles Aldrich, "Jefferson Davis and Black Hawk," *Midland Monthly* 5.

PAQUETTE HUMILIATES SUCKER   Henry Merrell, "Pioneer Life in Wisconsin," *WHC,* vol. 7.

NEAPOPE'S CALL ALARMS CAMP   Wakefield, *History of the War;* Justice diary; *History of Jo Daviess County.*

GENERAL HENRY'S SPEECH   Wakefield, *History of the War.*

REUNION AT BLUE MOUND   Wakefield, *History of the War;* Cooke, *Scenes and Adventures in the Army.*

HENRY DODGE-THOMAS FORD FEUD   Ford, *History of Illinois.*

WISCONSIN HEIGHTS AS A WHITE DEFEAT   Armstrong, *Sauks and the Black Hawk War.*

FIRE IN THE GALENA STOCKADE   *History of Jo Daviess County.*

TWELVE *Bad Axe*

STREET ALERTS THE SIOUX   Alfred Brunson, "Memoir of T. P. Burnett," *WHC*, vol. 2.

ATKINSON ARMY CROSSES THE WISCONSIN   Cooke, *Scenes and Adventures in the Army;* Smith, "Indian Campaign of 1932"; Justice diary; Shaw journal; Wakefield, *History of the War.*

SAUK MASSACRED AT MOUTH OF WISCONSIN   Ritner to Loomis July 29, 1832, ISL; Augustin Grignon, "Seventy-two Years' Recollection of Wisconsin," *WHC*, vol. 3.

WARRIOR EXPEDITION   Fonda, "Early Reminiscences of Wisconsin"; Brunson, "Memoir of T. P. Burnett"; James B. Estes's account, Smith, *History of Wisconsin.* Throckmorton report, Drake, *Life and Adventures of Black Hawk.* Indian version of *Warrior* incident, testimony of Weesheet, August 27, 1832, and of Kishkasshoi, August 19, 1832, "Minutes of Examination of Indian Prisoners," ISL.

BATTLE OF BAD AXE   Wakefield, *History of the War;* Shaw journal; Bracken, "Further Strictures"; Smith, "Indian Campaign of 1832"; Cooke, *Scenes and Adventures in the Army;* H. S. Townsend speech, *Vernon County Censor* (August 10, 1898), clipping at WHS; Joseph Dickson, "Personal Narrative," *WHC*, vol. 5; Davis, *Good Old Times; History of Edgar County* (Chicago, 1879). Official reports of Taylor and the militia brigade commanders, ISL. Atkinson's reports to Scott, August 3 and 9, 1832, ISL. Atkinson's official report on the war, November 19, 1832, ISL. Macomb report on the war, November 1832, in *American State Papers,* vol. 5.

THIRTEEN *Pax Americana*

SCOTT TO HENRY   Stevens, "A Forgotten Hero."

ATKINSON TO DODGE   George W. Jones, "Robert S. Black and the Black Hawk War," *WHC*, vol. 10.

REYNOLDS'S QUEST FOR REMUNERATION   Greene and Alvord, eds., *Governors' Letter Books.*

CHOLERA EPIDEMIC AT ROCK ISLAND   *Sangamo Journal* (October 13, 1832); J. S. Gallagher letter, August 31, 1832, WHS; William Chapman letter, September 6, 1832, USMA.

SCOTT AT ROCK ISLAND   Elliott, *Winfield Scott;* Scott's *Memoirs.*

SUBSEQUENT SPREAD OF CHOLERA   Chambers, *Conquest of Cholera.*

INDIAN SPEECHES AT PRAIRIE DU CHIEN   Drake, *Life and Adventures of Black Hawk.*

BLACK HAWK PARTY ESCORTED TO ST. LOUIS   Robert Anderson, "Reminiscences of the Black Hawk War"; *Sangamo Journal* (September 15, 1832).

JEFFERSON DAVIS IN THE NORTHWEST   P. L. Scanlan, "The Military Record of Jefferson Davis in Wisconsin," *Wisconsin Magazine of History* 24; Matson, *Shabena.*

THE PROPHET IN CHAINS   Brown, *History of Illinois.*

TREATY NEGOTIATIONS   Hagan, *Sac and Fox Indians;* Docket No. 83, Indian Claims Commission, ISL.

TEXT OF TREATY   Kappler, ed., *Indian Affairs.*

BLACK HAWK'S EASTERN TOUR   Jackson's introduction to Black Hawk's autobiography; Drake, *Life and Adventures of Black Hawk; Niles' Weekly Register* (June 29, 1833); Frankfort *Commonwealth* (July 30, 1833); "Black Hawk Scraps from Old Newspapers," *WHC,* vol. 10; Allan Nevins, ed., *The Diary of Philip Hone,* vol. 1 (New York, 1927).

BLACK HAWK AT JEFFERSON BARRACKS   Maximilian, Prince of Wied, *Travels in the Interior of North America* (London, 1843).

JACKSON IN INDIAN HEADDRESS   Marquis James, *The Life of Andrew Jackson* (Indianapolis, Ind., 1937).

PHRENOLOGICAL ANALYSIS   Stevens, *Black Hawk War.*

Portraits of Black Hawk appear in Hagan, *Sac and Fox Indians,* and in Donald Jackson's summary of the war, *The Palimpsest* 43 (no. 2).

BLACK HAWK'S RETURN TO ROCK ISLAND   Spencer, *Reminiscences of Pioneer Life;* Hagan, *Sac and Fox Indians;* Drake, *Life and Adventures of Black Hawk.*

Epilogue

WAR FEVER, WINTER OF 1832–33   Reynolds's address at opening session of Illinois legislature, Archives Department, State of Illinois; *Sangamo Journal* (December, 1832–January, 1833); *Galenian* (December, 1832–January, 1833).

HARDSHIPS AMONG THE WINNEBAGO   Kinzie, *Wau-bun.*

MISSIONARY AMONG THE SAUK AND FOX   Chapin, "Sketch of Cutting Marsh."

1836 TREATY   Pelzer, *Henry Dodge;* Hagan, *Sac and Fox Indians;* Catlin, *Letters and Notes.*

TEXTS OF TREATIES   Kappler, ed., *Indian Affairs.*

EASTERN TOUR, 1837   Drake, *Life and Adventures of Black Hawk.*

BLACK HAWK IN IOWA   Cole, *I Am a Man;* Ebenezer Childs, "Recollections of Wisconsin Since 1820," *WHC,* vol. 4.

Accounts of ROBBING BLACK HAWK'S GRAVE are abundant but contradictory. *History of Peoria County;* J. F. Snyder, "The Burial and Resurrection of Black Hawk," *ISHS* 4; Willard Barrows, "The Death of Black Hawk," *WHC,* vol. 5; Armstrong, *Sauks and the Black Hawk War.*

KEOKUK SEQUEL   Vertical file, Keokuk Public Library.

Hagan, *Sac and Fox Indians,* provides an account of the Sauk and Fox nation from the Black Hawk War to the 1920s.

RUSSELL'S ABORTED TREATISE ON THE WAR   John Russell papers, ISL.

DAVENPORT MURDER   Armstrong, *Sauks and the Black Hawk War.*

Sources for Quoted Materials

‹‹

Page 5

"For the nation, there is an unrequited account": Catlin, *Letters and Notes*, vol. 2, p. 256.

Page 17

"Ain't no game like Ingins": Quoted in Arthur Moore, *The Frontier Mind* (Lexington, Ky., 1957), p. 95.

"a tissue of blunders": Quoted in Hudson Strode, *Jefferson Davis, American Patriot* (New York, 1955), p. 74.

"an affair of fatigue": Quoted in Roland, *Albert Sidney Johnston*, p. 46.

Page 18

". . . an excess of the *Indian ill-will*": Reynolds, *My Own Times*, p. 337.

". . . origin in avarice": Drake, *Life and Adventures of Black Hawk*, p. 199.

". . . fraught with dishonor": Thwaites, "The Story of the Black Hawk War," *WHC*, vol. 12, p. 261.

". . . cold-blooded series of murders": Armstrong, *Sauks and the Black Hawk War*, p. 105.

Page 21

". . . a most complete whipping": G. W. Featherstonhaugh, *A Canoe Voyage up the Minnay Sotor* (London, 1847), vol. 2, p. 179.

Page 22

"a prominent part of the entertainment": Ibid., p. 197.

"animals of an inferior type": Francisco Arese, *A Trip to the Prairies and in the Interior of North America* (1837–1838) (New York, 1934), p. 46.

"sons of Cain": Charles Dickens, *American Notes.*

"Ostrogoths": Arese, p. 25.

"Everyone has come to make money": De Tocqueville, "Notebook E," *Journey to America* (New Haven, Conn., 1960).

"A propensity to cheat and deceive": Faux, *Memorable Days in America* (London, 1823), p. 125.

"You can't get on no how": Featherstonhaugh, p. 166.

Page 23

"The whites . . . more pagan": Latrobe, *Rambler in North America*, vol. 2, p. 153.

"Providence will be best pleased": Reynolds, *The Pioneer History of Illinois*, p. 24.

"A democracy is but a mob": Quoted in de Tocqueville, *Journey to America*, "Non-Alphabetic Notebooks 2 & 3."

Page 25

"The people of St. Louis": Forsyth to George Davenport, July 11, 1832, Augustana College.

"Washington will have it so": Lockwood, "Early Times and Events in Wisconsin," *WHC*, vol. 2, p. 153.

Page 26

"yelling and dancing like devils": Baird, "Indian Customs and Early Recollections," *WHC*, vol. 9, p. 326.

"neither civil nor military authorities": Ibid.

Page 27

"His flag, your flag": Minutes of Council, June 14, 1830, Sac and Fox Agency File, Iowa Historical Society.

Page 28

"if the Government is not early in stopping them": Quoted in Brunson, "Memoir of T. P. Burnett," *WHC*, vol. 2, p. 255.

"preserve the pledged faith": Summary in Johnston field journal, April 1, 1832, ISL.

Page 29

"fiercest Indians in our country": McCall, *Letters from the Frontier*, letter of June 17, 1831.

Page 31

"North Carolina had no one": Quoted in Nichols, *General Henry Atkinson,* p. 80.

Page 32

"*rowdyism* was the order of the day": Cooke, *Scenes and Adventures in the Army,* p. 17.

Page 34

"I can hardly think that Black Hawk": Atkinson to Gaines, April 7, 1832, Atkinson Letter Book, ISL.

Page 38

"the largest and best built Indian town": Carver, *Travels Through the Interior Parts of North America,* p. 47.

Page 40

"The Saucks . . . certainly do not pay that respect": Quoted in Missouri Historical Society, *Glimpses of the Past,* vol. 2, p. 111.

Page 42

". . . wrested from the Government": Quoted in Pease, *Frontier State,* p. 184.

Page 43

"You take the buzzard": Featherstonhaugh, *Canoe Voyage,* vol. 2, p. 3.

Page 44

"undue familiarities": Armstrong, *Sauks and the Black Hawk War,* p. 59.

Page 45

"the chiefs of your villages": Quoted in Jackson, *Black Hawk* (hereafter cited as Black Hawk), p. 55n.

Page 46

"The writer has no doubt": Isaac Galland, *Chronicles of the North American Savage,* vol. 1, p. 53.

"It was known to all": *Iowa Journal of History and Politics* 10:109.

"They had been drunk": Black Hawk, p. 54.

Page 47

"Whole assent is necessary": Carver, p. 257.

"The man was not a chief": *Iowa Journal of History and Politics* 10:110.

Page 49

"I will leave it to the people": Black Hawk, p. 54.

"wet groceries and gewgaws": Armstrong, p. 92.

"Bad Deeds": *Territorial Papers of the United States,* vol. 13, p. 165.

"a sober, honest, faithful young man": Quoted in Jackson, "William Ewing," *Agricultural History* 31:2.

"supposedly shot by the guard": Esarey, ed., *Messages and Letters of William Henry Harrison,* vol. 1, p. 132n.

Page 50

"degrading to the institution": Jackson, "William Ewing," p. 5.

"It is astonishing to me": Jackson, ed., *Journals of Zebulon Montgomery Pike,* vol. 1, p. 22.

"He presented us an American flag": Black Hawk, p. 52.

Page 51

"Tell my Great Father": Catlin, *Letter and Notes,* vol. 2, p. 174.

Page 52

"wretched pen": Quoted in the *Palimpsest* 47:33.

"If you do not join your friends": Black Hawk, p. 58.

Page 53

"war of extirpation": Quoted in Hagan, *Sac and Fox Indians,* p. 47.

"quiet and friendly": Ibid.

"*I had not discovered one good trait*": Black Hawk, p. 60.

Page 54

"If you do not immediately strike": "Papers of the Dominion Archives of Ottawa," *MPC,* vol. 16, p. 196.

Page 55

"on the final extermination of the Osages": Black Hawk, p. 49.

"She is a good woman": Ibid., p. 73.

"probably the handsomest man in the world": Quoted in *Iowa Journal of History and Politics* 10:262.

Page 56

"I was tired of being with them": Black Hawk, p. 68.

"a banditti of ruffians": Forsyth, "Journal of a Voyage from St. Louis to the Falls of St. Anthony in 1819," *WHC*, vol. 6, p. 197.

Page 58

". . . she had gone off": Quoted in Scanlin, *Prairie du Chien,* p. 118.
"A great battle": B. W. Brisbois, "Traditions and Recollections of Prairie du Chien," *WHC,* vol. 9, p. 296.

Page 59

". . . plenty of whiskey": Black Hawk, p. 78.

Page 60

"I had a good opinion of this war chief": Ibid., p. 79.
". . . the women even jumped on board": Quoted in Black Hawk, p. 79n.

Page 61

"than if all the goods": Duncan to T. G. Anderson, *WHC,* vol. 9, p. 232.

Page 62

"The satisfaction afforded the Indians": Ibid.
"I was prepared to meet them": Black Hawk, p. 80.

Page 64

"I shall fight the Big Knives": "Bulger Papers," *WHC,* vol. 13, p. 132.

Page 66

"What do we know of the laws": Black Hawk, p. 87.

Page 67

". . . a *bad spirit* has taken his place": Black Hawk, p. 88.

Page 68

"a great jubilee": Fonda, "Early Reminiscences of Wisconsin," *WHC,* vol. 5, p. 236.

Page 69

". . . a great many boxes of money": Catlin, *Letters and Notes,* vol. 2, p. 171.

Page 70

"a wild weird scene": John Bush, "Minutes of Annual Meeting, 1895," *MPC,* vol. 26, p. 320.

Page 71

"I cannot see how [they] could exist": Quoted in Hagan, *Sac and Fox Indians,* p. 90.

". . . a perfect ignoramus": Quoted in Blair, *Indian Tribes of the Upper Mississippi Valley,* vol. 2, p. 189.

Page 73

"Westward the Jug of Empire": Twain, *Life on the Mississippi,* chap. 60.

"They would not move from the land": Quoted in *The Black Hawk War,* ISL, vol. 35, p. 27.

". . . those Indians will be removed": Ibid., p. 28.

Page 74

"a very quiet, peaceable neighbor": Spencer, *Reminiscences of Pioneer Life,* p. 27. The quotations cited in this volume are from the reprint edited by Milo M. Quaife as *The Early Day of Rock Island and Davenport* (Chicago, 1942).

Page 75

"It appears hard to me": Quoted in Hagan, p. 111.

". . . dividing our corn-fields": Black Hawk, p. 99.

"the bare recollection of such extravagance": Galland, *Chronicles of the North American Savage* (June 1835).

Page 76

"I now promised this party": Black Hawk, p. 99.

"We dare not resent any of these things": Quoted in Thomas Mc-Kenny and James Hall, *History of the Indian Tribes of North America* (Philadelphia, 1836), p. 73.

Page 77

"never lost a cent's worth": Quoted in Armstrong, *Sauks and the Black Hawk War,* p. 17.

Page 78

"You will stand alone in the world": Minutes of Council, June 16, 1830, Sac and Fox Agency File.

"We always take notice of your words": Ibid., June 14, 1830.

"By the Eternal": Ibid., p. 142.

Page 79

"Permit me to observe": Letter, June 14, 1830, Sac and Fox Agency File.

Page 80

"attempted stabbing": Petition to Governor Reynolds, January 5, 1831, Sac and Fox Agency File.

Page 81

"rights of the citizens": Resolutions of the Legislature of Illinois, February 5, 1831, Sac and Fox Agency File.

"I had considerable talk with them": Letter, May 28, 1831, Sac and Fox Agency File.

Page 82

"almost destroyed all our crops": Quoted in Stevens, *Black Hawk War*, p. 82.

"In this place as well as other sections": Letter of August 4, 1831, Governor Reynolds Correspondence, Archives Department, State of Illinois.

Page 83

". . . a state of actual invasion of the State": Letter of May 26, 1831; quoted in Stevens, p. 85.

"Should the hostile band be sustained": Letter of May 29, 1831; quoted in Stevens, p. 89.

". . . advancement of his own political views": McCall, *Letters from the Frontier*, letter of July 1, 1831.

Page 84

"Runners were sent": Black Hawk, p. 106.

Page 85

"bounding from the earth": McCall, letter of June 17, 1831.

". . . to *refuse* any, and every offer": Black Hawk, p. 110.

Page 86

"I am a red-skin": McCall, letter of June 17, 1831.

Page 87

"for all the women were on my side": Black Hawk, p. 108.

"Our women have worked the fields": McCall, letter of June 17, 1831.

"manly conduct and soldierly deportment": Black Hawk, p. 113.

"linsey-woolsey Excellency": McCall, letter of July 1, 1831.

Page 89

"I would have remained": Black Hawk, p. 114.

"The enemy having escaped": Ford, *History of Illinois,* p. 164.

"I had a field of twenty acres": Spencer, *Reminiscences of Pioneer Life,* p. 49.

Page 90
"The sound of his heel upon the floor": McCall, letter of July 5, 1831.

Page 91
"The country rings around with loud alarms": Quoted in "Porte Crayon," *Harper's Monthly* 17:212.

Page 92
"log pen": Armstrong, *Sauks and the Black Hawk War,* p. 203.

Page 93
"expecting to meet the soldiers at Rock river": Black Hawk, p. 119.

Page 94
"is determined to make war": Atkinson file of letters received, ISL.
"that he would rather kill Genl Gaines": Atkinson file of letters received, ISL.

Page 95
"they seemed but a short distance from us": Spencer, *Reminiscences of Pioneer Life,* p. 52.

Page 96
"if things assume a more threatening aspect": Letter of April 13, 1832, Atkinson letter book, ISL.
". . . the frontier is in great danger": Letter of April 13, 1832, Atkinson letter book, ISL.

Page 97
"Fellow citizens": Reynolds, *My Own Times,* p. 352.

Page 98
". . . a mere school of titles": Quoted in Pease, *Frontier State,* p. 41.

Page 99
"some sitting, some lying": Jamison, "Independent Military Companies of Sangamon County," *ISHS* 3:23.

Page 100
". . . not mind shooting an Indian": Woods, *Two Years Residence in the Settlement on the English Prairie,* p. 152.

". . . taken by contract for $50,000": Hoffman, *A Winter in the Far West,* p. 86.

". . . a brother is to be loved, and an Indian to be hated": *The Confidence Man,* chap. 26.

Page 101

". . . chicken-stealing expedition": Herndon, *Herndon's Lincoln,* vol. 1, p. 93.

". . . cypher to the rule of three": Ford, *History of Illinois,* p. 148.

Page 102

"pliant demagogue": Pease, p. 136.

"the nightly alarm of hostile Indians": Reynolds, *My Own Times,* p. 7.

Page 103

"one of the greatest men": Reynolds, *Pioneer History of Illinois,* p. 150.

"the greatest achievement of human intellect": Reynolds, *My Own Times,* p. 104.

Page 104

"a pusillanimous fear of giving offence": Ford, p. 114.

"Now I want you and all your friends": Ibid., p. 112.

"I must stir or git beat": Pease, p. 136.

"he could preach to one set of men": Ford, p. 145.

Page 105

"heavy fall of rain": Entry of April 25, 1832, Browning diary, ISL.

". . . full of patriotism mixed with whiskey": Charles Ballew to Ninevah Shaw, May 15, 1832, Shaw papers, ISL.

Page 106

"The whole time that I was out": Orr, "The Indian War," *ISHS* 5:78.

Page 107

"Go to the devil, Sir!": Herndon, vol. 1, p. 94.

". . . bloody struggles with the mosquitoes": Quoted in Jackson, "Lincoln in the Black Hawk War," *WHC,* vol. 14, p. 126.

"Then came the Black Hawk War": Ibid., p. 121.

"never spoke in malice of Lincoln": Snyder to Frank Stevens, April 1, 1916, Stevens Collection, ISL.

Page 108

" 'This company is dismissed": Tarbell, *Life of Abraham Lincoln,* vol. 1, p. 76.

". . . that man could throw a grizzly bear": Quoted in Moore, "Lincoln as a Wrestler," *Transactions of the Illinois State Historical Society* 9:434.

Page 109

"The mighty Napoleon": Orr, "The Indian War," p. 74.

"right cold and tempestuous": May 2, 1832, Browning diary.

Page 110

"a show of bridges": May 3, 1832, Browning diary.

"I believe the same army": Reynolds, *My Own Times,* p. 356.

"It was considered dangerous": Ibid., p. 357.

Page 111

"12 blasts": May 5, 1832, Reynolds letter book, ISL.

Page 113

"The yoke of oxen": Armstrong, *Sauks and the Black Hawk War,* p. 310.

"decidedly hostile": Atkinson letter book, ISL.

Page 114

"ignorant of fear": Fonda, "Early Reminiscences of Wisconsin," *WHC,* vol. 5, p. 241.

Page 115

"they are so decidedly hostile": Atkinson letter book, ISL.

"I am rather of the opinion": Ibid.

". . . more sinned against": Smith, "Indian Campaign of 1832," *WHC,* vol. 10, p. 155.

Page 116

"If your hearts are good": Quoted in Black Hawk, p. 121n.

"We have no bad feelings": Neapope to Atkinson, April 26, 1832, Atkinson file of letters received, ISL.

"I do not command the Indians": Black Hawk to Atkinson, April 26, 1832, Atkinson file of letters received, ISL.

"he hoped to brake or wear it out": "A Diary of the Black Hawk War," *Iowa Journal of History and Politics* 8:266.

"I and others were principal chiefs": Minutes of the Examination of the Prisoners, August 20, 1832, ISL.

Page 117

"I told them that the white flag was mine": Gratiot diary, April 25, 1832, *Mississippi Valley Historical Review* 12:398.

Page 118

"He returns you the letter": Gratiot to Atkinson, April 27, 1832, Atkinson file of letters received, ISL.

"They said the object of his mission": Black Hawk, p. 120.

"Gratiot's men pulled for their lives": Washburne, "Col. Henry Gratiot," *WHC*, vol. 10, p. 254.

"*War is declared*": Quoted in John Dixon to I. Stillman, April 28, 1832, Reynolds letter book, ISL.

Page 119

"they must be checked at once": Atkinson to Macomb, April 27, 1832, Atkinson letter book, ISL.

Page 120

". . . as active as a swarming hive": Cooke, *Scenes and Adventures in the Army*, p. 158.

"I did not call on the Governor": Atkinson letter book, ISL.

Page 121

"to harmonize and conciliate": Reynolds, *My Own Times,* p. 359.

Page 122

"I never heard of . . . any depredation": Quoted in Kett, *History of Jo Daviess County,* p. 282.

"If any man thinks I am a coward": Quoted in Jackson, "Lincoln in the Black Hawk War," *WHC*, vol. 14, p. 123.

Page 123

"at the ends of their halter-straps": Armstrong, p. 311.

". . . stuffing themselves with beef": Davis, *Good Old Times,* p. 101.

"The troops under the command of Major Stillman": Reynolds letter book, ISL.

Page 124

"stealing hogs, burning hay": Stillman to Reynolds, January 4, 1832, Greene and Alvord, eds., *Governors' Letter Books 1818–1834,* vol. 1, p. 199.

"any lawless & violent mode": Reynolds to Stillman, January 25, 1832, ibid., p. 200.

". . . Warm work is expected": Stillman to Colonel Ellis Foster, April 29, 1832, Reynolds letter book, ISL.

Page 125

"I thought they might discover the enemy": Quoted in John Nicolay and John Hay, *Abraham Lincoln* (New York, 1890), vol. 1, p. 91.

Page 126

"I concluded to tell my people": Black Hawk, p. 122.

"exasperated militia": Atkinson file of letters received, ISL.

Page 127

"such accuracy and precision of military movements": Quoted in Ford, *History of Illinois*, p. 172.

"such horrid and tragical stories": Reynolds, *My Own Times*, p. 363.

". . . we got most beautifully whipped": County history file, Mrs. Ellen Whitney Collection, ISL.

Page 128

"Everybody offered everybody a drink": Davis, p. 102.

"corned pretty heavily": *Sangamo Journal*, August 25, 1832.

"I immediately started three young men": Black Hawk, p. 122.

Page 129

". . . the guard came in": Davis, p. 103.

"Get ready, boys": *History of Peoria County*, p. 130.

"Me good Pottawattomie": Davis, p. 103.

"I heard there were some Americans near": Minutes of the Examination of the Prisoners, August 20, 1832, ISL.

Page 130

"It's all nonsense": Ibid.

"The enemy *retreated*": Black Hawk, p. 123.

". . . like swarms of summer insects": *Sangamo Journal*, June 14, 1832.

Page 131

"our lines never again formed": Ibid.

"If you run into an Indian ambuscade": *History of Peoria County*, p. 131.

Page 132

"Mr. Indian, I surrender": Armstrong, p. 319.

". . . Stop and fight!": Davis, p. 105.

"prevented a perfect massacre": Letter of R. H. McGoon, September 23, 1854, WHS.

Page 133

"with our army . . . the blind man": Davis, p. 113.

"hopelessly crazed": Stevens, *Black Hawk War,* p. 136.

"were as drunk as he was": Kett, *History of Jo Daviess County,* p. 283.

"I never was so much surprised": Black Hawk, p. 126.

Page 134

"It is impossible to inform you the number": Letter of May 15, 1832, ISL.

"to cover the retreat": Whiteside and Reynolds to Atkinson, May 15, 1832, Atkinson file of letters received, ISL.

"The honor of serving my country": Wakefield, *"History of the War,"* p. 23.

Page 135

"You have been appraised": Letter of May 15, 1832, Atkinson file of letters received, ISL.

"with more order and silence": Orr, "The Indian War," *ISHS* 5:75.

Page 136

"a partial cause of the disasters": Reynolds, *My Own Times,* p. 368.

Page 137

"Remember Stillman's Run!": Atwood, *Story of the Battle of Stillman's Run* (pamphlet).

"doubtless by way of challenge": Orr, p. 74.

"horribly lengthened countenance": Ibid., p. 75.

". . . I will stay with you in future": Letter of May 17, 1832, Buckmaster-Curran papers, ISL.

Page 139

"You have no idea": Quoted in Dyer, *Zachary Taylor,* p. 79.

Page 140

"Contrary to my wish": Letter of May 18, 1832, Atkinson file of letters received, ISL.

"that disgraceful affair of Stillman's": Quoted in Hamilton, *Wisconsin Magazine of History* 24:309.

"Only one man was killed near the ground": Quoted in Roland, *Albert Sidney Johnston,* p. 38.

"where a hundred men ought to have repulsed": Smith, "Indian Campaign of 1832," *WHC,* vol. 10, p. 157.

"ought to have prevented it": Hamilton, p. 309.

Page 141

"has not only encouraged the Indians": Atkinson letter book, ISL.

"the little and degenerate son": Gara, "William S. Hamilton," *Wisconsin Magazine of History* 41:27.

Page 142

". . . none of y'r d———d foolish pride": Hoffman, *A Winter in the Far West,* p. 44.

"the ravages of the Tiger": Gara, p. 28.

Page 143

". . . visits of mourning": Orr, "The Indian War," *ISHS* 5:75.

"fresh from the bleeding heads": Ibid., p. 76.

". . . perfectly dry": Ibid.

Page 145

"Had he *killed* the Indian": Scanlan, *Indian Creek Massacre,* p. 29.

"abused him in a shameful manner": Matson, *Shabena,* p. 113.

Page 146

"The tomahawk soon ended the cries": Quoted in Stevens, *Black Hawk War,* p. 155.

Page 147

"We were trying to hide": Quoted in Stevens, p. 150.

"to protect the settlements": Order no. 20, May 19, 1832, Atkinson order book, ISL.

"their naked persons": Ford, *History of Illinois,* p. 178.

"squeaked like geese": Ibid.

Page 148

"Murder! Murder!": Wakefield, *History of the War,* p. 58.

"Never mind Susan": Ibid., p. 59.

"Strong men turned pale": Quoted in Quaife, *Chicago and the Old Northwest,* p. 326.

Page 149
"a crowded caravansary": Andreas, *History of Cook County, Illinois,* p. 118.

Page 152
"a war of extermination": *Galenian,* May 23, 1832.

Page 153
"declaring martial law": Letter of May 26, 1832, Atkinson letter book, ISL.

"he could whip the United States troops": Strode to Atkinson, May 27, 1832, Atkinson file of letters received, ISL.

Page 154
"in great danger of being overcome": Bliss to Stephenson, May 28, 1832, ISL.

"Should your order have been couched": Stephenson to Bliss, May 28, 1832, ISL.

"probably slaughtered by Indians": *Galenian,* May 30, 1832.

"I was out of work": Herndon, *Herndon's Lincoln,* p. 120.

Page 155
"poured out a regular tirade": Armstrong, *Sauks and the Black Hawk War,* p. 379.

"What part have *you* played": Ibid.

"deep feelings of mortification": Reynolds, *My Own Times,* p. 375.

"I am not able to lay before the public": Wakefield, p. 24.

"some cause connected with the local politics": Smith, "Indian Campaign of 1832," *WHC,* vol. 10, p. 155.

Page 156
"The whole country . . . is infested": Letter of May 30, 1832, Atkinson letter book, ISL.

Page 157
". . . in the most imminent danger": Quoted in Ballard, *Tales of Early Niles* (pamphlet).

"not [to] return to this place": "Papers of Gen. John R. Williams," *MPC,* vol. 31, p. 368.

"Resolved": Ibid., p. 321.

"There is no danger": Ibid., p. 326.

Page 158

"quiet the fears of the timid": Ibid., p. 383.

"a right smart power": Little, "A History of the Black Hawk War," *MPC*, vol. 5, p. 160.

"he was ready to meet death": Little, p. 153.

Page 159

"all the troops should be presed through": "Papers of Gen. John R. Williams," p. 387.

Page 160

"grand magnificent halts": Ibid., p. 160.

"a good watch": Brown, "Autobiographical Notes," *MPC*, vol. 30, p. 455.

Page 161

"What a fuss": Davenport to R. Farnham, June 8, 1832, ISL.

Page 162

"perfectly panic stricken": Taylor to Atkinson, June 1, 1832, Atkinson file of letters received, ISL.

Page 163

"The more I see of the militia": Atkinson file of letters received, ISL.

"straight as an Indian": Pelzer, *Henry Dodge*, p. 19.

Page 164

"First give them presents": Ibid., p. 32.

"completely armed with rifles and pistols": Lyman, *John Marsh*, p. 142.

Page 165

"the captain of an aggressive civilization": Pelzer, p. 45.

Page 166

"I do not think I would even take the trouble": Kinzie, *Wau-bun*, p. 474.

"This is the third Indian war": Ibid., p. 483.

"They did not love the Americans": Kinzie, p. 468.

Page 167

"mild in peace": *Galenian,* May 30, 1832.

"the highest reward": Gratiot diary, p. 400.

Page 168

"half famished, half naked": John Messersmith in Smith, *History of Wisconsin,* vol. 3, p. 225.

"The Indians cleared off a piece of ground": Quoted in Stevens, *Black Hawk War,* p. 151.

Page 169

"I tryed to please and comfort them": Quoted in Gratiot diary, p. 403.

Page 170

"soft-shelled": Parkinson, "Pioneer Life in Wisconsin," *WHC,* vol. 2, p. 339.

"No man, either civilized or savage": *Galenian,* June 7, 1832.

Page 171

"It is but too true": *Galenian,* May 30, 1832.

". . . time for revelry and for homicide": Edwin Jerome, "Incidents in the Black Hawk War," *MPC,* vol. 1, p. 51.

Page 172

"The scene was horrid beyond description": Letter of Horatio Newhall, June 8, 1832, Newhall papers, ISL.

"Take this gun": May B. Rouse, *Galena's Old Stockade* (pamphlet).

Page 173

". . . quartered in his one-horse fort": Quoted in Stevens, p. 174.

"even were they to pass in sight": Taylor to Atkinson, June 13, 1832, Atkinson file of letters received, ISL.

Page 174

"To Arms! To Arms!": *Galenian,* June 12, 1832.

"We are not to have peace": Quoted in Pelzer, p. 56.

"are not blamable": Letter of September 18, 1831, Newhall papers.

"I hope no vestige": Letter of April 29, 1832, Newhall papers.

". . . a War of *extermination* should be waged": Clark to Lewis Cass, June 8, 1832, ISL.

Page 175

"I am 'bullet proof'": Letter of June 22, 1832, Washburne, ed., *Edwards Papers*, vol. 3, p. 590.

"the laudable motives": Letter of July 6, 1832, Green and Alvord, eds., *Governors' Letter Books*, p. 205.

Page 176

"dirt and discomfort": *Prose Writings of William Cullen Bryant*, p. 16.

Page 177

"the greatest public event": Stella P. Lyles, "Shawneetown," *ISHS* 22:174.

Page 178

". . . persons vending ardent spirits": Order no. 35, June 17, 1832, Atkinson order book, ISL.

Page 179

"to a fiendish degree": Stevens, "A Forgotten Hero," *Transactions of the Illinois State Historical Society*, p. 79.

Page 181

"from Lake Kashkenon": Quoted in Gratiot diary, p. 394.

Page 182

"Blood flows here": Reynolds to Edwards, June 22, 1832, Washburne, ed., *Edwards Papers*, vol. 3, p. 590.

Page 183

"Their mode of warfare is such": Johnston field journal, ISL.

Page 184

"at one bound he sprang": Bracken and Parkinson, "Pecatonica Battle Controversy," *WHC*, vol. 2, p. 367.

"wild excitement and disorder": Parkinson, "Pioneer Life in Wisconsin," *WHC*, vol. 2, p. 346.

"charge them sword in hand": Ibid., p. 347.

Page 185

"most terrific yells": Ibid.

"There's an Indian": Bracken, p. 371.

"had never heard a hostile gun": Ibid.

"That's my hair!": Parkinson, "Notes on the Black Hawk War," *WHC*, vol. 10, p. 391.

". . . have I behaved like a soldier": Bracken, p. 373.

Page 187

"the annals of border warfare": Ibid., p. 372.

Page 188

"Let me give them a pop": Spencer, *Reminiscences of Pioneer Life*, p. 67.

Page 189

"small events and little men": Ford, *History of Illinois,* p. 1.

Page 190

". . . almost ready to fight Taylor": Stevens, *Black Hawk War,* p. 198.

". . . You need not obey his orders": Ibid.

Page 192

"Our situation is a delicate one": Ebeneezer Brigham memo, June 23, 1832, WHS.

"whooping and halloing": Wakefield, *History of the War,* p. 34.

Page 193

"drove round the fort like a fury": Brunson, "A Methodist Circuit Rider," *WHS*, vol. 15, p. 278.

"a chronicle of shame": *Rambler in North America,* vol. 2, p. 188.

". . . an end to his bravery": Black Hawk, p. 130.

Page 194

"tumultuous retreat": Parkinson, "Pioneer Life in Wisconsin," p. 352.

"The chief . . . addressed his warriors": Black Hawk, p. 130.

Page 195

"as we had run the bear into his hole": Ibid., p. 131.

"It was not within my power": Letter of June 26, 1832, Atkinson file of letters received, ISL.

Page 196

"I remember just how those men looked": Quoted in Tarbell, *Life of Abraham Lincoln,* vol. 1, p. 87.

Page 197

". . . the most difficult country": Atkinson to Scott, July 11, 1832, Atkinson letter book, ISL.

Page 198

"damned all to posterity": Cooke, *Scenes and Adventures in the Army*, p. 162.

"little man": *Galenian*, July 11, 1832.

Page 200

"Give me two infantry companies mounted": Kinzie, *Wau-bun*, p. 523.

Page 201

"dead horses, burnt wagons": Bruckner, "A Brief History of the War," *MPC*, vol. 12, p. 429.

"a precaution . . . always after famous for": Wakefield, *History of the War*, p. 43.

Page 202

"Capt. Early seemed always a little too *early*": Armstrong, *Sauks and the Black Hawk War*, p. 443.

"a melancholy and sadness": Reynolds, *My Own Times*, p. 394.

"To Colonel W. S. Hamilton": *Galenian*, July 11, 1832.

". . . hunting a shadow": Reynolds, p. 394.

Page 203

"The old fellow told all he knew": Wakefield, p. 44.

"foolish, blind, and a skeleton": Lieutenant M. L. Clark to William Clark, July 7, 1832; quoted in Swart, *Footsteps of Our Founding Fathers* (pamphlet), p. 15.

"To shorten his days": Wakefield, p. 44.

"as a contrary course": Order no. 48, July 5, 1832, Atkinson order book, ISL.

Page 204

"generally more dangerous to their friends": Cooke, p. 164.

Page 205

"My horse cannot be found": Lt. Clark letter, in Swart, p. 15.

Page 206

"becoming quite discontented": James Justice diary, July 10, 1832, ISL.

"remain there till further orders": Order no. 52, Atkinson order book, ISL.

Page 207

"or leave his bones on the field": *Galenian,* July 18, 1832.

"We let her float all night": Baringer, ed., *Lincoln Day by Day,* vol. 1, p. 29.

"The privations and sufferings of the citizens": Letter of July 20, 1832, Green and Alvord, eds., *Governors' Letter Books,* p. 220.

Page 208

"not throw themselves upon me": Atkinson to George Boyd, July 12, 1832, Atkinson letter book, ISL.

"the greatest difficulty in subduing him": Atkinson to Scott, July 11, 1832, Atkinson letter book, ISL.

"sweepings of cities": Quoted in Cooke, p. 167.

"but for the waste of provisions": Atkinson report on the war, November 19, 1832, ISL.

Page 209

"venetian blinds and panel doors": Kinzie, p. 473.

"We were soon roused from our slumbers": Justice diary, July 14, 1832, ISL.

Page 210

"generally unfit anyway": Ewing to Atkinson, July 14, 1832, Atkinson file of letters received, ISL.

"Between Henry and Stephenson": Bracken and Parkinson, "Pecatonica Battle Controversy," *WHC,* vol. 2, p. 406.

Page 211

"a wild goose chase": Quoted in Armstrong, *Sauks and the Black Hawk War,* p. 446.

"draw twelve days' rations": Order no. 51, July 9, 1832, Atkinson order book, ISL.

Page 213

"The dead bodies of deserters": *Niles' Weekly Register,* July 28, 1832.

Page 214

"someone is to blame": Letter of June 12, 1832, ISL.

". . . the whole country . . . should be freed": Letter of June 15, 1832, ISL.

Page 215

"to handle regulars": Elliott, *Winfield Scott,* p. 263.

Page 216

"the defense of the frontier": Pelzer, *Henry Dodge,* p. 67.

Page 217

"3 drachms of oyster shells": *A History of the Army Medical Service at the United States Military Academy,* p. 42.

Page 218

"all mutilating and scalping": Quoted in Elliott, p. 265.

Page 219

"crowded almost to suffocation": *Niles' Weekly Register,* August 11, 1832.

Page 220

"the disease had become so violent": Walker, "Early Days on the Lakes," *Publications of the Buffalo Historical Society* 5:311.

Page 221

". . . some have died in the woods": *Niles' Weekly Register,* July 28, 1832.

Page 222

"I was thrown down on the deck": *Niles' Weekly Register,* August 11, 1832.

Page 223

"gulped down half a bottle of wine": Scott, *Memoirs,* p. 218.

Page 224

". . . almost frantic with joy": Walker letter in Wentworth, *Early Chicago,* p. 75.

". . . sufficient to rack the senses of a devil": Quoted in letter from David B. Harris, July 31, 1832, Duke University.

Page 225

"Account settled by death": Wentworth, p. 73.

"with more precipitate haste": Quoted in Andreas, *History of Cook County, Illinois,* p. 120.

"a rapidity . . . unprecedented": U.S. Congress, *American State Papers,* Class V, vol. 5, p. 31.

Page 226

"he had never felt his entire helplessness": Quoted in Quaife, *Chicago and the Old Northwest,* p. 331.

"Our prospects are deplorable": Atkinson file of letters received, ISL.

Page 227

". . . the battles . . . will never be forgotten": Communication to Legislature at opening session of 1832, Archives Department, State of Illinois.

Page 228

"muddy triangle": Bruckner, "A Brief History of the War," p. 432.

"instructed to pursue the enemy": Atkinson report on the war, November 19, 1832, ISL.

Page 229

"rushing, rumbling sound": Cooke, p. 168.

"the schoolboy puzzle": Cooke, *Scenes and Adventures in the Army,* p. 163.

". . . meet your entire approbation": Henry to Atkinson, July 19, 1832, Atkinson file of letters received, ISL.

"a very barrony place": Justice diary, July 17, 1832, ISL.

Page 230

". . . new life to every heart": Wakefield, *History of the War,* p. 64.

Page 231

"We were forced to dig *roots*": Black Hawk, p. 133.

Page 232

"The soldiers had begun to dispair": Justice diary, July 21, 1832, ISL.

Page 233

"delightful view": Justice diary, July 21, 1832, ISL.

"If those lakes were any where else": Wakefield, p. 66.

"popped him on the spot": *History of Grant County, Wisconsin,* p. 431.

Page 234

"If you don't like being scalped": Ibid.

"It is not common for *editors* to fight": *Galenian,* August 1, 1832.

Page 235

"with blows and curses": Bracken, "Further Strictures," *WHC*, vol. 2, p. 408.

Page 236

"The heads of the Indians": *Galenian,* August 1, 1832.

Page 237

"Our men stood firmly": Ibid.

". . . the enemy were not disposed to pursue": Black Hawk, p. 134.

Page 238

"a feat of most consummate management": Quoted in Aldrick, "Jefferson Davis and Black Hawk," *Midland Monthly* 5: 409.

Page 239

"I'll kick you": Merrell, "Pioneer Life in Wisconsin," *WHC*, vol. 7, p. 391.

"harangueed the soldiers": Justice diary, July 22, 1832.

". . . You are fighting a set of demons!": Wakefield, p. 71.

"Friends, we fight no more": *History of Jo Daviess County,* p. 294.

Page 240

"Stillman is not here!": Brown, *History of Illinois,* p. 368.

Page 241

"before which Tippecanoe, etc": Cooke, p. 171.

"Let Dodge have it": Armstrong, *Sauks and the Black Hawk War,* p. 460.

Page 243

"Kill the nits": *History of Crawford and Clark Counties, Illinois.*

Page 244

"The Dr. Mr. General": Johnston field journal, July 25, 1832, ISL.

"more dissatisfaction": Wakefield, *History of the War,* p. 75.

"the alps": Shaw journal, July 30, 1832, ISL.

Page 245

"unintelligible exclamations": Cooke, *Scenes and Adventures in the Army,* p. 173.

"the most difficult country imaginable": Atkinson report on the war, November 19, 1832, ISL.

Page 246

"shooting a squirrel at the top": Shaw journal, July 30, 1832, ISL.

"in wading swamps & marshes": Quoted in Dyer, *Zachary Taylor*, p. 80.

"the corpses, not of warriors only": Cooke, p. 177.

"these gallant knights of the whip": Ibid., p. 178.

"all were in profound ignorance": Ibid., p. 179.

Page 248

"anxious to get a pop": Fonda, "Early Reminiscences of Wisconsin," *WHC*, vol. 5, p. 261.

"Run and get me the white flag": Kishkasshoi's testimony, Minutes of the Examination of the Prisoners, August 19, 1832, ISL.

"I will save you and the children": Ibid.

"Is there any chief there": Weesheet's testimony, Minutes of the Examination of the Prisoners, August 27, 1832.

Page 249

"Run and hide": Black Hawk, p. 137.

"mowed a swath clean through them": Fonda, p. 261.

"As we neared them": Brown, *History of Illinois*, p. 370.

"The Winnebago, on the steam boat": Black Hawk, p. 137.

Page 250

"starve in this dreary waste": Wakefield, p. 81.

"in grim defiance": Cooke, p. 179.

"small but highly appreciative audience": *Vernon County Censor*, August 17, 1898, WHS.

"The query was": Speech of H. S. Townsend, ibid.

Page 251

"They have been hard pressed": Letter of August 1, 1832, Atkinson letter book, ISL.

Page 252

"there was pretty hot work": Shaw journal, August 2, 1832, ISL.

"Tell Atkinson I'll not obey his order": Townsend, *Vernon County Censor*.

"dazed and wild": Ibid.

Page 253

". . . fast getting rid of those demons": Wakefield, p. 83.

Page 254

"very uncomfortable circumstances": Cooke, p. 186.

"Three squaws were shot on that race": Townsend, *Vernon County Censor*.

"The Ruler of the Universe": Wakefield, p. 88.

Page 256

"Dodge is giving them hell!": Fonda, p. 262.

"Before we could get back again": Quoted in Brown, p. 130.

Page 257

"White man . . . have mercy": Townsend, *Vernon County Censor*.

Page 259

"he attempted to destroy himself": Fonda, p. 264.

Page 260

"the sodden scalps of corpses": Cooke, p. 190.

Page 261

"It filled my heart with gratitude": Wakefield, p. 94.

Page 262

"I do not permit the criers": Keokuk to Reynolds, November 30, 1832; quoted in Drake, *Life and Adventures of Black Hawk*, p. 132.

". . . disposed to reverse the old maxim": *Sangamo Journal*, September 1, 1832.

"Dodge, you have saved me!" Quoted in Jones, "Robert S. Black and the Black Hawk War," *WHC*, vol. 10, p. 230.

Page 263

"worse to manage than the Seminoles": Quoted in Dyer, *Zachary Taylor*, p. 85.

"And as to myself the pecuniary consideration": Green and Alvord, eds., *Governors' Letter Books*, p. 217.

Page 264

"receive the SAME PAY": *Sangamo Journal*, July 26, 1832.

"Uncle Sam can't do better with his loose change": *Sangamo Journal,* January 12, 1833.

Page 265

". . . every soldier or Ranger": Quoted in Elliott, *Winfield Scott,* p. 270.

"puked and purged all night": *Sangamo Journal,* October 13, 1832.

Page 266

"and *die,* if the Great Spirit saw proper": Black Hawk, p. 139.

Page 267

". . . we have done what you told us to do": Quoted in Drake, p. 172.

". . . soldiers sometimes stick the ends of their guns": Quoted in Drake, p. 175.

"Black Hawk is an Indian": Quoted in Brown, *History of Illinois,* p. 372.

Page 268

"An Indian who is as bad as the white man": Quoted in John Hauberg, "Black Hawk's Mississippi," *ISHS* 22:130.

Page 269

". . . treated us all with much kindness": Black Hawk, p. 140.

"infirm of body and imbecile of mind": Item in *Sangamo Journal,* September 15, 1832.

"Make me so": Quoted in Brown, p. 376.

"Was the White Beaver afraid": Black Hawk, p. 142.

Page 271

"making an unjust war": Minutes of Conference, September 19, 1832, Docket no. 83, Indian Claims Commission.

"an evill Genious": Quoted in Hagan, *Sac and Fox Indians,* p. 197.

"will be worth more": Letter of September 22, 1832, ISL.

Page 272

"for no other fault than defending": Forsyth report on the Black Hawk War, October 11, 1832, Forsyth Papers, WHS.

Page 273

"the spirit of forbearance and liberality": *Memoirs,* p. 226.

"spirit of proper liberality": Letter of October 11, 1832, ISL.

"They have sceded to the United States": Letter of September 24, 1832, Docket no. 83, Indians Claims Commission.

Page 274

"much shouting of delight": *Memoirs,* p. 226

"chief, in the name of the President": Scott and Reynolds to Clark, September 22, 1832, Docket no. 83, Indian Claims Commission.

"a forlorn crew": Quoted in Drake, p. 202.

Page 275

"I prefer riding on horseback": Black Hawk, p. 145.

"I thought he ought to have known this before": Ibid., p. 146.

"I don't think those fellows": James, *Life of Andrew Jackson,* p. 663.

Page 276

"What can you do against us": Quoted in Drake, p. 208.

Page 277

"I see the strength of the white man": Ibid.

"would excite the envy of the phrenologist": Quoted in Stevens, *Black Hawk War,* p. 19.

"We watched with anxiety": Black Hawk, p. 147.

"warmly kissed him": *Niles' Weekly Register,* June 29, 1833.

Page 278

"I la-zee": Ibid.

"with the exception of Lafayette's arrival": *The Diary of Philip Hone* (New York, 1927), vol. 1, p. 94.

"ruffian like appearance": Quoted in Black Hawk, p. 14.

Page 279

". . . heartily tired of crowds": Ibid.

". . . they will begin to drive . . . our people": Black Hawk, p. 150.

". . . unable to utter a word": Quoted in Drake, p. 221.

"I am a man—an old man": Ibid.

Page 281

". . . how most effectually to cheat them": Quoted in Hagan, *Sac and Fox Indians,* p. 214.

Page 282

"If we have another war": *Sangamo Journal,* January 12, 1833.

Page 283

"missionaries would only make them worse": Chapin, "Sketch of Cutting Marsh," *WHC*, vol. 15, p. 112.

"Often when looking at their condition": Ibid., p. 151.

"Such a specimen of neatness and good order": Ibid., p. 117.

Page 284

"But our way is best": Ibid., p. 119.

"Why that is just like the Indians": Ibid., p. 142.

"The poor dethroned monarch": Catlin, *Letters and Notes,* vol. 2, p. 217.

Page 285

"safe state stocks": Kappler, ed., *Indian Affairs,* p. 367.

Page 286

"A few summers ago I was fighting": Quoted in Cole, *I Am a Man,* p. 270.

Page 287

"*Nesso Chemokemon":* Quoted in Drake, *Life and Adventures of Black Hawk,* p. 245.

"with the apparent curiosity of a child": *History of Peoria County,* p. 144.

Page 288

"may in time be idolized as a saint": Keokuk (Iowa) *Daily Gate City,* March 20, 1885.

Page 290

"a thorough backwoodsman": Quoted in Pelzer, *Henry Dodge,* p. 83.

Page 295

"unjustified assault of white settlers": Undated clipping, WHS.

Index

Index